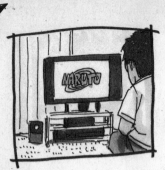

Thanks to everyone's support, the *Naruto* anime will also celebrate its tenth anniversary next year. I am eternally indebted to everyone on the animation staff! And I also have nothing but words of gratitude to all you readers who have continuously supported *Naruto*! ...No, really, I'm dead serious!!

岸本斉史

—Masashi Kishimoto, 2011

Author/artist Masashi Kishimoto was born in 1974 in rural Okayama Prefecture, Japan. After spending time in art college, he won the Hop Step Award for new manga artists with his manga **Karakuri** (Mechanism). Kishimoto decided to base his next story on traditional Japanese culture. His first version of **Naruto**, drawn in 1997, was a one-shot story about fox spirits; his final version, which debuted in **Weekly Shonen Jump** in 1999, quickly became the most popular ninja manga in Japan.

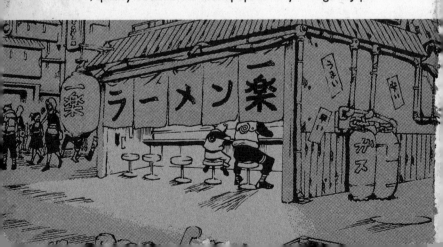

NARUTO VOL. 58
SHONEN JUMP Manga Edition

STORY AND ART BY MASASHI KISHIMOTO

Translation/Mari Morimoto
English Adaptation/Joel Enos
Touch-up Art & Lettering/John Hunt
Design/Sam Elzway
Editor/Joel Enos

Printed in the U.S.A.

Published by VIZ Media, LLC
P.O. Box 77010
San Francisco, CA 94107

10 9 8 7 6 5 4 3 2 1
First printing, September 2012

www.viz.com

THE WORLD'S
MOST POPULAR MANGA

SHONEN JUMP MANGA EDITION

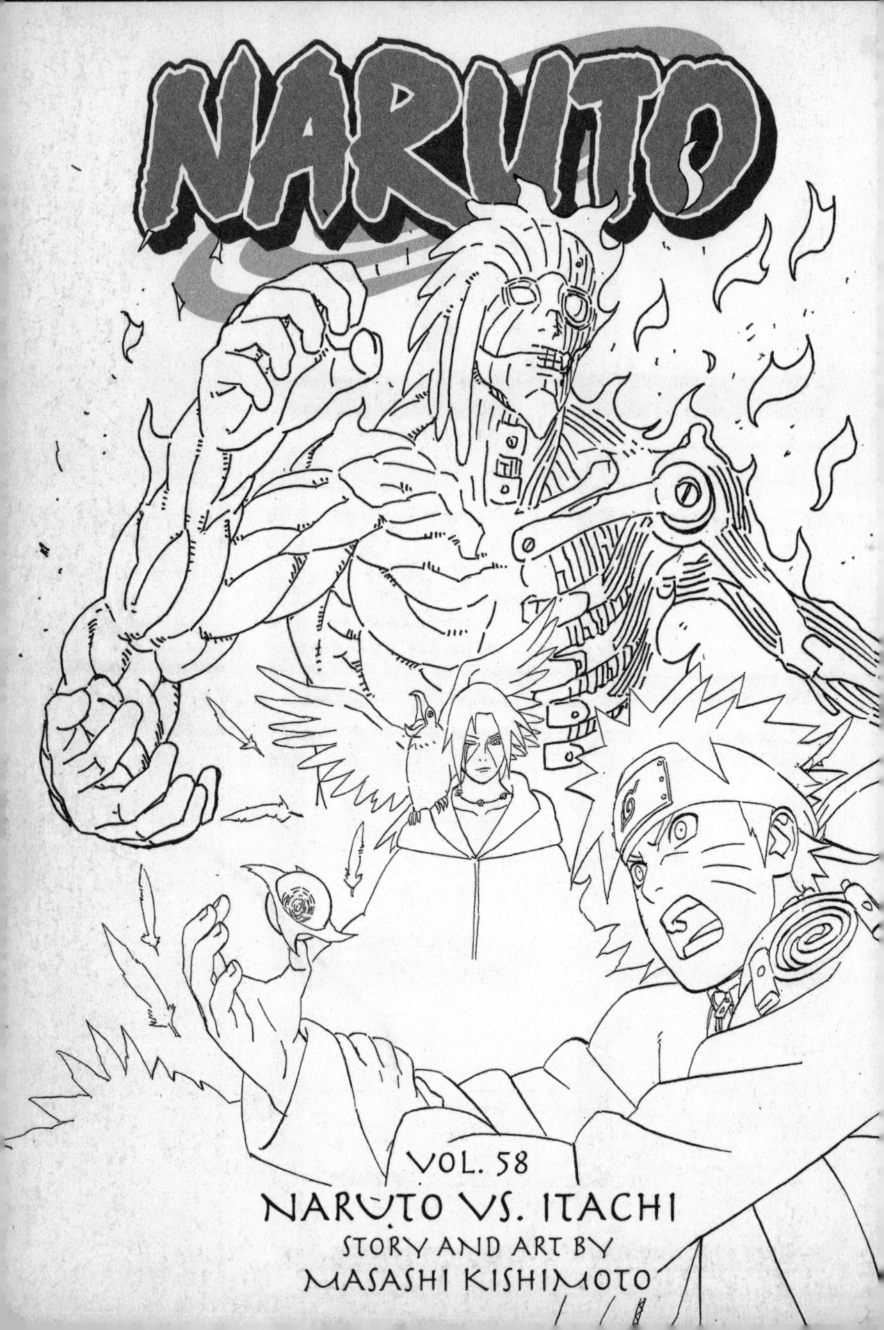
NARUTO

VOL. 58

NARUTO VS. ITACHI

STORY AND ART BY
MASASHI KISHIMOTO

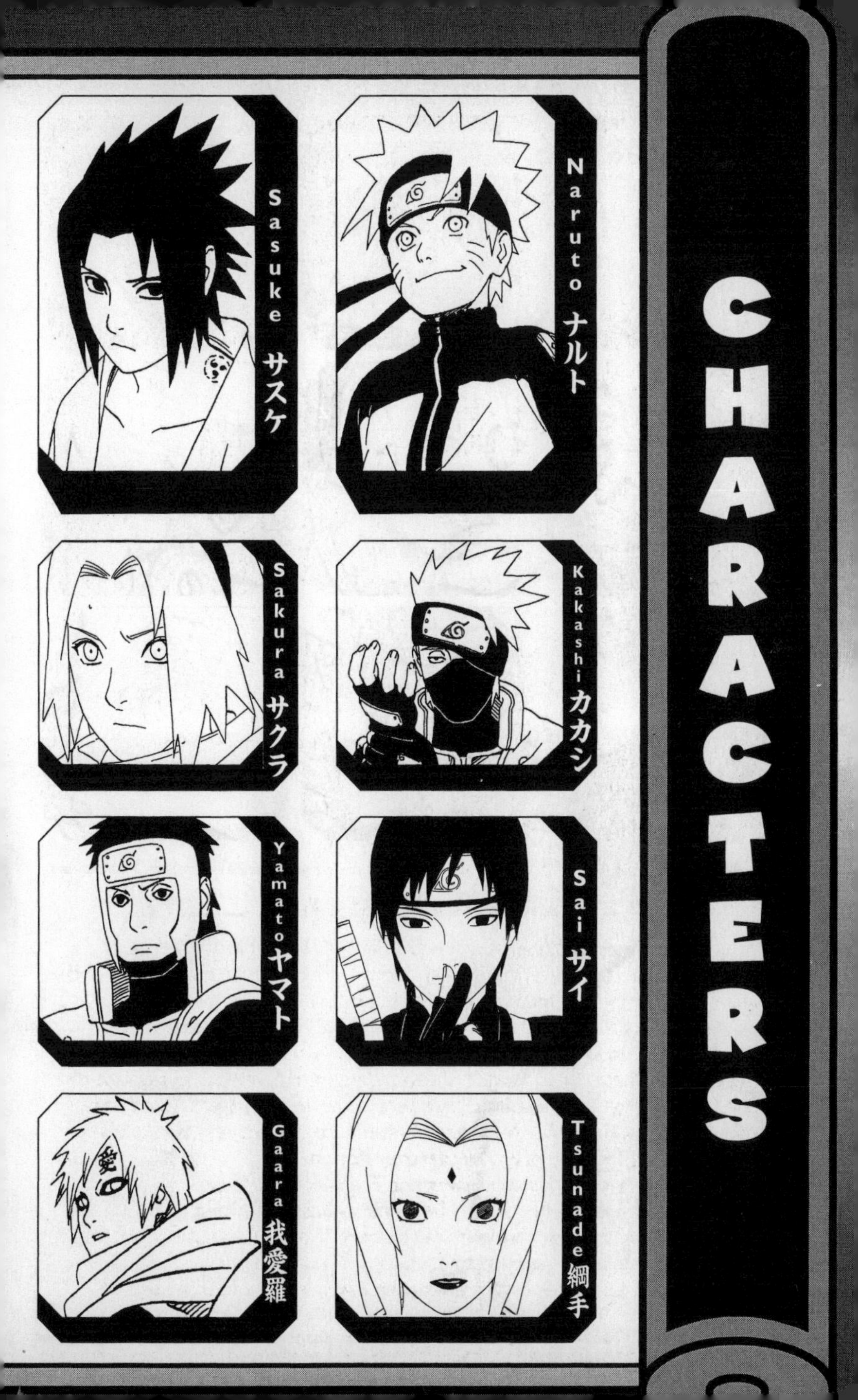
CHARACTERS
Naruto ナルト
Sasuke サスケ
Kakashi カカシ
Sakura サクラ
Sai サイ
Yamato ヤマト
Tsunade 綱手
Gaara 我愛羅

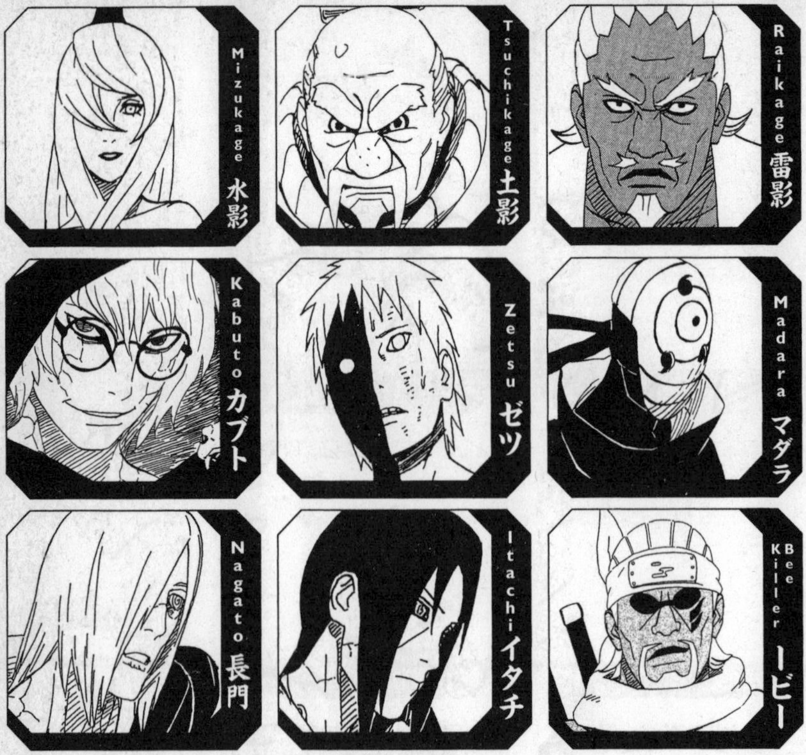
Raikage 雷影
Tsuchikage 土影
Mizukage 水影
Madara マダラ
Zetsu ゼツ
Kabuto カブト
Killer Bee ービー
Itachi イタチ
Nagato 長門

THE STORY SO FAR...

Naruto, the biggest troublemaker at the Ninja Academy in the Village of Konohagakure, finally becomes a ninja along with his classmates Sasuke and Sakura. They grow and mature through countless trials and battles. However, Sasuke, unable to give up his quest for vengeance, leaves Konohagakure to seek out power from the renegade ninja Orochimaru.

Two years pass. Naruto grows up and engages in fierce battles against the Tailed Beast-targeting Akatsuki. Elsewhere, after winning the heroic battle against Itachi and learning his older brother's true intentions, Sasuke allies with the Akatsuki and sets out to destroy Konoha.

Upon Madara's declaration of war, the Five Kage put together an Allied Shinobi Force. The Fourth Great Ninja War against the Akatsuki begins. After Naruto learns that the war was launched with him as the target, he and Bee break out of the training grounds. They then dissuade Tsunade and Raikage, who had come to stop them, and rush towards the battlefield!!

VOL. 58
NARUTO VS. ITACHI

CONTENTS

Number 545: The Immortal Corps

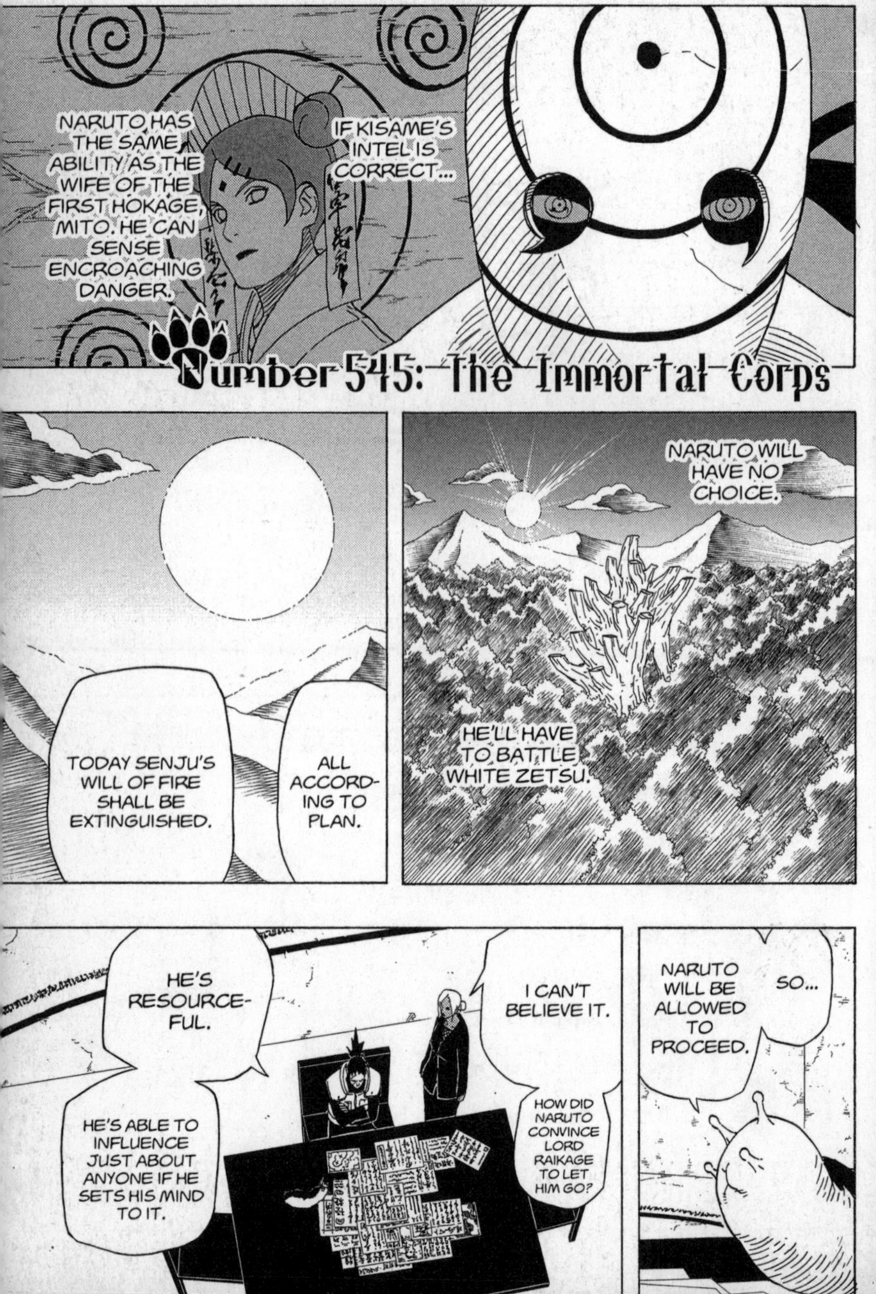
IF KISAME'S INTEL IS CORRECT...
NARUTO HAS THE SAME ABILITY AS THE WIFE OF THE FIRST HOKAGE, MITO. HE CAN SENSE ENCROACHING DANGER.
NARUTO WILL HAVE NO CHOICE.
HE'LL HAVE TO BATTLE WHITE ZETSU.
ALL ACCORD-ING TO PLAN.
TODAY SENJU'S WILL OF FIRE SHALL BE EXTINGUISHED.
SO...
NARUTO WILL BE ALLOWED TO PROCEED.
I CAN'T BELIEVE IT.
HOW DID NARUTO CONVINCE LORD RAIKAGE TO LET HIM GO?
HE'S RESOURCE-FUL.
HE'S ABLE TO INFLUENCE JUST ABOUT ANYONE IF HE SETS HIS MIND TO IT.

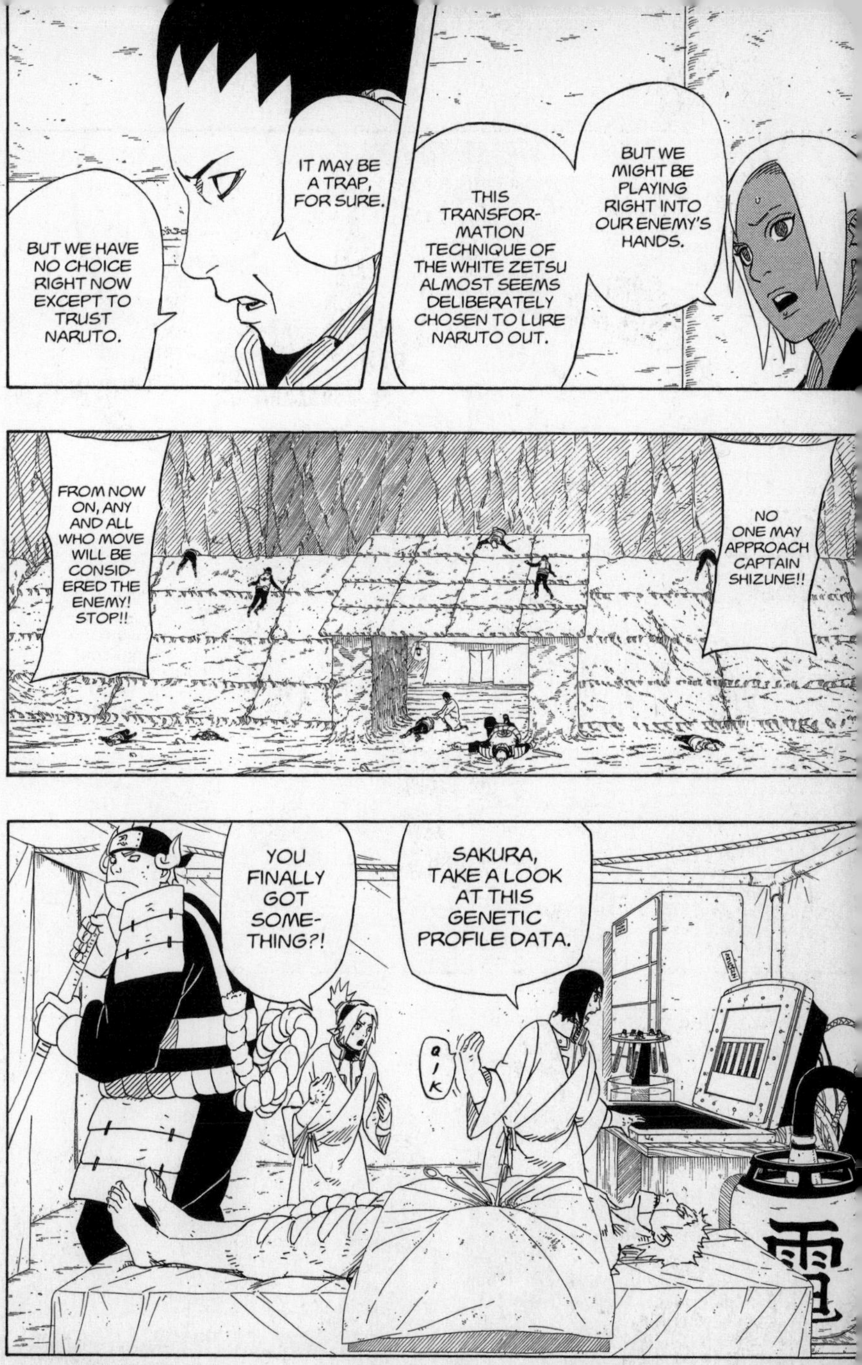
BUT WE MIGHT BE PLAYING RIGHT INTO OUR ENEMY'S HANDS.
THIS TRANSFORMATION TECHNIQUE OF THE WHITE ZETSU ALMOST SEEMS DELIBERATELY CHOSEN TO LURE NARUTO OUT.
IT MAY BE A TRAP, FOR SURE.
BUT WE HAVE NO CHOICE RIGHT NOW EXCEPT TO TRUST NARUTO.
NO ONE MAY APPROACH CAPTAIN SHIZUNE!!
FROM NOW ON, ANY AND ALL WHO MOVE WILL BE CONSIDERED THE ENEMY! STOP!!
SAKURA, TAKE A LOOK AT THIS GENETIC PROFILE DATA.
QIK
YOU FINALLY GOT SOMETHING?!

READ THIS WAY

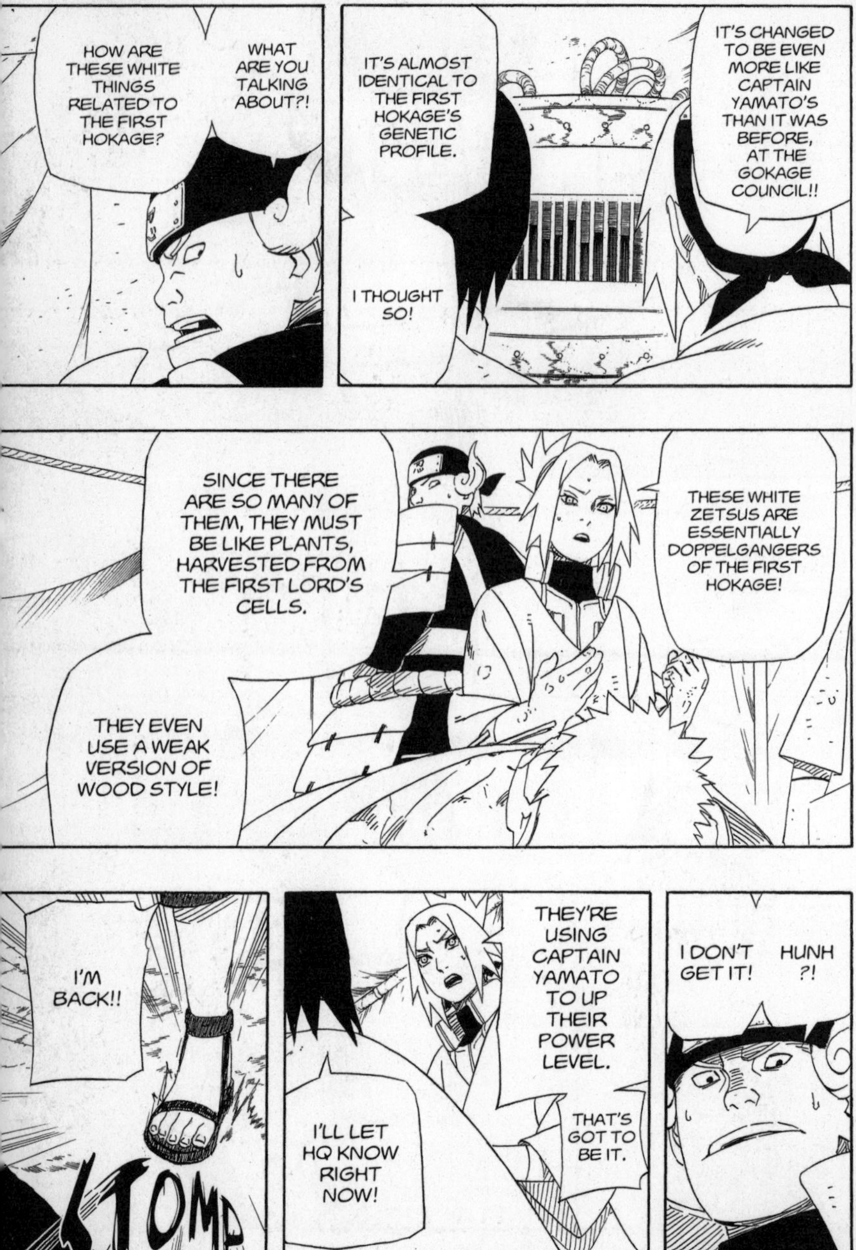
IT'S CHANGED TO BE EVEN MORE LIKE CAPTAIN YAMATO'S THAN IT WAS BEFORE, AT THE GOKAGE COUNCIL!!
IT'S ALMOST IDENTICAL TO THE FIRST HOKAGE'S GENETIC PROFILE.
I THOUGHT SO!
WHAT ARE YOU TALKING ABOUT?!
HOW ARE THESE WHITE THINGS RELATED TO THE FIRST HOKAGE?
THESE WHITE ZETSUS ARE ESSENTIALLY DOPPELGANGERS OF THE FIRST HOKAGE!
SINCE THERE ARE SO MANY OF THEM, THEY MUST BE LIKE PLANTS, HARVESTED FROM THE FIRST LORD'S CELLS.
THEY EVEN USE A WEAK VERSION OF WOOD STYLE!
HUNH ?!
I DON'T GET IT!
THEY'RE USING CAPTAIN YAMATO TO UP THEIR POWER LEVEL.
THAT'S GOT TO BE IT.
I'LL LET HQ KNOW RIGHT NOW!
I'M BACK!!
STOMP

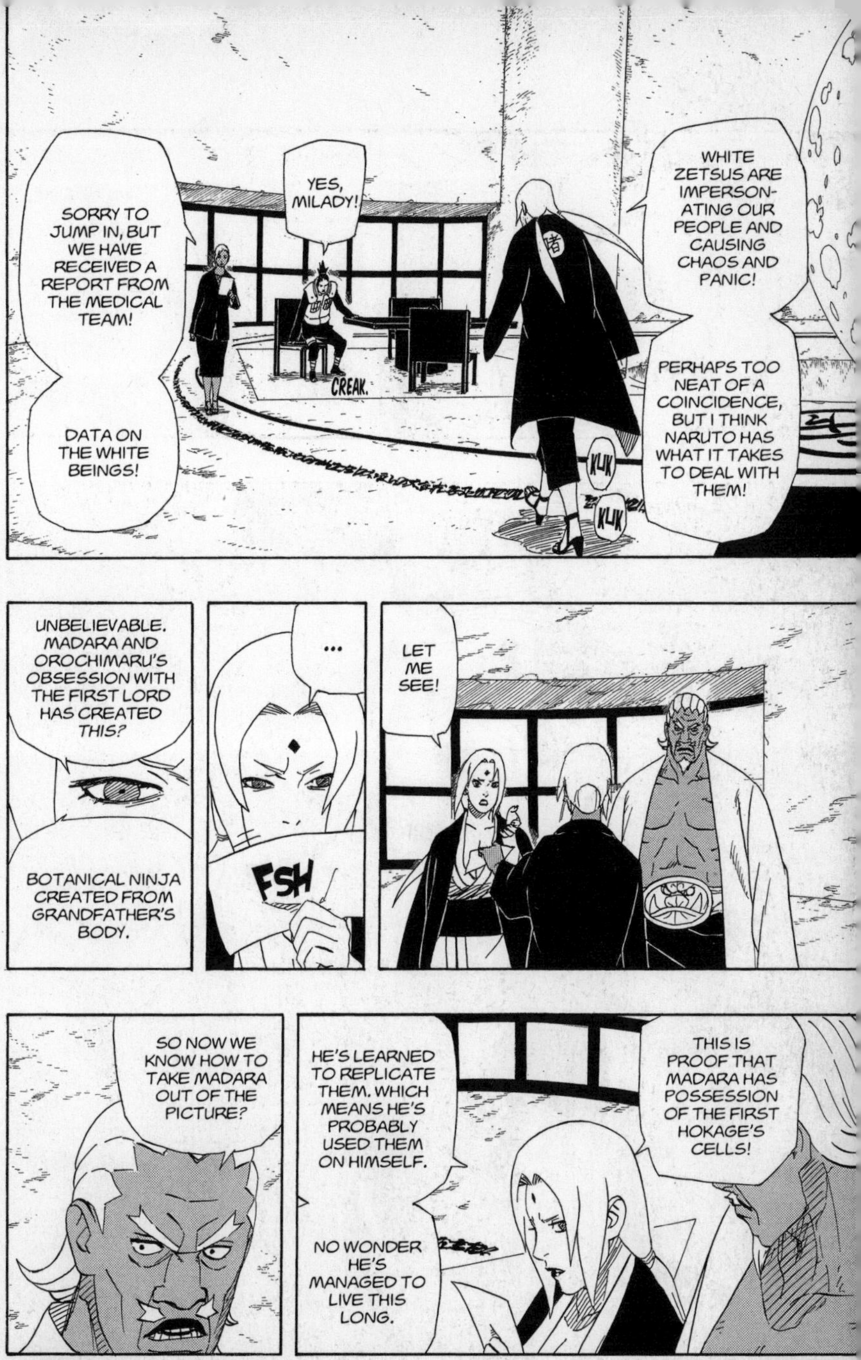
WHITE ZETSUS ARE IMPERSON-ATING OUR PEOPLE AND CAUSING CHAOS AND PANIC!
PERHAPS TOO NEAT OF A COINCIDENCE, BUT I THINK NARUTO HAS WHAT IT TAKES TO DEAL WITH THEM!
KUK
KUK
YES, MILADY!
CREAK.
SORRY TO JUMP IN, BUT WE HAVE RECEIVED A REPORT FROM THE MEDICAL TEAM!
DATA ON THE WHITE BEINGS!
LET ME SEE!
...
FSH
UNBELIEVABLE. MADARA AND OROCHIMARU'S OBSESSION WITH THE FIRST LORD HAS CREATED THIS?
BOTANICAL NINJA CREATED FROM GRANDFATHER'S BODY.
THIS IS PROOF THAT MADARA HAS POSSESSION OF THE FIRST HOKAGE'S CELLS!
HE'S LEARNED TO REPLICATE THEM. WHICH MEANS HE'S PROBABLY USED THEM ON HIMSELF.
NO WONDER HE'S MANAGED TO LIVE THIS LONG.
SO NOW WE KNOW HOW TO TAKE MADARA OUT OF THE PICTURE?

READ THIS WAY

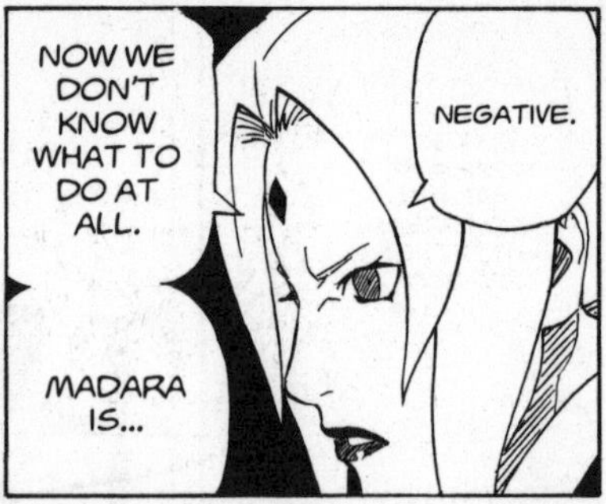
NEGATIVE.
NOW WE DON'T KNOW WHAT TO DO AT ALL.
MADARA IS...

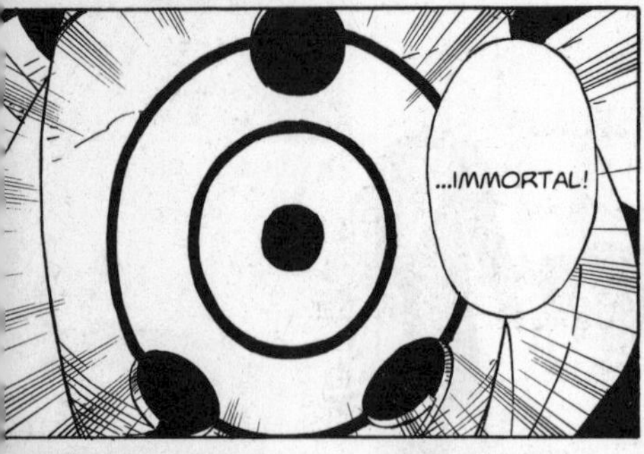
...IMMORTAL!

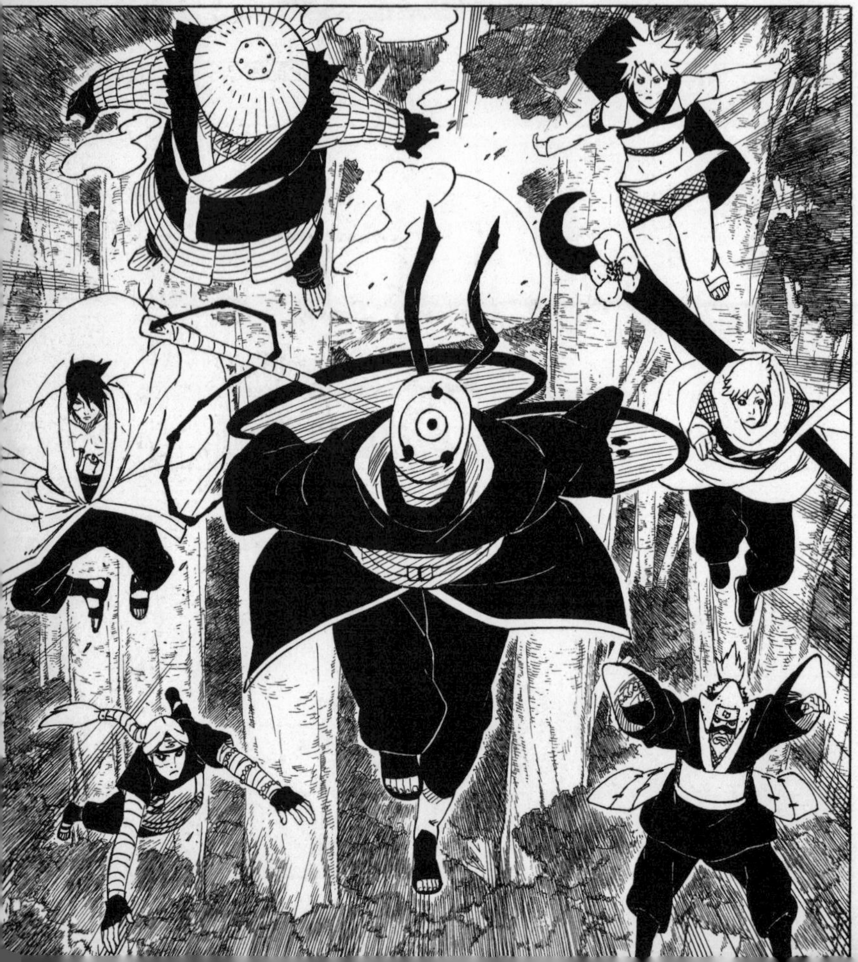

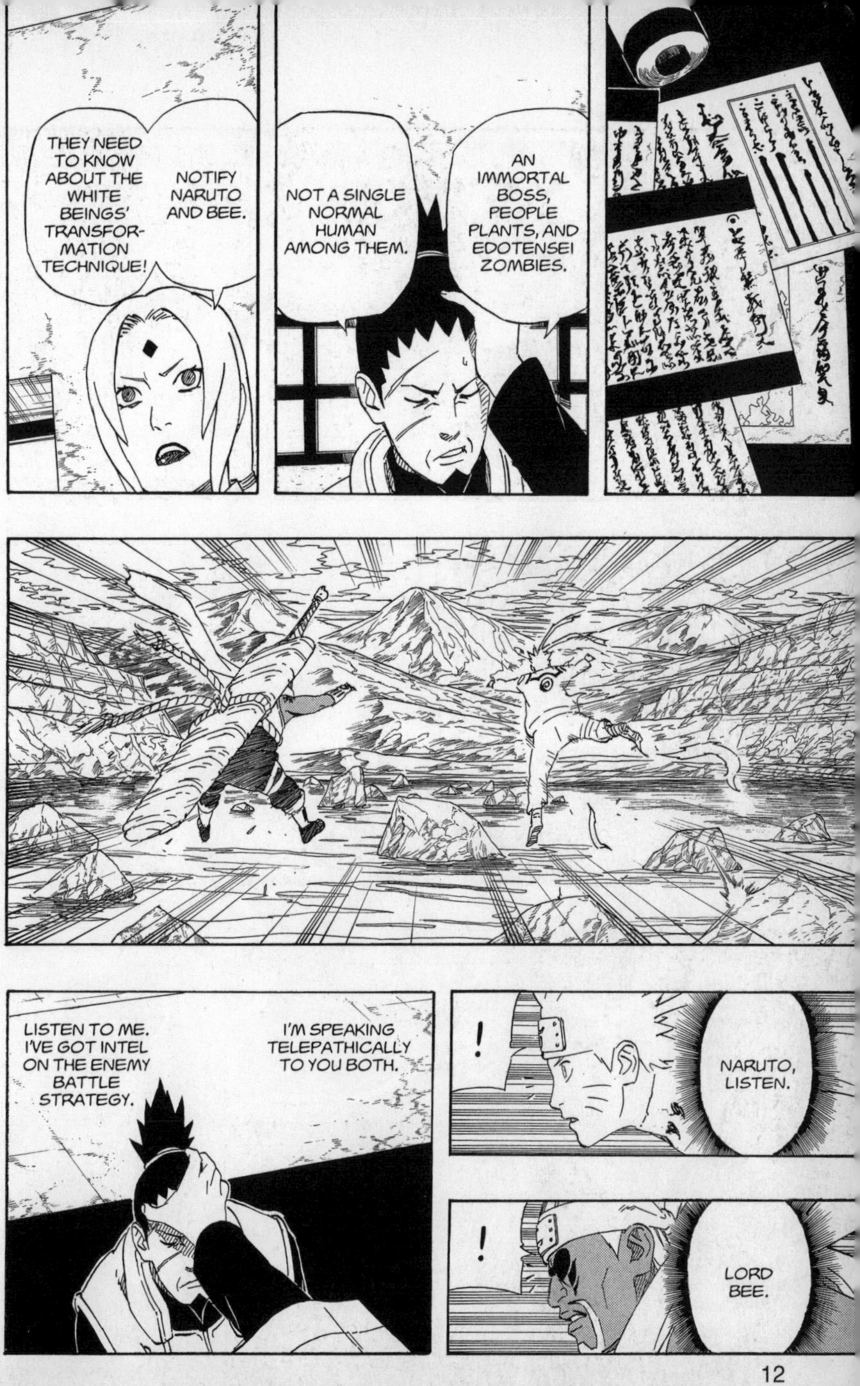
AN IMMORTAL BOSS, PEOPLE PLANTS, AND EDOTENSEI ZOMBIES.
NOT A SINGLE NORMAL HUMAN AMONG THEM.
NOTIFY NARUTO AND BEE.
THEY NEED TO KNOW ABOUT THE WHITE BEINGS' TRANSFORMATION TECHNIQUE!
!
NARUTO, LISTEN.
!
LORD BEE.
I'M SPEAKING TELEPATHICALLY TO YOU BOTH.
LISTEN TO ME. I'VE GOT INTEL ON THE ENEMY BATTLE STRATEGY.

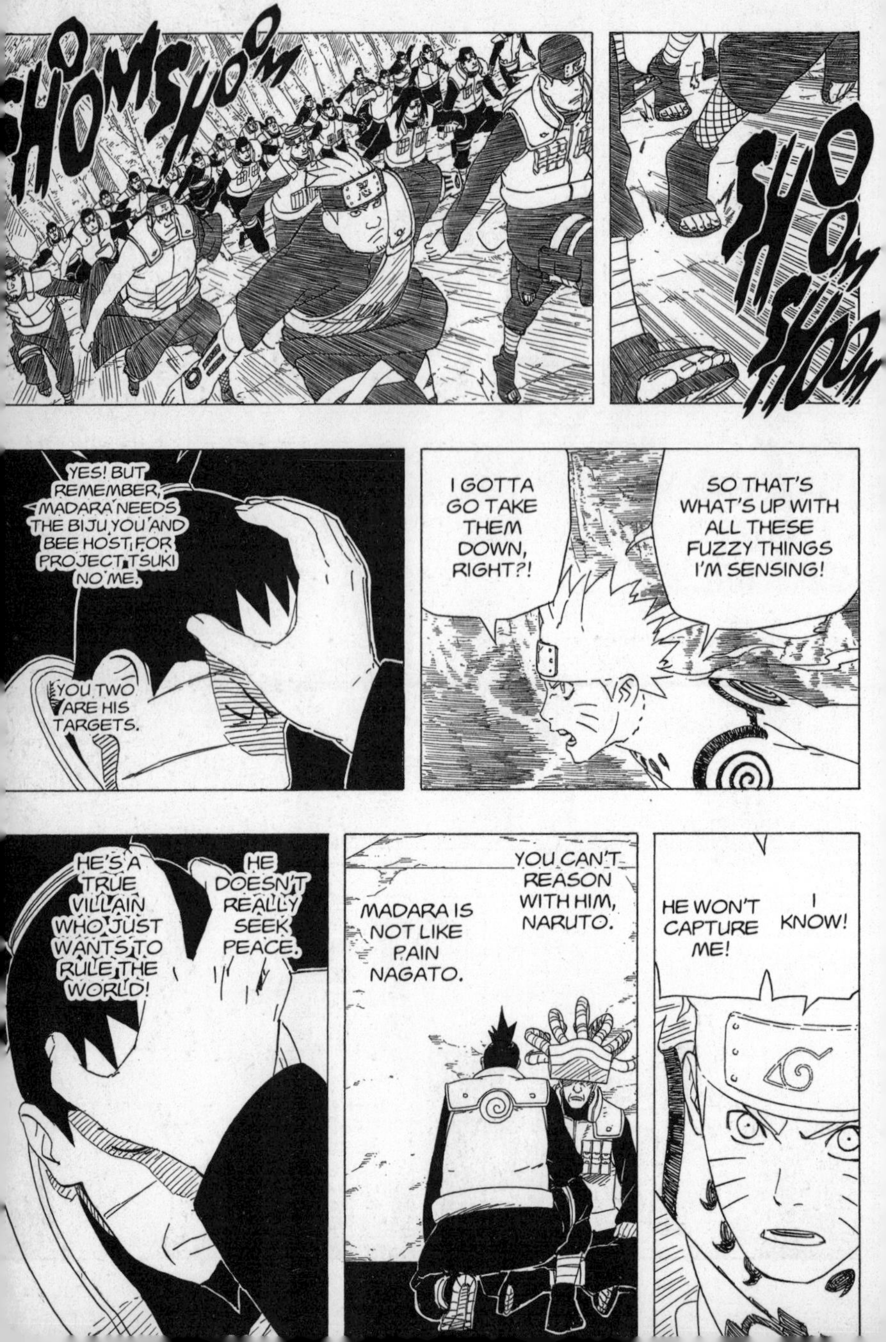
SHOOM SHOOM
SHOOM SHOOM
SO THAT'S WHAT'S UP WITH ALL THESE FUZZY THINGS I'M SENSING!
I GOTTA GO TAKE THEM DOWN, RIGHT?!
YES! BUT REMEMBER, MADARA NEEDS THE BIJU YOU AND BEE HOST FOR PROJECT TSUKI NO ME.
YOU TWO ARE HIS TARGETS.
I KNOW!
HE WON'T CAPTURE ME!
YOU CAN'T REASON WITH HIM, NARUTO.
MADARA IS NOT LIKE PAIN NAGATO.
HE DOESN'T REALLY SEEK PEACE.
HE'S A TRUE VILLAIN WHO JUST WANTS TO RULE THE WORLD!

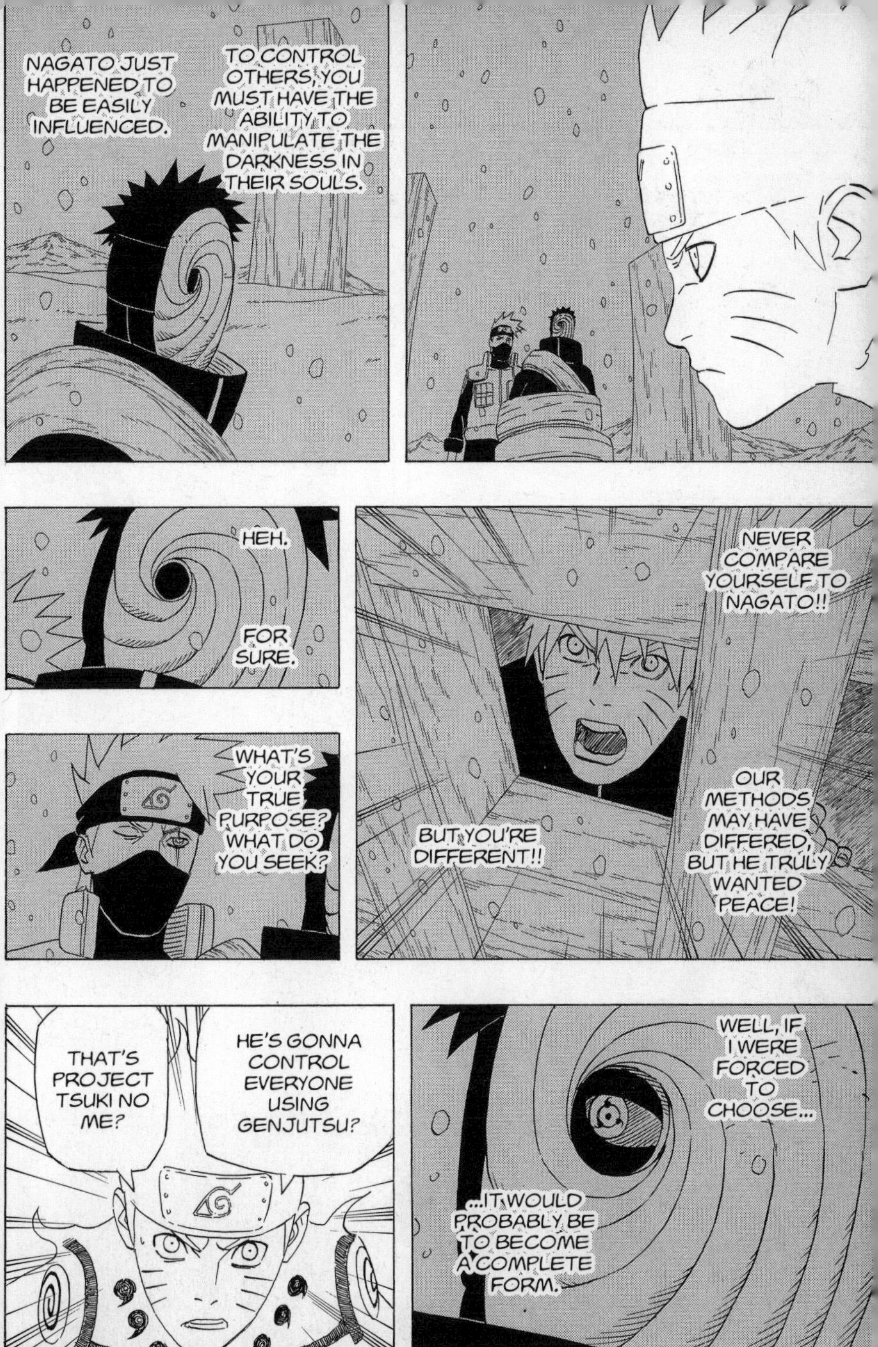
TO CONTROL OTHERS, YOU MUST HAVE THE ABILITY TO MANIPULATE THE DARKNESS IN THEIR SOULS.
NAGATO JUST HAPPENED TO BE EASILY INFLUENCED.
NEVER COMPARE YOURSELF TO NAGATO!!
OUR METHODS MAY HAVE DIFFERED, BUT HE TRULY WANTED PEACE!
BUT YOU'RE DIFFERENT!!
HEH.
FOR SURE.
WHAT'S YOUR TRUE PURPOSE? WHAT DO YOU SEEK?
WELL, IF I WERE FORCED TO CHOOSE...
...IT WOULD PROBABLY BE TO BECOME A COMPLETE FORM.
HE'S GONNA CONTROL EVERYONE USING GENJUTSU?
THAT'S PROJECT TSUKI NO ME?

READ THIS WAY

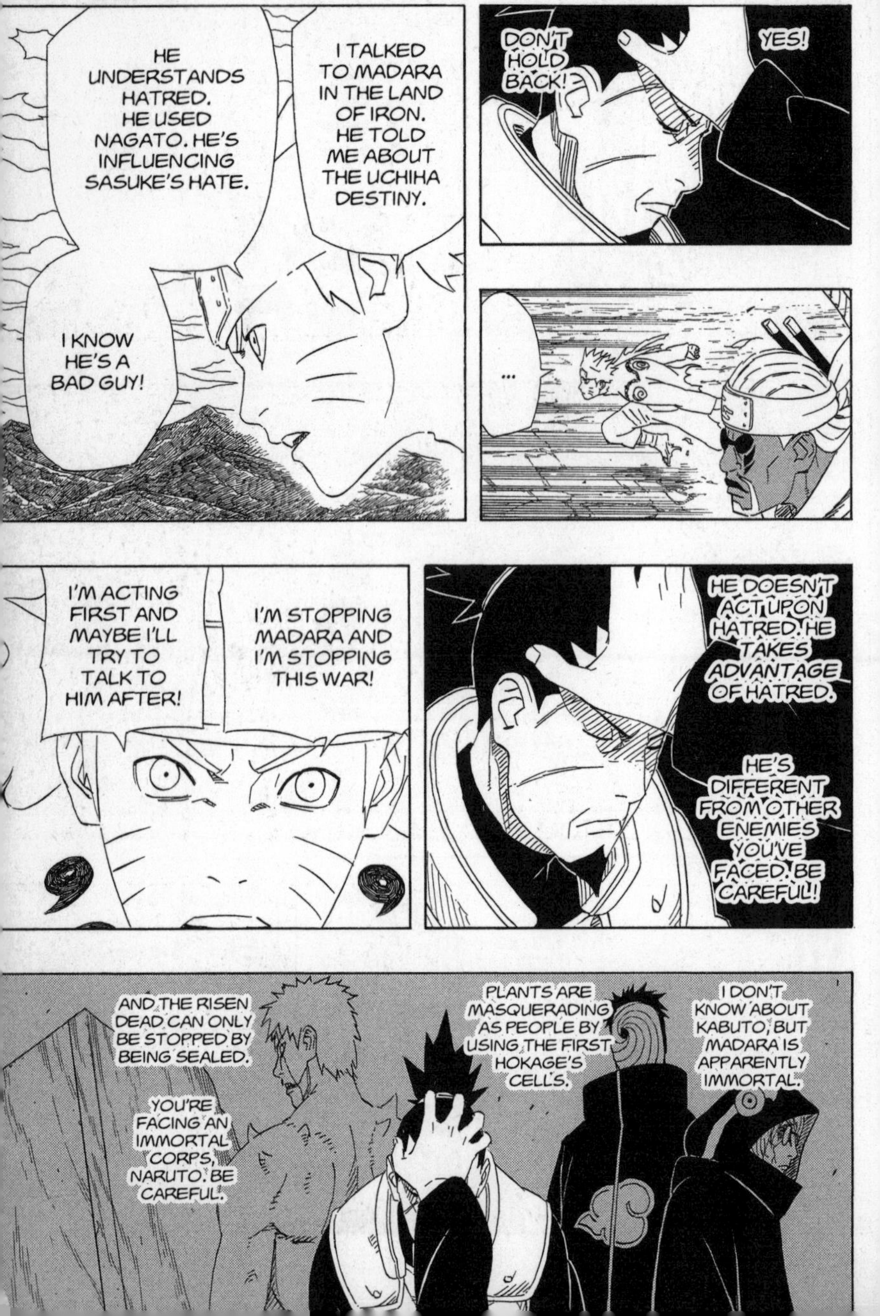
YES!
DON'T HOLD BACK!
...
I TALKED TO MADARA IN THE LAND OF IRON. HE TOLD ME ABOUT THE UCHIHA DESTINY.
HE UNDERSTANDS HATRED. HE USED NAGATO. HE'S INFLUENCING SASUKE'S HATE.
I KNOW HE'S A BAD GUY!
HE DOESN'T ACT UPON HATRED. HE TAKES ADVANTAGE OF HATRED.
HE'S DIFFERENT FROM OTHER ENEMIES YOU'VE FACED. BE CAREFUL!
I'M STOPPING MADARA AND I'M STOPPING THIS WAR!
I'M ACTING FIRST AND MAYBE I'LL TRY TO TALK TO HIM AFTER!
I DON'T KNOW ABOUT KABUTO, BUT MADARA IS APPARENTLY IMMORTAL.
PLANTS ARE MASQUERADING AS PEOPLE BY USING THE FIRST HOKAGE'S CELLS.
AND THE RISEN DEAD CAN ONLY BE STOPPED BY BEING SEALED.
YOU'RE FACING AN IMMORTAL CORPS, NARUTO. BE CAREFUL.

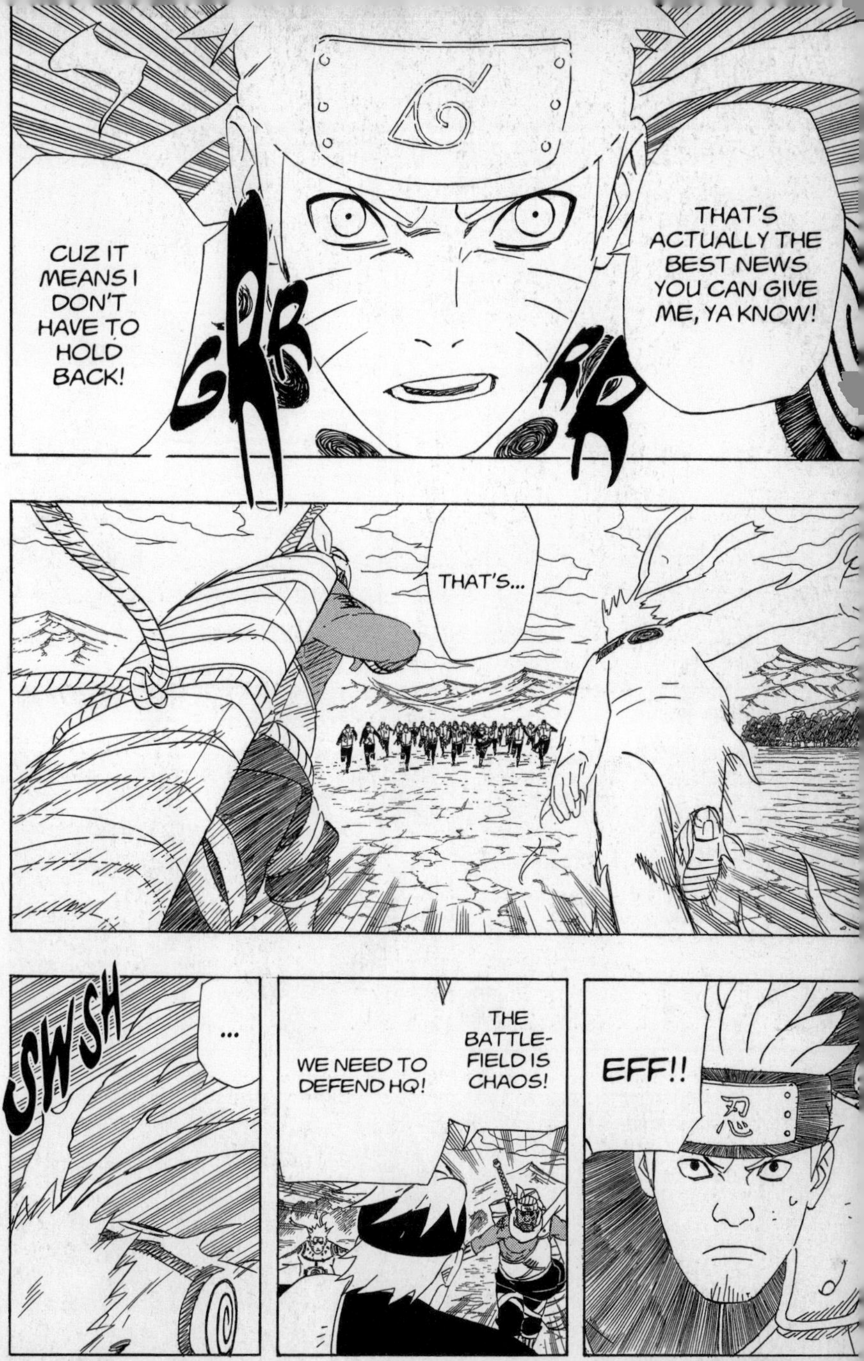
THAT'S ACTUALLY THE BEST NEWS YOU CAN GIVE ME, YA KNOW!
CUZ IT MEANS I DON'T HAVE TO HOLD BACK!
GRRRR
THAT'S...
EFF!!
THE BATTLE-FIELD IS CHAOS!
WE NEED TO DEFEND HQ!
...
SWSH

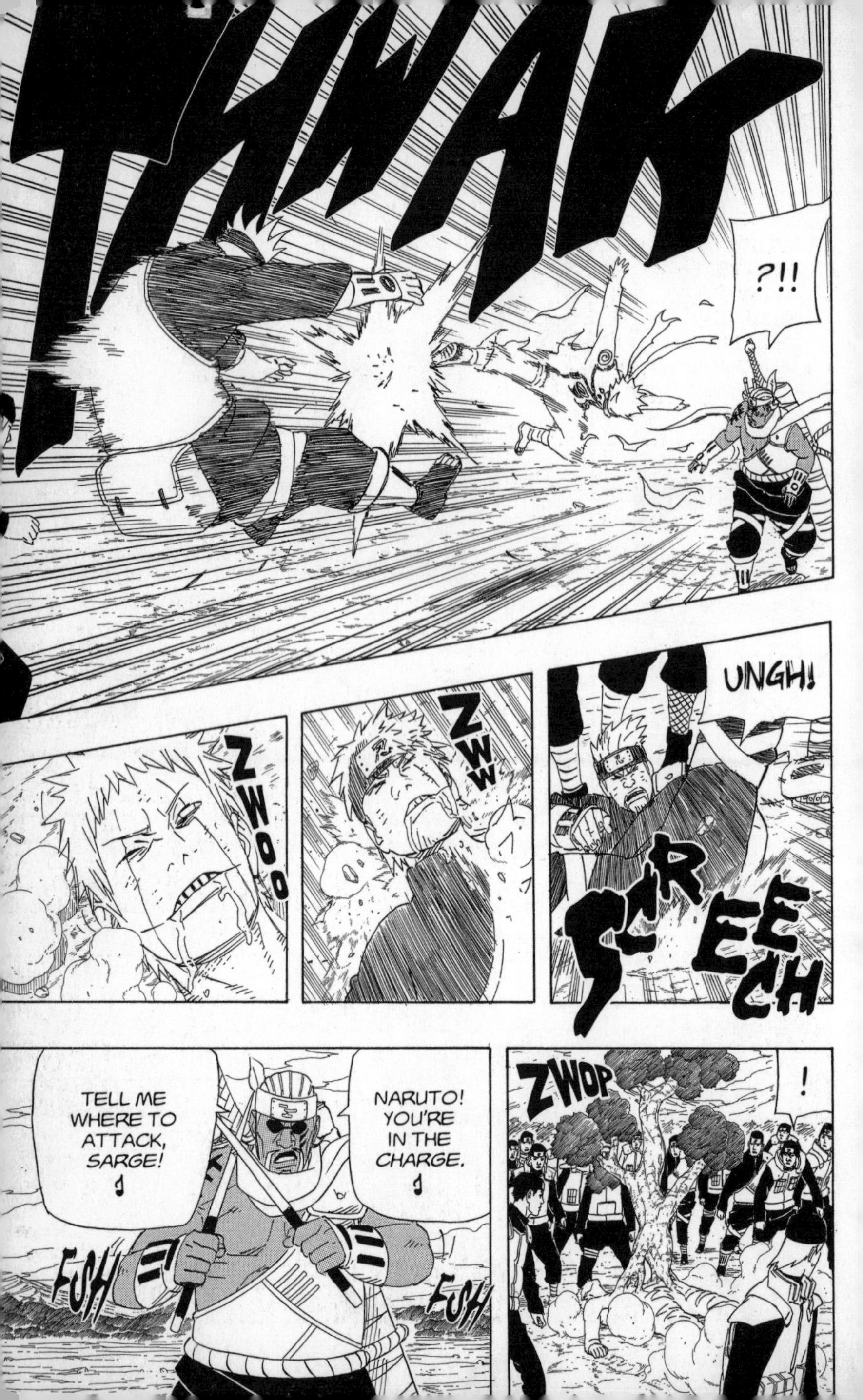
THWAK
?!!
UNGH!
SCREECH
ZWW
ZWOO
ZWOP
!
NARUTO! YOU'RE IN THE CHARGE.
TELL ME WHERE TO ATTACK, SARGE!
FSH
FSH

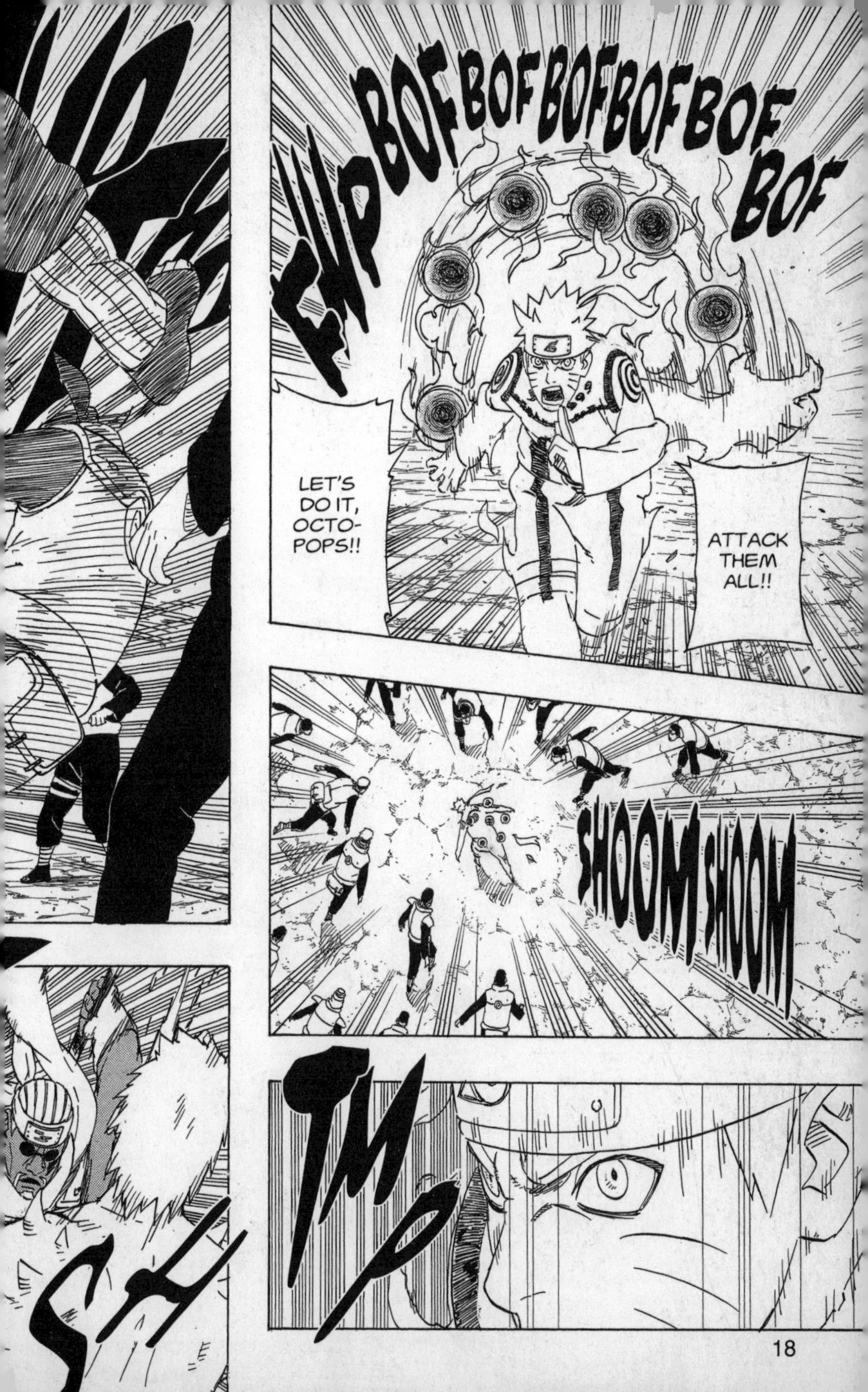
FWIP BOF BOF BOF BOF BOF BOF BOF
ATTACK THEM ALL!!
LET'S DO IT, OCTO-POPS!!
SHOOM SHOOM
THMP

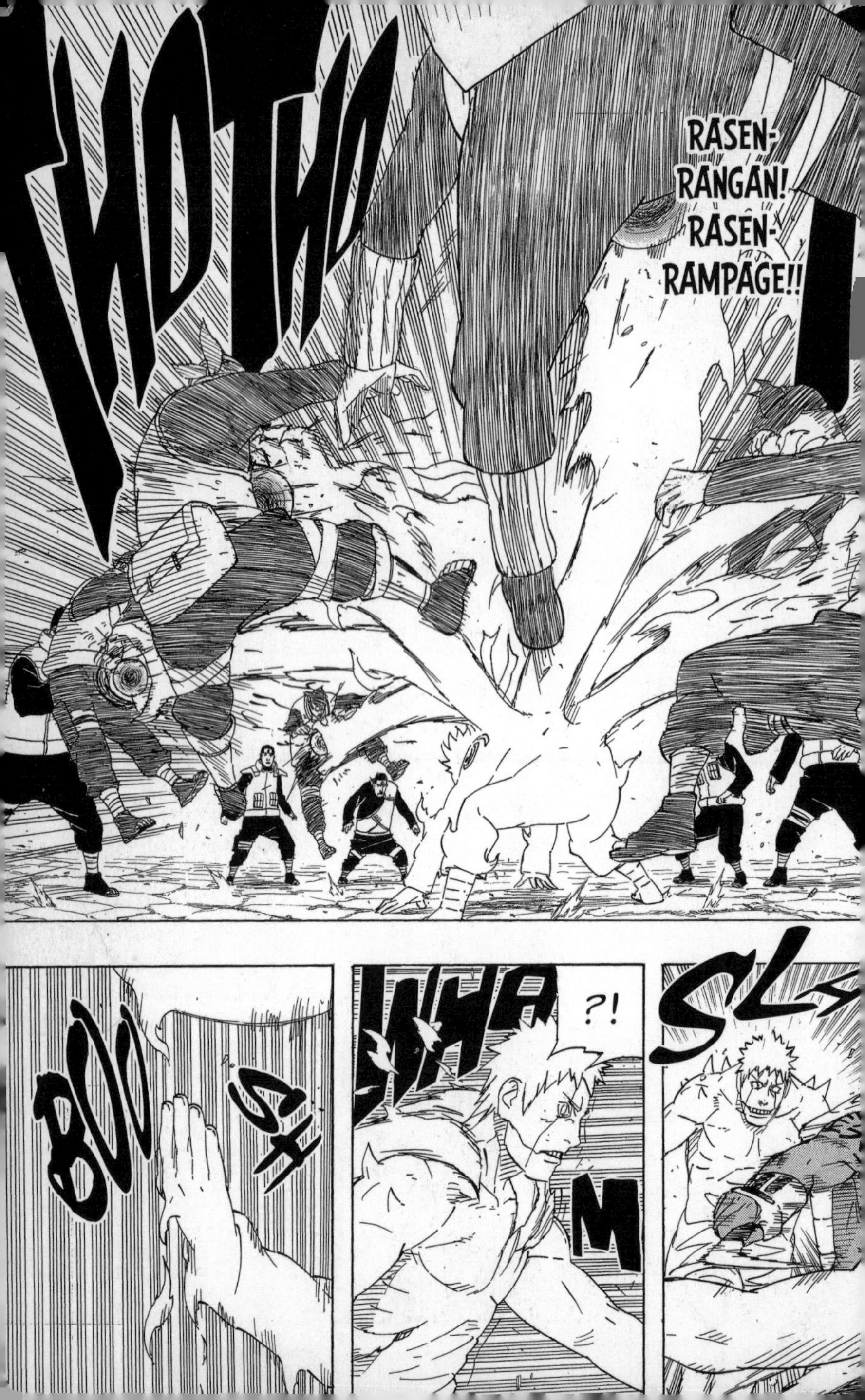
RASEN-RANGAN! RASEN-RAMPAGE!!
?!
BOOSH

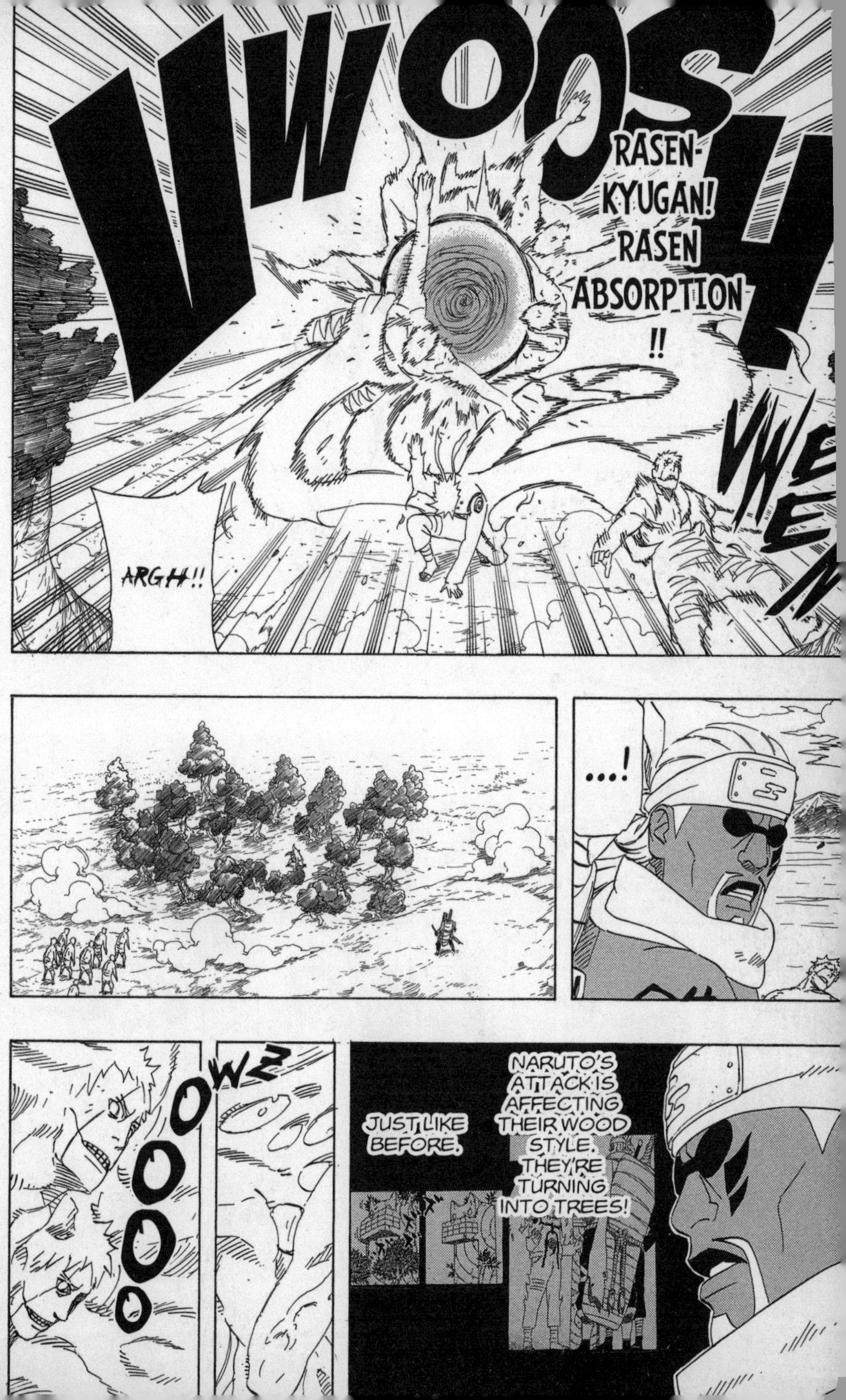
RASEN-KYUGAN! RASEN ABSORPTION!!
VWOOSH
VWEEN
ARGH!!
...!
NARUTO'S ATTACK IS AFFECTING THEIR WOOD STYLE. THEY'RE TURNING INTO TREES!
JUST LIKE BEFORE.
OOOOOWZ

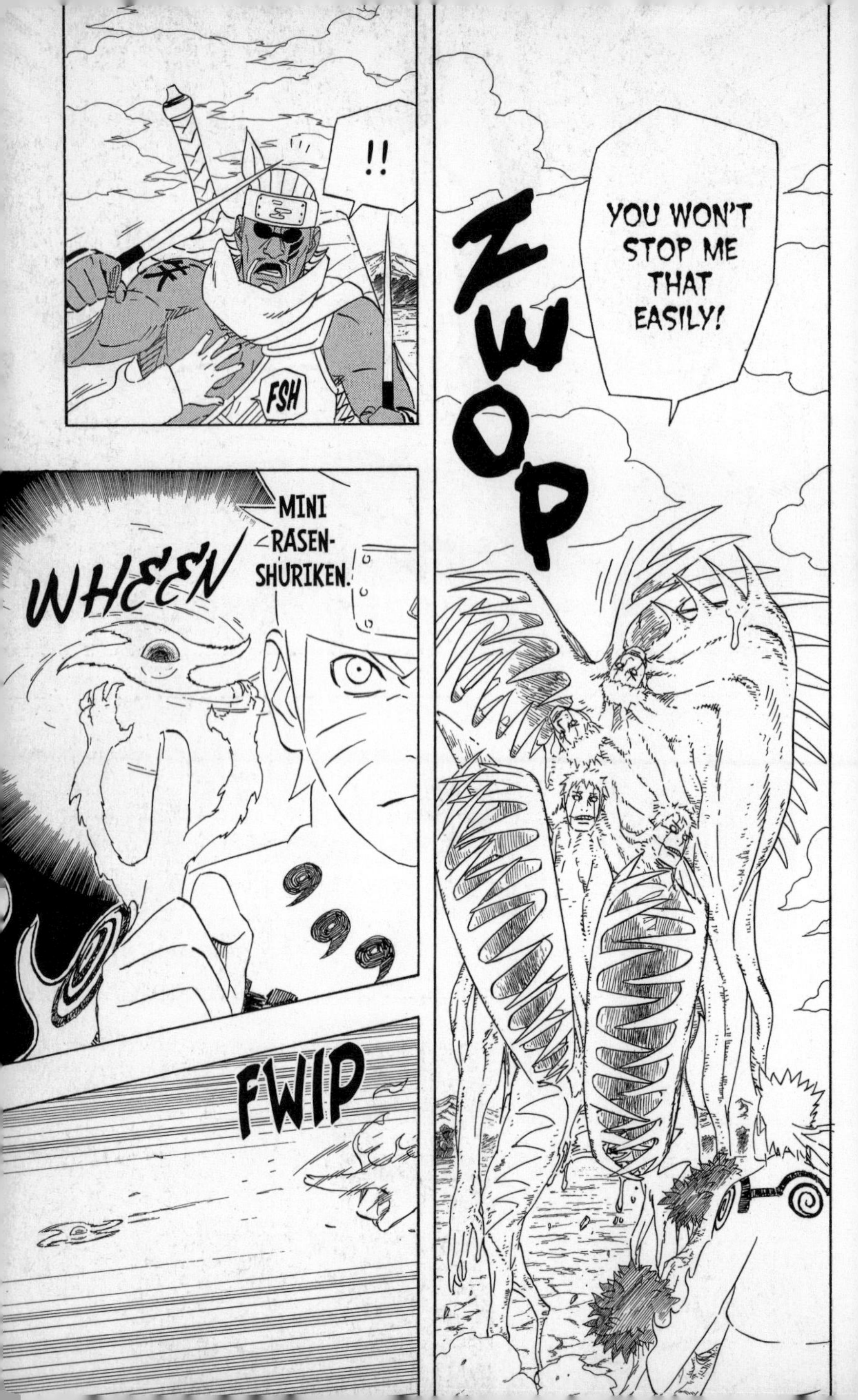

ZWOP
YOU WON'T STOP ME THAT EASILY!
!!
FSH
MINI RASEN-SHURIKEN.
WHEEN
FWIP

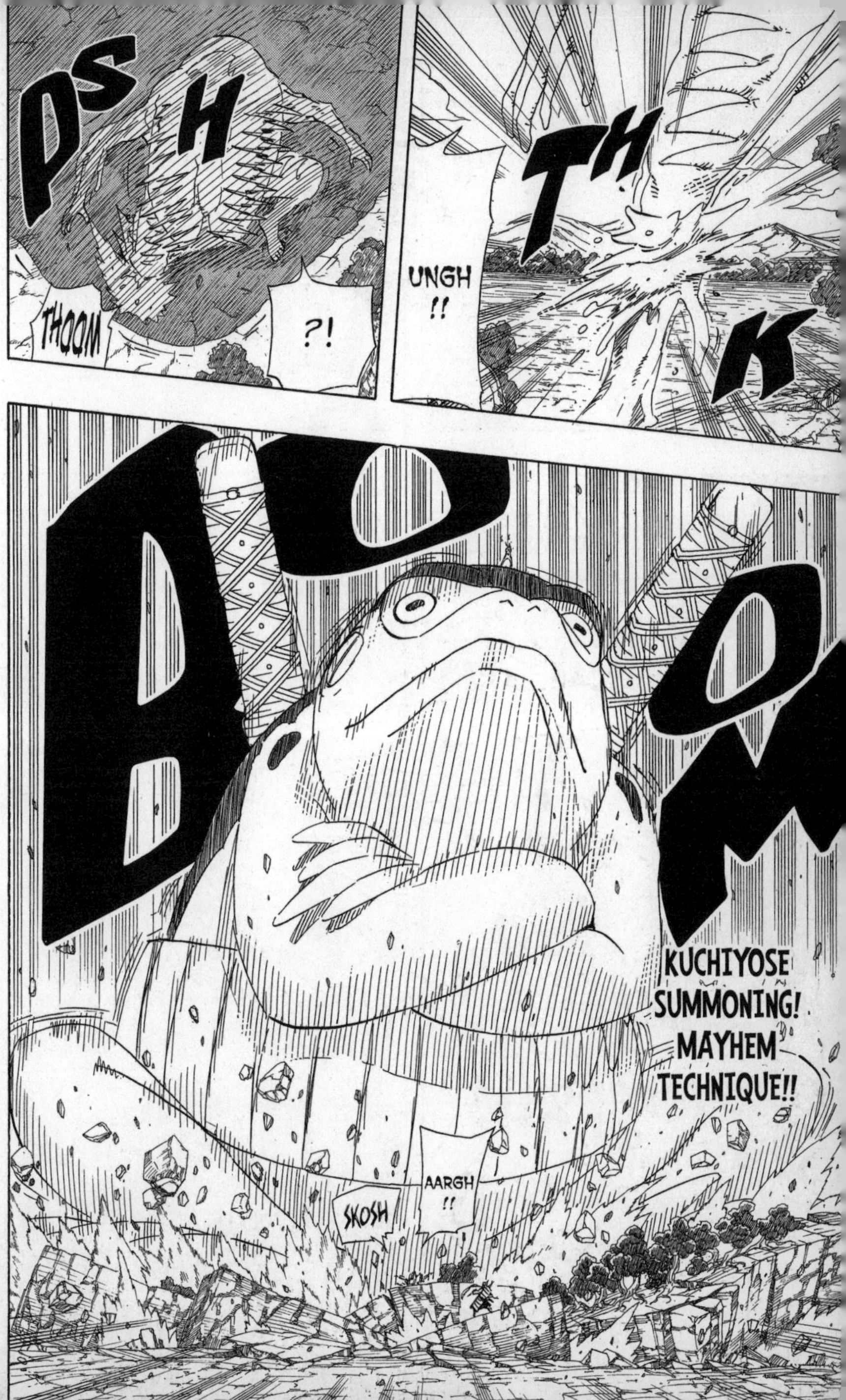
THK
UNGH !!
PSH
THOOM
?!
KUCHIYOSE SUMMONING! MAYHEM TECHNIQUE!!
AARGH !!
SKOSH

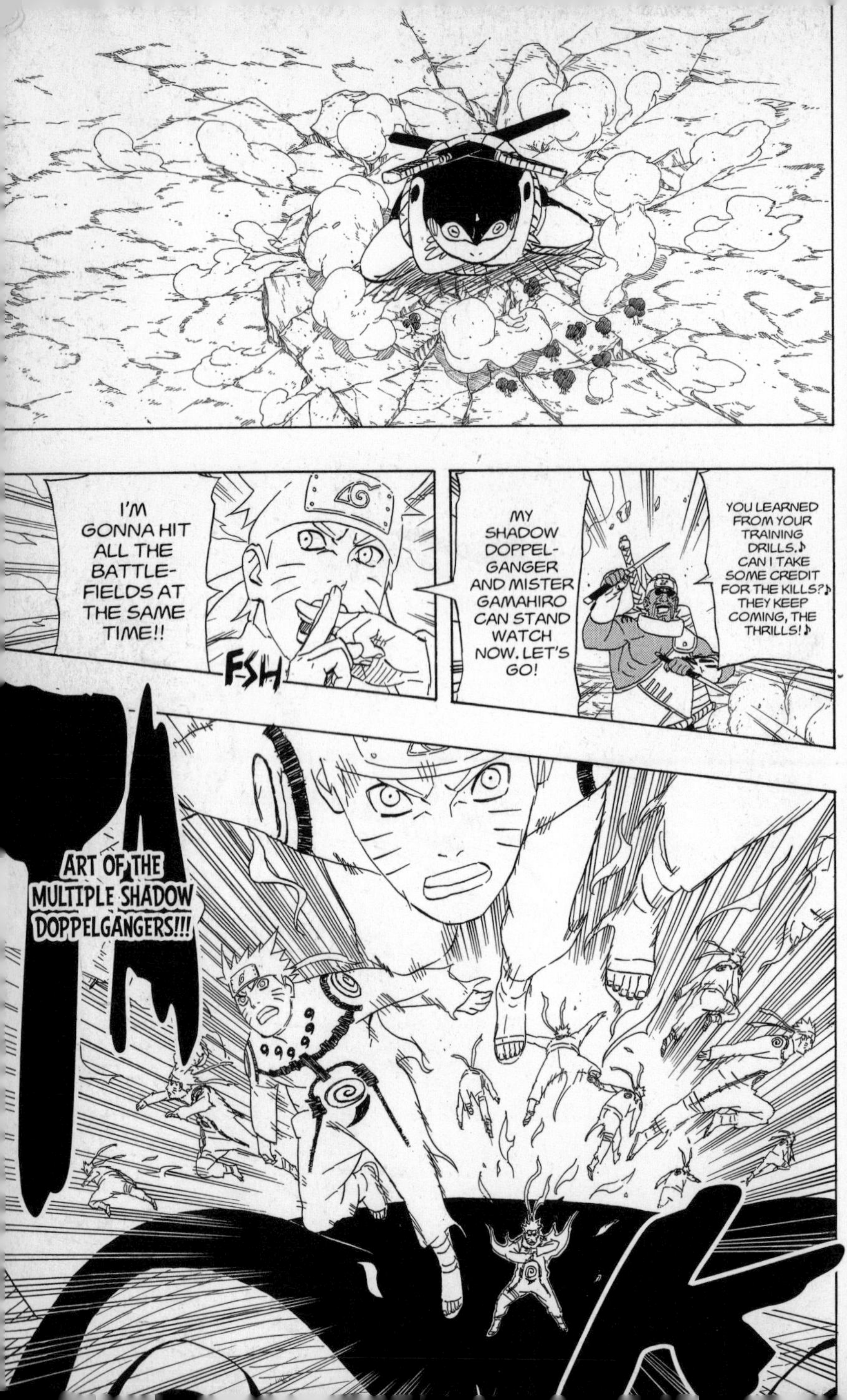
YOU LEARNED FROM YOUR TRAINING DRILLS.♪ CAN I TAKE SOME CREDIT FOR THE KILLS?♪ THEY KEEP COMING, THE THRILLS!♪
MY SHADOW DOPPEL-GANGER AND MISTER GAMAHIRO CAN STAND WATCH NOW. LET'S GO!
I'M GONNA HIT ALL THE BATTLE-FIELDS AT THE SAME TIME!!
FSH
ART OF THE MULTIPLE SHADOW DOPPELGANGERS!!!

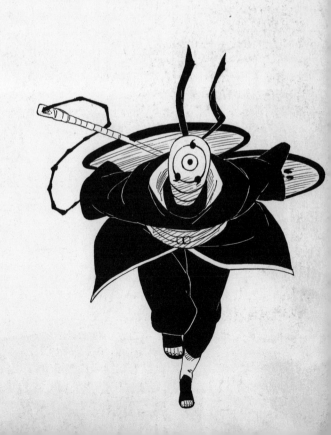

Number 546: Kage Showdown!!

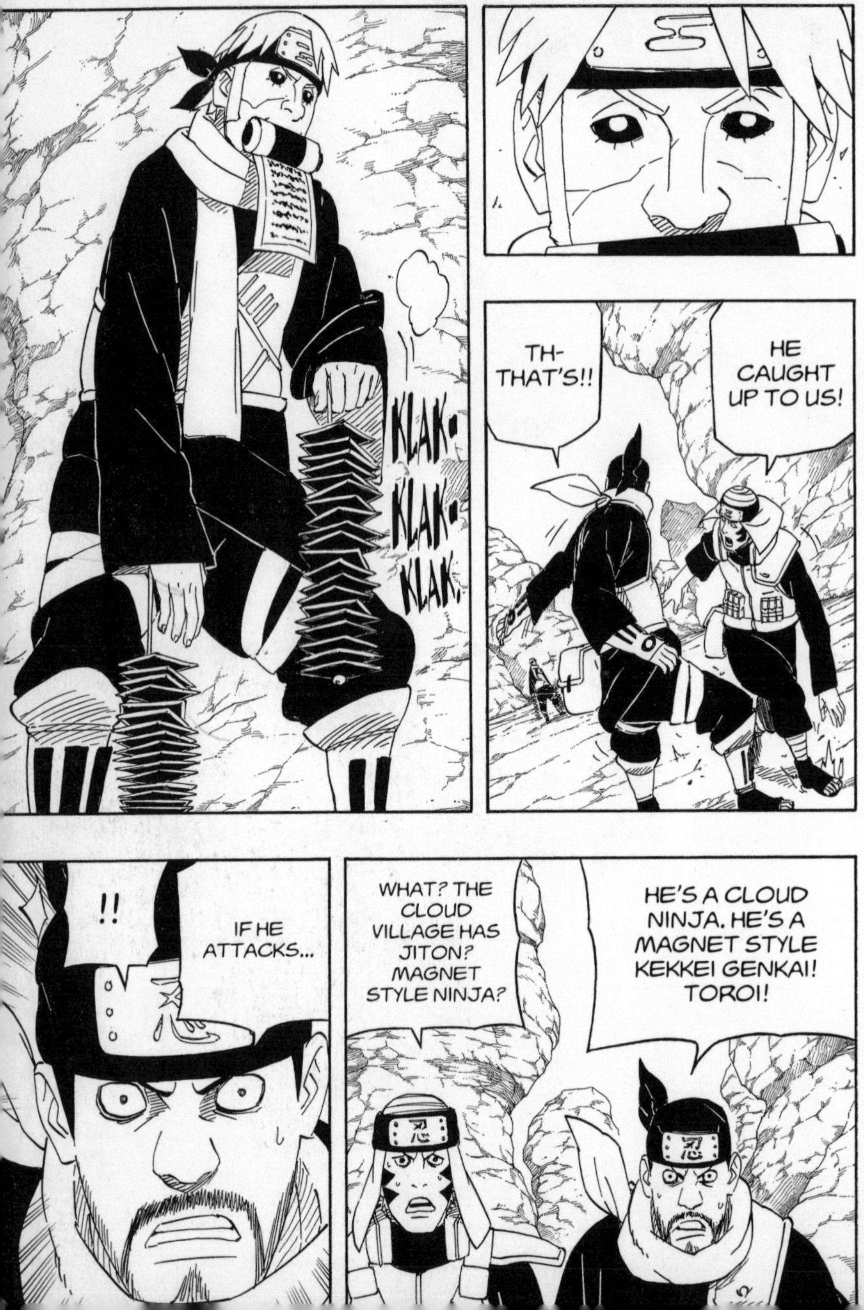
HE CAUGHT UP TO US!
TH- THAT'S!!
KLAK KLAK KLAK
HE'S A CLOUD NINJA. HE'S A MAGNET STYLE KEKKEI GENKAI! TOROI!
WHAT? THE CLOUD VILLAGE HAS JITON? MAGNET STYLE NINJA?
IF HE ATTACKS...
!!

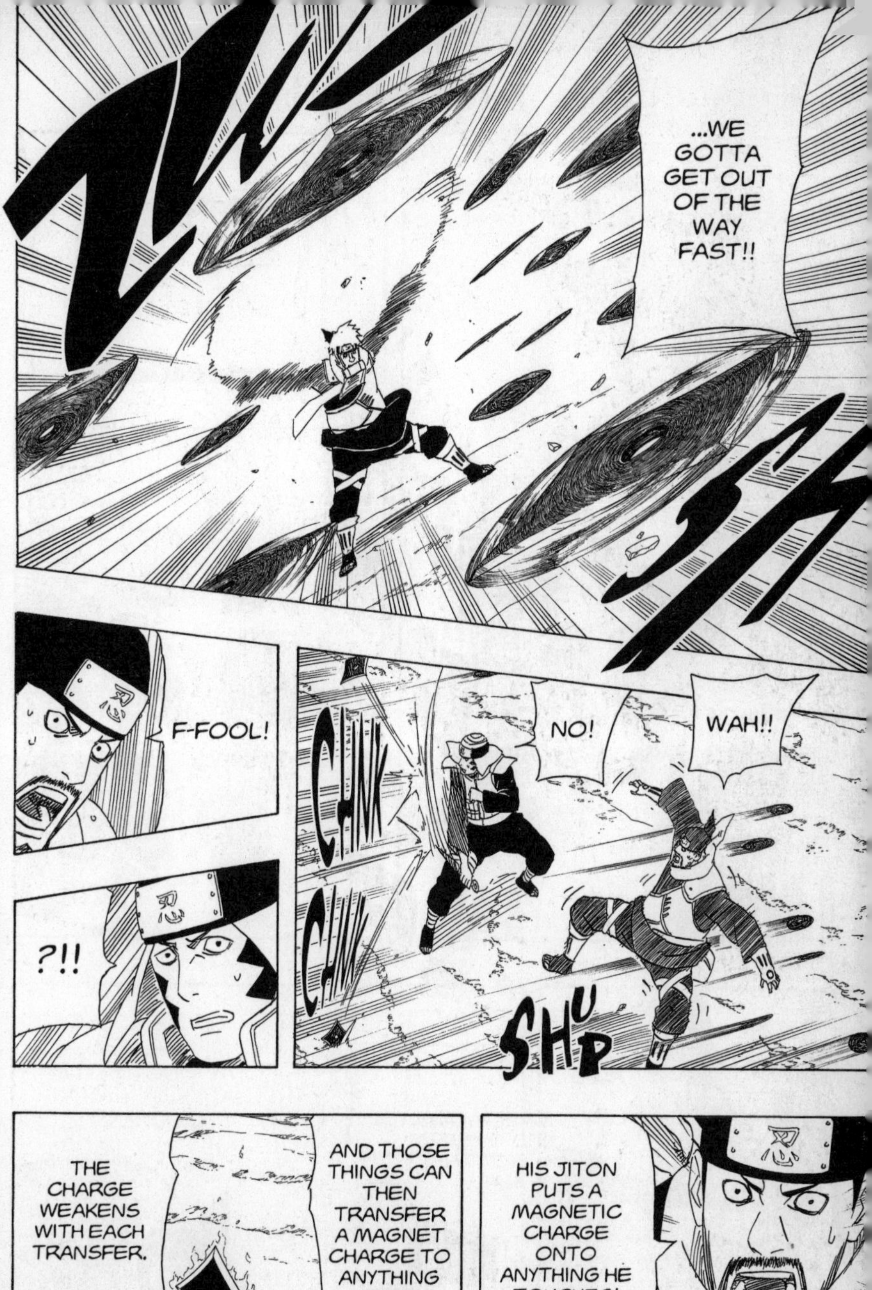
...WE GOTTA GET OUT OF THE WAY FAST!!
WAH!!
NO!
CHINK
CHINK
SHUP
F-FOOL!
?!!
HIS JITON PUTS A MAGNETIC CHARGE ONTO ANYTHING HE TOUCHES!
AND THOSE THINGS CAN THEN TRANSFER A MAGNET CHARGE TO ANYTHING THEY TOUCH!
THE CHARGE WEAKENS WITH EACH TRANSFER.

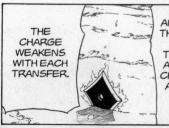

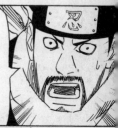

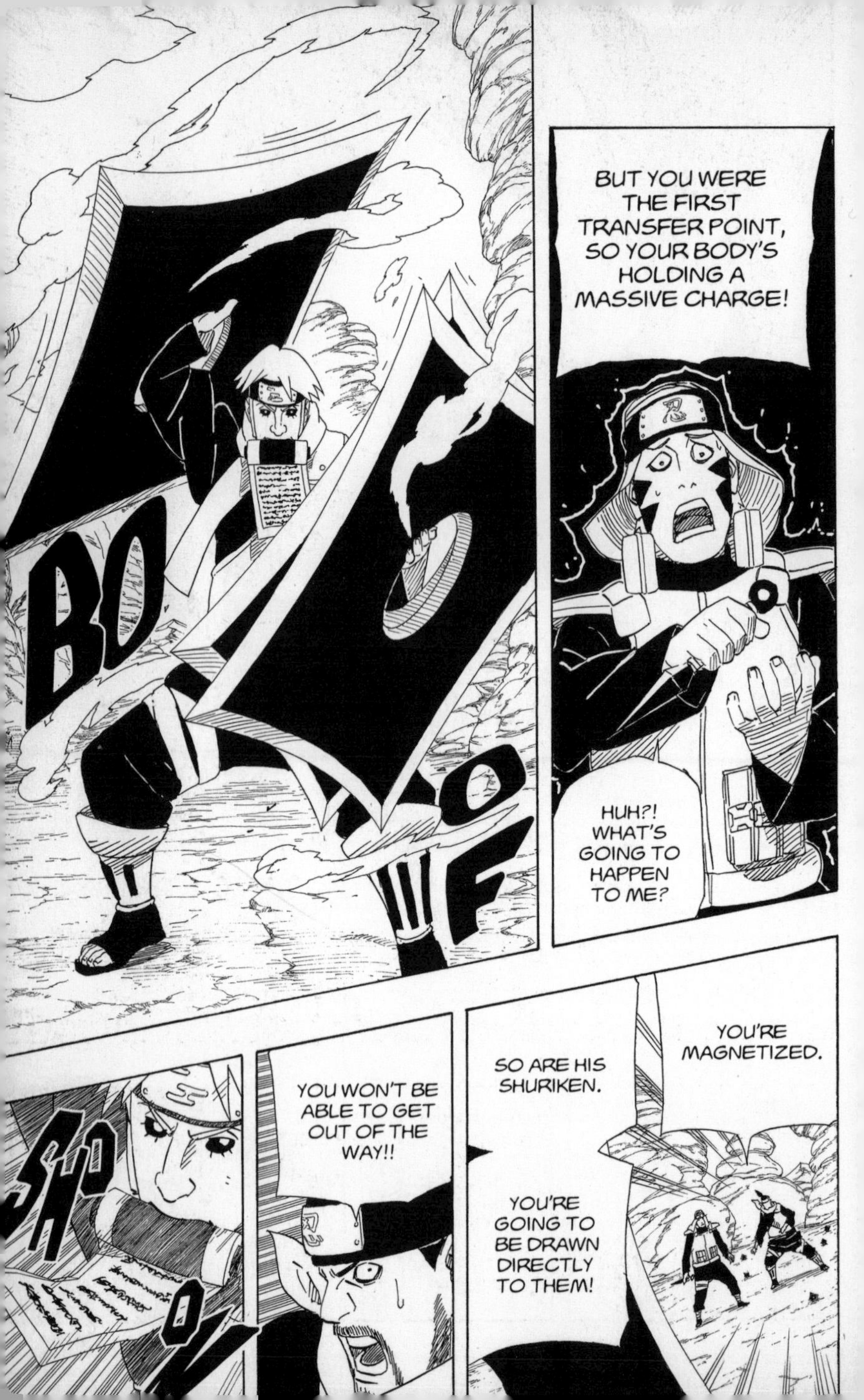
BUT YOU WERE THE FIRST TRANSFER POINT, SO YOUR BODY'S HOLDING A MASSIVE CHARGE!
HUH?! WHAT'S GOING TO HAPPEN TO ME?
BOOF
YOU'RE MAGNETIZED.
SO ARE HIS SHURIKEN.
YOU'RE GOING TO BE DRAWN DIRECTLY TO THEM!
YOU WON'T BE ABLE TO GET OUT OF THE WAY!!
SHOO

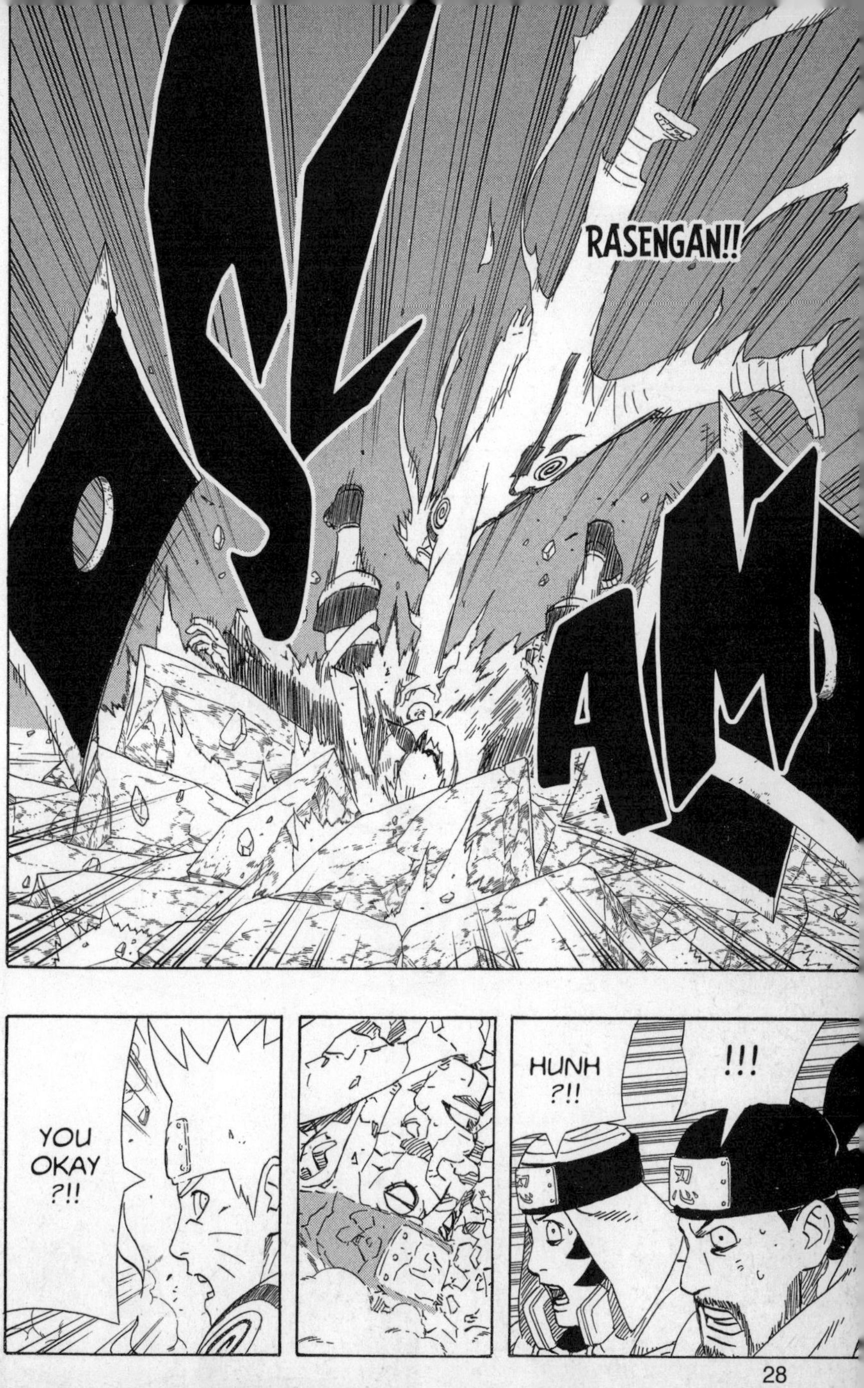
RASENGAN!!
!!!
HUNH ?!!
YOU OKAY ?!!

READ THIS WAY

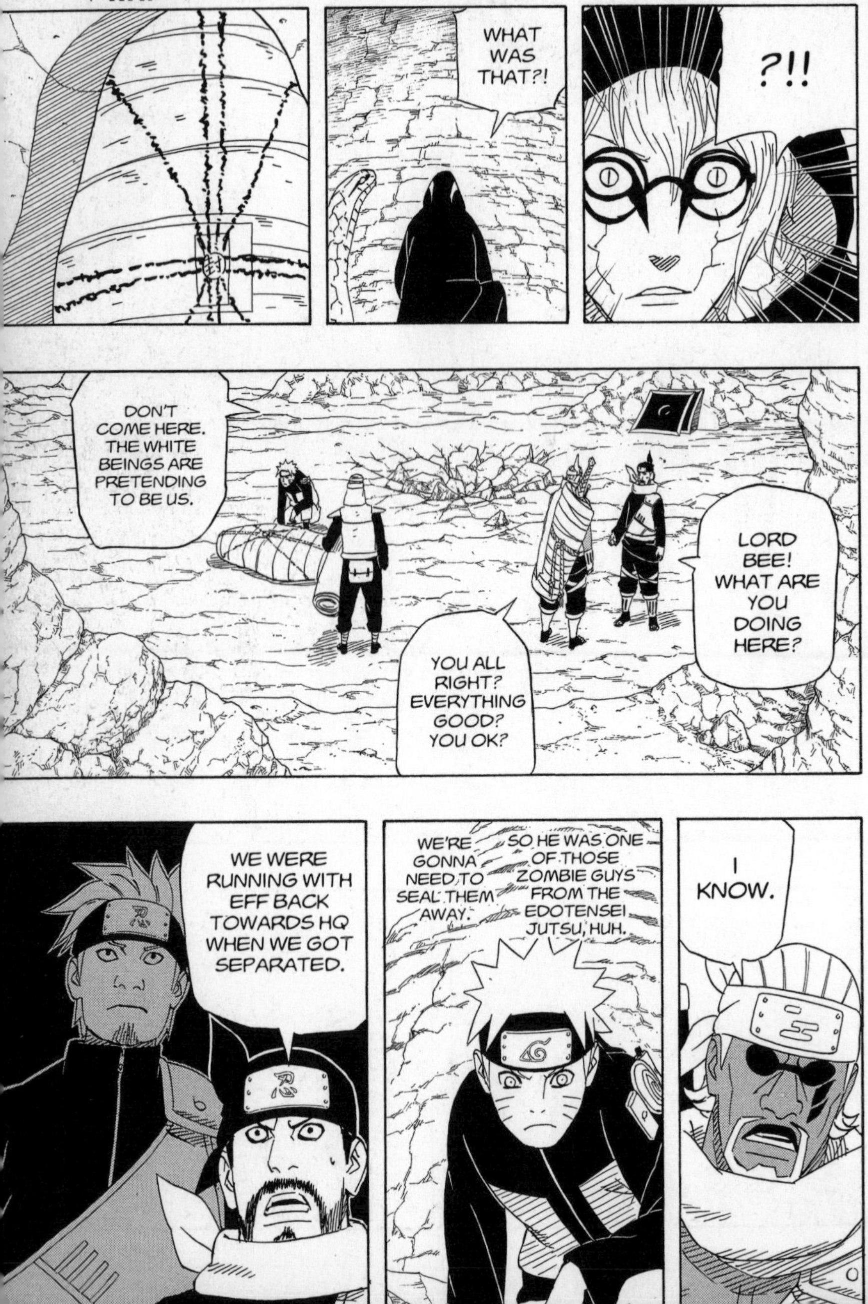
?!!
WHAT WAS THAT?!
LORD BEE! WHAT ARE YOU DOING HERE?
YOU ALL RIGHT? EVERYTHING GOOD? YOU OK?
DON'T COME HERE. THE WHITE BEINGS ARE PRETENDING TO BE US.
I KNOW.
SO HE WAS ONE OF THOSE ZOMBIE GUYS FROM THE EDOTENSEI JUTSU, HUH.
WE'RE GONNA NEED TO SEAL THEM AWAY.
WE WERE RUNNING WITH EFF BACK TOWARDS HQ WHEN WE GOT SEPARATED.

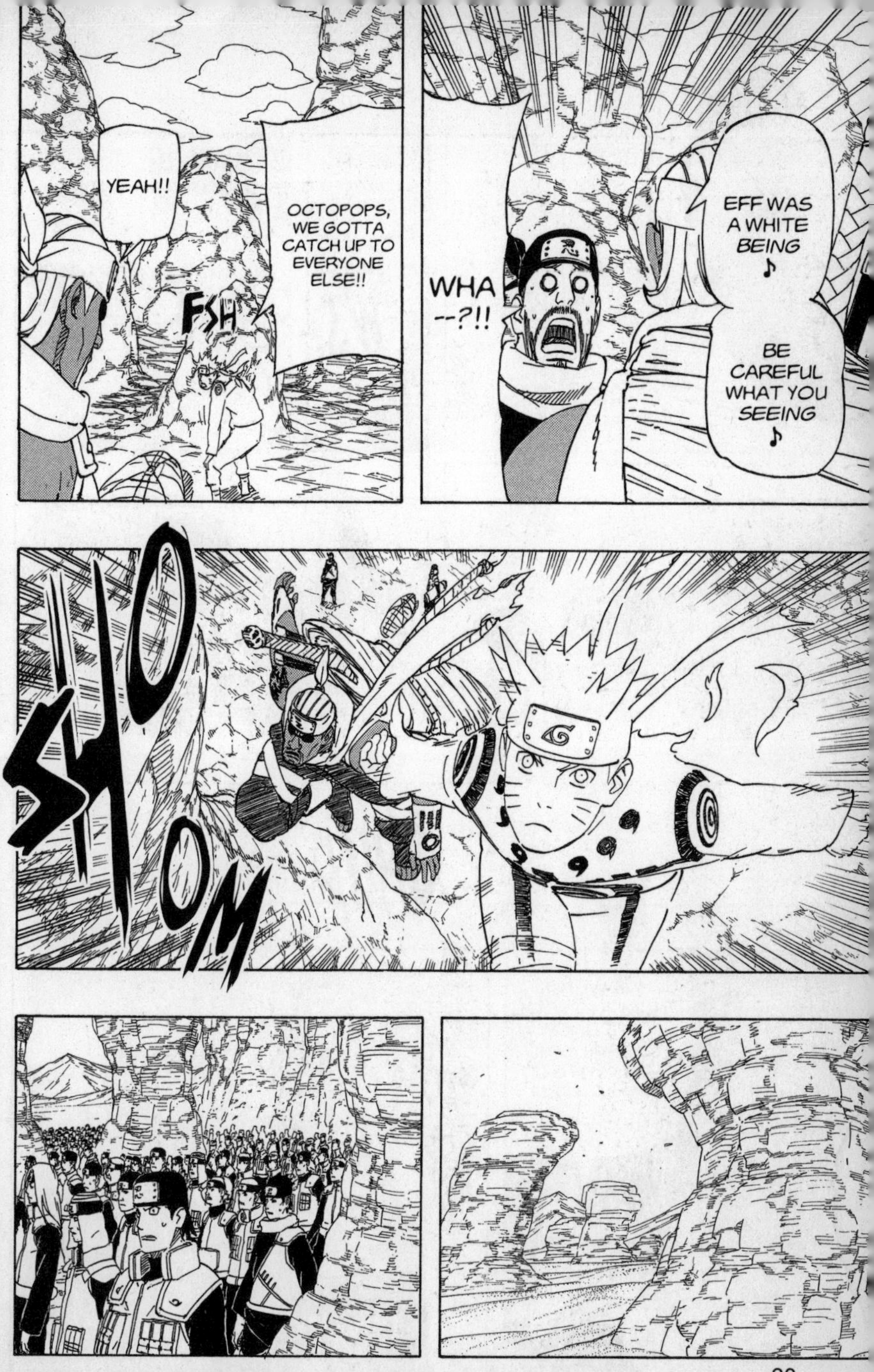
EFF WAS A WHITE BEING ♪
BE CAREFUL WHAT YOU SEEING ♪
WHA--?!!
OCTOPOPS, WE GOTTA CATCH UP TO EVERYONE ELSE!!
YEAH!!
FSH
SHOOM

READ THIS WAY

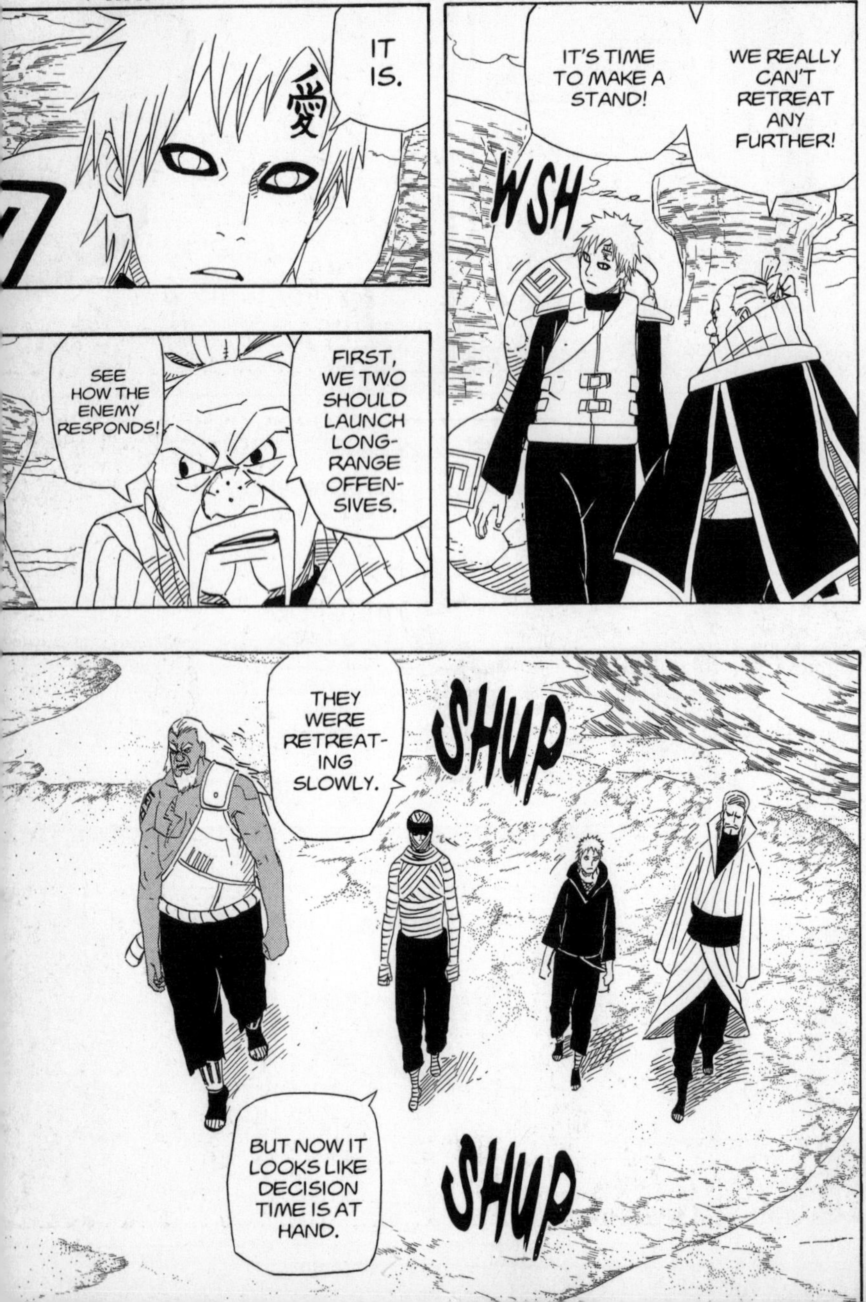
WE REALLY CAN'T RETREAT ANY FURTHER!
IT'S TIME TO MAKE A STAND!
WSH
IT IS.
FIRST, WE TWO SHOULD LAUNCH LONG-RANGE OFFENSIVES.
SEE HOW THE ENEMY RESPONDS!
SHUP
THEY WERE RETREATING SLOWLY.
SHUP
BUT NOW IT LOOKS LIKE DECISION TIME IS AT HAND.

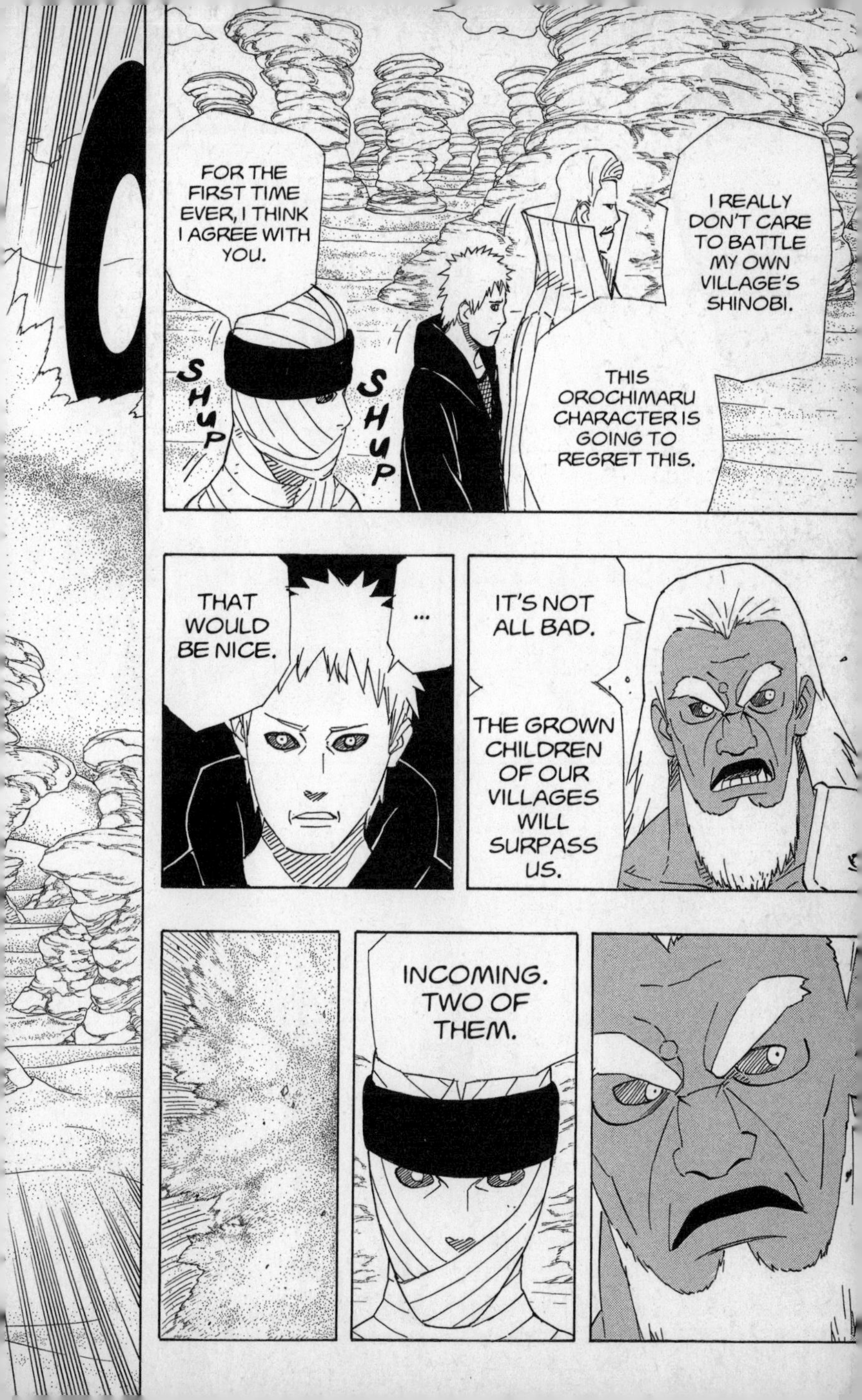
I REALLY DON'T CARE TO BATTLE MY OWN VILLAGE'S SHINOBI.
THIS OROCHIMARU CHARACTER IS GOING TO REGRET THIS.
FOR THE FIRST TIME EVER, I THINK I AGREE WITH YOU.
SHUP
SHUP
IT'S NOT ALL BAD.
THE GROWN CHILDREN OF OUR VILLAGES WILL SURPASS US.
...
THAT WOULD BE NICE.
INCOMING. TWO OF THEM.

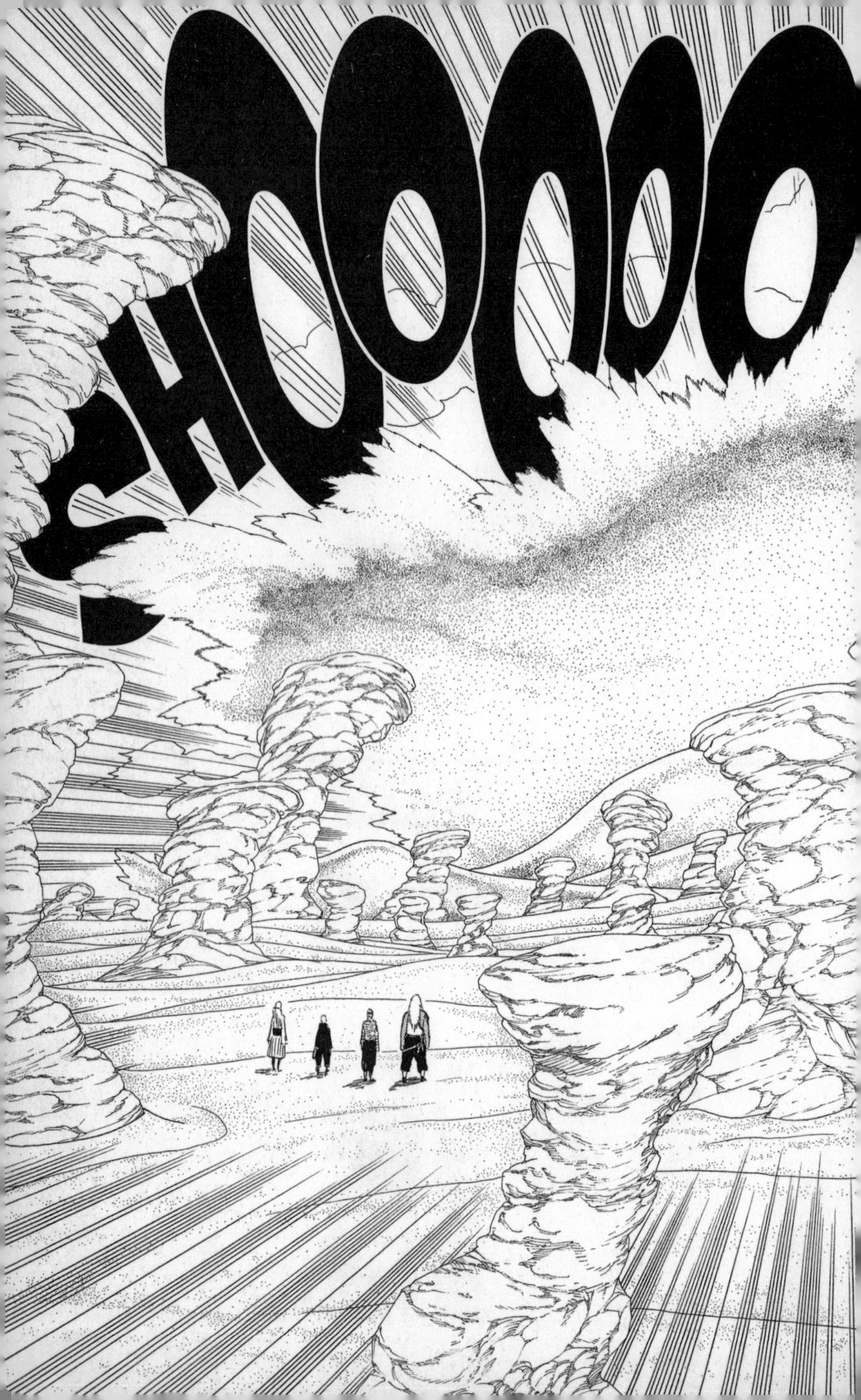
SHOOOOOO

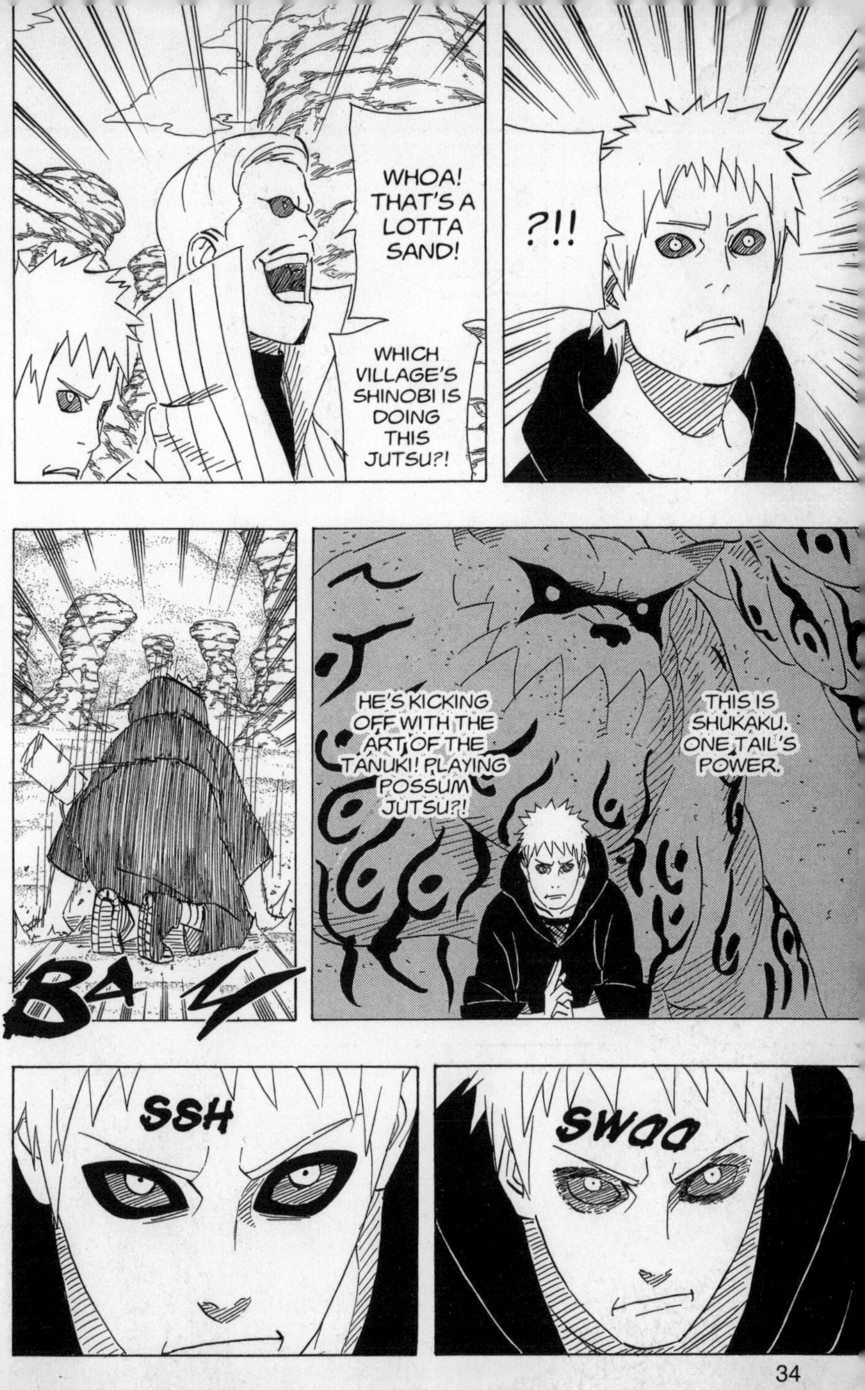
?!!
WHOA! THAT'S A LOTTA SAND!
WHICH VILLAGE'S SHINOBI IS DOING THIS JUTSU?!
THIS IS SHUKAKU. ONE TAIL'S POWER.
HE'S KICKING OFF WITH THE ART OF THE TANUKI! PLAYING POSSUM JUTSU?!
BAM
SWAA
SSH

READ THIS WAY

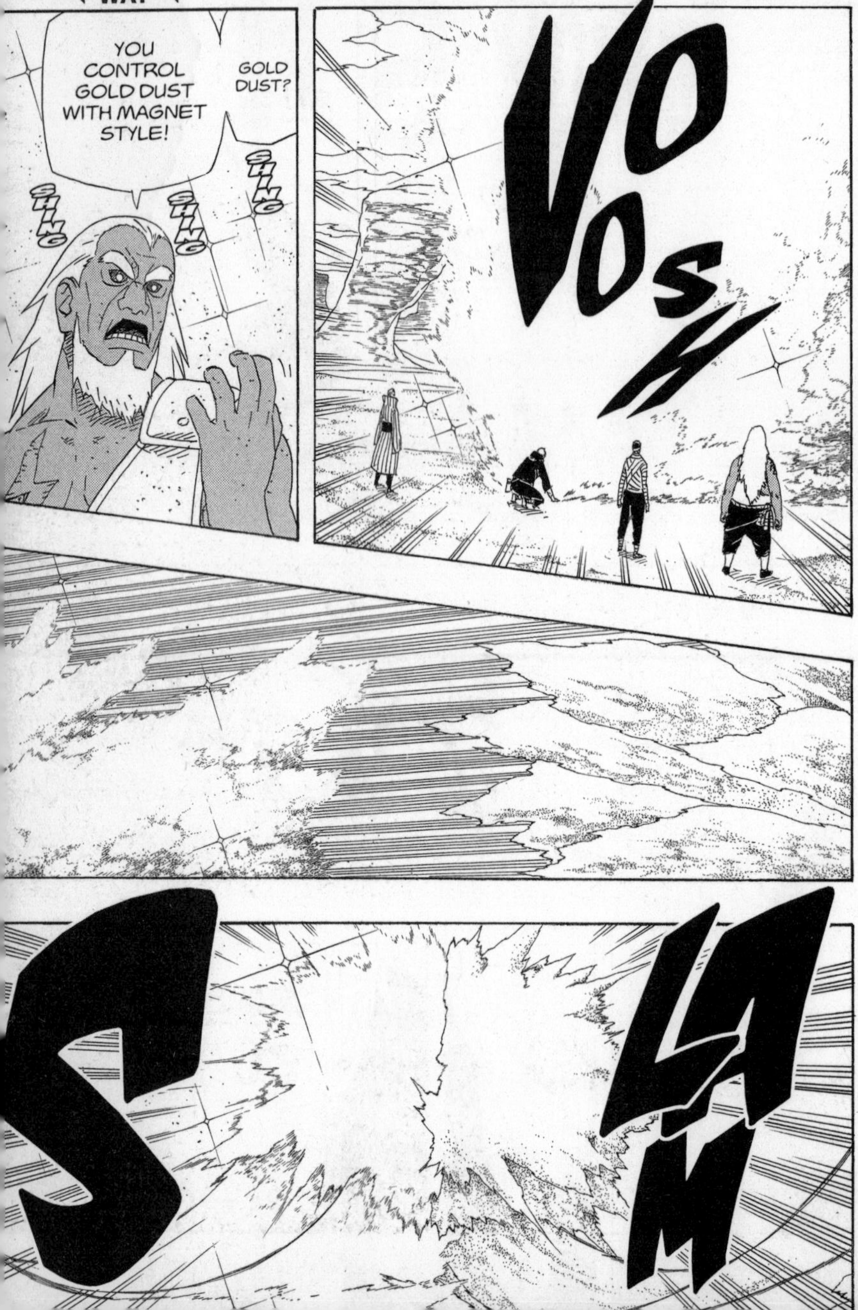
VOOSH
GOLD DUST?
YOU CONTROL GOLD DUST WITH MAGNET STYLE!
SHING
SHING
SHING
SLAM

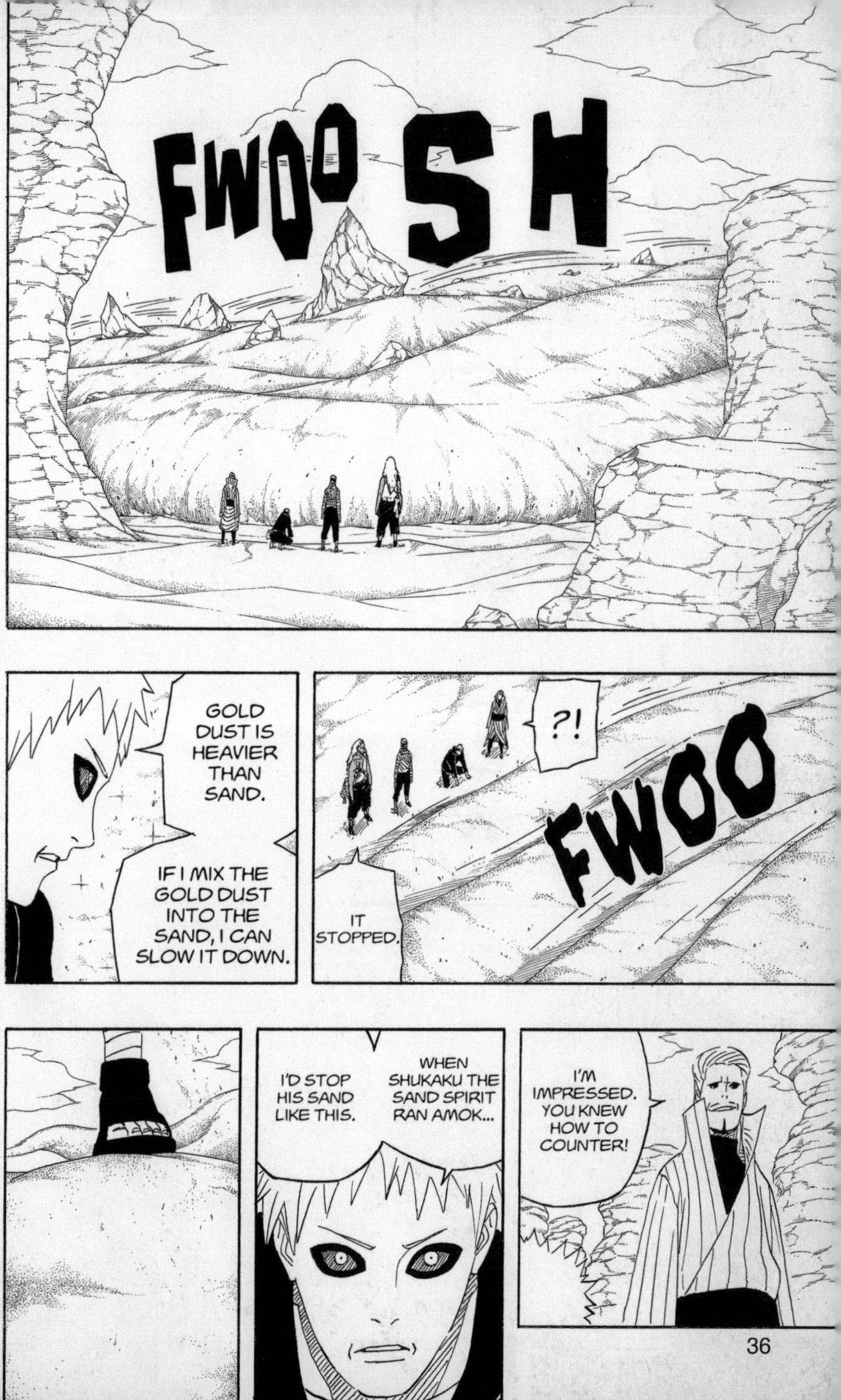
FWOOSH
FWOO
?!
IT STOPPED.
GOLD DUST IS HEAVIER THAN SAND.
IF I MIX THE GOLD DUST INTO THE SAND, I CAN SLOW IT DOWN.
I'M IMPRESSED. YOU KNEW HOW TO COUNTER!
WHEN SHUKAKU THE SAND SPIRIT RAN AMOK...
I'D STOP HIS SAND LIKE THIS.

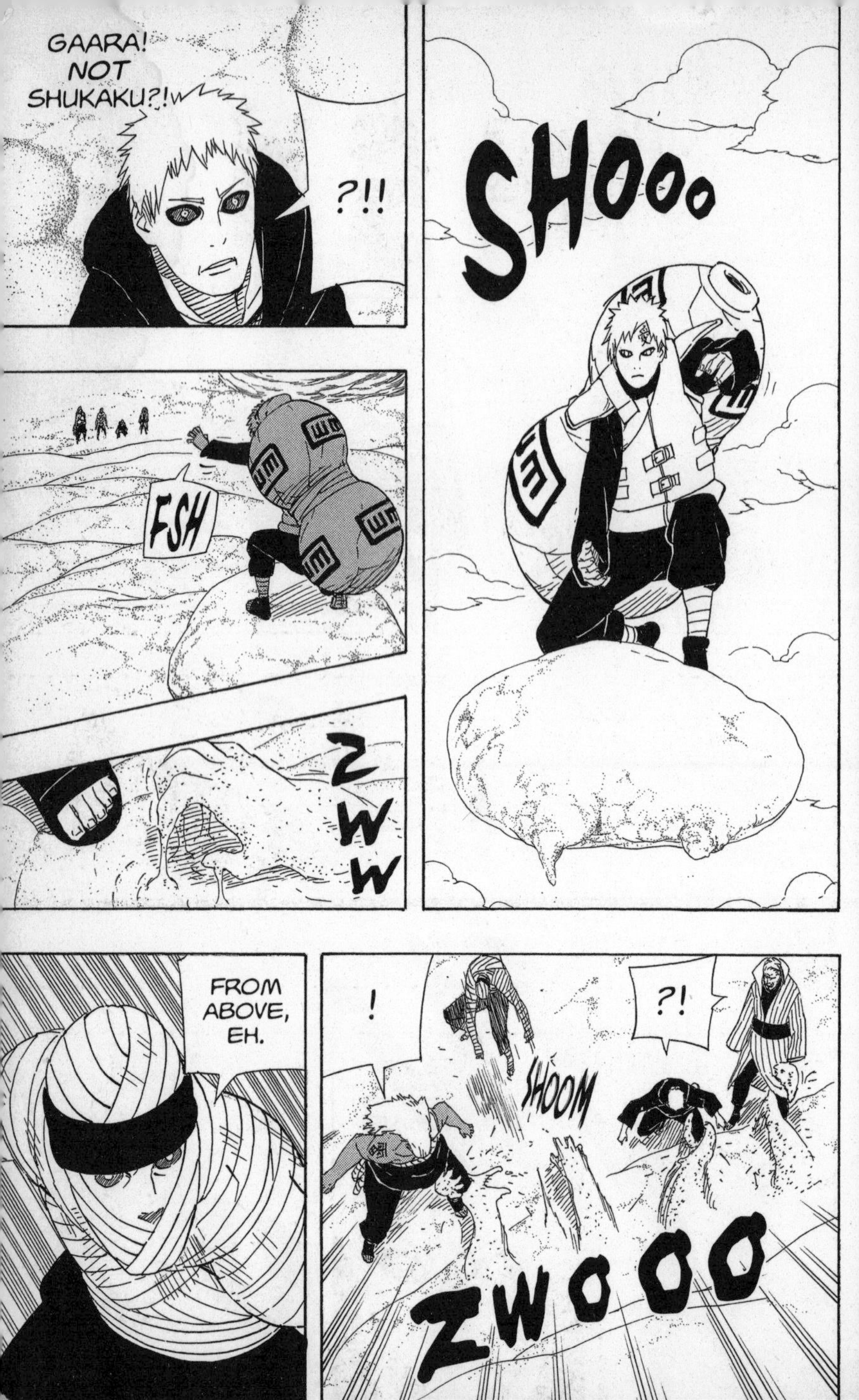
SHOOO
GAARA! NOT SHUKAKU?!
?!!
FSH
ZWW
?!
!
SHOOM
ZWOOO
FROM ABOVE, EH.

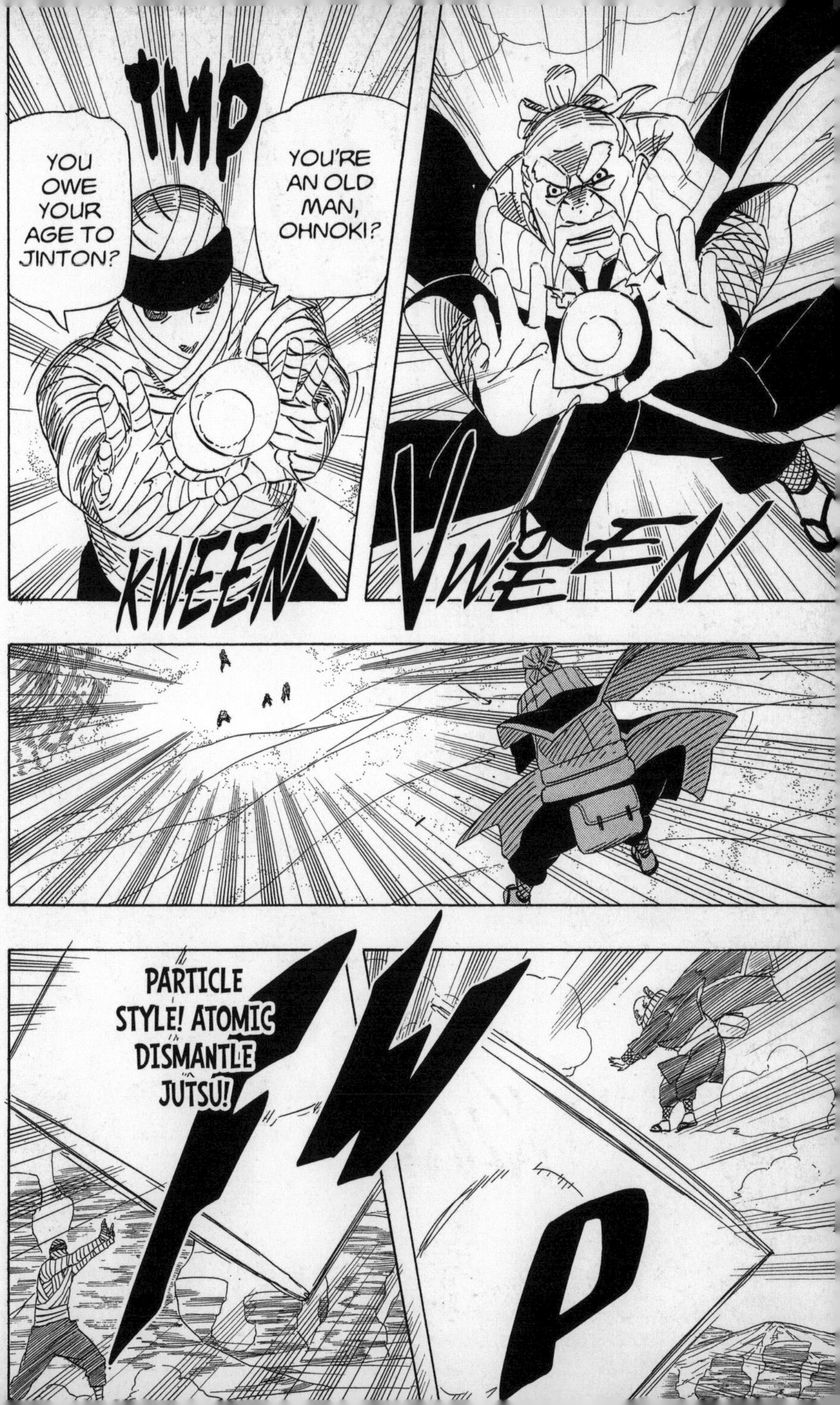
VWEEN
YOU'RE AN OLD MAN, OHNOKI?
TMP
YOU OWE YOUR AGE TO JINTON?
KWEEN
FWP
PARTICLE STYLE! ATOMIC DISMANTLE JUTSU!

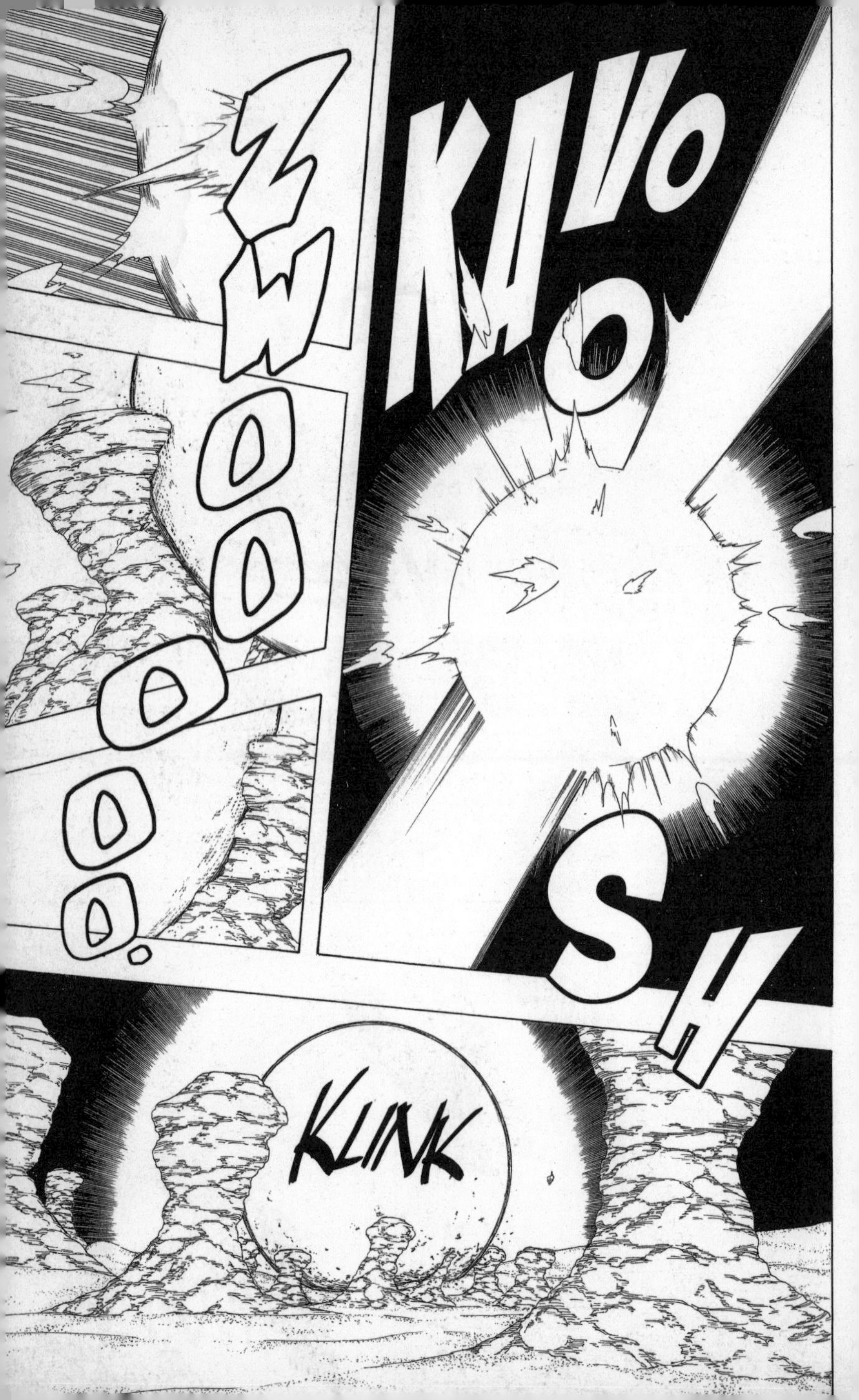
KAVOOSH
ZWOOOOO.
KLINK

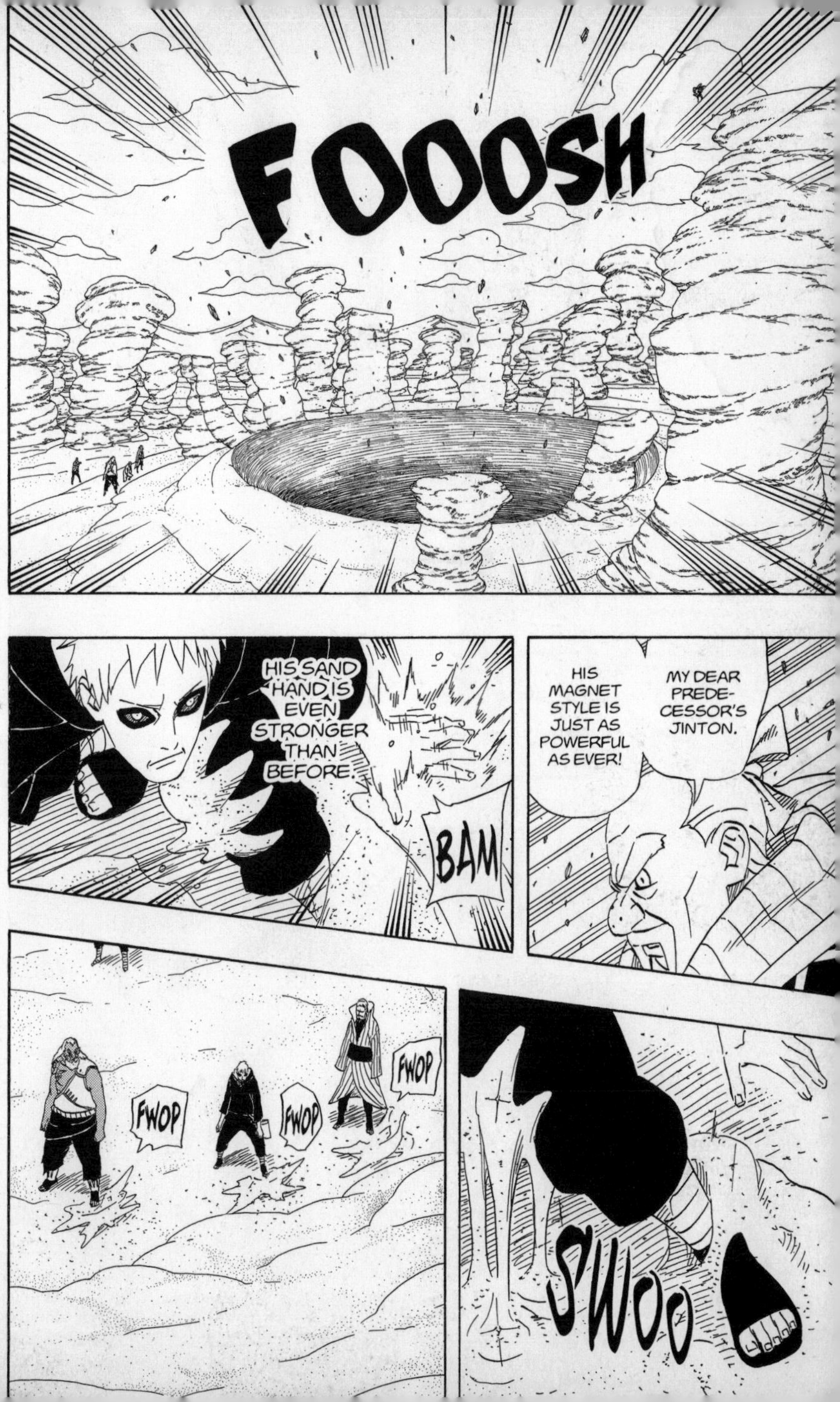
FOOOSH
MY DEAR PREDE-CESSOR'S JINTON.
HIS MAGNET STYLE IS JUST AS POWERFUL AS EVER!
HIS SAND HAND IS EVEN STRONGER THAN BEFORE.
BAM
SWOO
FWOP
FWOP
FWOP

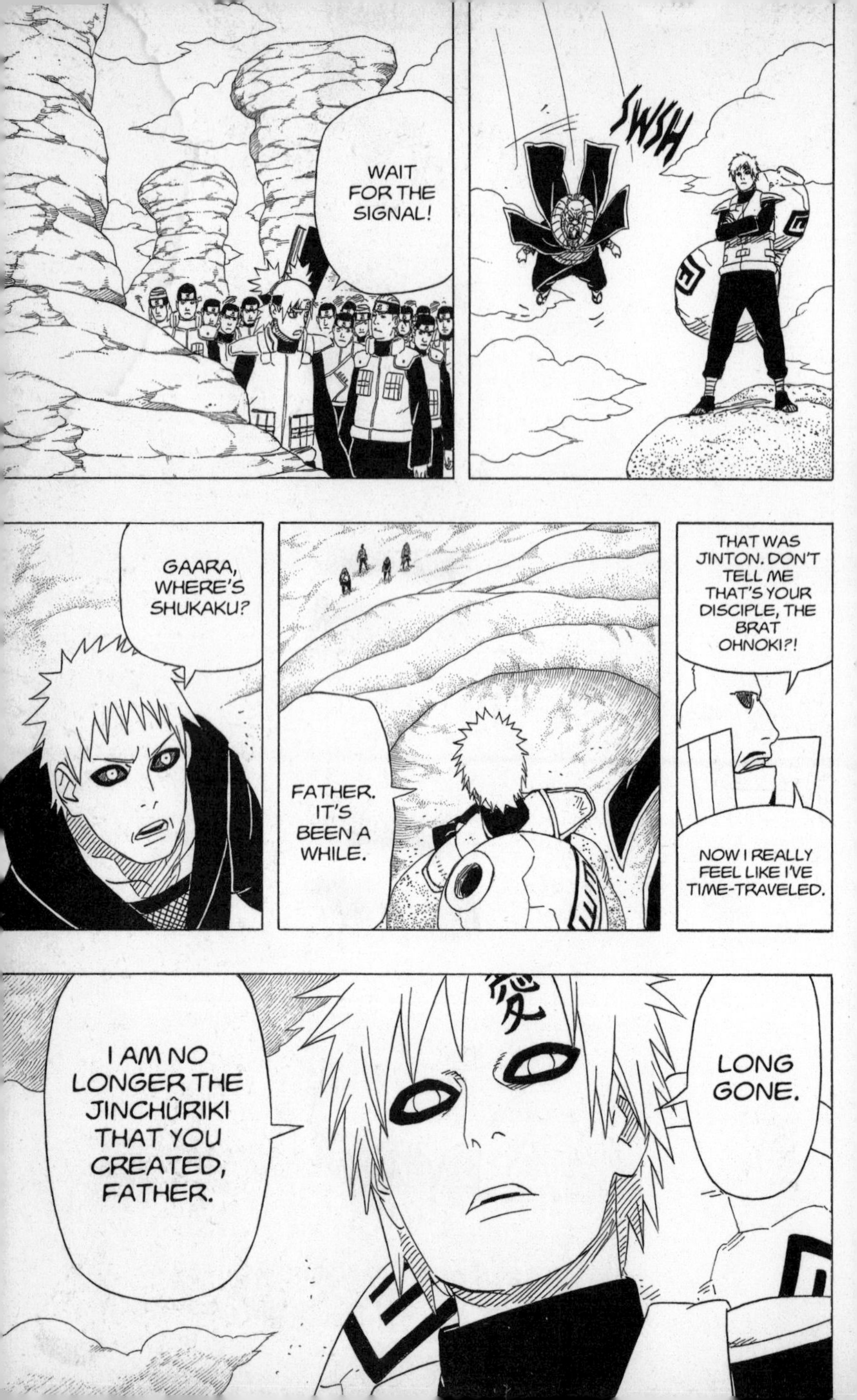
SWSH
WAIT FOR THE SIGNAL!
THAT WAS JINTON. DON'T TELL ME THAT'S YOUR DISCIPLE, THE BRAT OHNOKI?!
NOW I REALLY FEEL LIKE I'VE TIME-TRAVELED.
FATHER. IT'S BEEN A WHILE.
GAARA, WHERE'S SHUKAKU?
LONG GONE.
I AM NO LONGER THE JINCHÛRIKI THAT YOU CREATED, FATHER.

NARUTO

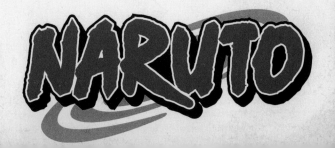

Number 547: Valued Treasures!!

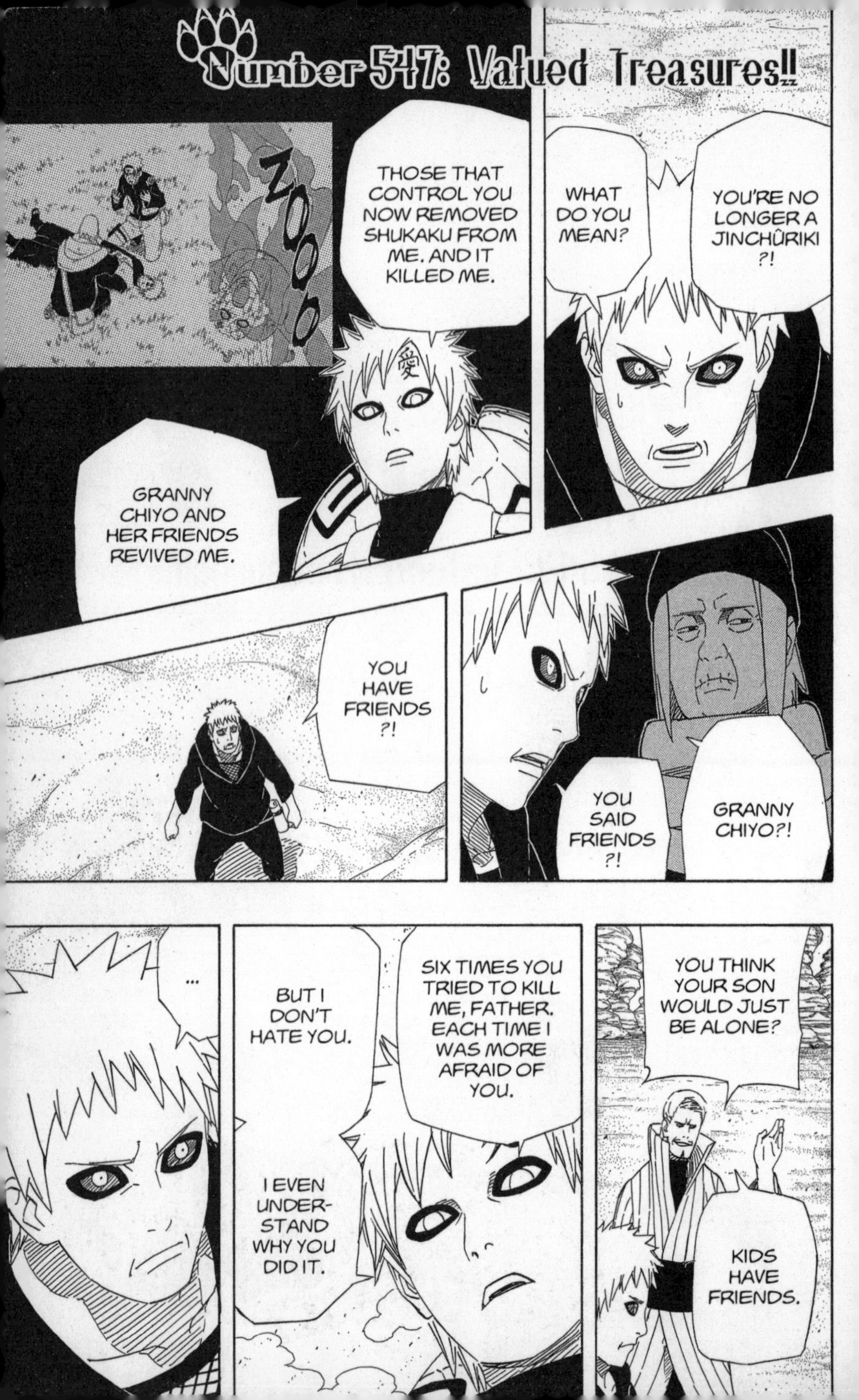

YOU'RE NO LONGER A JINCHÛRIKI ?!
WHAT DO YOU MEAN?
THOSE THAT CONTROL YOU NOW REMOVED SHUKAKU FROM ME. AND IT KILLED ME.
GRANNY CHIYO AND HER FRIENDS REVIVED ME.
GRANNY CHIYO?!
YOU SAID FRIENDS ?!
YOU HAVE FRIENDS ?!
YOU THINK YOUR SON WOULD JUST BE ALONE?
KIDS HAVE FRIENDS.
SIX TIMES YOU TRIED TO KILL ME, FATHER. EACH TIME I WAS MORE AFRAID OF YOU.
BUT I DON'T HATE YOU.
I EVEN UNDER-STAND WHY YOU DID IT.
...

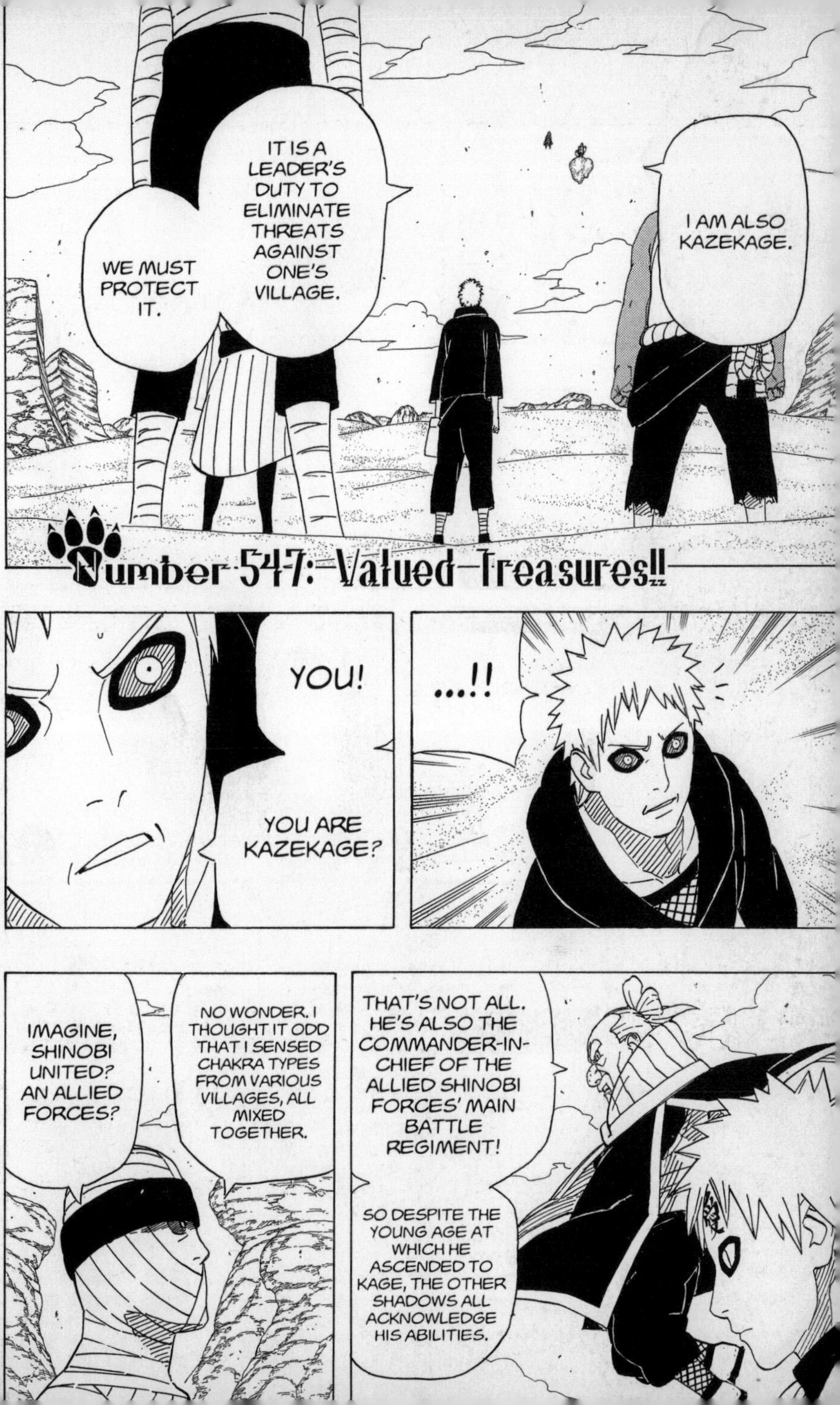
I AM ALSO KAZEKAGE.
IT IS A LEADER'S DUTY TO ELIMINATE THREATS AGAINST ONE'S VILLAGE.
WE MUST PROTECT IT.
Number 547: Valued Treasures!!
...!!
YOU!
YOU ARE KAZEKAGE?
THAT'S NOT ALL. HE'S ALSO THE COMMANDER-IN-CHIEF OF THE ALLIED SHINOBI FORCES' MAIN BATTLE REGIMENT!
SO DESPITE THE YOUNG AGE AT WHICH HE ASCENDED TO KAGE, THE OTHER SHADOWS ALL ACKNOWLEDGE HIS ABILITIES.
NO WONDER. I THOUGHT IT ODD THAT I SENSED CHAKRA TYPES FROM VARIOUS VILLAGES, ALL MIXED TOGETHER.
IMAGINE, SHINOBI UNITED? AN ALLIED FORCES?

READ THIS WAY

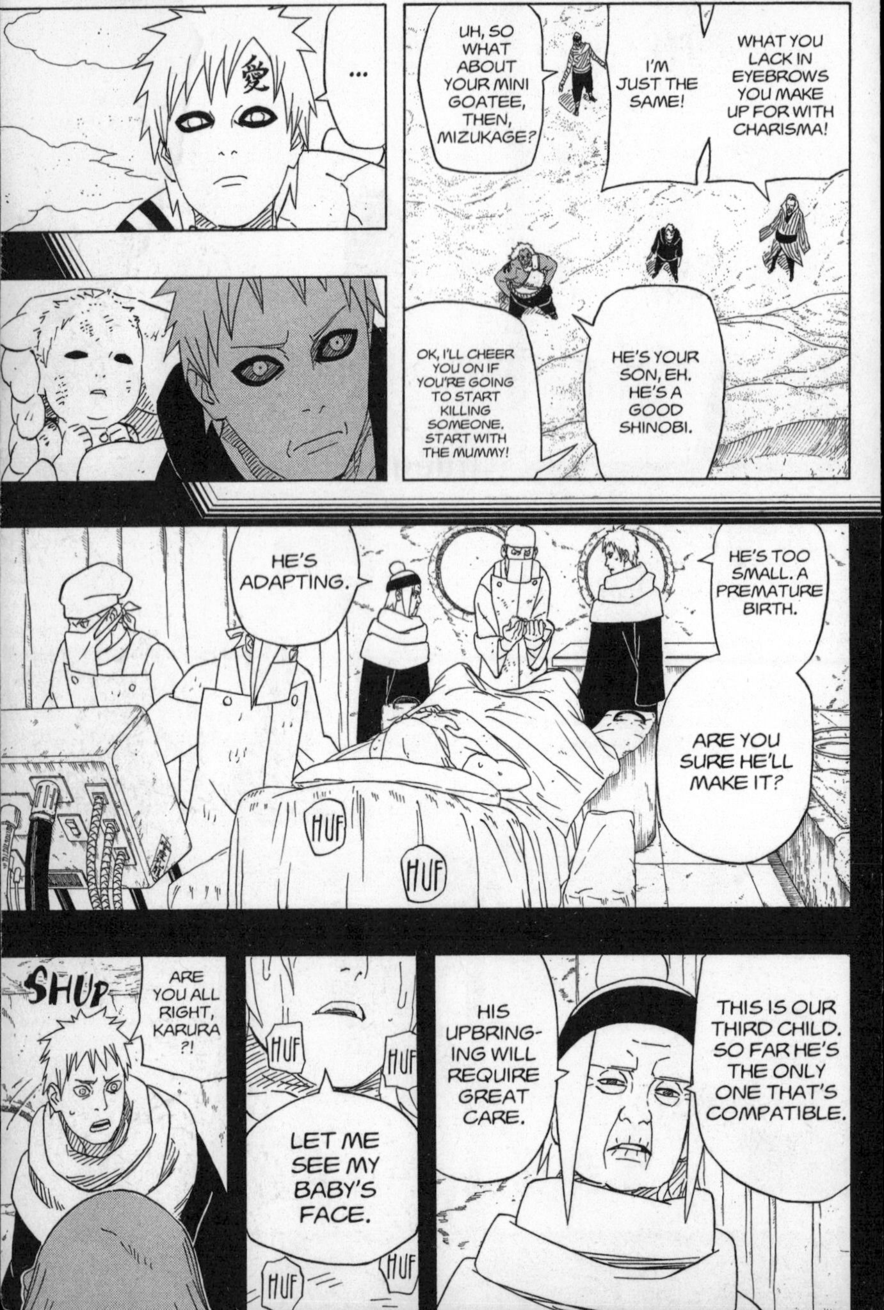
WHAT YOU LACK IN EYEBROWS YOU MAKE UP FOR WITH CHARISMA!
I'M JUST THE SAME!
UH, SO WHAT ABOUT YOUR MINI GOATEE, THEN, MIZUKAGE?
HE'S YOUR SON, EH. HE'S A GOOD SHINOBI.
OK, I'LL CHEER YOU ON IF YOU'RE GOING TO START KILLING SOMEONE. START WITH THE MUMMY!
...
HE'S TOO SMALL. A PREMATURE BIRTH.
ARE YOU SURE HE'LL MAKE IT?
HE'S ADAPTING.
HUF
HUF
THIS IS OUR THIRD CHILD. SO FAR HE'S THE ONLY ONE THAT'S COMPATIBLE.
HIS UPBRINGING WILL REQUIRE GREAT CARE.
HUF
HUF
LET ME SEE MY BABY'S FACE.
HUF
HUF
SHUP
ARE YOU ALL RIGHT, KARURA?!

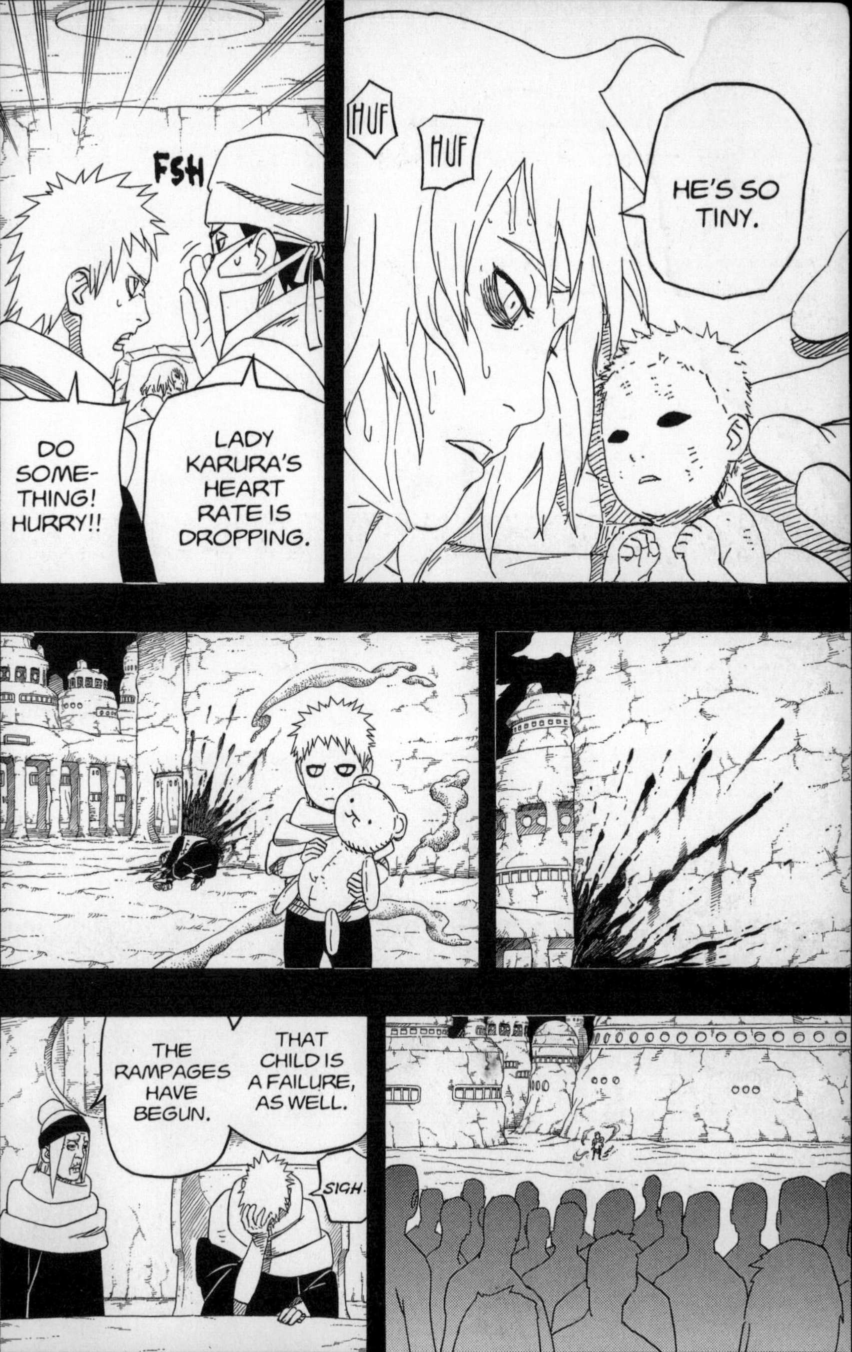
HUF
HUF
HE'S SO TINY.
FSH
LADY KARURA'S HEART RATE IS DROPPING.
DO SOME-THING! HURRY!!
THAT CHILD IS A FAILURE, AS WELL.
THE RAMPAGES HAVE BEGUN.
SIGH.

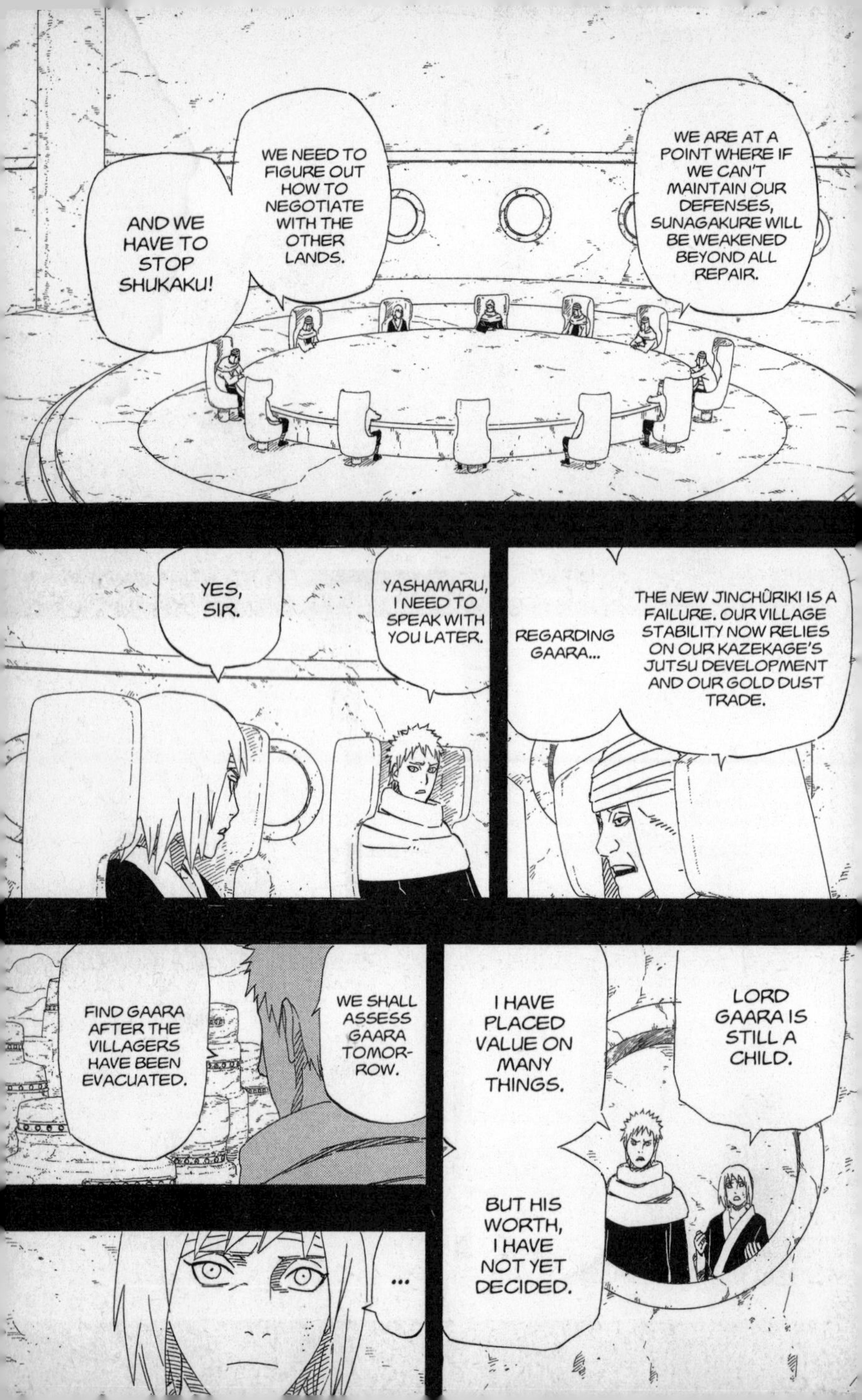
WE ARE AT A POINT WHERE IF WE CAN'T MAINTAIN OUR DEFENSES, SUNAGAKURE WILL BE WEAKENED BEYOND ALL REPAIR.
WE NEED TO FIGURE OUT HOW TO NEGOTIATE WITH THE OTHER LANDS.
AND WE HAVE TO STOP SHUKAKU!
THE NEW JINCHÛRIKI IS A FAILURE. OUR VILLAGE STABILITY NOW RELIES ON OUR KAZEKAGE'S JUTSU DEVELOPMENT AND OUR GOLD DUST TRADE.
REGARDING GAARA...
YASHAMARU, I NEED TO SPEAK WITH YOU LATER.
YES, SIR.
LORD GAARA IS STILL A CHILD.
I HAVE PLACED VALUE ON MANY THINGS.
BUT HIS WORTH, I HAVE NOT YET DECIDED.
WE SHALL ASSESS GAARA TOMORROW.
FIND GAARA AFTER THE VILLAGERS HAVE BEEN EVACUATED.
...

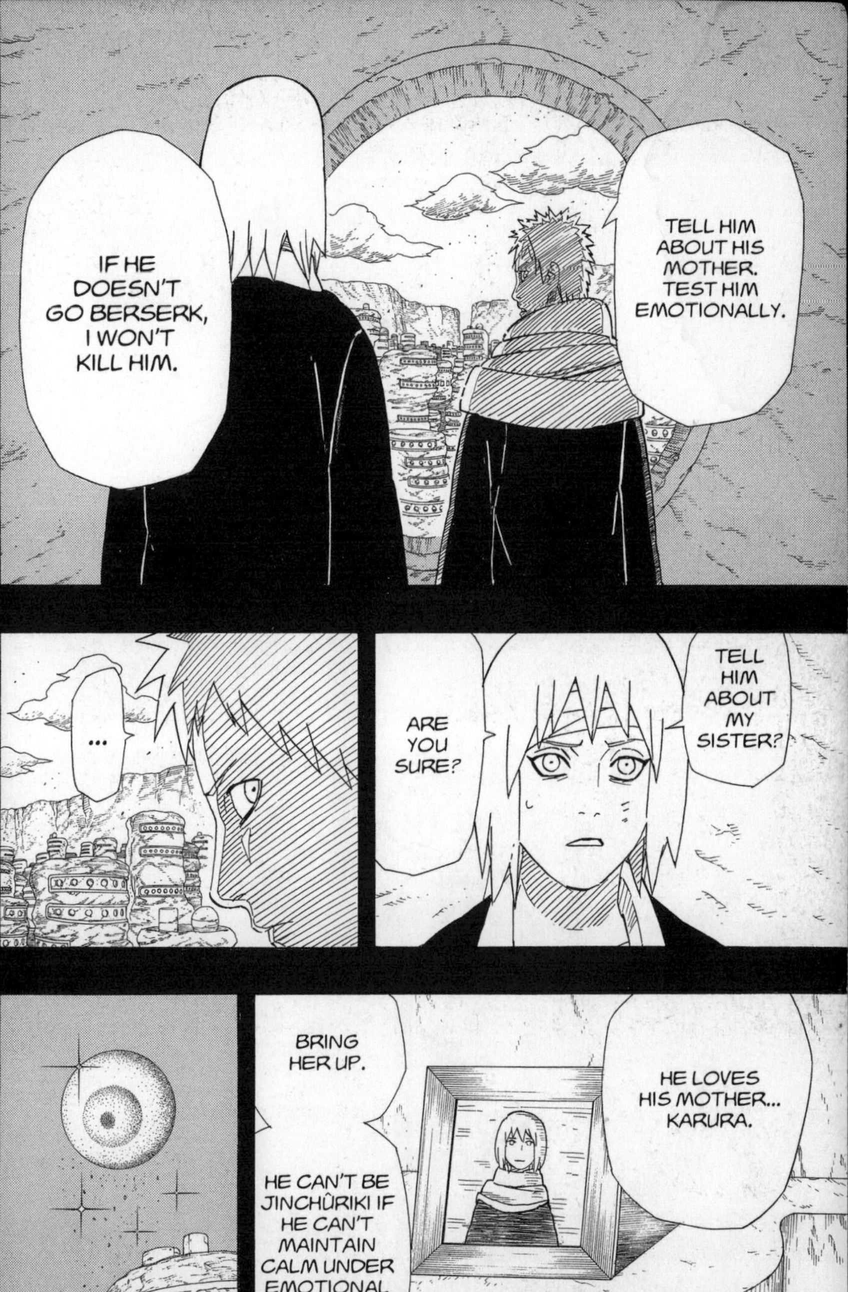
TELL HIM ABOUT HIS MOTHER. TEST HIM EMOTIONALLY.
IF HE DOESN'T GO BERSERK, I WON'T KILL HIM.
TELL HIM ABOUT MY SISTER?
ARE YOU SURE?
...
HE LOVES HIS MOTHER... KARURA.
BRING HER UP.
HE CAN'T BE JINCHÛRIKI IF HE CAN'T MAINTAIN CALM UNDER EMOTIONAL DURESS.

READ THIS WAY

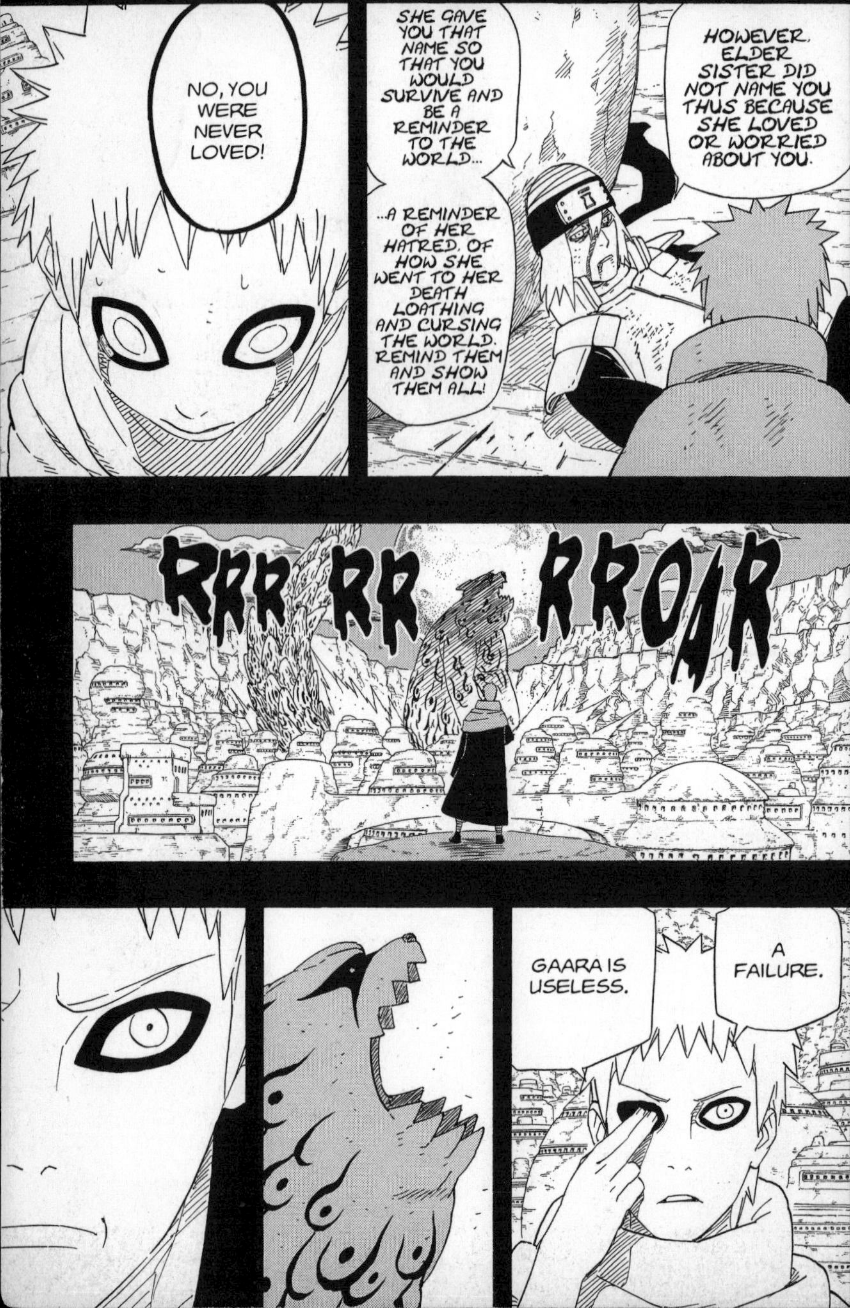
HOWEVER, ELDER SISTER DID NOT NAME YOU THUS BECAUSE SHE LOVED OR WORRIED ABOUT YOU.
SHE GAVE YOU THAT NAME SO THAT YOU WOULD SURVIVE AND BE A REMINDER TO THE WORLD...
...A REMINDER OF HER HATRED, OF HOW SHE WENT TO HER DEATH LOATHING AND CURSING THE WORLD. REMIND THEM AND SHOW THEM ALL!
NO, YOU WERE NEVER LOVED!
RRRRR RROAR
A FAILURE.
GAARA IS USELESS.

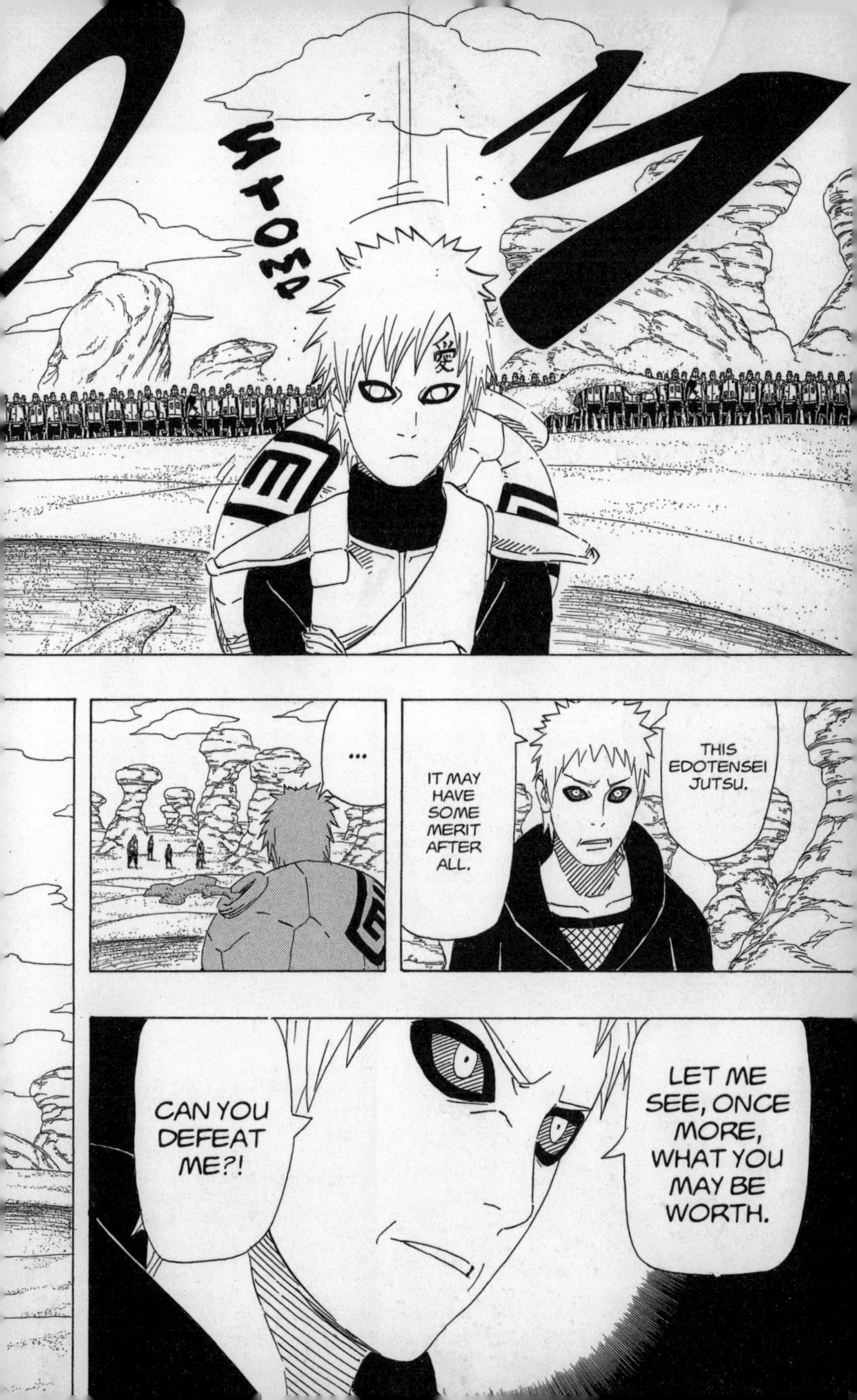
STOMP
THIS EDOTENSEI JUTSU.
IT MAY HAVE SOME MERIT AFTER ALL.
...
LET ME SEE, ONCE MORE, WHAT YOU MAY BE WORTH.
CAN YOU DEFEAT ME?!

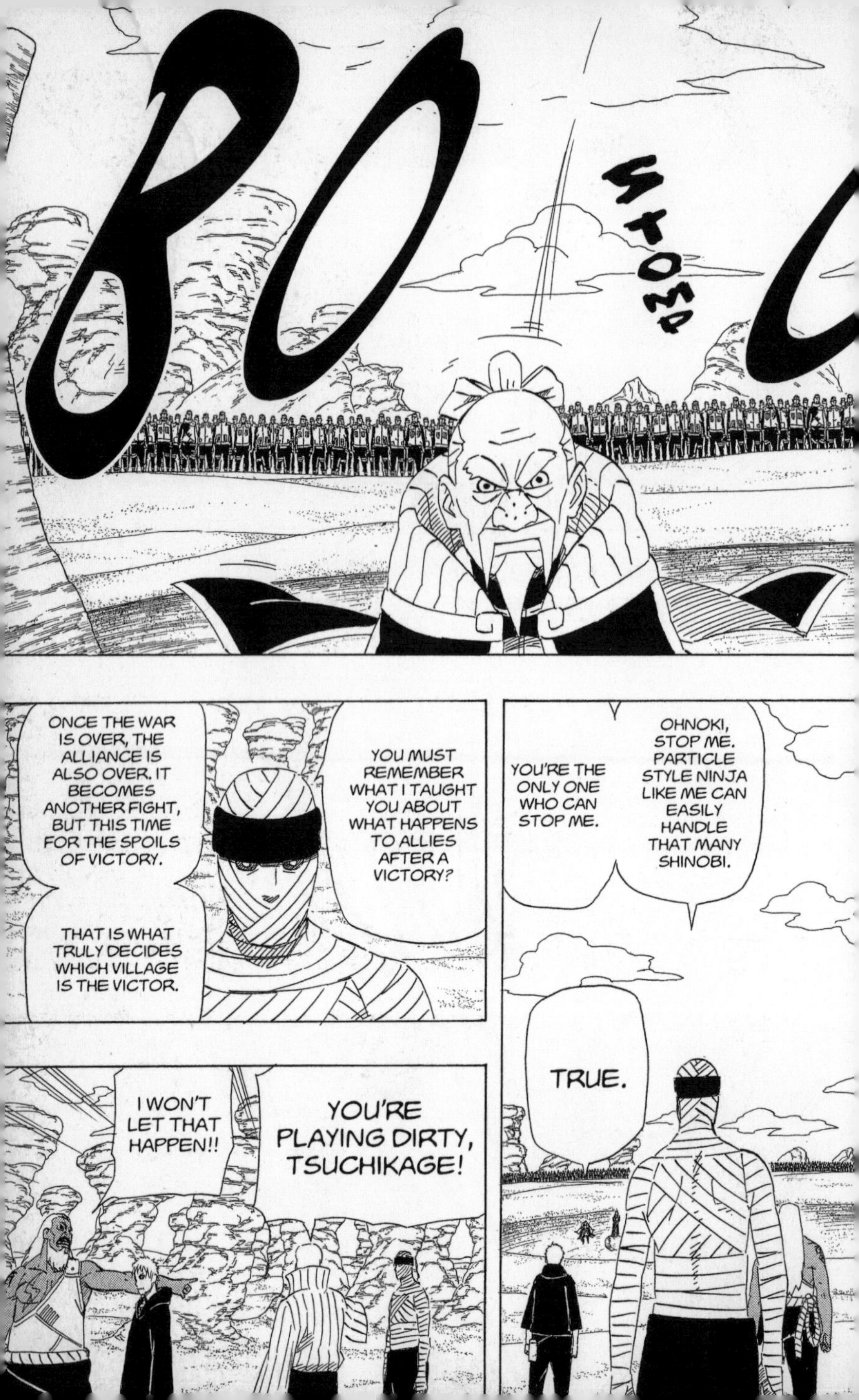
STOMP
OHNOKI, STOP ME. PARTICLE STYLE NINJA LIKE ME CAN EASILY HANDLE THAT MANY SHINOBI.
YOU'RE THE ONLY ONE WHO CAN STOP ME.
TRUE.
YOU MUST REMEMBER WHAT I TAUGHT YOU ABOUT WHAT HAPPENS TO ALLIES AFTER A VICTORY?
ONCE THE WAR IS OVER, THE ALLIANCE IS ALSO OVER. IT BECOMES ANOTHER FIGHT, BUT THIS TIME FOR THE SPOILS OF VICTORY.
THAT IS WHAT TRULY DECIDES WHICH VILLAGE IS THE VICTOR.
YOU'RE PLAYING DIRTY, TSUCHIKAGE!
I WON'T LET THAT HAPPEN!!

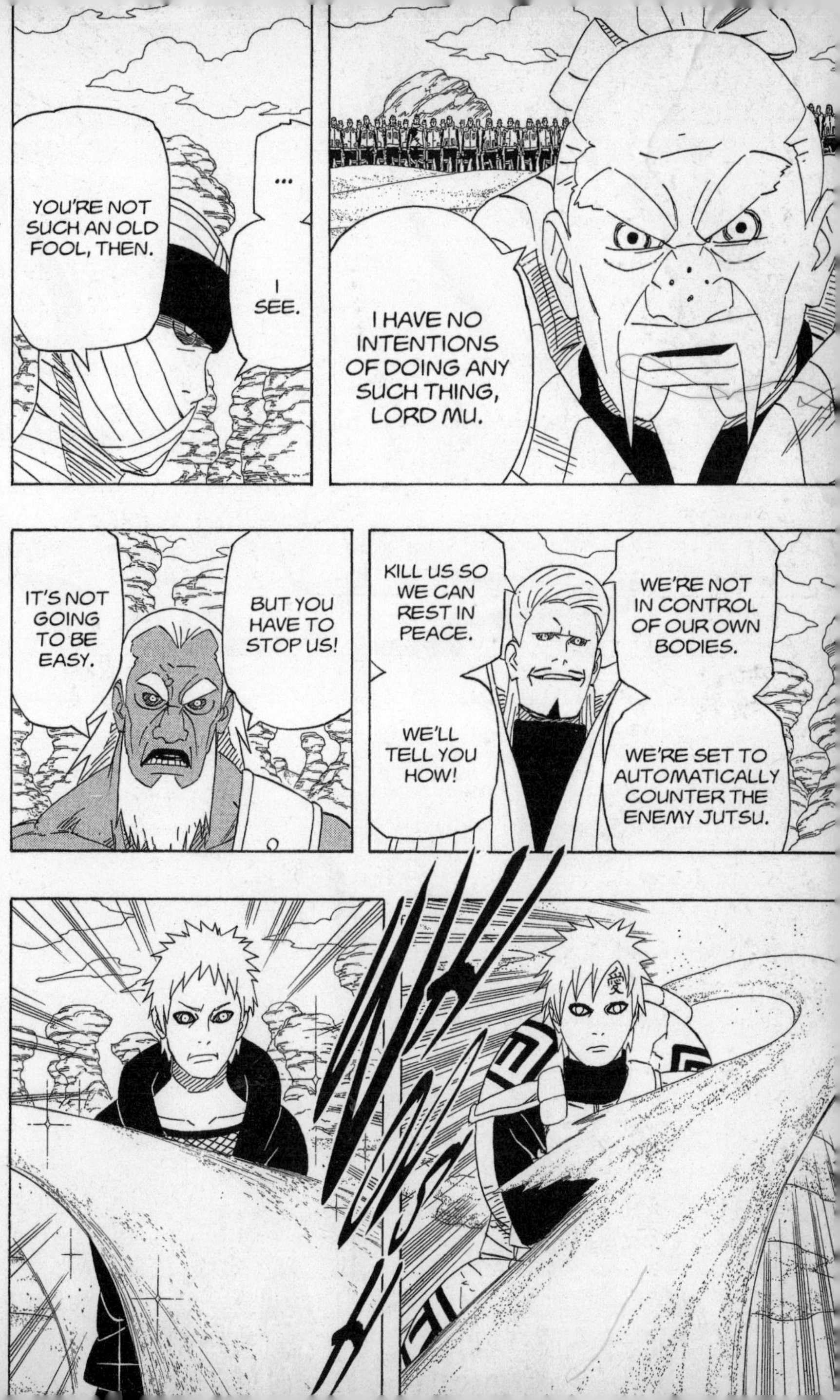
I HAVE NO INTENTIONS OF DOING ANY SUCH THING, LORD MU.
... I SEE.
YOU'RE NOT SUCH AN OLD FOOL, THEN.
WE'RE NOT IN CONTROL OF OUR OWN BODIES.
KILL US SO WE CAN REST IN PEACE.
WE'RE SET TO AUTOMATICALLY COUNTER THE ENEMY JUTSU.
WE'LL TELL YOU HOW!
BUT YOU HAVE TO STOP US!
IT'S NOT GOING TO BE EASY.

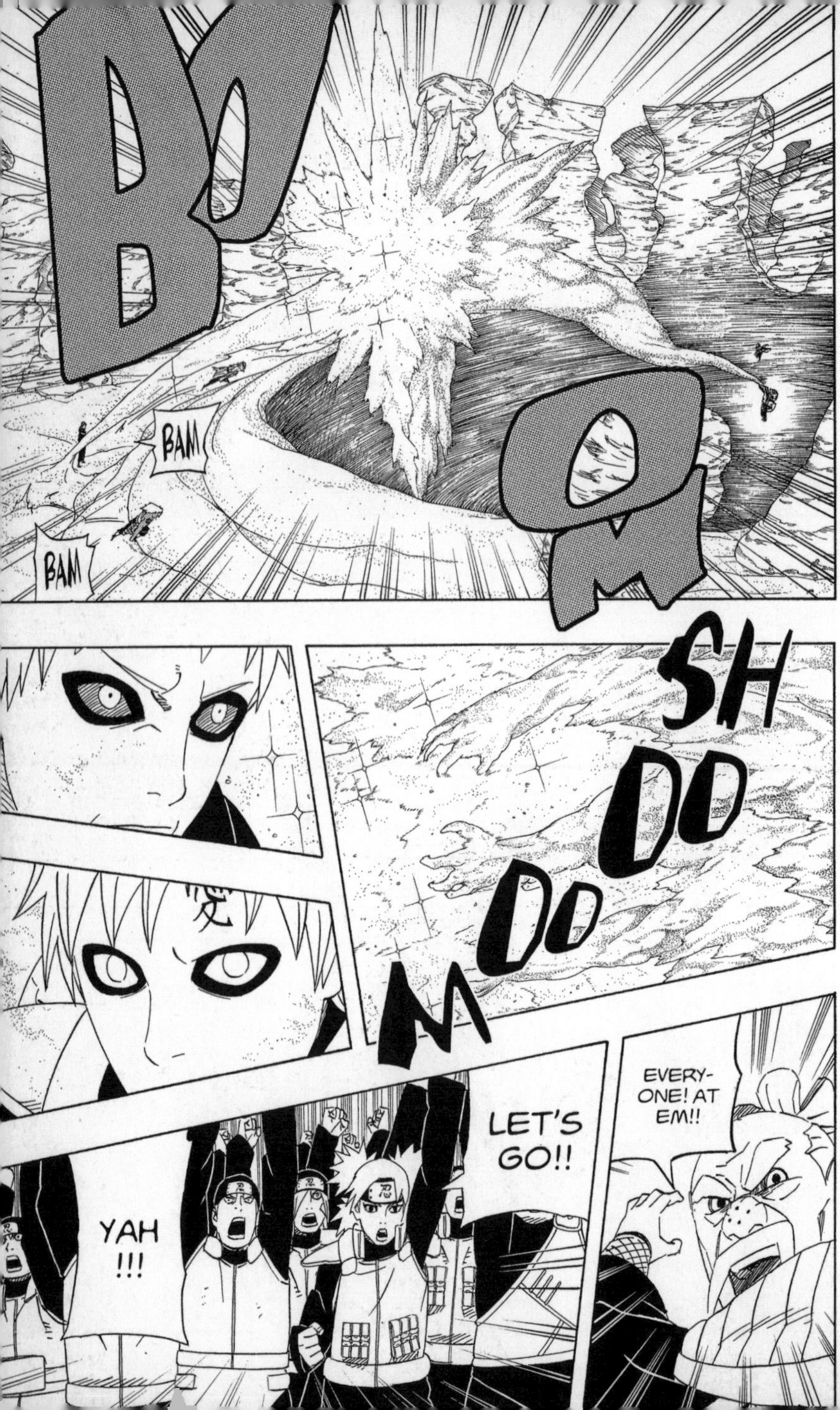
BOOOM
BAM
BAM
SHDODOM
EVERY-ONE! AT EM!!
LET'S GO!!
YAH !!!

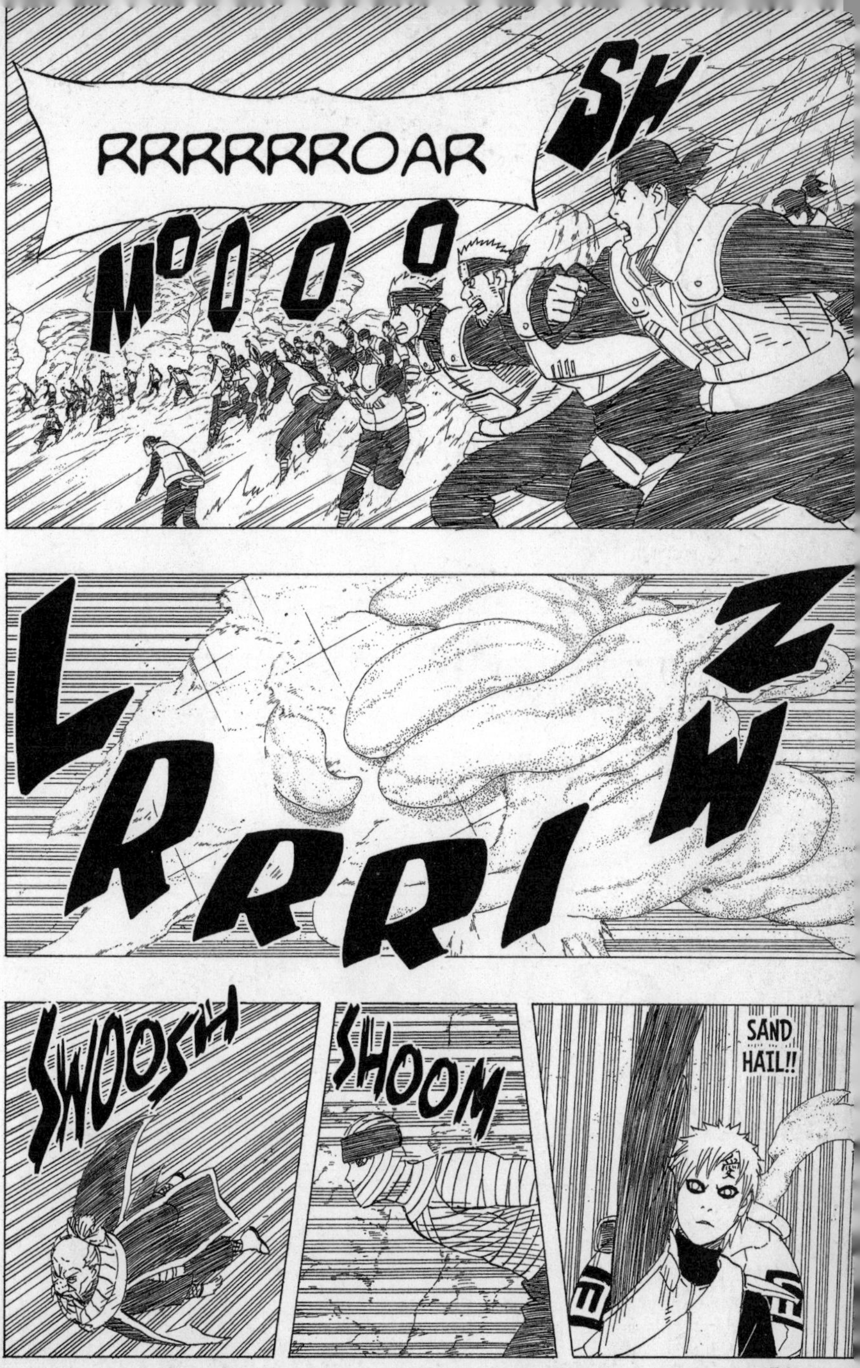
RRRRRROAR
SH
MOOOO
ZWIRRRL
SAND HAIL!!
SHOOM
SWOOSH

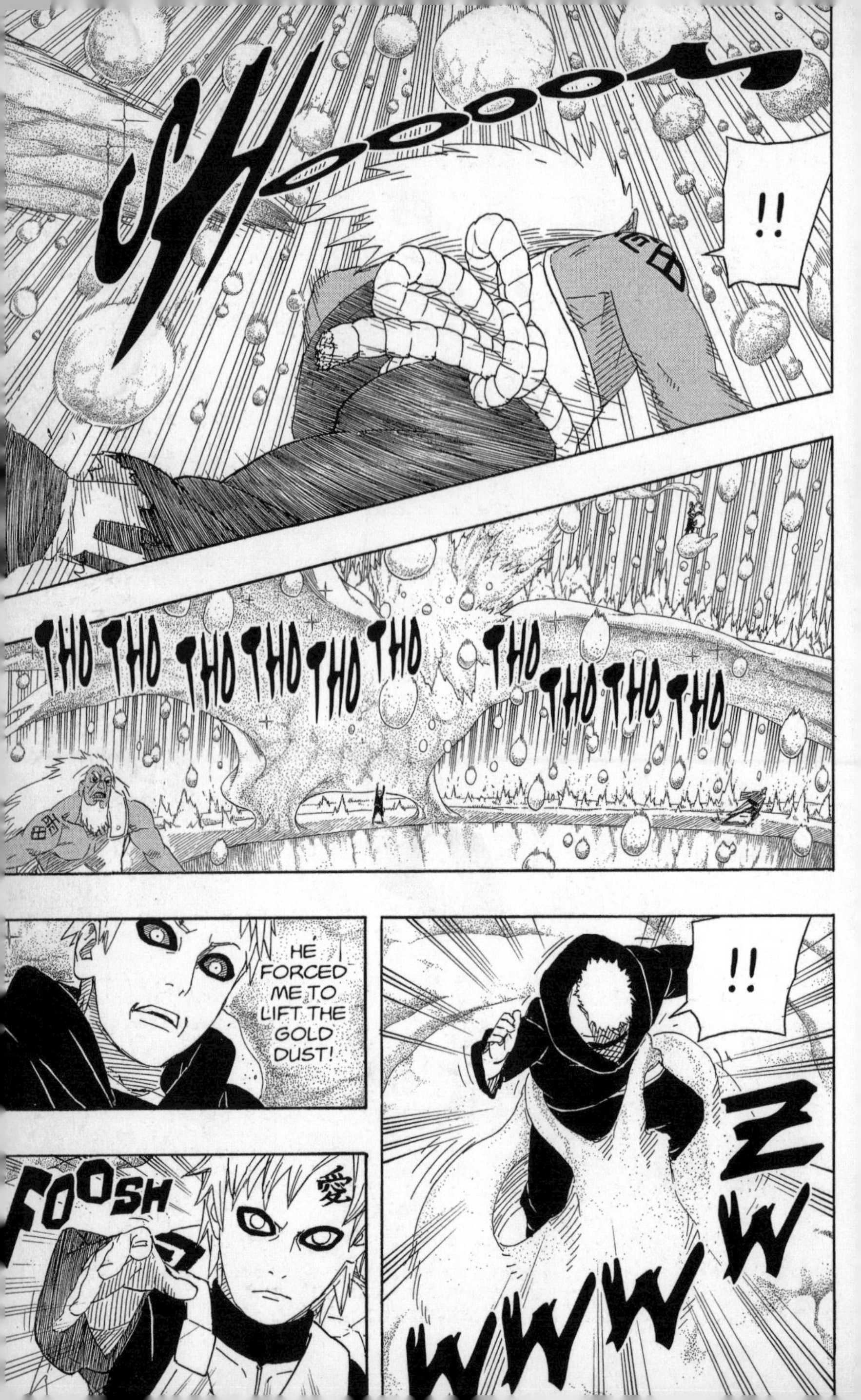
SHOOOOOM
!!
THO THO THO THO THO THO THO THO THO THO
!!
ZWWWWW
HE FORCED ME TO LIFT THE GOLD DUST!
FOOSH

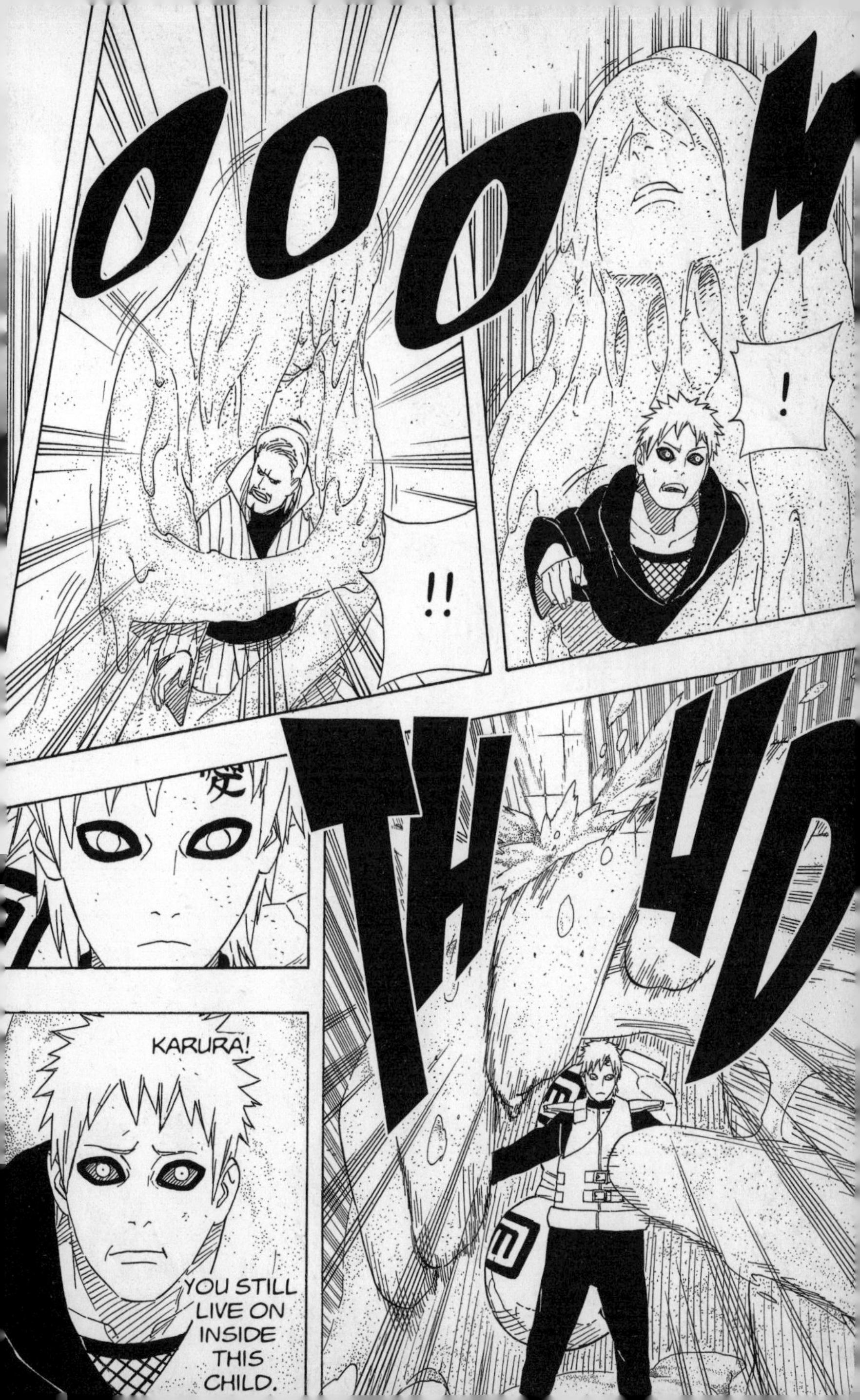
OOOOM
!
!!
THUD
KARURA!
YOU STILL LIVE ON INSIDE THIS CHILD.

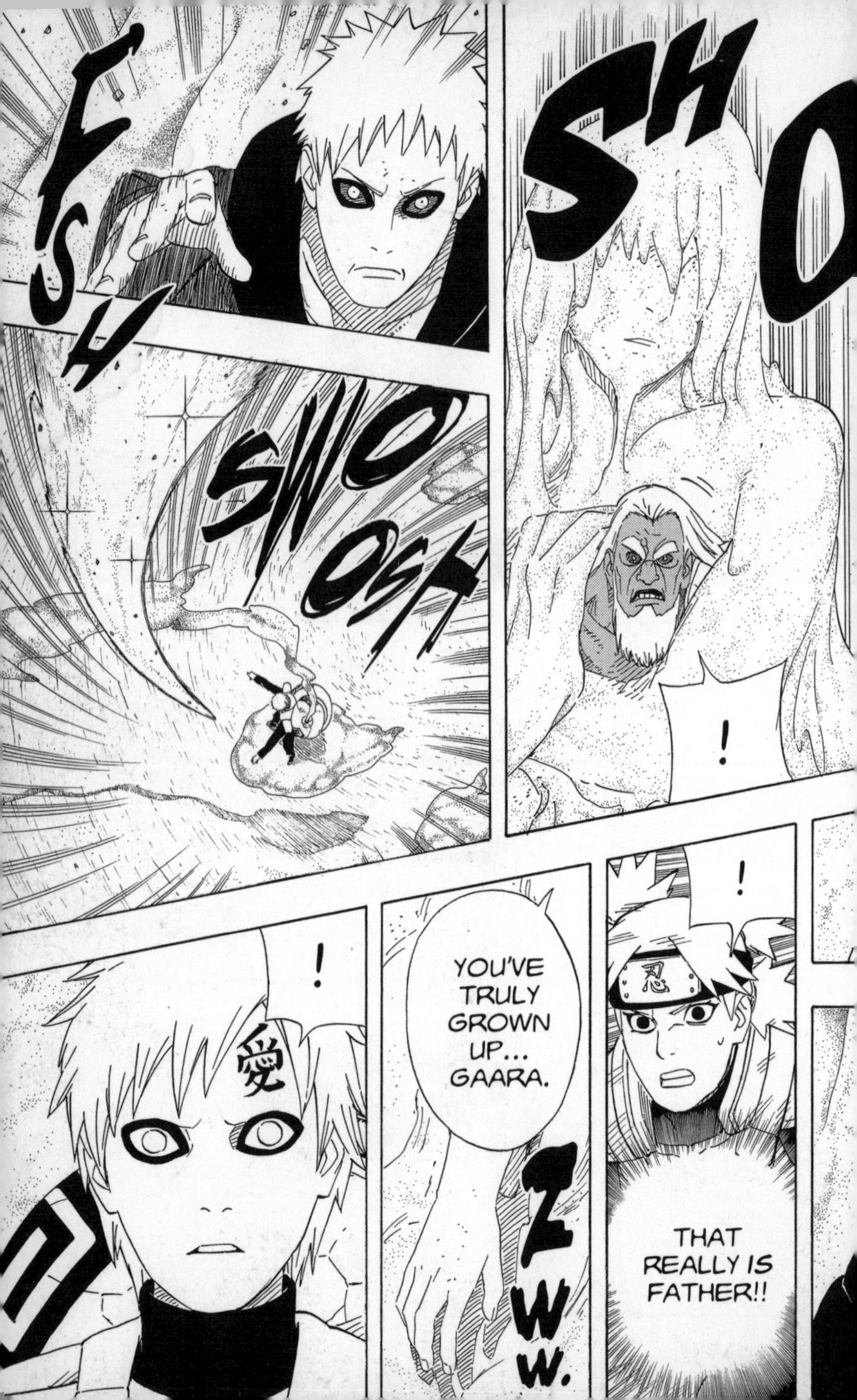
SHO
!
FSH
SWOOSH
!
THAT REALLY IS FATHER!!
YOU'VE TRULY GROWN UP... GAARA.
ZWW.
!

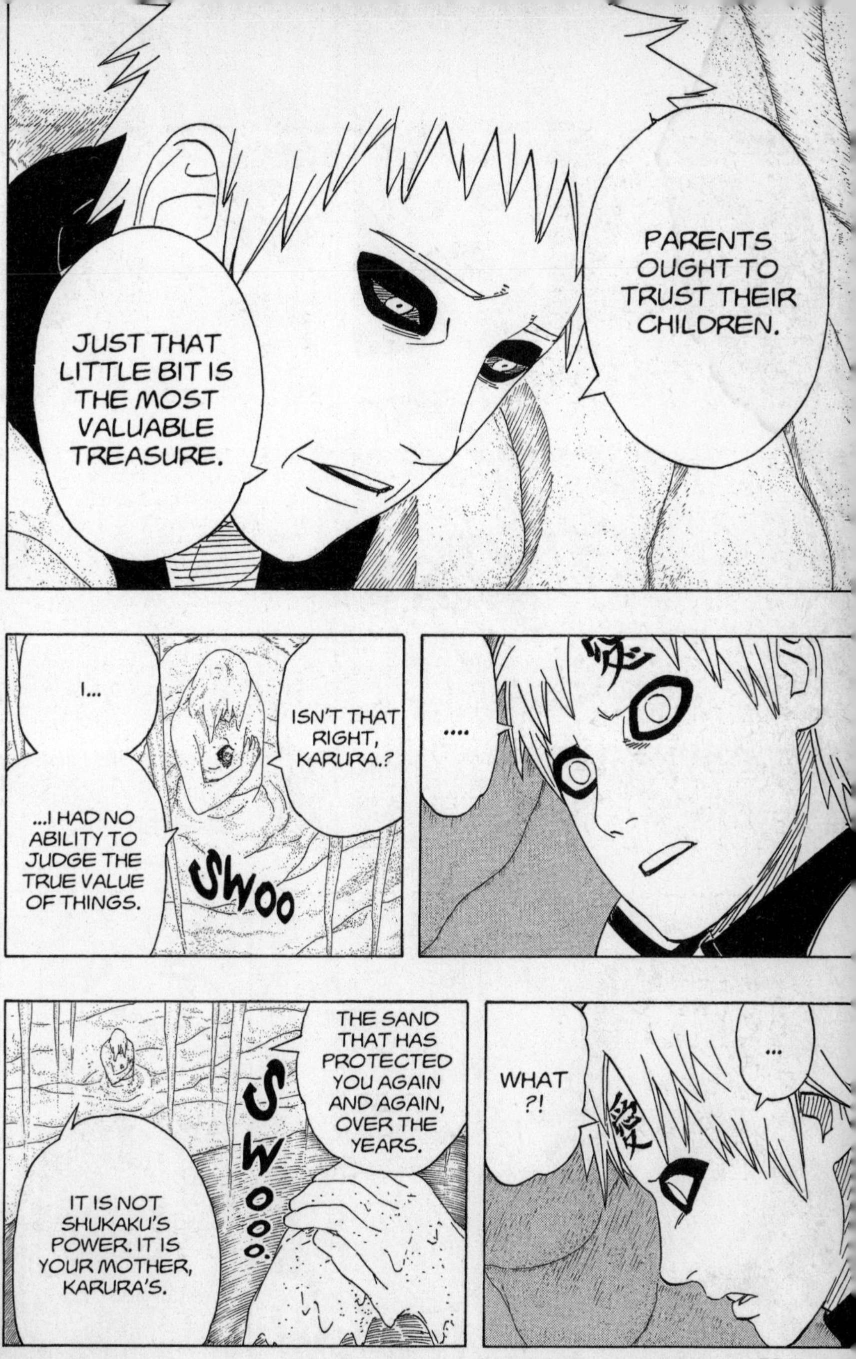
PARENTS OUGHT TO TRUST THEIR CHILDREN.
JUST THAT LITTLE BIT IS THE MOST VALUABLE TREASURE.
....
ISN'T THAT RIGHT, KARURA.?
I...
...I HAD NO ABILITY TO JUDGE THE TRUE VALUE OF THINGS.
SWOO
...
WHAT ?!
THE SAND THAT HAS PROTECTED YOU AGAIN AND AGAIN, OVER THE YEARS.
SWOOO
IT IS NOT SHUKAKU'S POWER. IT IS YOUR MOTHER, KARURA'S.

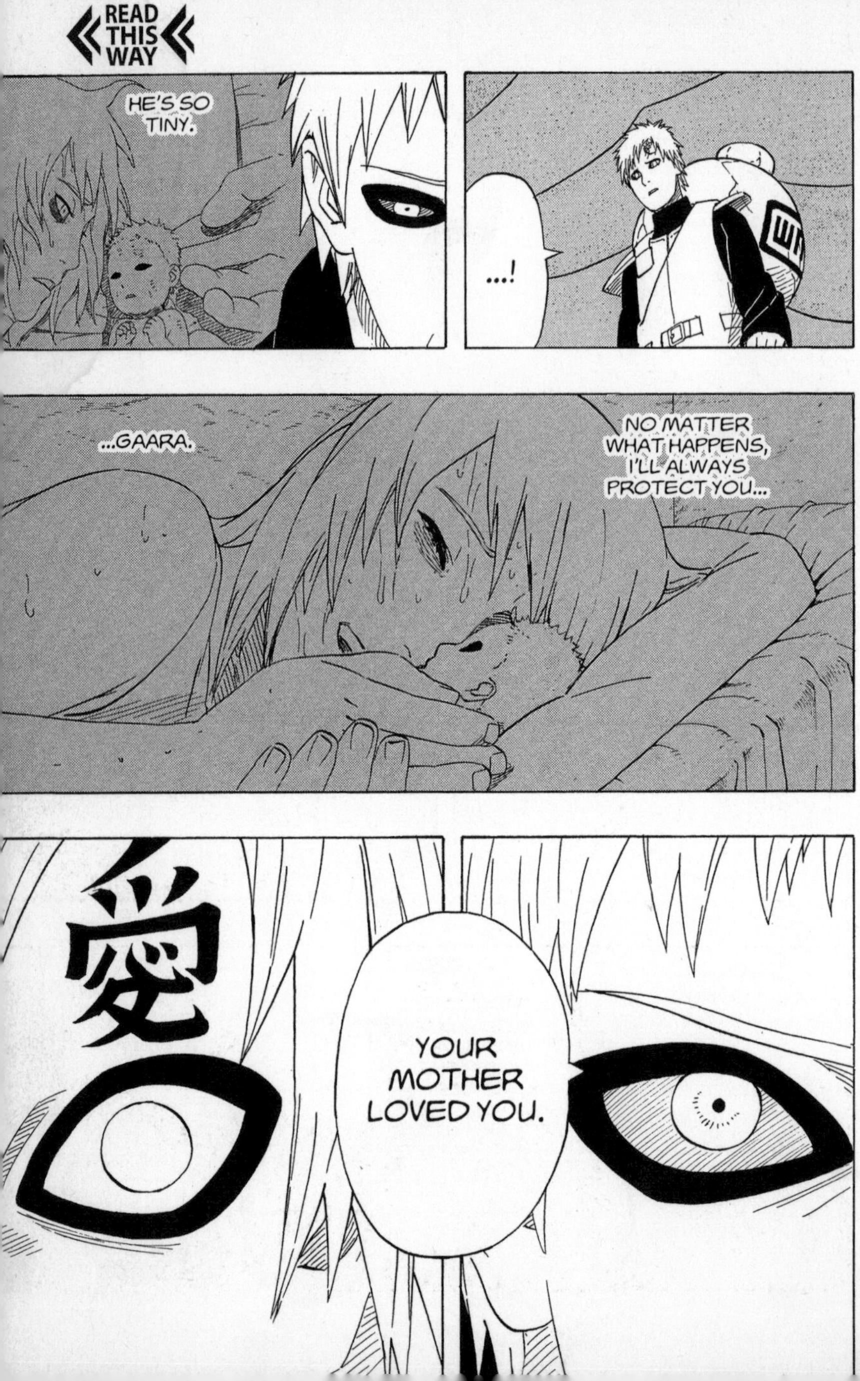
READ THIS WAY
...!
HE'S SO TINY.
NO MATTER WHAT HAPPENS, I'LL ALWAYS PROTECT YOU...
...GAARA.
YOUR MOTHER LOVED YOU.
愛

NARUTO

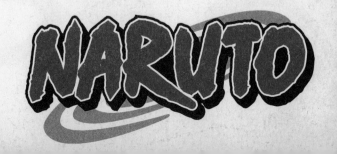

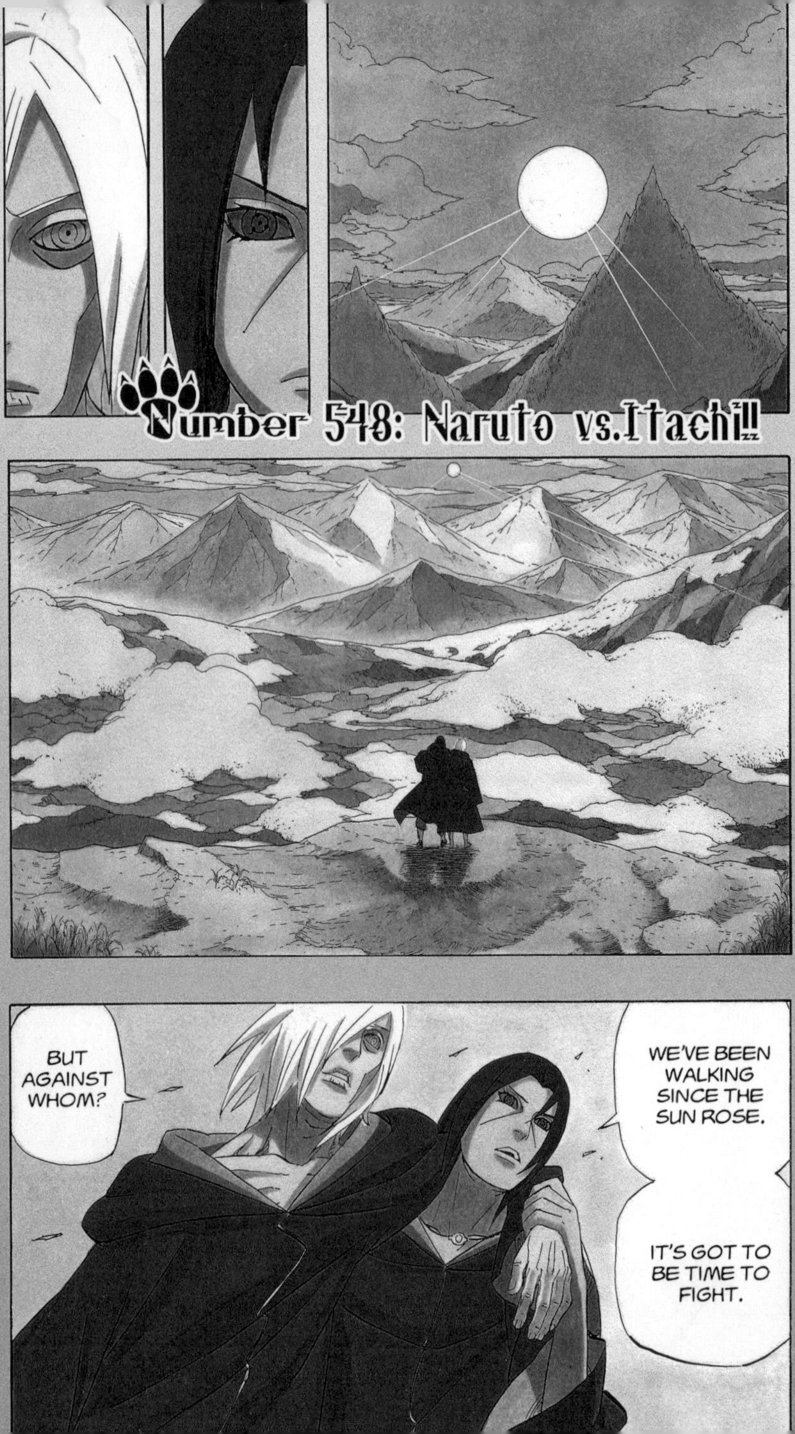
Number 548: Naruto vs.Itachi!!
WE'VE BEEN WALKING SINCE THE SUN ROSE.
IT'S GOT TO BE TIME TO FIGHT.
BUT AGAINST WHOM?

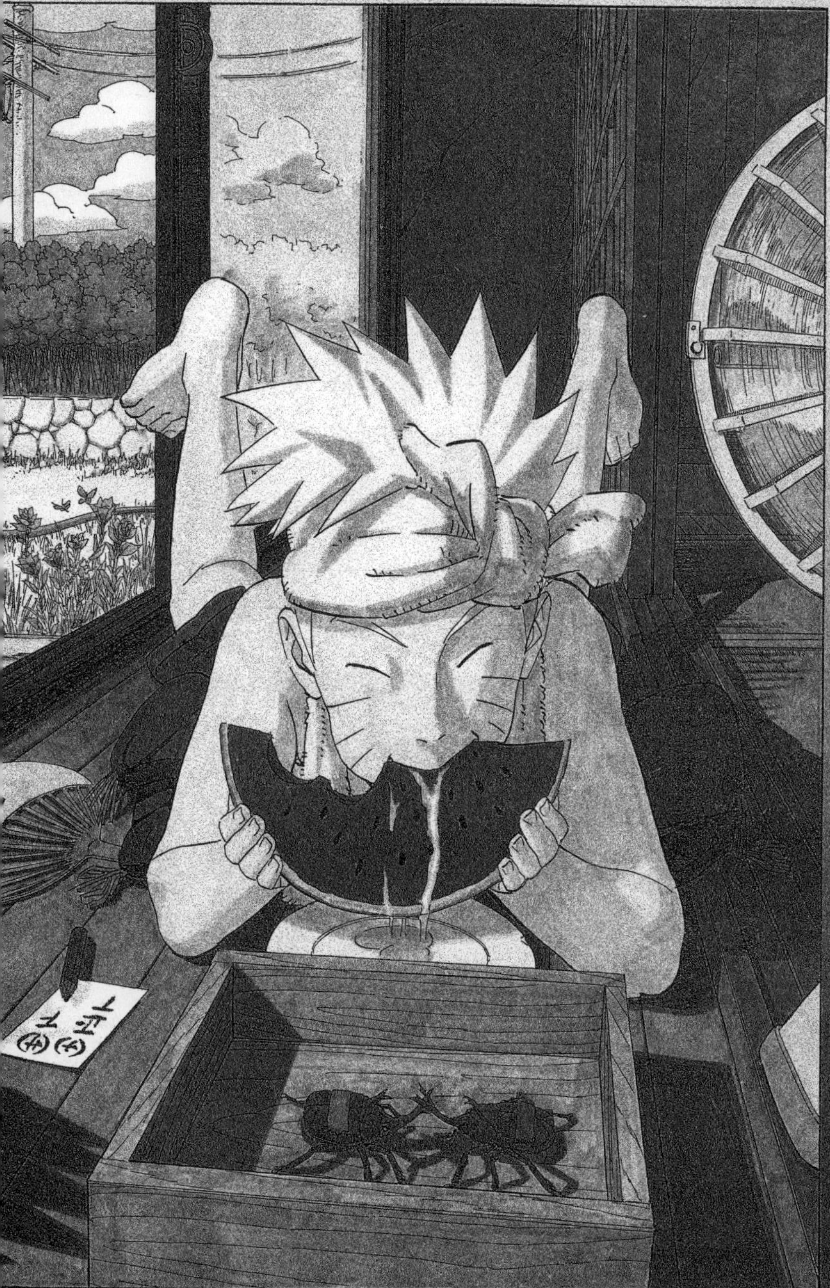

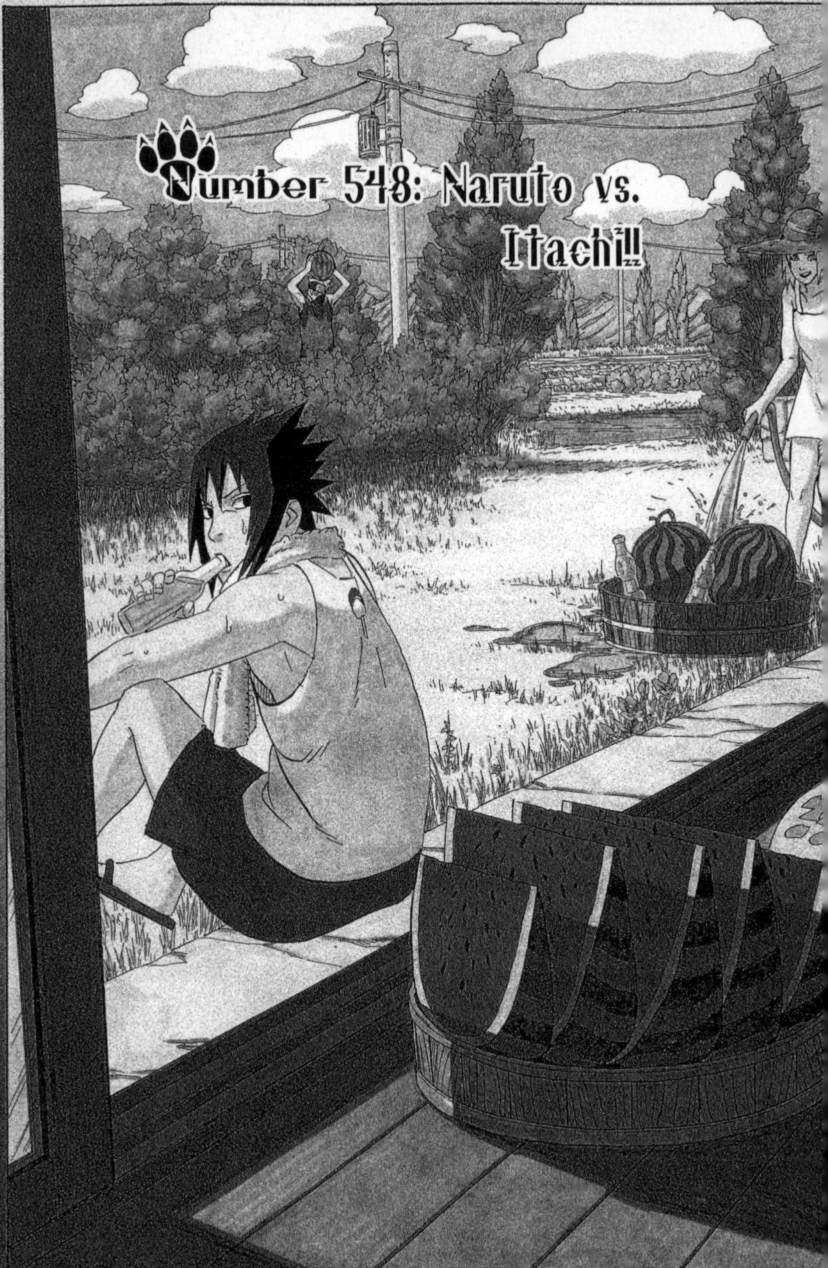
Number 548: Naruto vs. Itachi!!

NARUTO

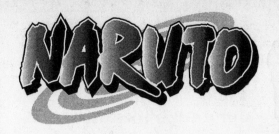

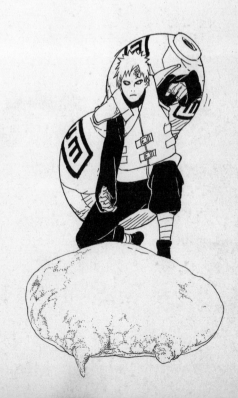

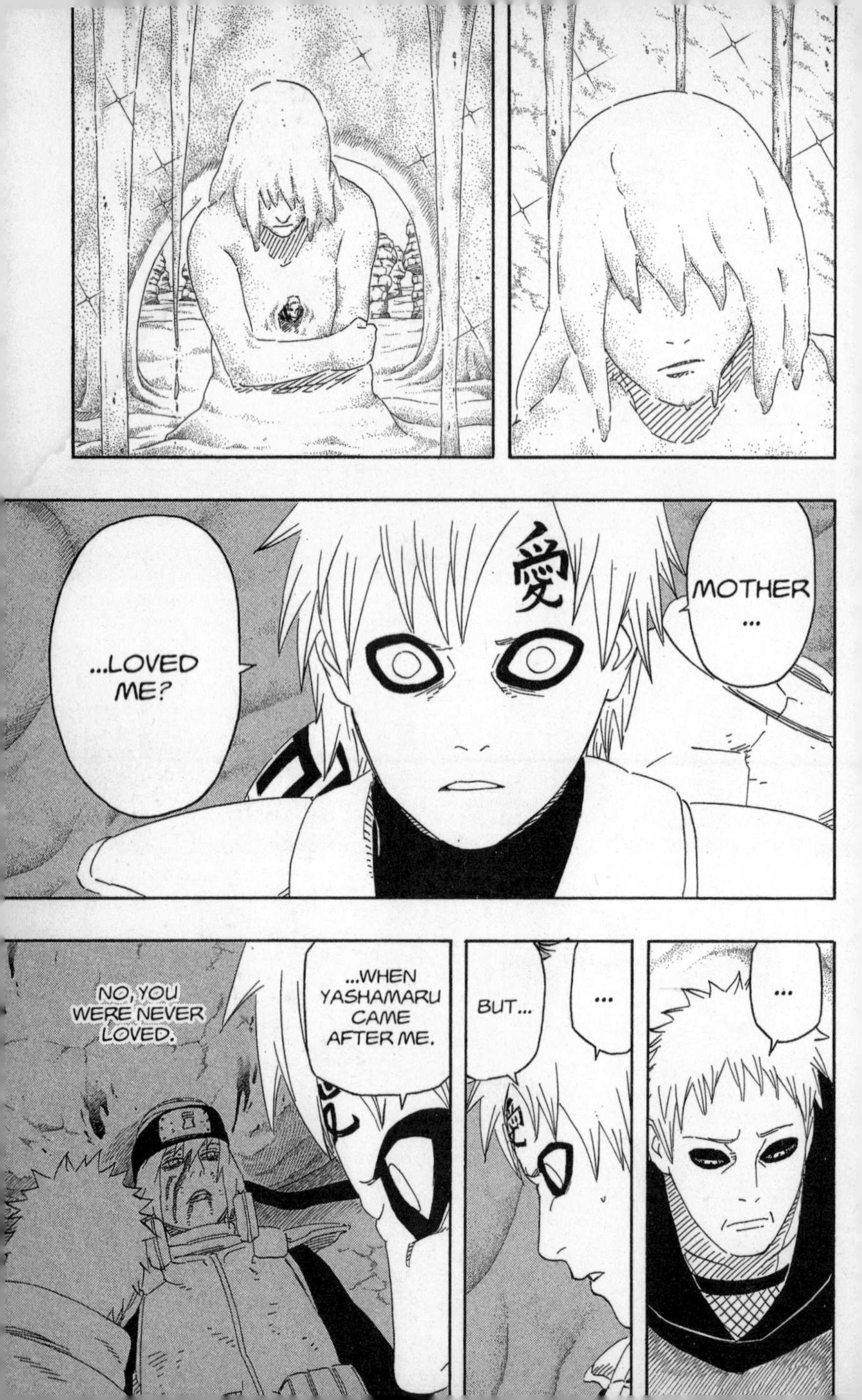
MOTHER ...
...LOVED ME?
...
...
BUT...
...WHEN YASHAMARU CAME AFTER ME.
NO, YOU WERE NEVER LOVED.

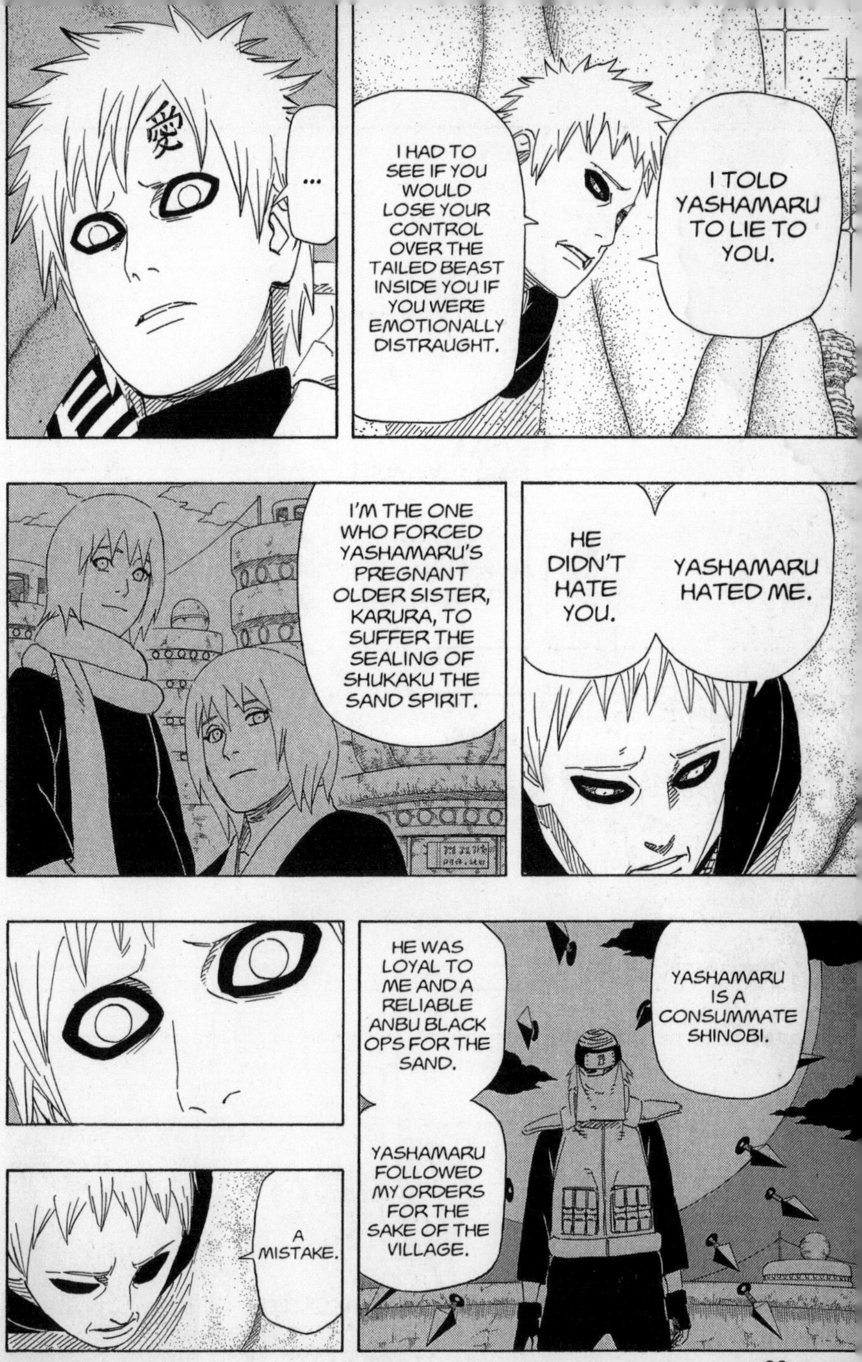
I TOLD YASHAMARU TO LIE TO YOU.
I HAD TO SEE IF YOU WOULD LOSE YOUR CONTROL OVER THE TAILED BEAST INSIDE YOU IF YOU WERE EMOTIONALLY DISTRAUGHT.
...
YASHAMARU HATED ME.
HE DIDN'T HATE YOU.
I'M THE ONE WHO FORCED YASHAMARU'S PREGNANT OLDER SISTER, KARURA, TO SUFFER THE SEALING OF SHUKAKU THE SAND SPIRIT.
YASHAMARU IS A CONSUMMATE SHINOBI.
HE WAS LOYAL TO ME AND A RELIABLE ANBU BLACK OPS FOR THE SAND.
YASHAMARU FOLLOWED MY ORDERS FOR THE SAKE OF THE VILLAGE.
A MISTAKE.

READ THIS WAY

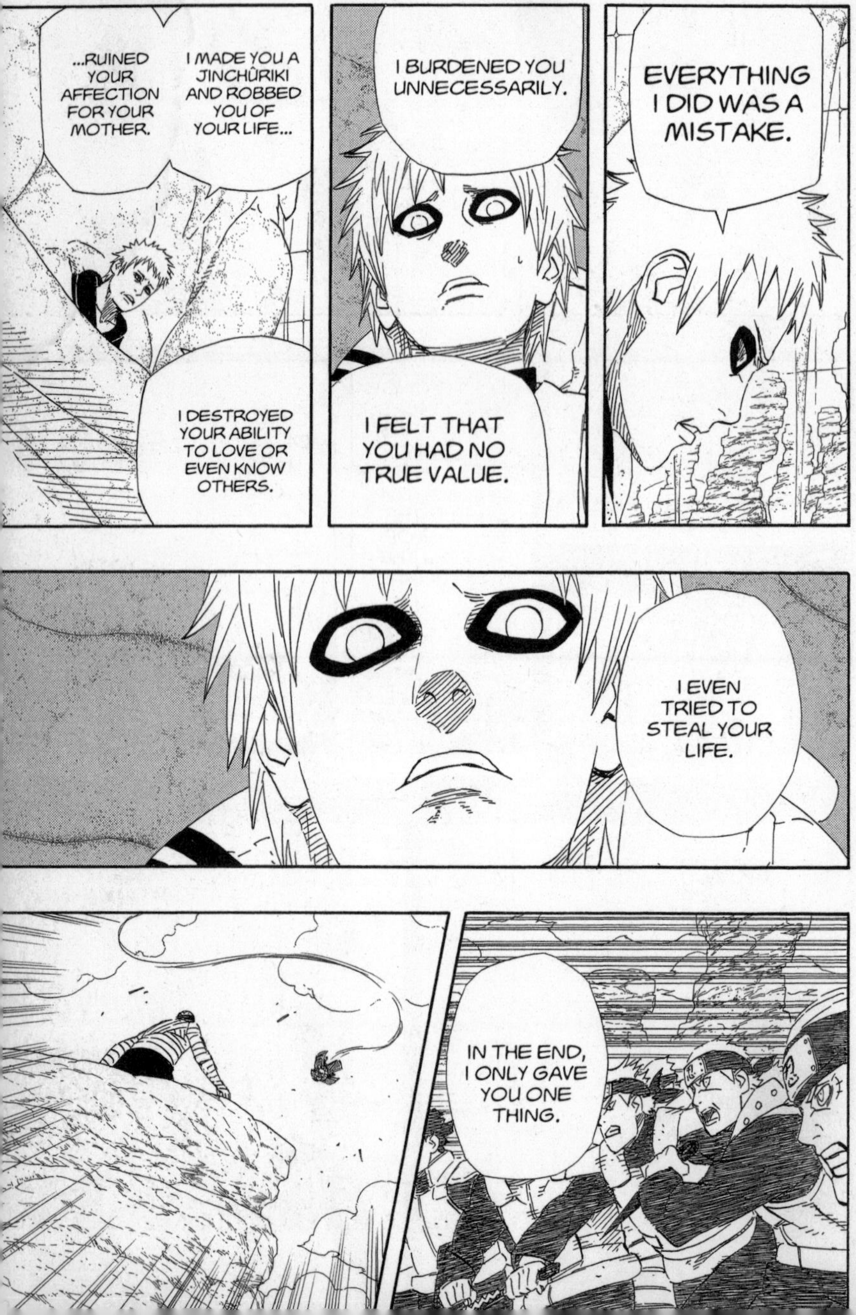
EVERYTHING I DID WAS A MISTAKE.
I BURDENED YOU UNNECESSARILY.
I FELT THAT YOU HAD NO TRUE VALUE.
I MADE YOU A JINCHÛRIKI AND ROBBED YOU OF YOUR LIFE...
...RUINED YOUR AFFECTION FOR YOUR MOTHER.
I DESTROYED YOUR ABILITY TO LOVE OR EVEN KNOW OTHERS.
I EVEN TRIED TO STEAL YOUR LIFE.
IN THE END, I ONLY GAVE YOU ONE THING.

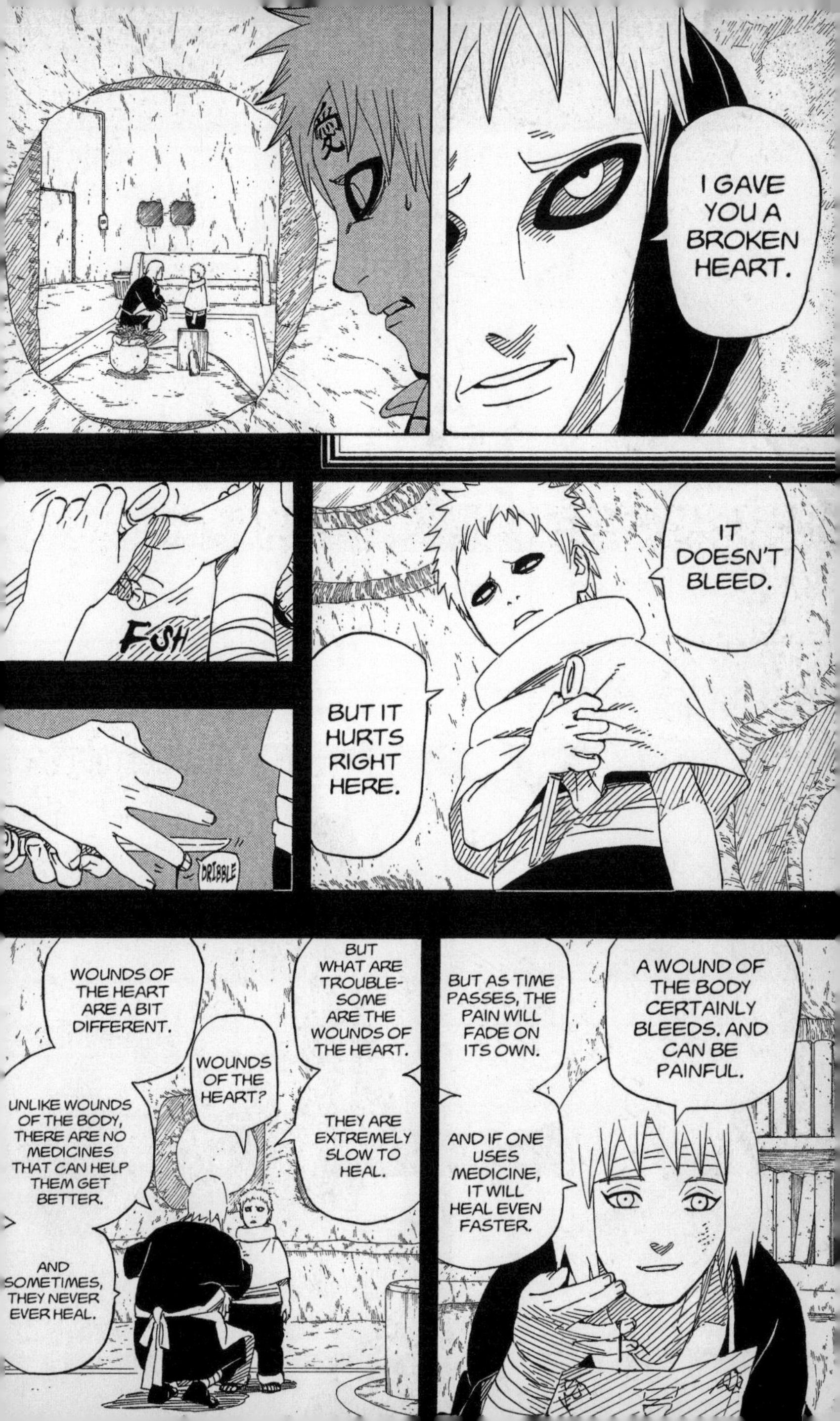
I GAVE YOU A BROKEN HEART.
IT DOESN'T BLEED.
BUT IT HURTS RIGHT HERE.
FSH
DRIBBLE
A WOUND OF THE BODY CERTAINLY BLEEDS. AND CAN BE PAINFUL.
BUT AS TIME PASSES, THE PAIN WILL FADE ON ITS OWN.
AND IF ONE USES MEDICINE, IT WILL HEAL EVEN FASTER.
BUT WHAT ARE TROUBLE-SOME ARE THE WOUNDS OF THE HEART.
THEY ARE EXTREMELY SLOW TO HEAL.
WOUNDS OF THE HEART?
WOUNDS OF THE HEART ARE A BIT DIFFERENT.
UNLIKE WOUNDS OF THE BODY, THERE ARE NO MEDICINES THAT CAN HELP THEM GET BETTER.
AND SOMETIMES, THEY NEVER EVER HEAL.

READ THIS WAY

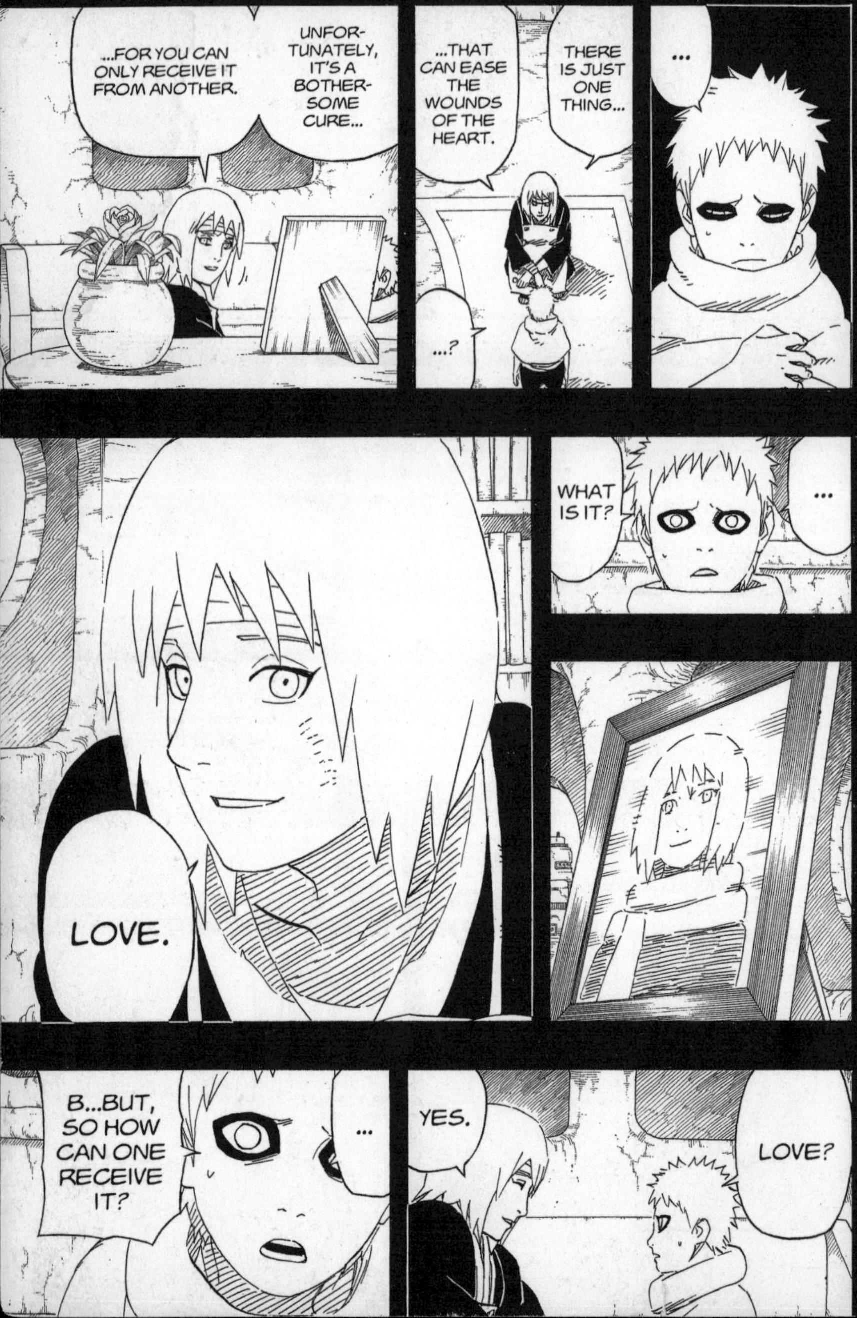
...
THERE IS JUST ONE THING...
...THAT CAN EASE THE WOUNDS OF THE HEART.
...?
UNFOR-TUNATELY, IT'S A BOTHER-SOME CURE...
...FOR YOU CAN ONLY RECEIVE IT FROM ANOTHER.
...
WHAT IS IT?
LOVE.
LOVE?
YES.
...
B...BUT, SO HOW CAN ONE RECEIVE IT?

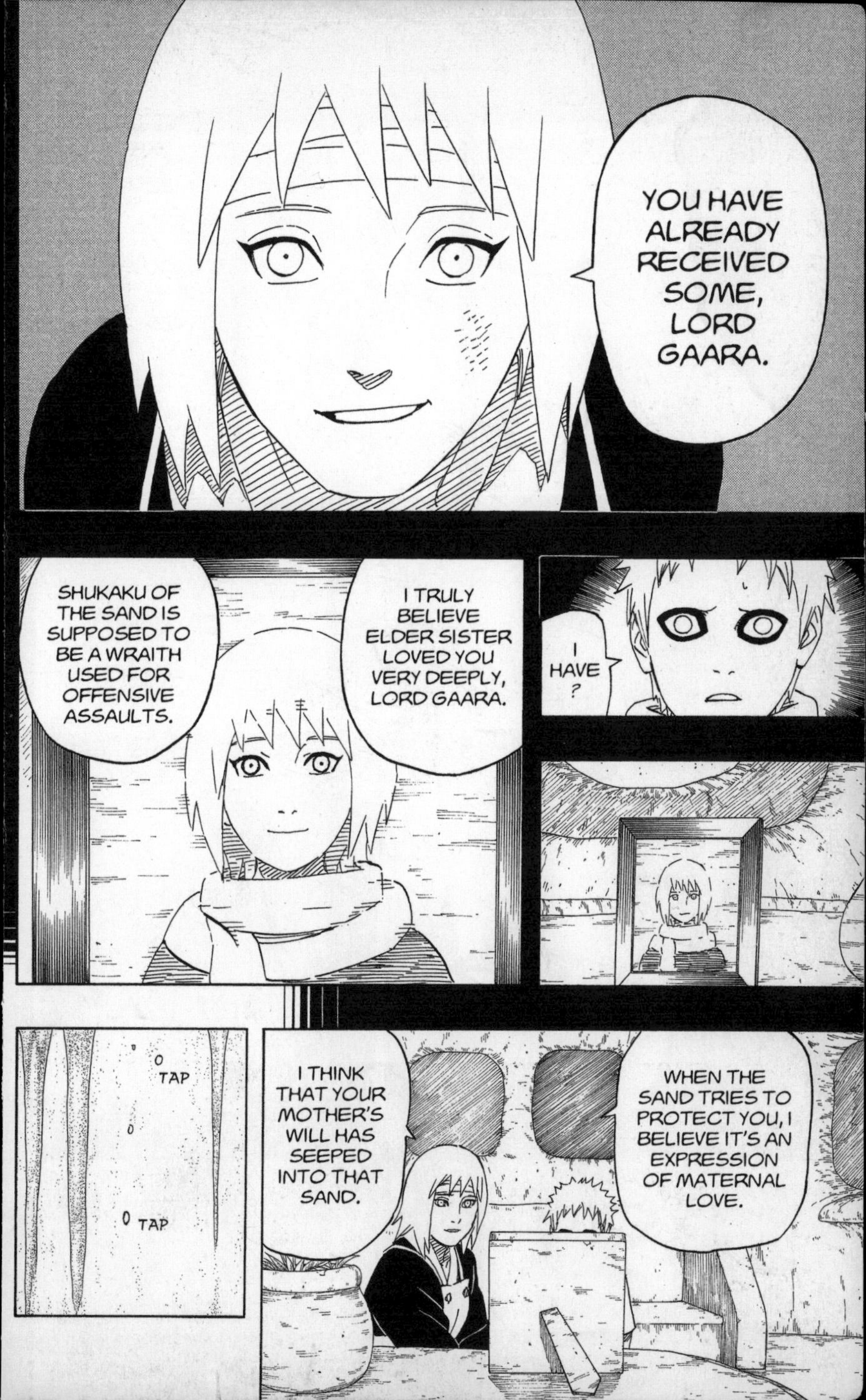
YOU HAVE ALREADY RECEIVED SOME, LORD GAARA.
I HAVE?
I TRULY BELIEVE ELDER SISTER LOVED YOU VERY DEEPLY, LORD GAARA.
SHUKAKU OF THE SAND IS SUPPOSED TO BE A WRAITH USED FOR OFFENSIVE ASSAULTS.
WHEN THE SAND TRIES TO PROTECT YOU, I BELIEVE IT'S AN EXPRESSION OF MATERNAL LOVE.
I THINK THAT YOUR MOTHER'S WILL HAS SEEPED INTO THAT SAND.
TAP
TAP

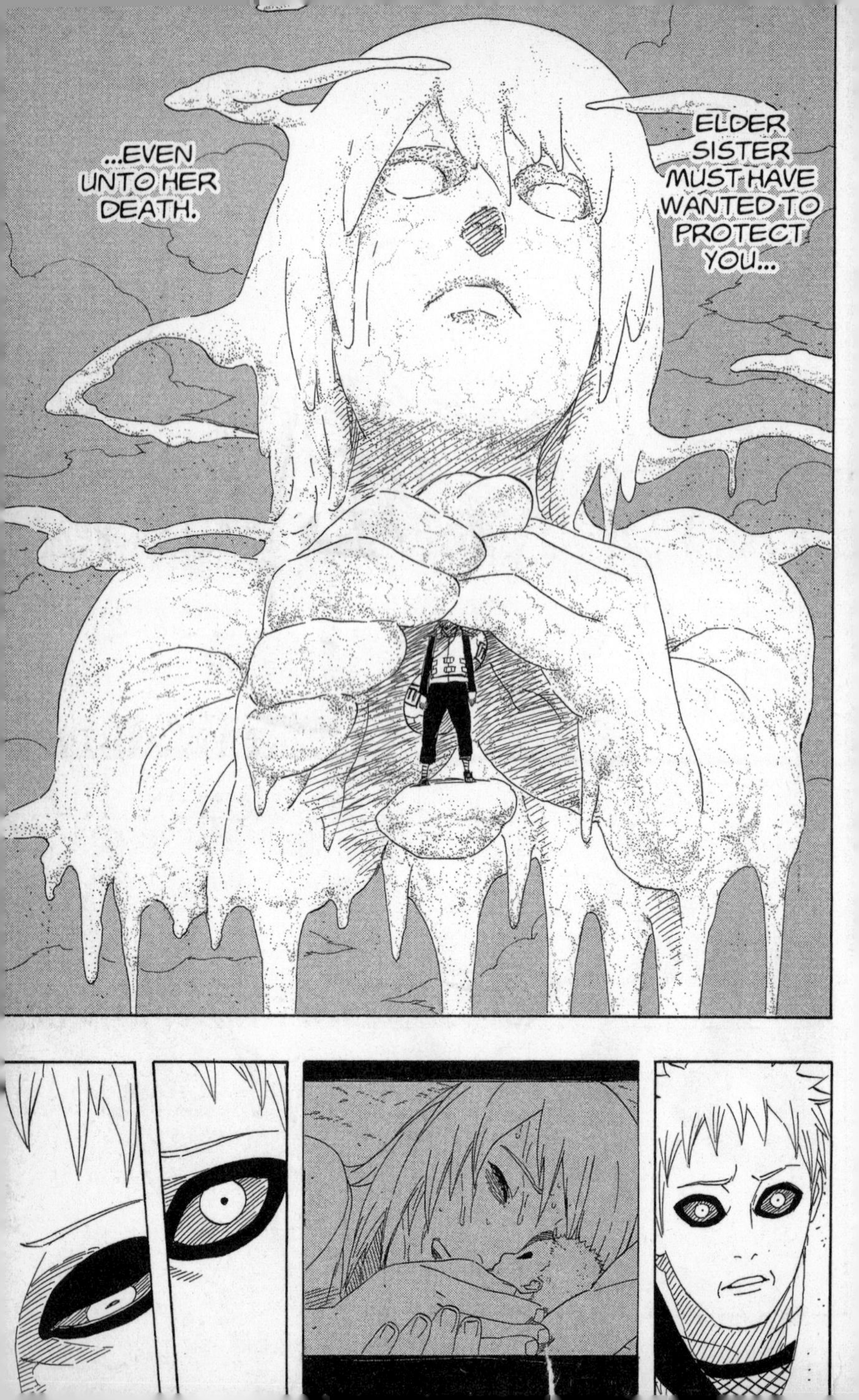
ELDER SISTER MUST HAVE WANTED TO PROTECT YOU...
...EVEN UNTO HER DEATH.

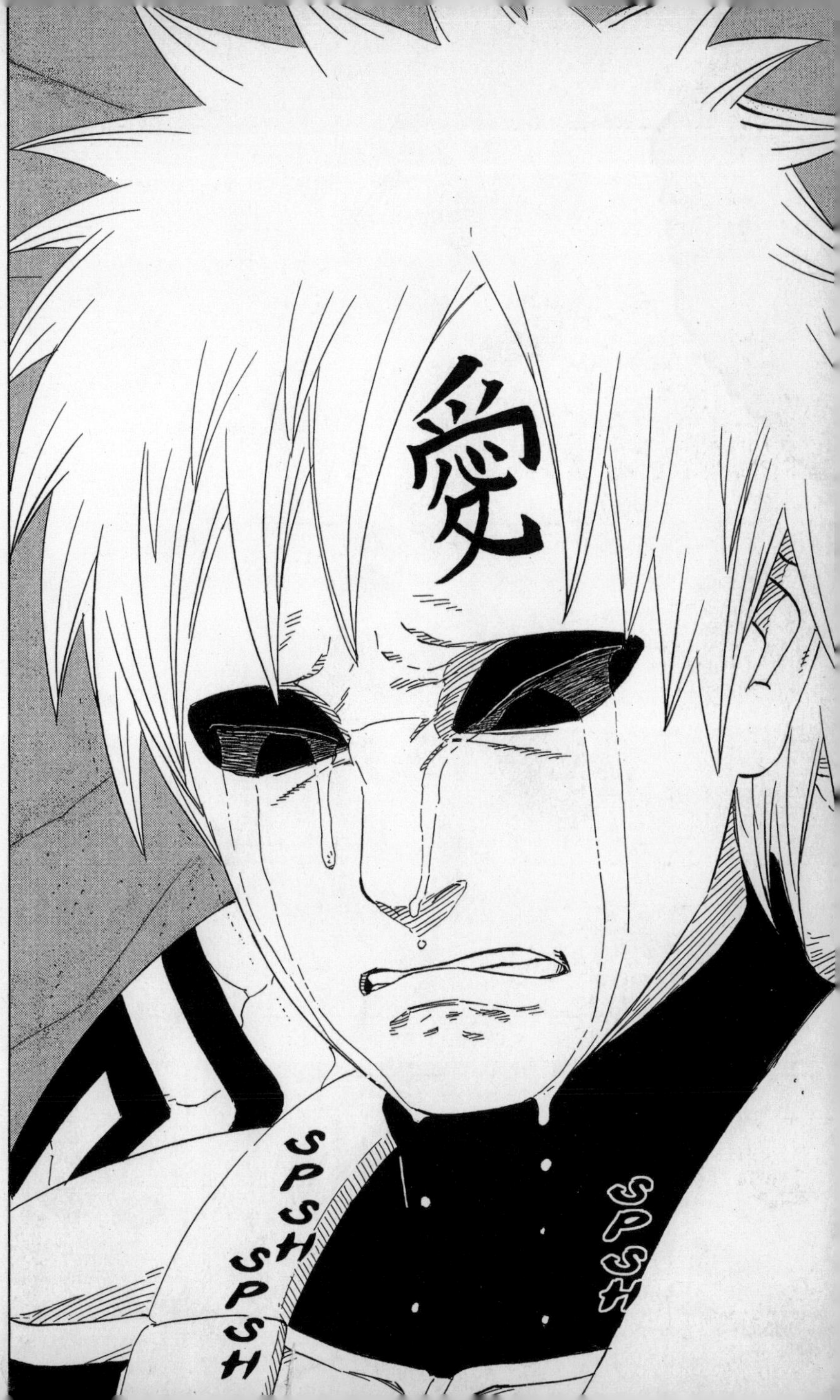
愛
SPSH
SPSH
SPSH
SPSH

READ THIS WAY

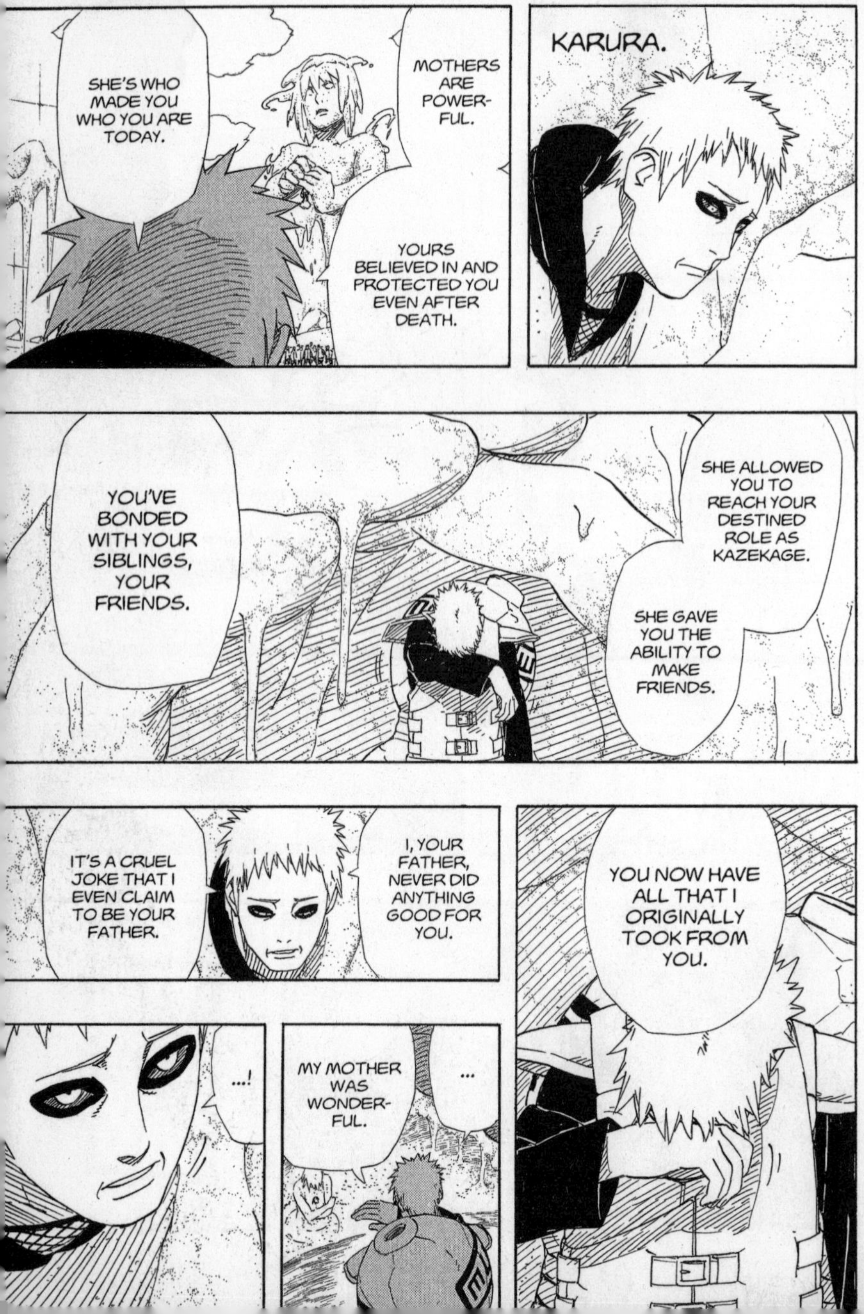
KARURA.
MOTHERS ARE POWER-FUL.
YOURS BELIEVED IN AND PROTECTED YOU EVEN AFTER DEATH.
SHE'S WHO MADE YOU WHO YOU ARE TODAY.
SHE ALLOWED YOU TO REACH YOUR DESTINED ROLE AS KAZEKAGE.
SHE GAVE YOU THE ABILITY TO MAKE FRIENDS.
YOU'VE BONDED WITH YOUR SIBLINGS, YOUR FRIENDS.
YOU NOW HAVE ALL THAT I ORIGINALLY TOOK FROM YOU.
I, YOUR FATHER, NEVER DID ANYTHING GOOD FOR YOU.
IT'S A CRUEL JOKE THAT I EVEN CLAIM TO BE YOUR FATHER.
...
MY MOTHER WAS WONDER-FUL.
...!

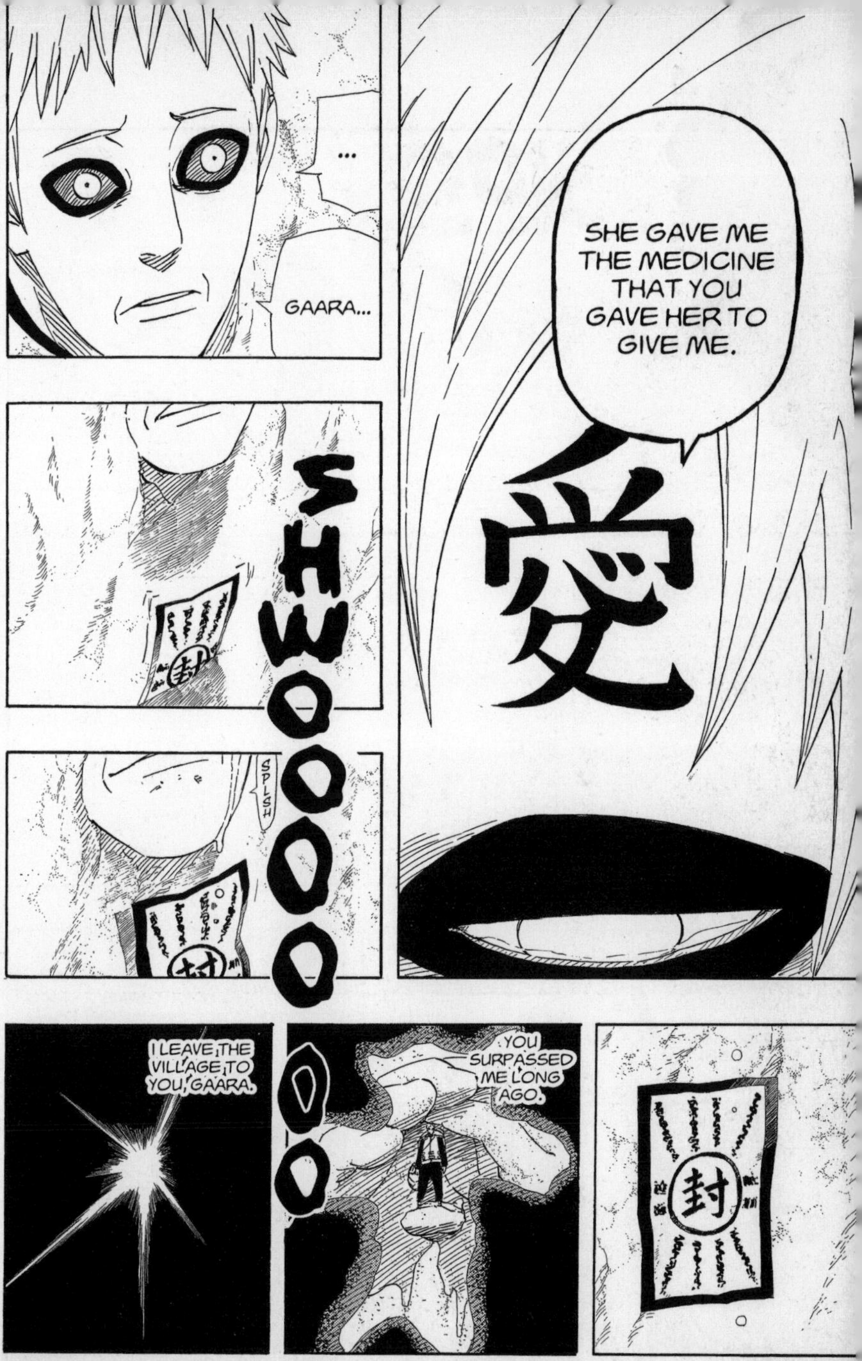

SHE GAVE ME THE MEDICINE THAT YOU GAVE HER TO GIVE ME.
愛
...
GAARA...
SHWOOOOOOO
SPLSH
YOU SURPASSED ME LONG AGO.
I LEAVE THE VILLAGE TO YOU, GAARA.

READ THIS WAY

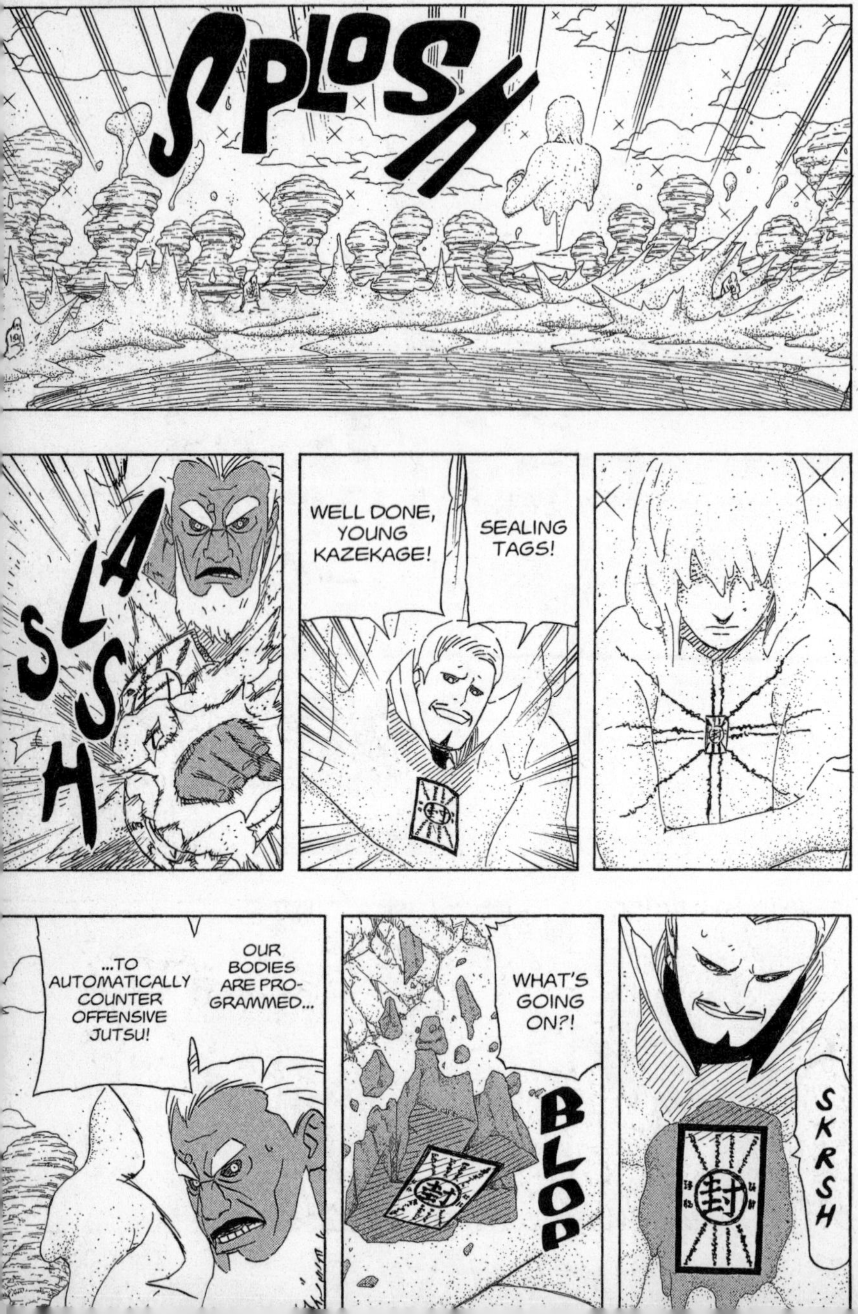
SPLOSH
SEALING TAGS!
WELL DONE, YOUNG KAZEKAGE!
SLASH
SKRSH
WHAT'S GOING ON?!
BLOP
OUR BODIES ARE PROGRAMMED...
...TO AUTOMATICALLY COUNTER OFFENSIVE JUTSU!

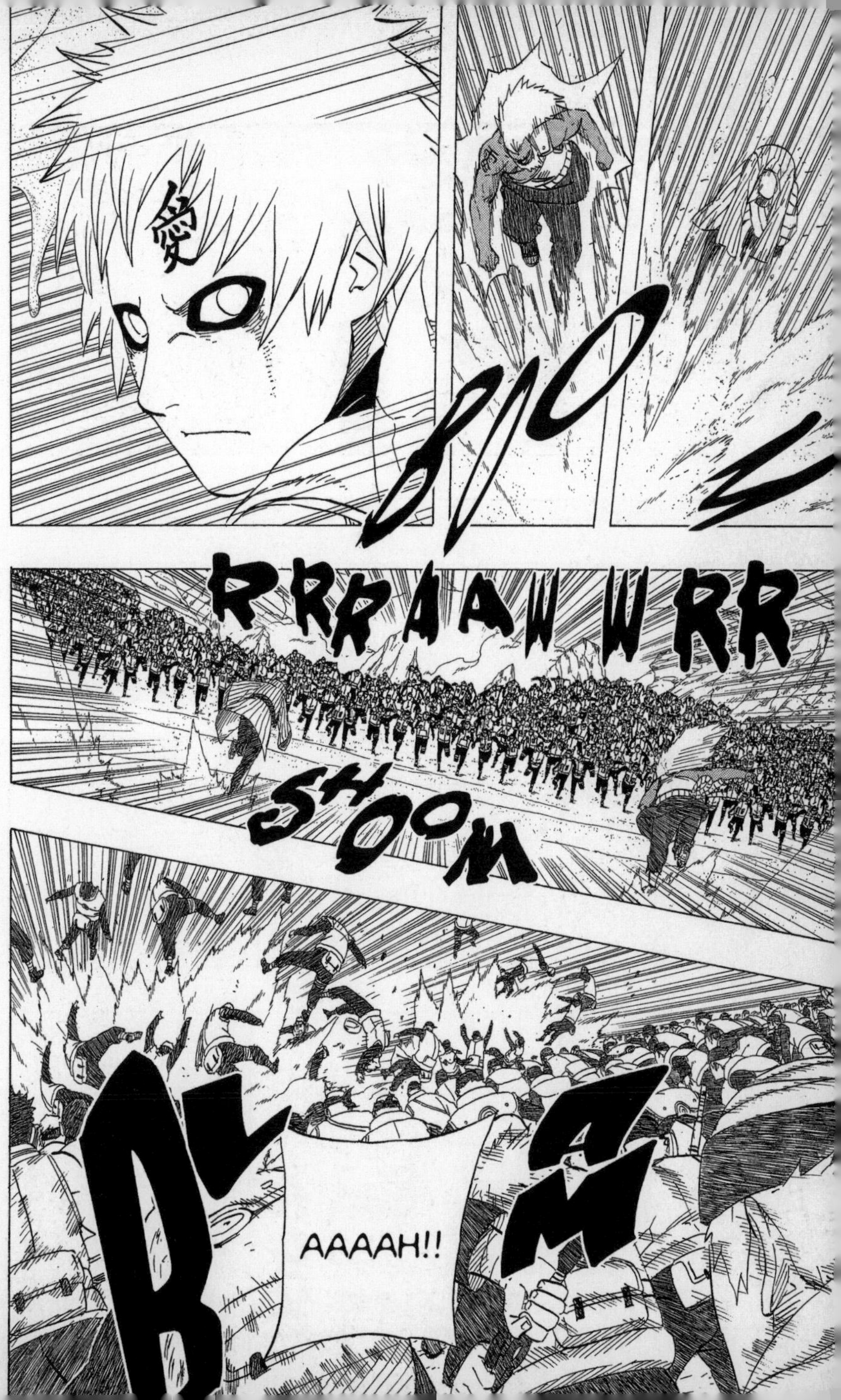
愛
BROOM
RRRAAWWRR
SHOOM
AAAAH!!

READ THIS WAY

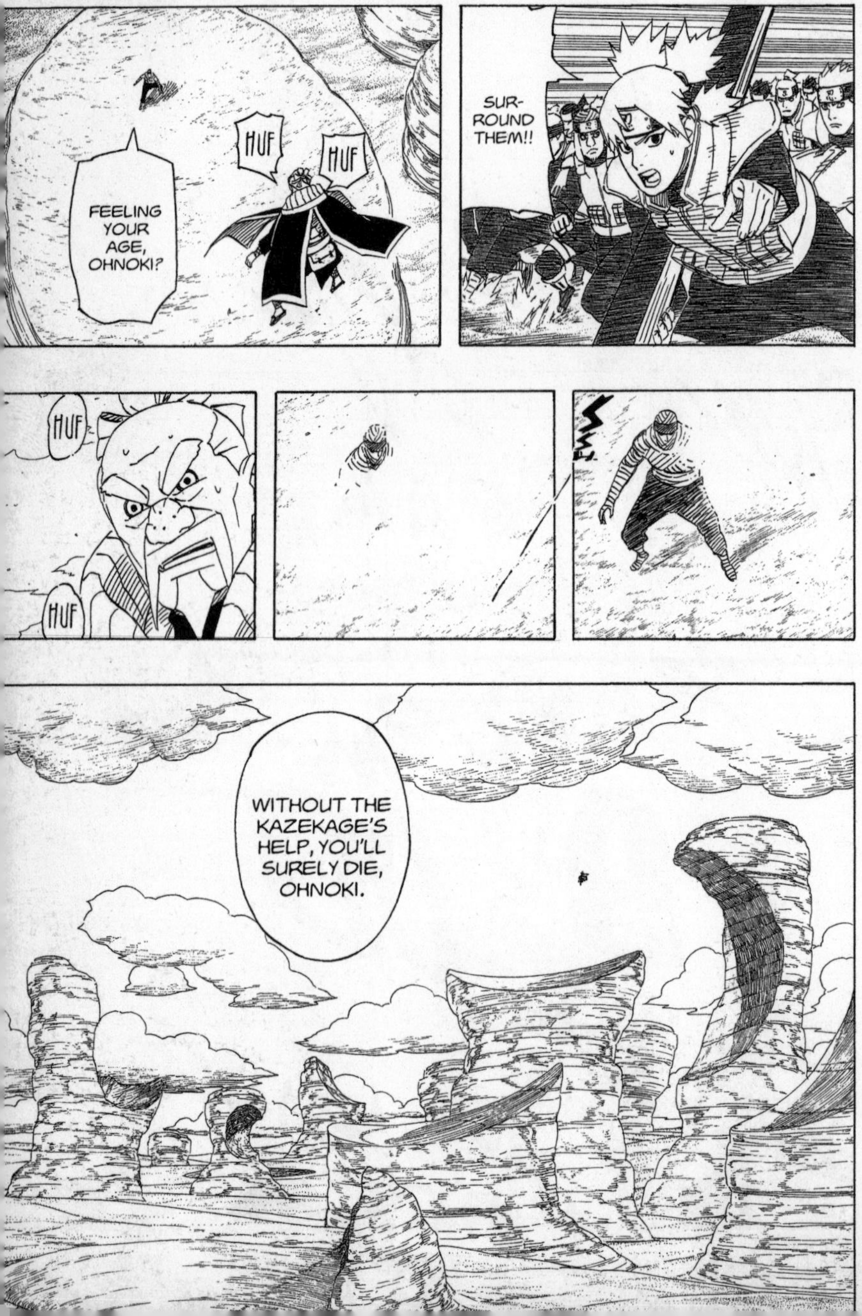

SUR-ROUND THEM!!
HUF
HUF
FEELING YOUR AGE, OHNOKI?
HUF
HUF
WITHOUT THE KAZEKAGE'S HELP, YOU'LL SURELY DIE, OHNOKI.

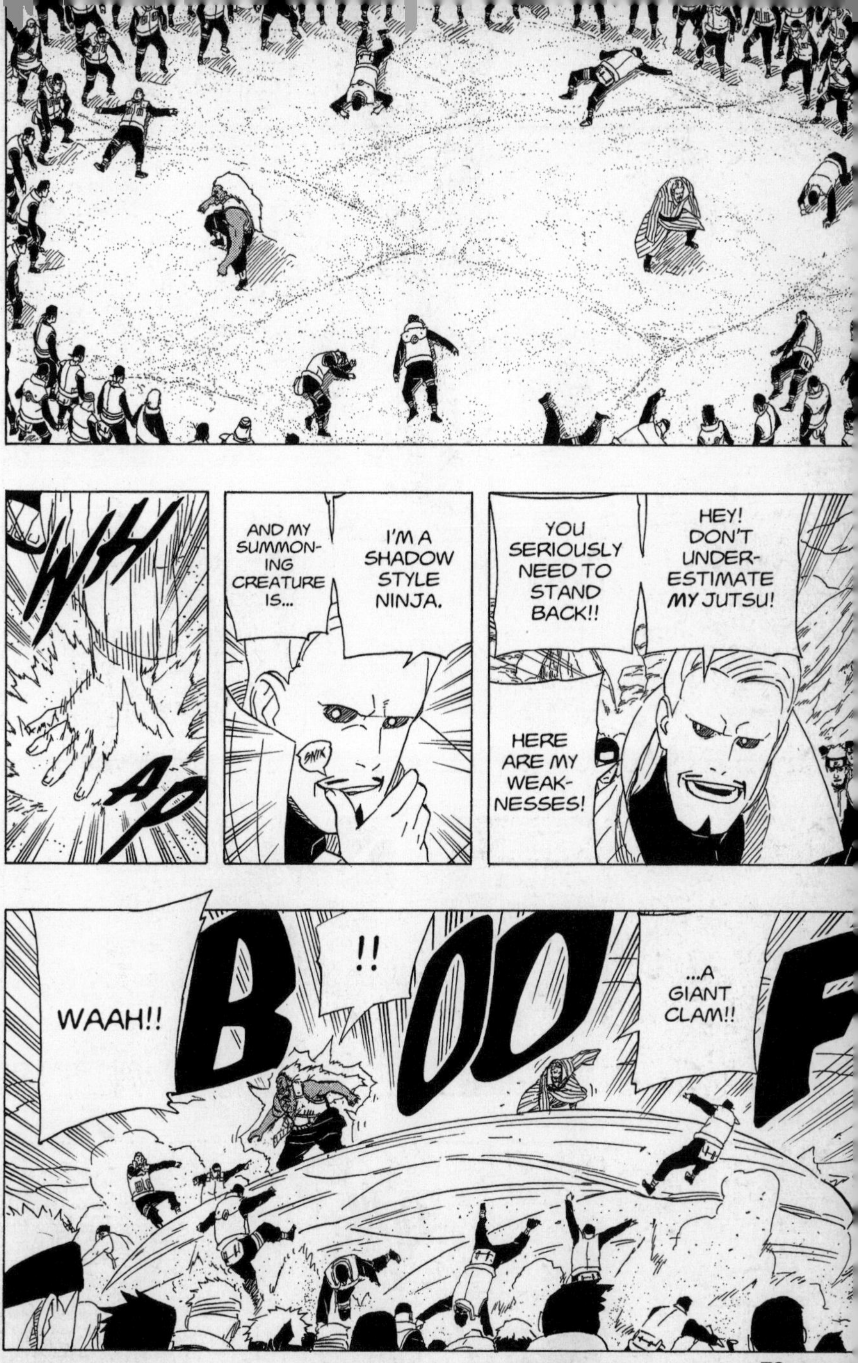
HEY! DON'T UNDERESTIMATE MY JUTSU!
YOU SERIOUSLY NEED TO STAND BACK!!
HERE ARE MY WEAKNESSES!
I'M A SHADOW STYLE NINJA.
AND MY SUMMONING CREATURE IS...
SNIK
WHAP
...A GIANT CLAM!!
!!
BOOF
WAAH!!

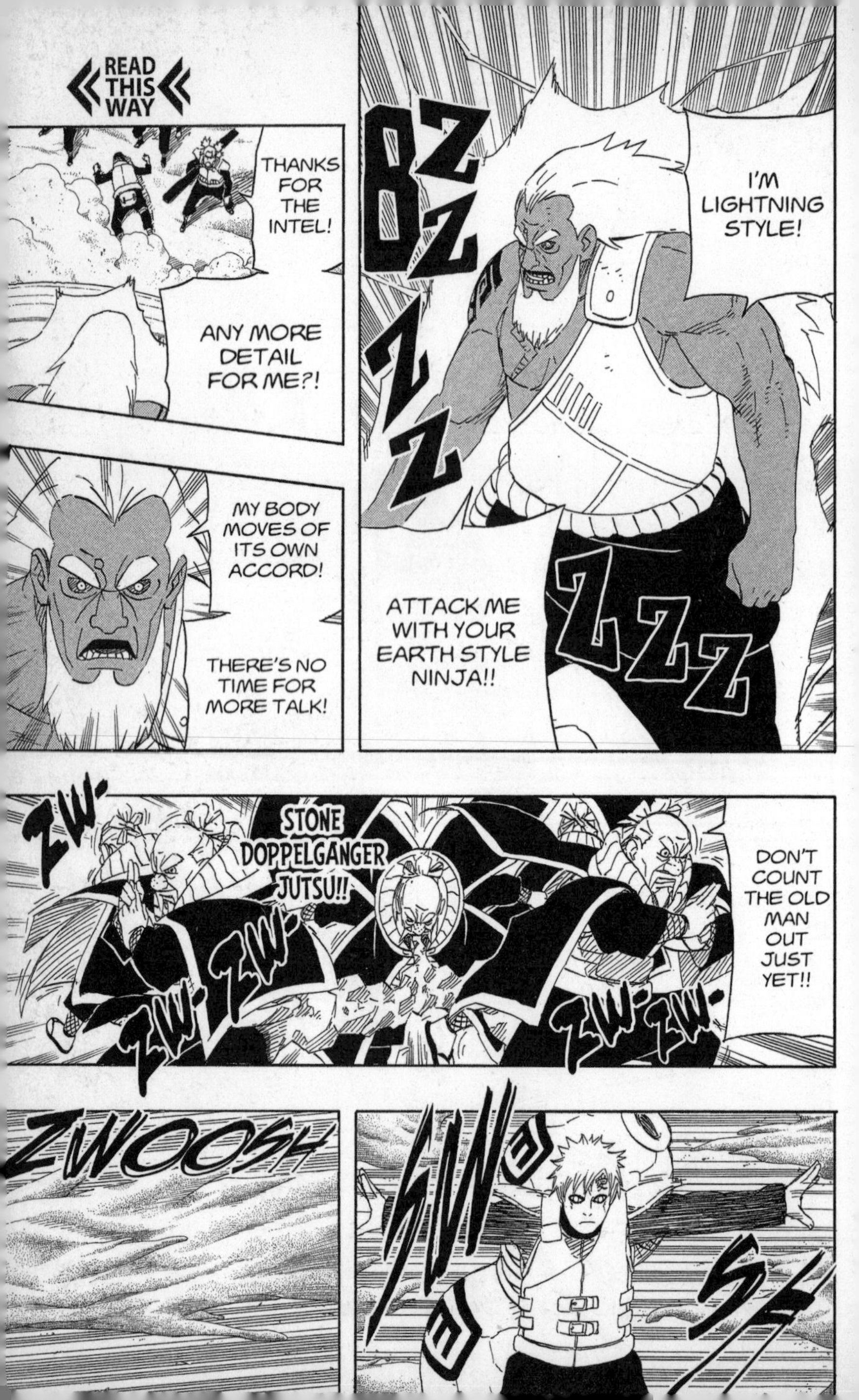
READ THIS WAY
BZZZ
I'M LIGHTNING STYLE!
ATTACK ME WITH YOUR EARTH STYLE NINJA!!
ZZZ
THANKS FOR THE INTEL!
ANY MORE DETAIL FOR ME?!
MY BODY MOVES OF ITS OWN ACCORD!
THERE'S NO TIME FOR MORE TALK!
DON'T COUNT THE OLD MAN OUT JUST YET!!
ZW- ZW-
STONE DOPPELGANGER JUTSU!!
ZW- ZW-
ZW-
SHWA
SH
ZWOOSH

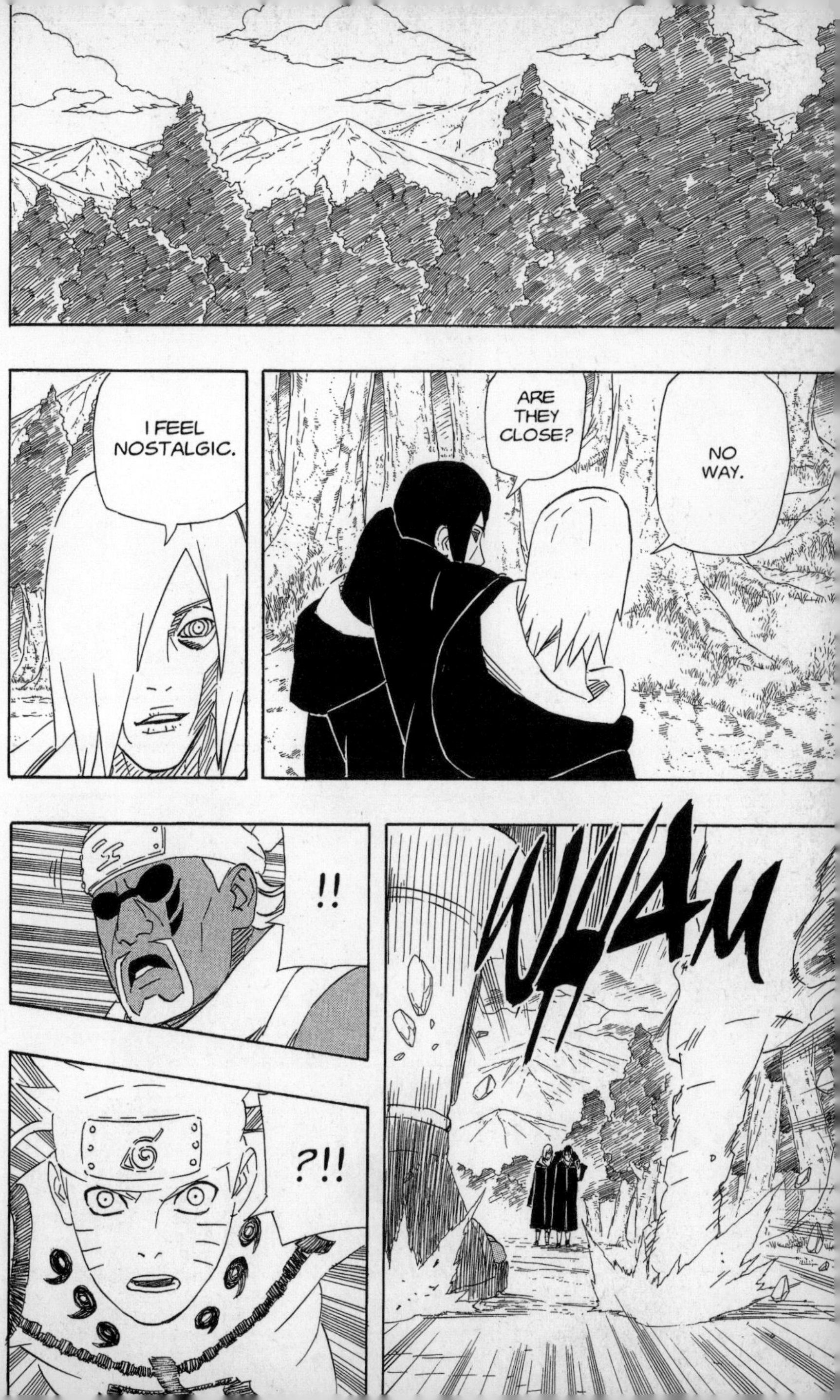
NO WAY.
ARE THEY CLOSE?
I FEEL NOSTALGIC.
WHAM
!!
?!!

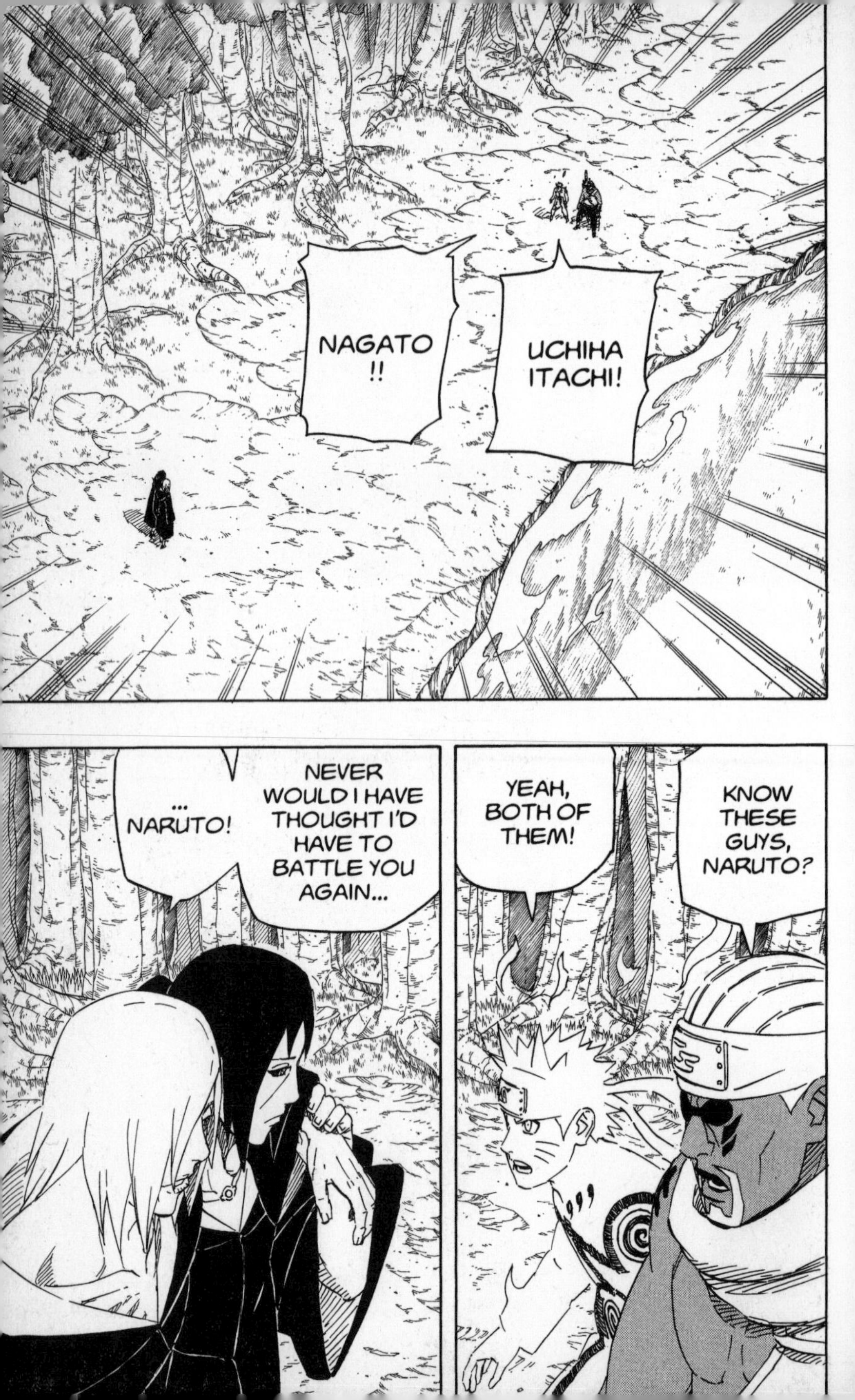
UCHIHA ITACHI!
NAGATO !!
KNOW THESE GUYS, NARUTO?
YEAH, BOTH OF THEM!
NEVER WOULD I HAVE THOUGHT I'D HAVE TO BATTLE YOU AGAIN...
... NARUTO!

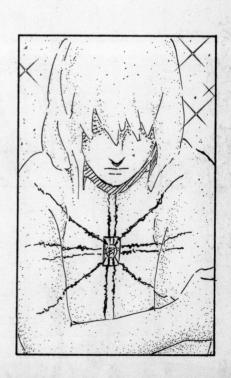

Number 549: Itachi's Question!!

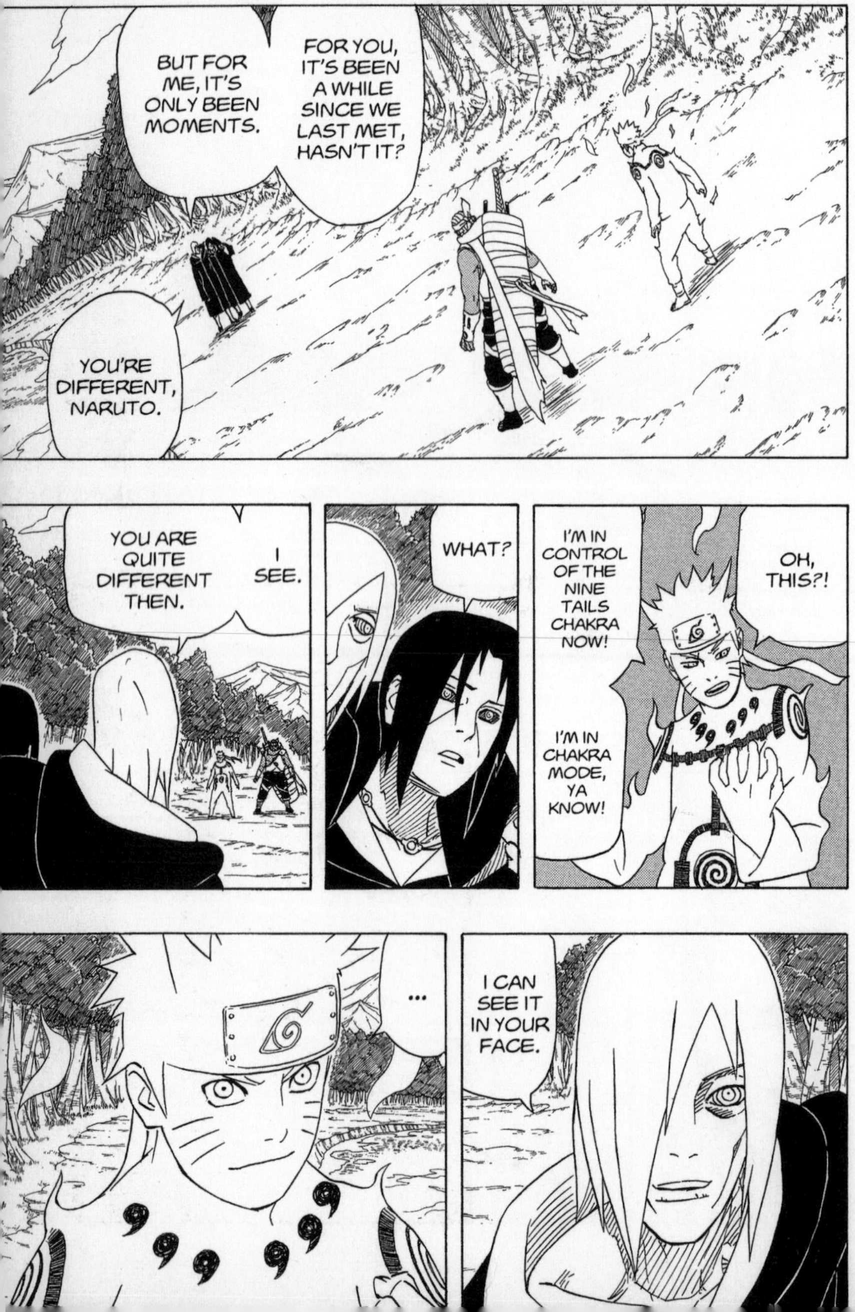
FOR YOU, IT'S BEEN A WHILE SINCE WE LAST MET, HASN'T IT?
BUT FOR ME, IT'S ONLY BEEN MOMENTS.
YOU'RE DIFFERENT, NARUTO.
OH, THIS?!
I'M IN CONTROL OF THE NINE TAILS CHAKRA NOW!
I'M IN CHAKRA MODE, YA KNOW!
WHAT?
I SEE.
YOU ARE QUITE DIFFERENT THEN.
I CAN SEE IT IN YOUR FACE.
...

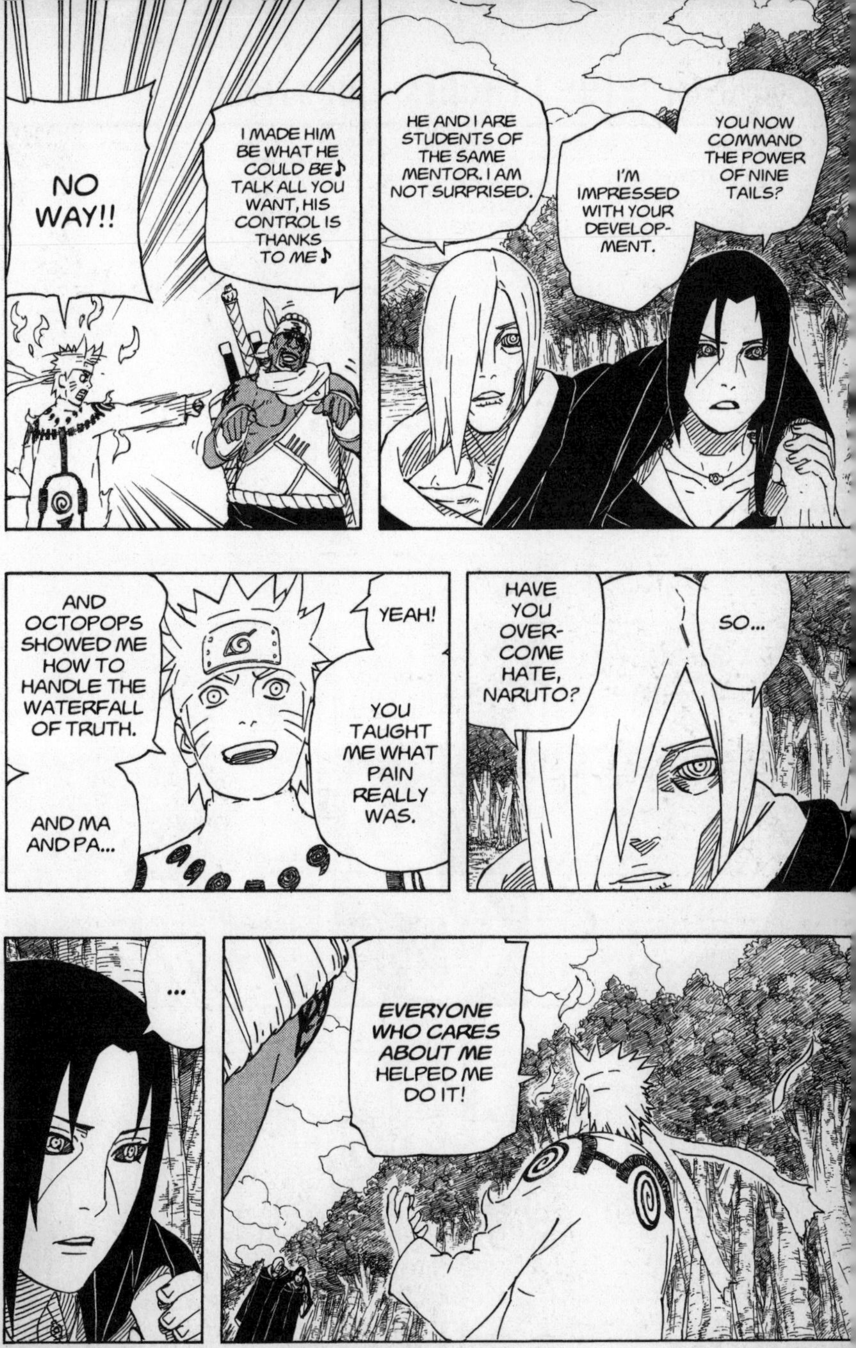
YOU NOW COMMAND THE POWER OF NINE TAILS?
I'M IMPRESSED WITH YOUR DEVELOPMENT.
HE AND I ARE STUDENTS OF THE SAME MENTOR. I AM NOT SURPRISED.
I MADE HIM BE WHAT HE COULD BE♪ TALK ALL YOU WANT, HIS CONTROL IS THANKS TO ME♪
NO WAY!!
SO...
HAVE YOU OVERCOME HATE, NARUTO?
YEAH!
YOU TAUGHT ME WHAT PAIN REALLY WAS.
AND OCTOPOPS SHOWED ME HOW TO HANDLE THE WATERFALL OF TRUTH.
AND MA AND PA...
EVERYONE WHO CARES ABOUT ME HELPED ME DO IT!
...

READ THIS WAY

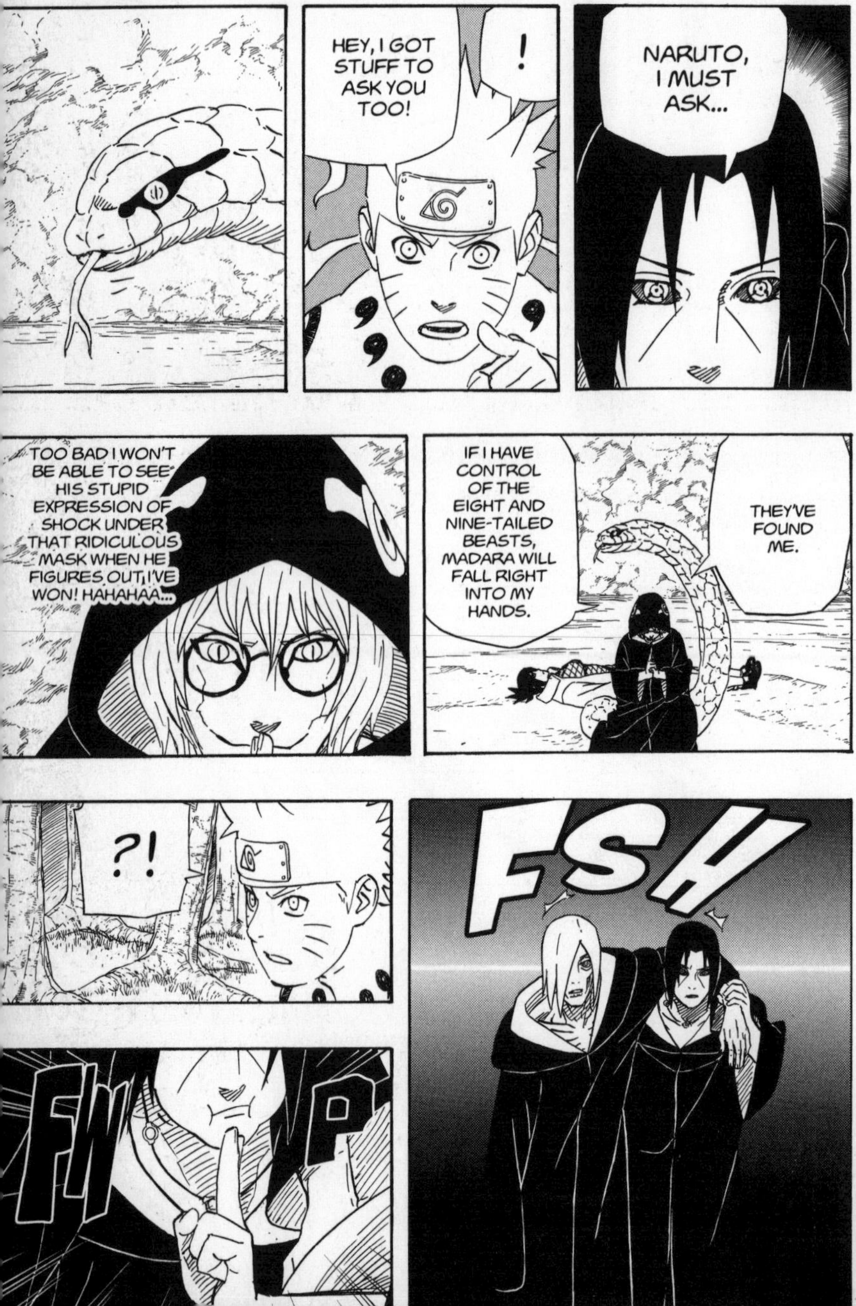
NARUTO, I MUST ASK...
!
HEY, I GOT STUFF TO ASK YOU TOO!
THEY'VE FOUND ME.
IF I HAVE CONTROL OF THE EIGHT AND NINE-TAILED BEASTS, MADARA WILL FALL RIGHT INTO MY HANDS.
TOO BAD I WON'T BE ABLE TO SEE HIS STUPID EXPRESSION OF SHOCK UNDER THAT RIDICULOUS MASK WHEN HE FIGURES OUT I'VE WON! HAHAHAA...
FSH
?!
FWIP

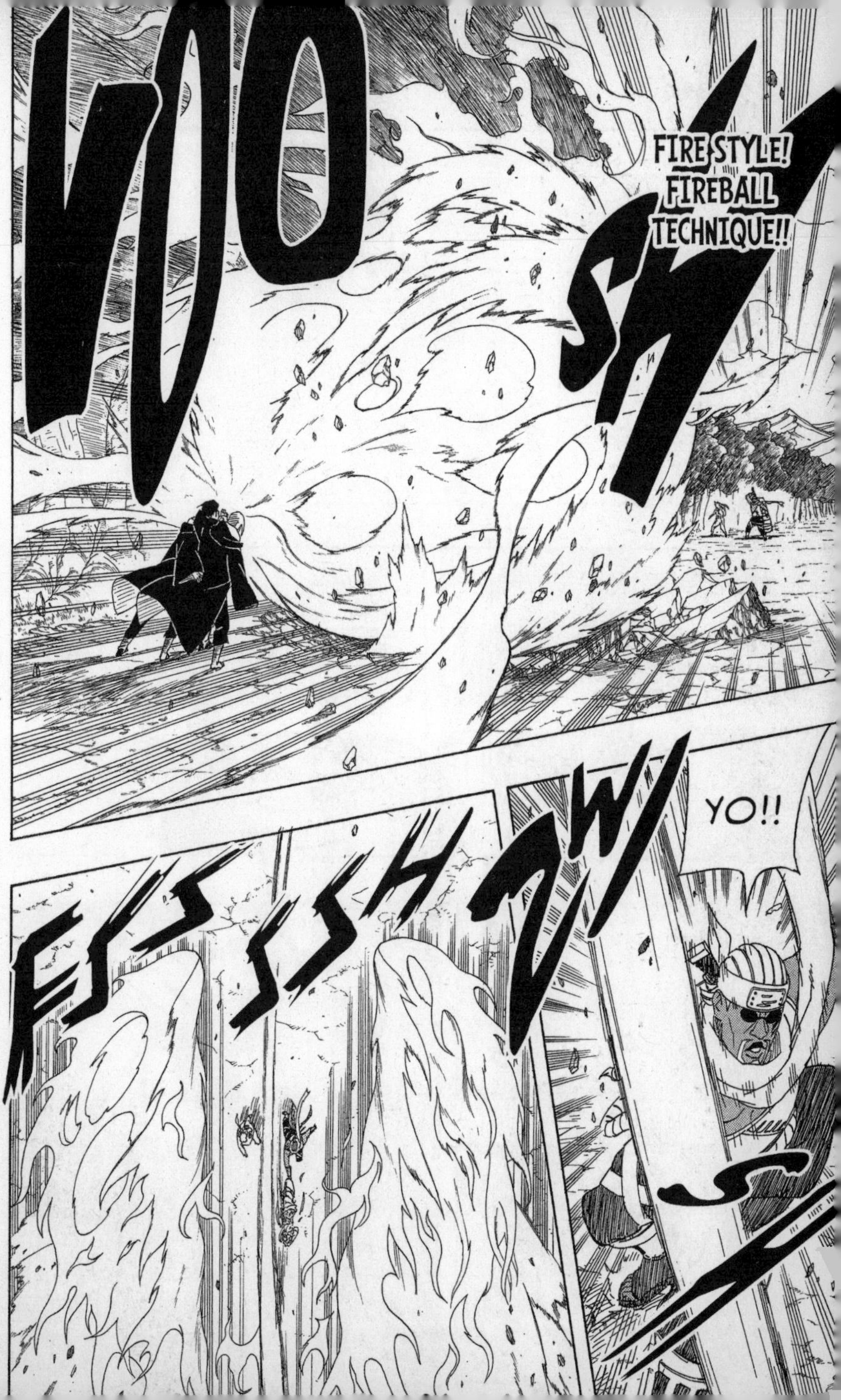
FIRE STYLE! FIREBALL TECHNIQUE!!
VOOSH
YO!!
FSSSHOW

READ THIS WAY

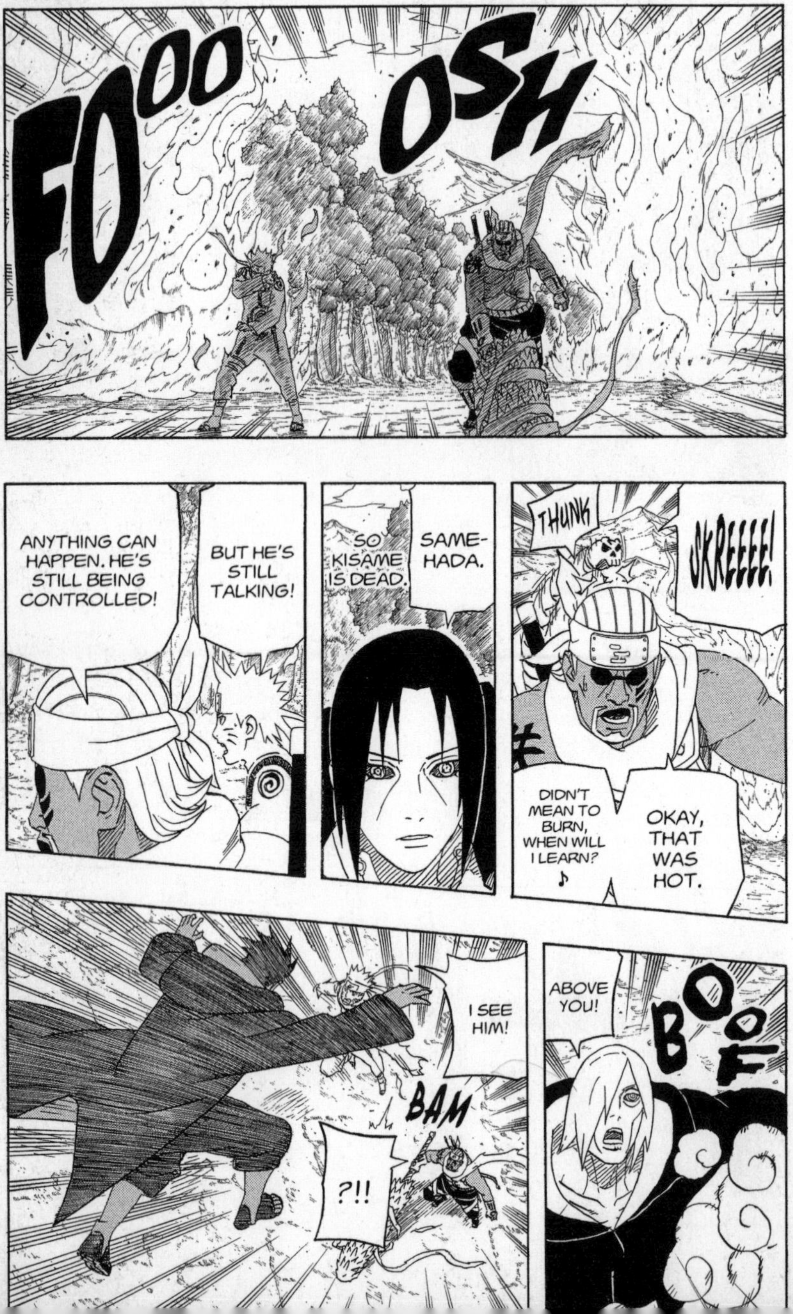
FOOOOSH
THUNK
SKREEEE!
OKAY, THAT WAS HOT.
DIDN'T MEAN TO BURN, WHEN WILL I LEARN? ♪
SAME-HADA.
SO KISAME IS DEAD.
BUT HE'S STILL TALKING!
ANYTHING CAN HAPPEN. HE'S STILL BEING CONTROLLED!
ABOVE YOU!
BOOF
I SEE HIM!
BAM
?!!

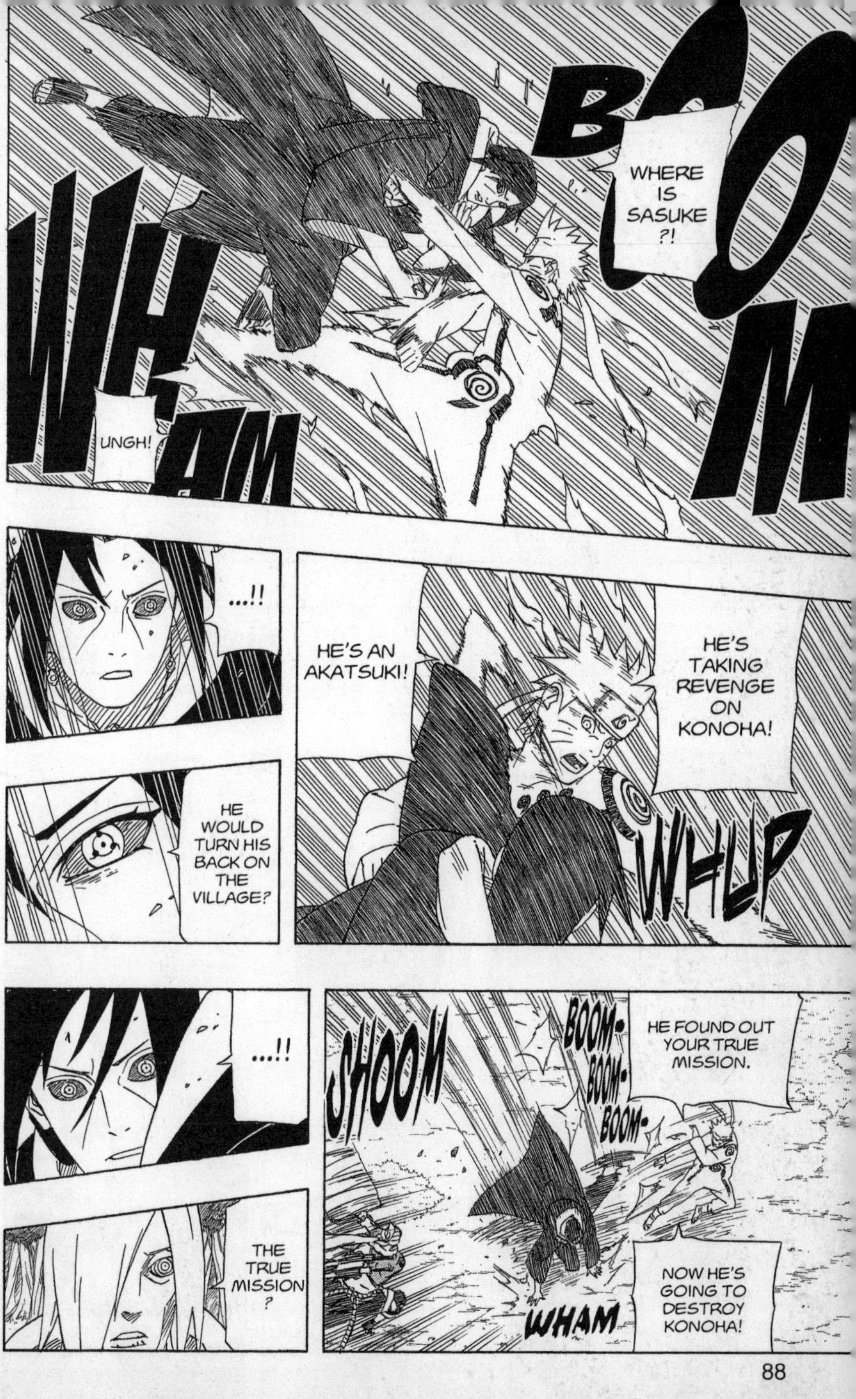
BOOM
WHERE IS SASUKE?!
WHAM
UNGH!
HE'S TAKING REVENGE ON KONOHA!
HE'S AN AKATSUKI!
WHUP
...!!
HE WOULD TURN HIS BACK ON THE VILLAGE?
HE FOUND OUT YOUR TRUE MISSION.
BOOM-BOOM-BOOM-
SHOOM
NOW HE'S GOING TO DESTROY KONOHA!
WHAM
...!!
THE TRUE MISSION?

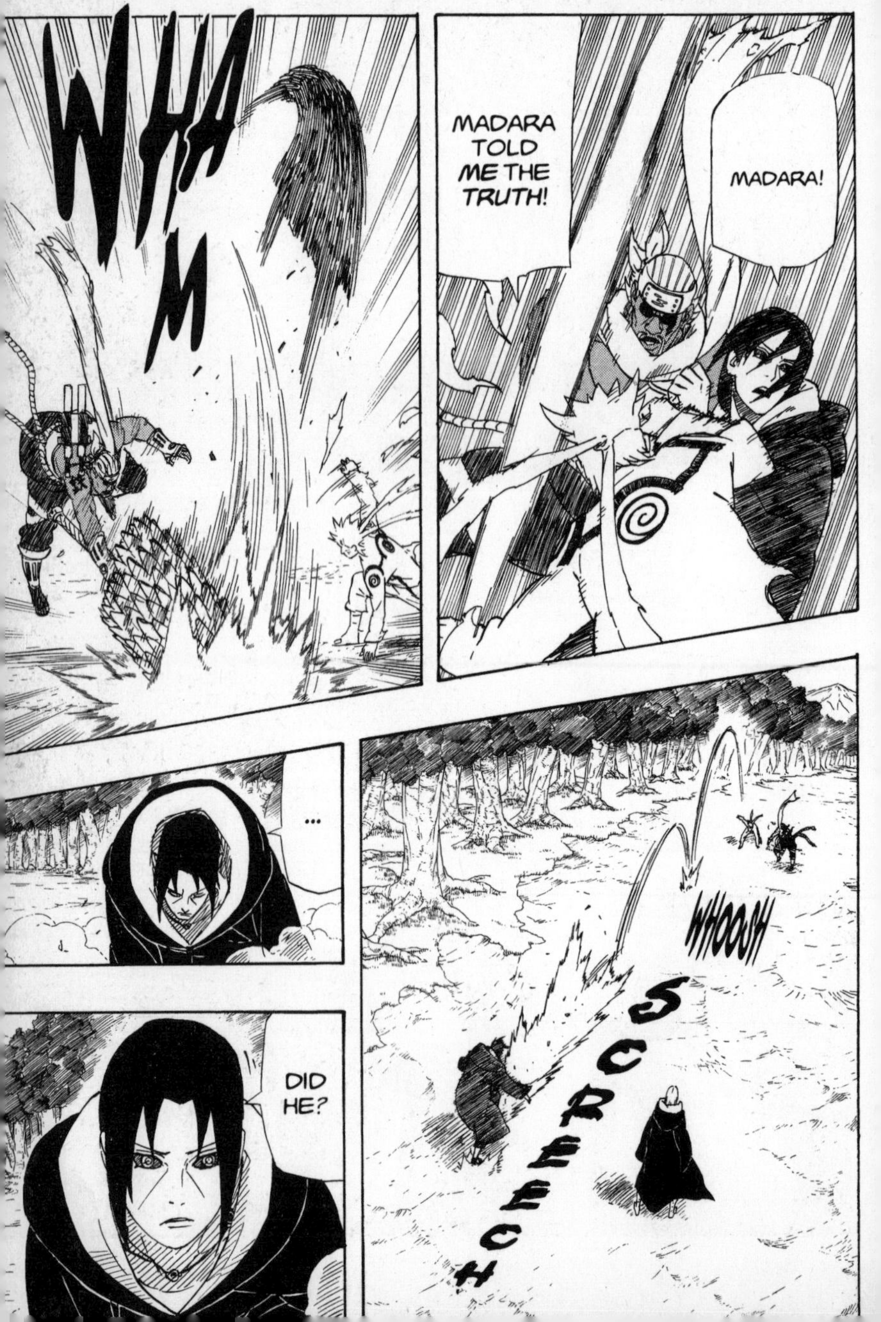
MADARA!
MADARA TOLD ME THE TRUTH!
WHAM
WHOOSH
SCREECH
...
DID HE?

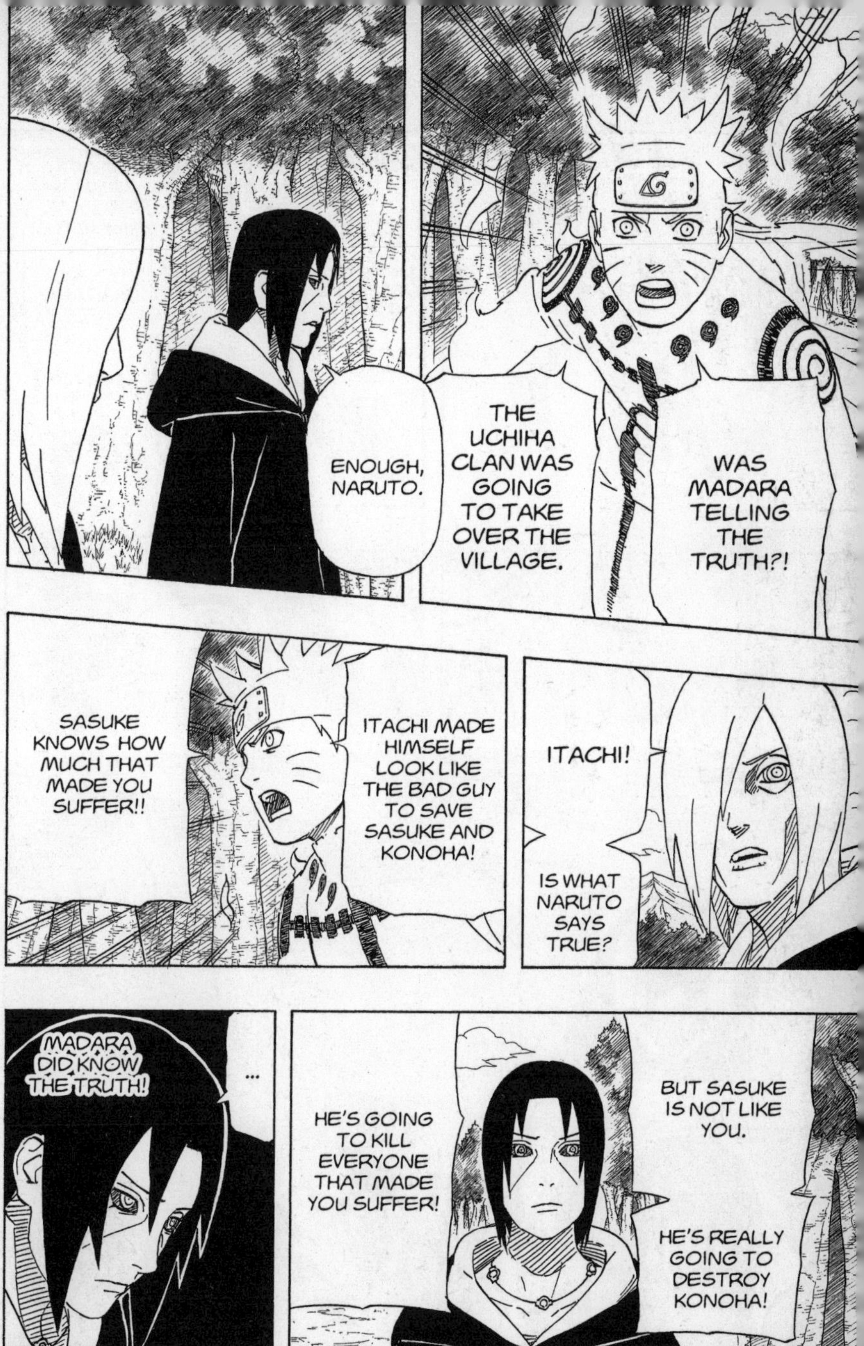
WAS MADARA TELLING THE TRUTH?!
THE UCHIHA CLAN WAS GOING TO TAKE OVER THE VILLAGE.
ENOUGH, NARUTO.
ITACHI!
IS WHAT NARUTO SAYS TRUE?
ITACHI MADE HIMSELF LOOK LIKE THE BAD GUY TO SAVE SASUKE AND KONOHA!
SASUKE KNOWS HOW MUCH THAT MADE YOU SUFFER!!
BUT SASUKE IS NOT LIKE YOU.
HE'S GOING TO KILL EVERYONE THAT MADE YOU SUFFER!
HE'S REALLY GOING TO DESTROY KONOHA!
...
MADARA DID KNOW THE TRUTH!

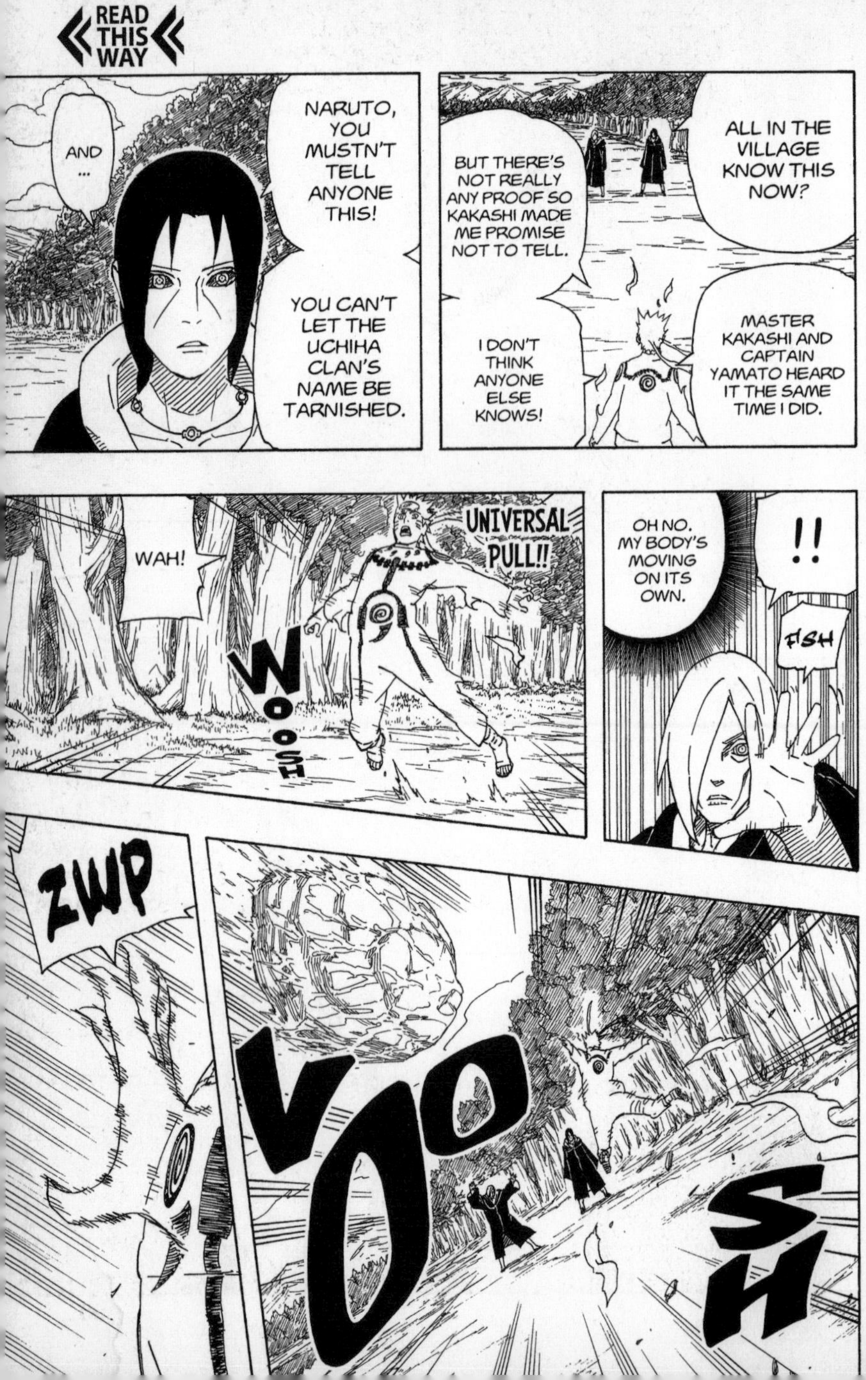
READ THIS WAY
ALL IN THE VILLAGE KNOW THIS NOW?
MASTER KAKASHI AND CAPTAIN YAMATO HEARD IT THE SAME TIME I DID.
I DON'T THINK ANYONE ELSE KNOWS!
BUT THERE'S NOT REALLY ANY PROOF SO KAKASHI MADE ME PROMISE NOT TO TELL.
NARUTO, YOU MUSTN'T TELL ANYONE THIS!
YOU CAN'T LET THE UCHIHA CLAN'S NAME BE TARNISHED.
AND ...
!!
FISH
OH NO. MY BODY'S MOVING ON ITS OWN.
UNIVERSAL PULL!!
WAH!
WOOSH
VOOSH
ZWP

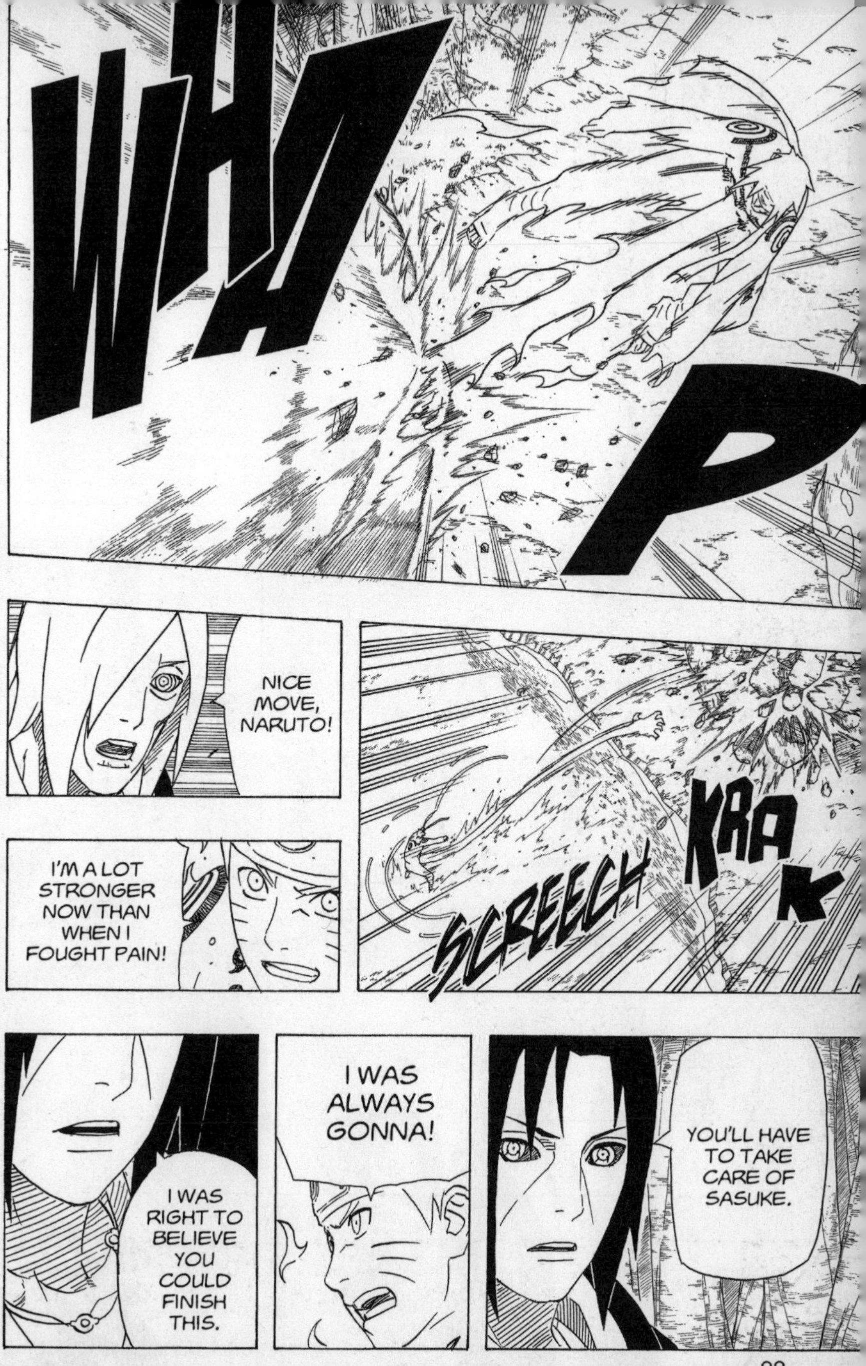
WHAP
KRAK
SCREECH
NICE MOVE, NARUTO!
I'M A LOT STRONGER NOW THAN WHEN I FOUGHT PAIN!
YOU'LL HAVE TO TAKE CARE OF SASUKE.
I WAS ALWAYS GONNA!
I WAS RIGHT TO BELIEVE YOU COULD FINISH THIS.

READ THIS WAY

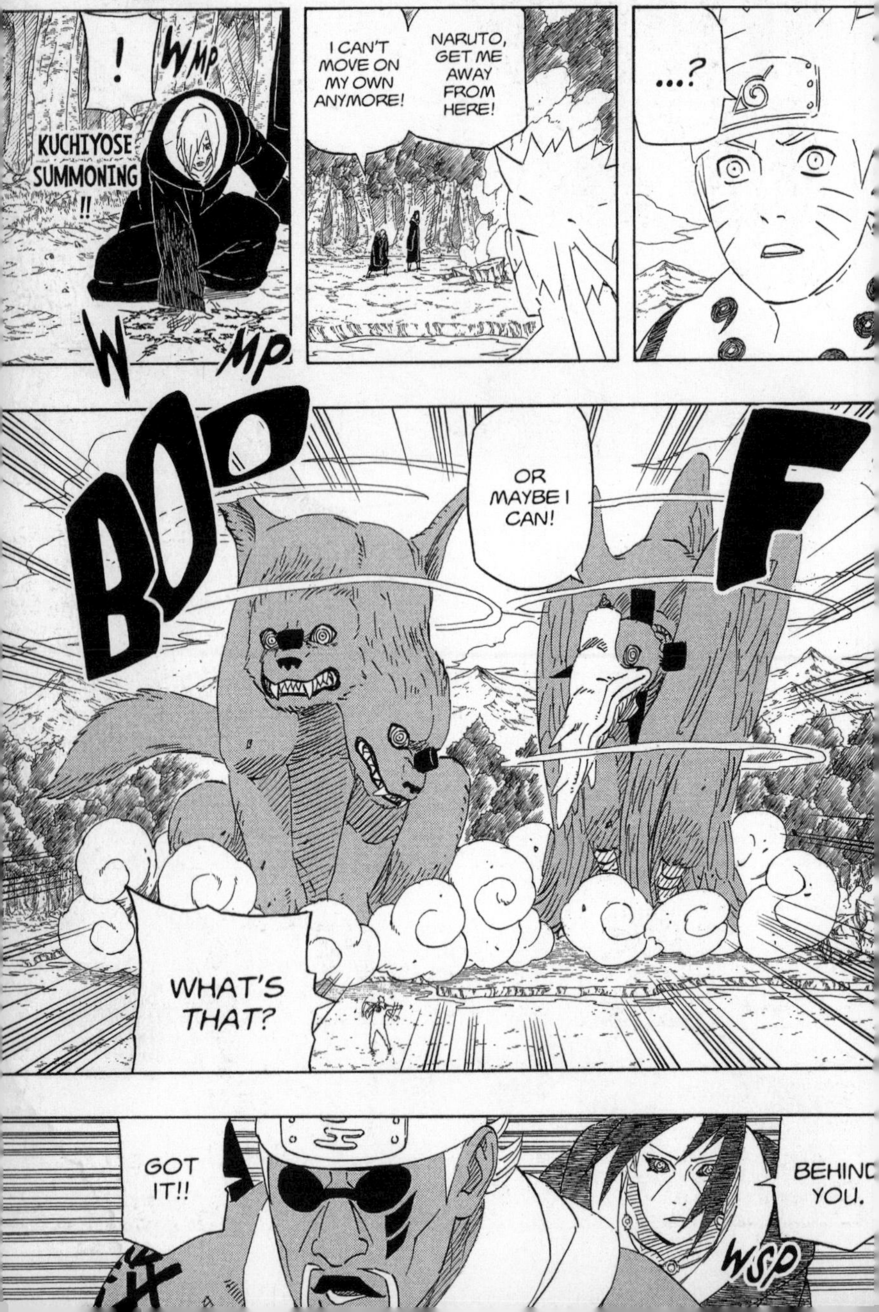
...?
NARUTO, GET ME AWAY FROM HERE!
I CAN'T MOVE ON MY OWN ANYMORE!
!
WMP
KUCHIYOSE SUMMONING!!
WMP
OR MAYBE I CAN!
BOOF
WHAT'S THAT?
BEHIND YOU.
WSP
GOT IT!!

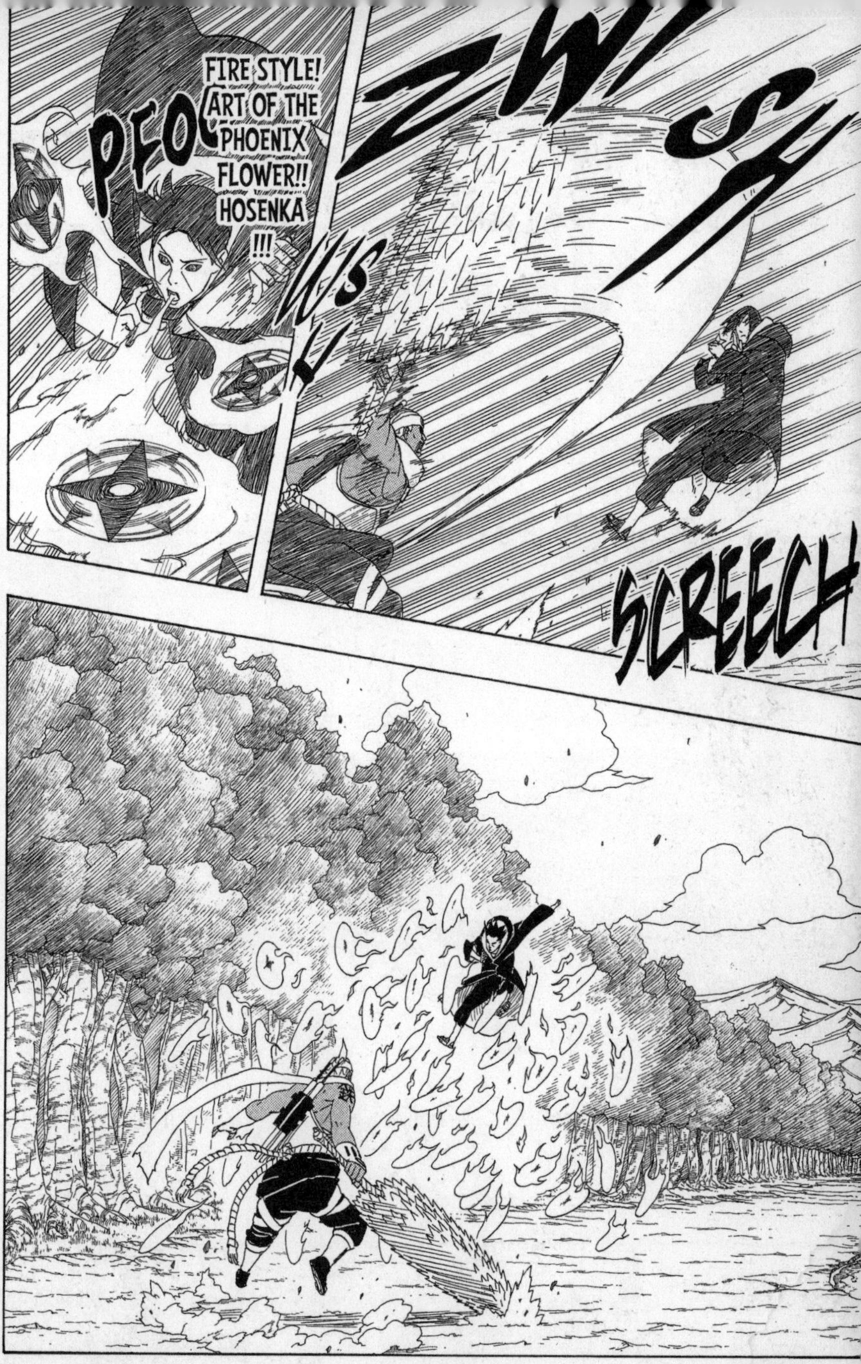
ZWISH
WUSH
SCREECH
PFO
FIRE STYLE! ART OF THE PHOENIX FLOWER!! HOSENKA!!!

READ THIS WAY

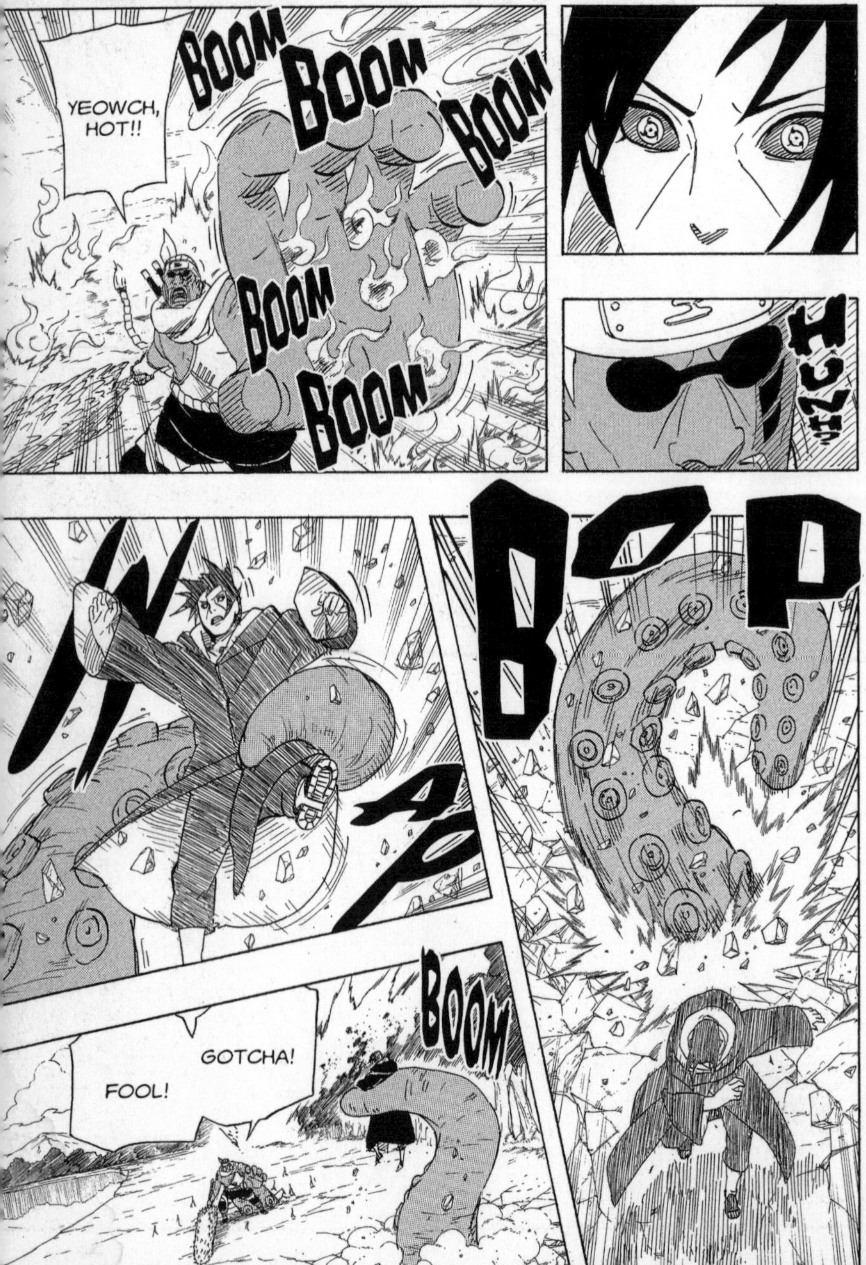
BOOM
BOOM
BOOM
BOOM
BOOM
YEOWCH, HOT!!
BOP
BOOM
GOTCHA!
FOOL!

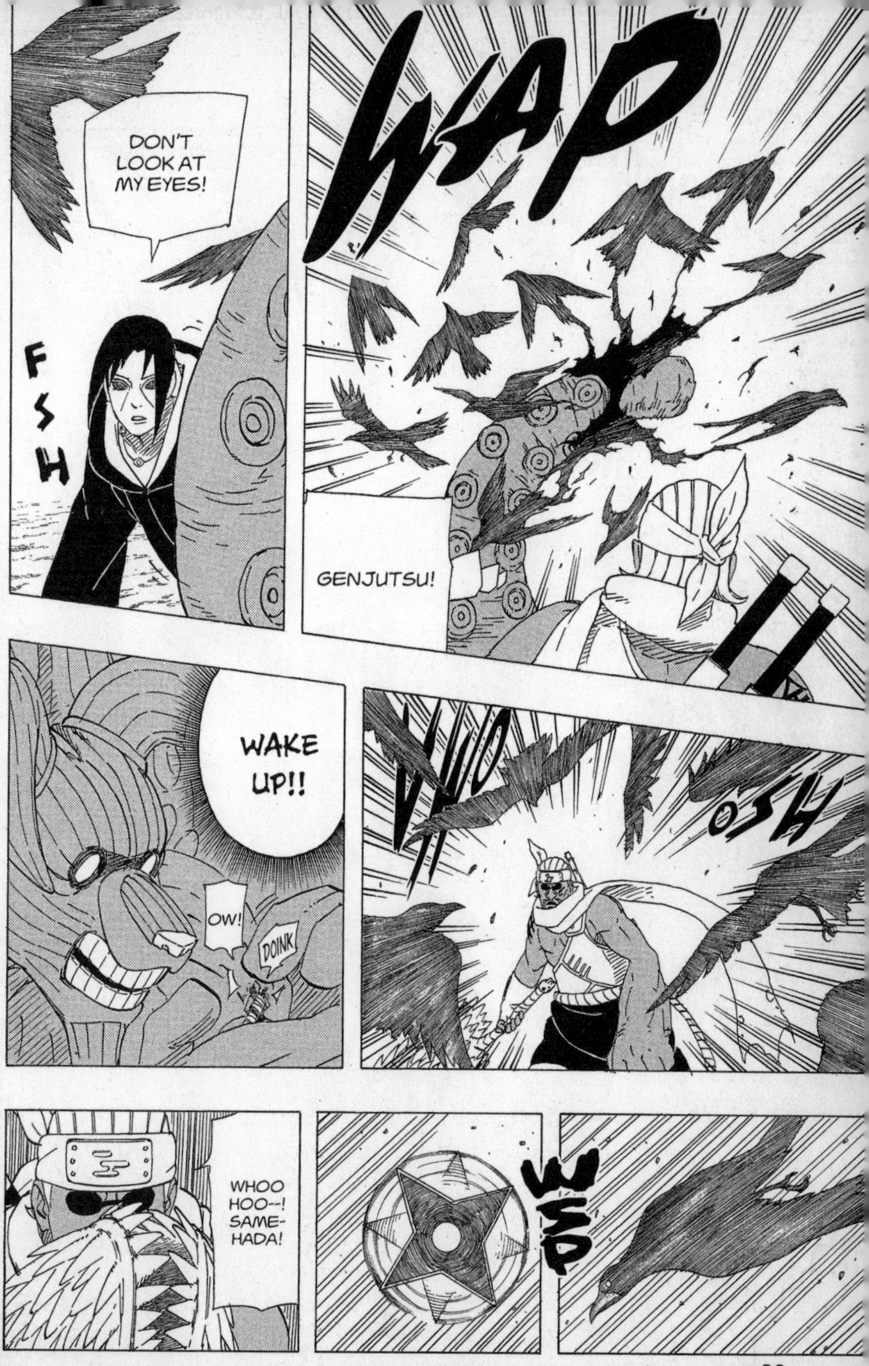
WAP
GENJUTSU!
DON'T LOOK AT MY EYES!
FSH
OSH
WAKE UP!!
OW!
DOINK
WHOO HOO--! SAME-HADA!

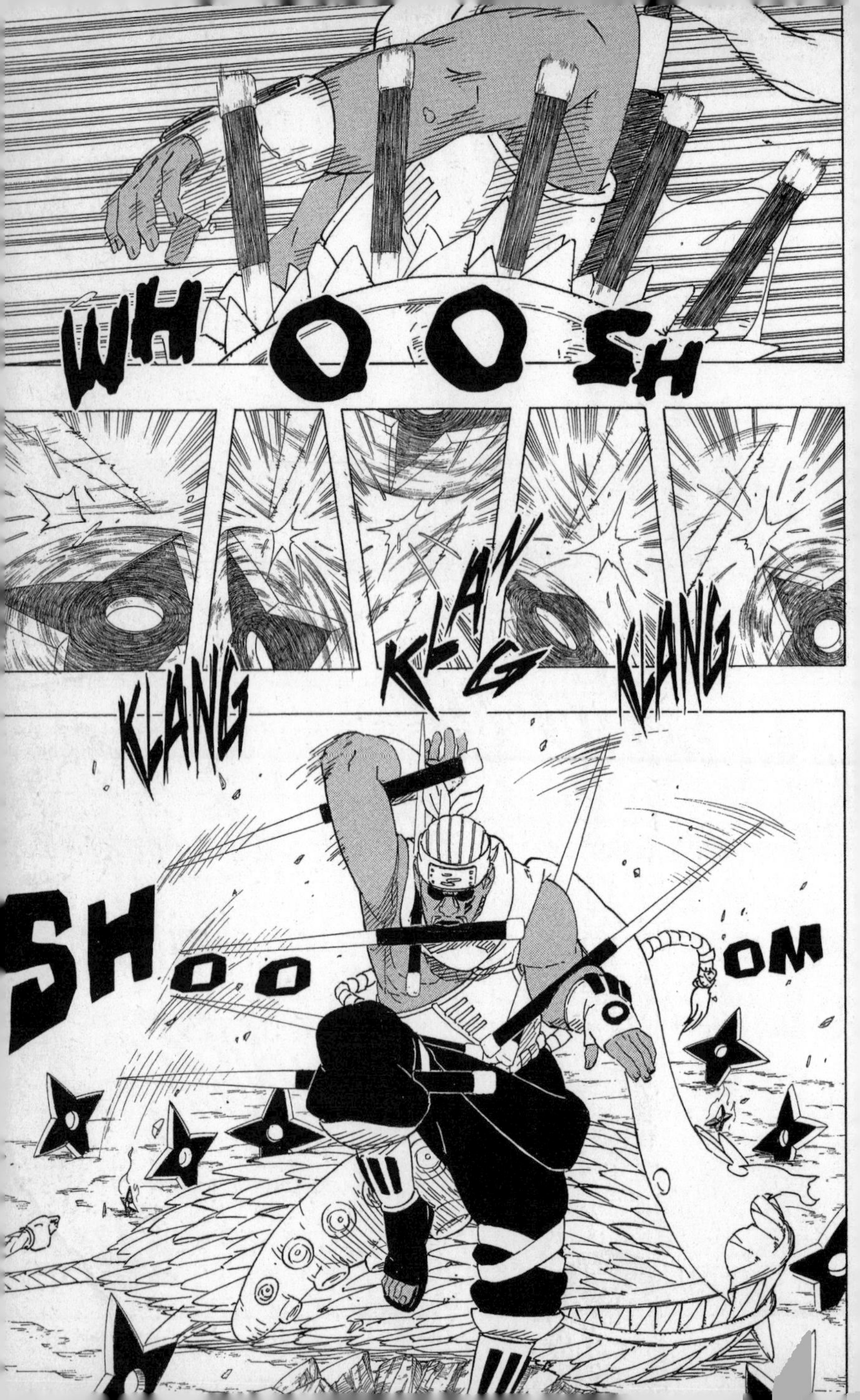
WHOOSH
KLANG
KLANG
KLANG
SHOOOOM

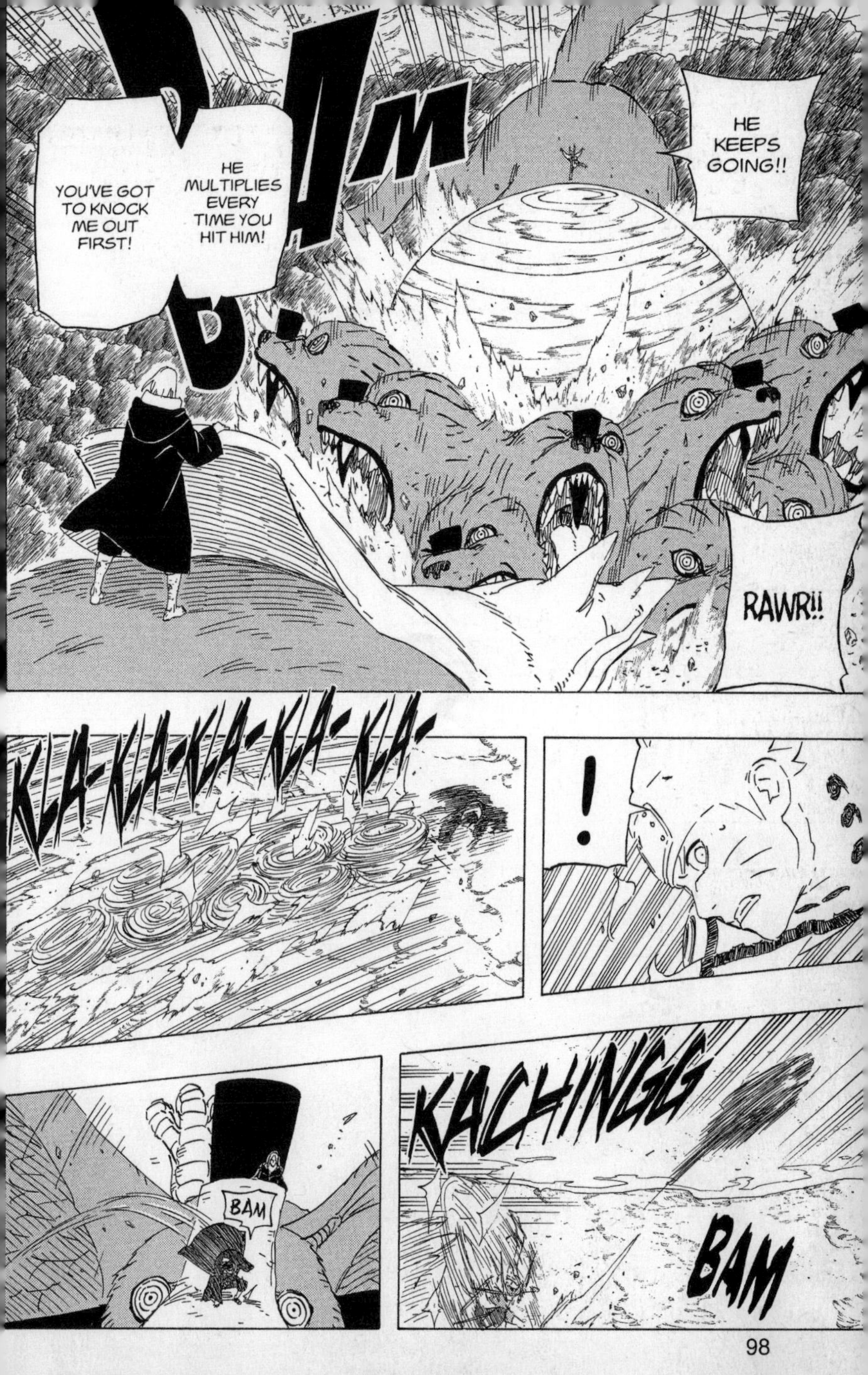
HE KEEPS GOING!!
HE MULTIPLIES EVERY TIME YOU HIT HIM!
YOU'VE GOT TO KNOCK ME OUT FIRST!
RAWR!!
!
KLA-KLA-KLA-KLA-KLA-
KACHINGG
BAM
BAM

READ THIS WAY

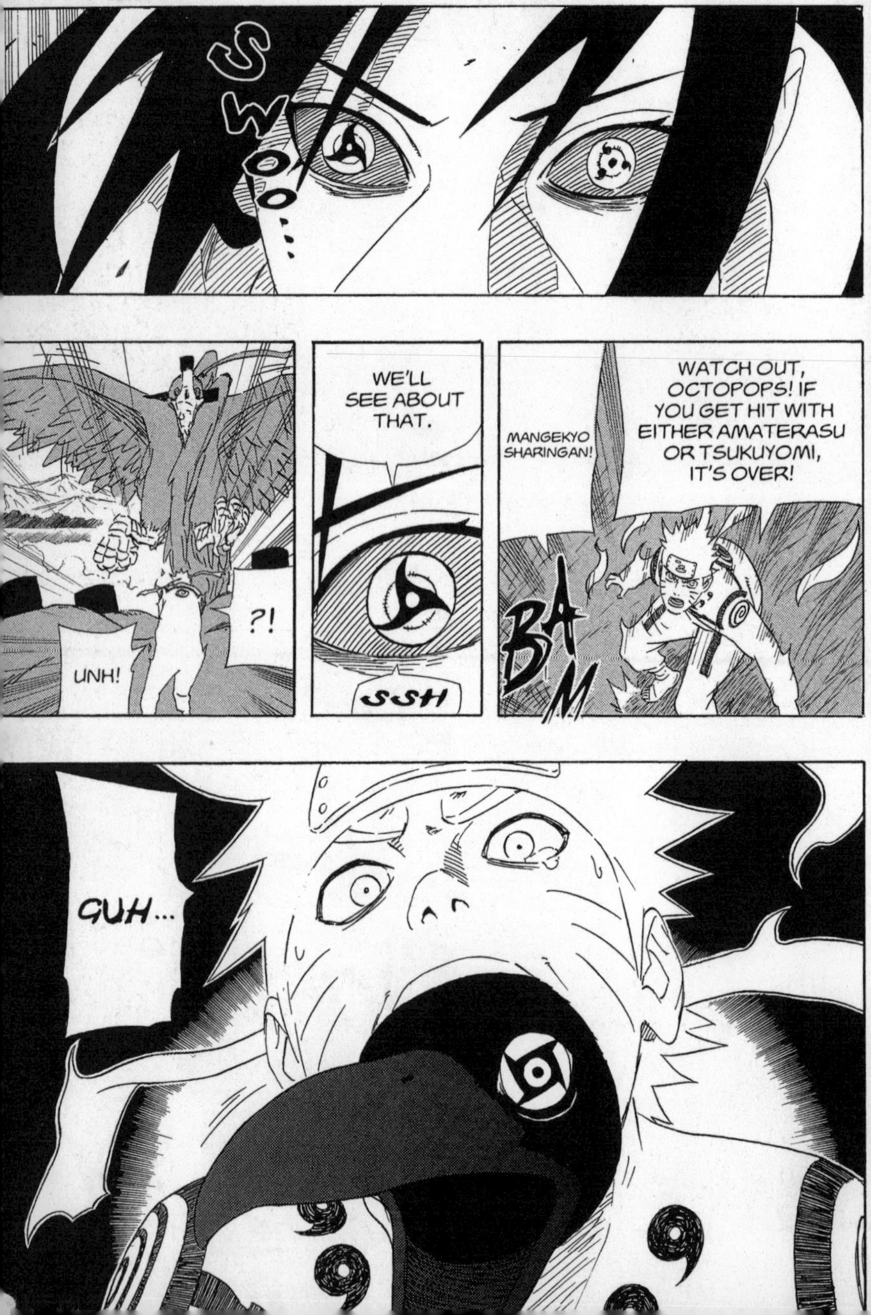
SWOOO...
WATCH OUT, OCTOPOPS! IF YOU GET HIT WITH EITHER AMATERASU OR TSUKUYOMI, IT'S OVER!
MANGEKYO SHARINGAN!
BAM
WE'LL SEE ABOUT THAT.
SSH
?!
UNH!
GUH...

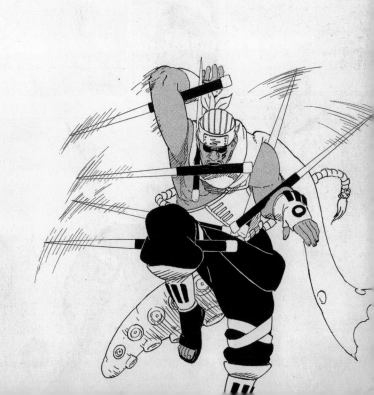

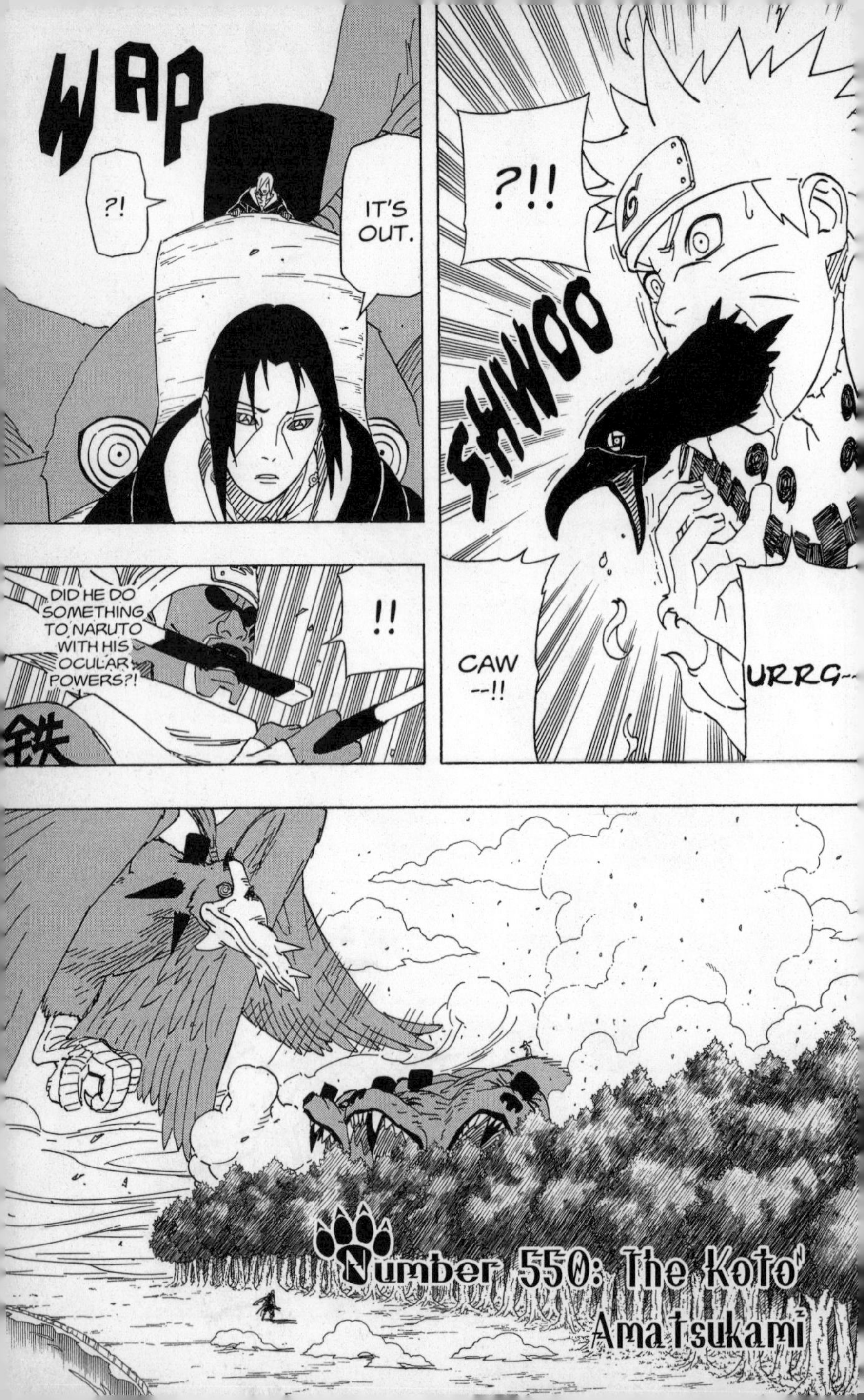
?!!
SHWOO
URRG--
CAW --!!
WAP
IT'S OUT.
?!
!!
DID HE DO SOMETHING TO NARUTO WITH HIS OCULAR POWERS?!
鉄
Number 550: The Koto Amatsukami

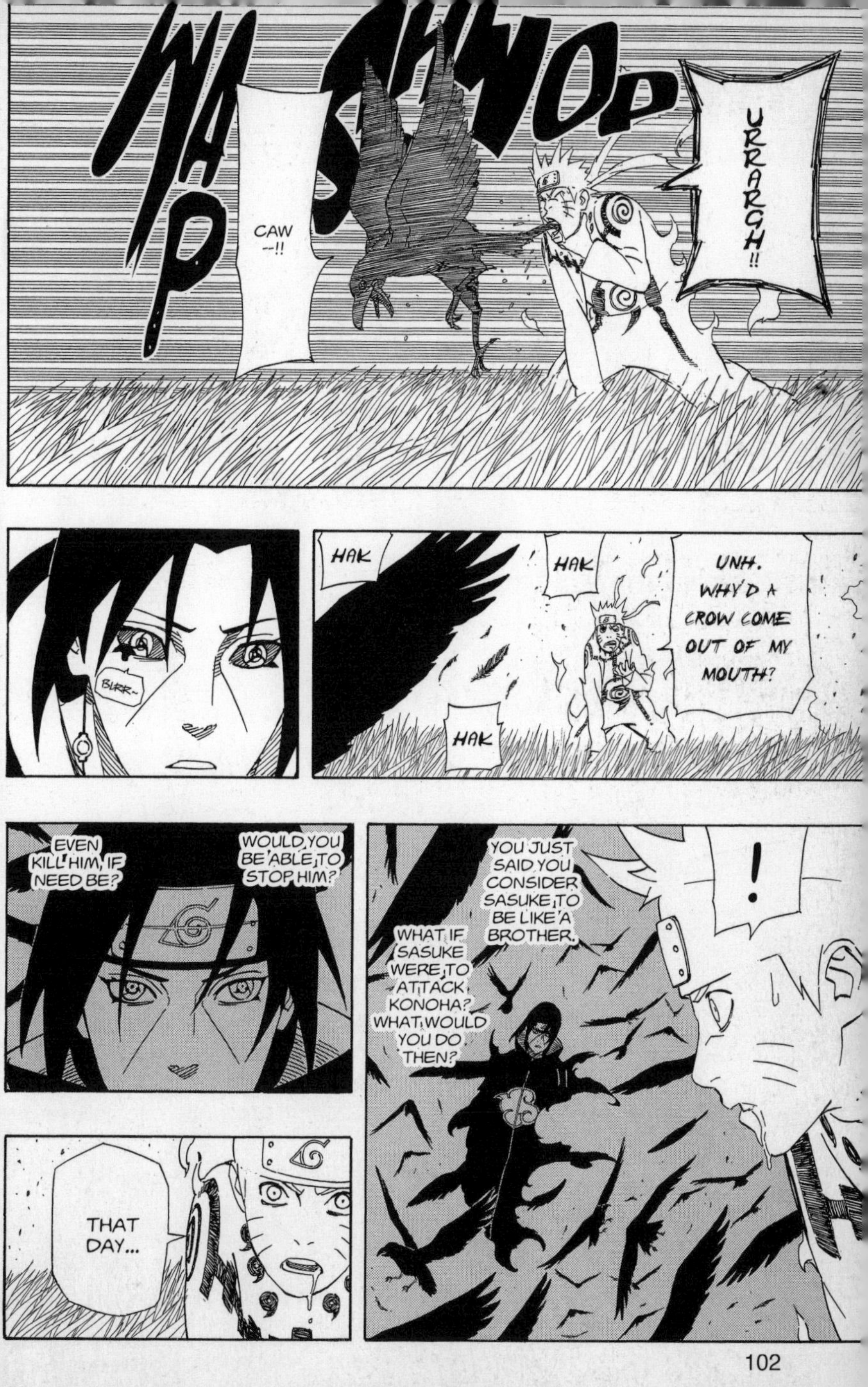
URRARGH!!
SHWOOP
CAW --!!
WHAP
UNH. WHY'D A CROW COME OUT OF MY MOUTH?
HAK
HAK
HAK
BLRR~
!
YOU JUST SAID YOU CONSIDER SASUKE TO BE LIKE A BROTHER.
WHAT IF SASUKE WERE TO ATTACK KONOHA? WHAT WOULD YOU DO THEN?
WOULD YOU BE ABLE TO STOP HIM?
EVEN KILL HIM, IF NEED BE?
THAT DAY...

READ THIS WAY

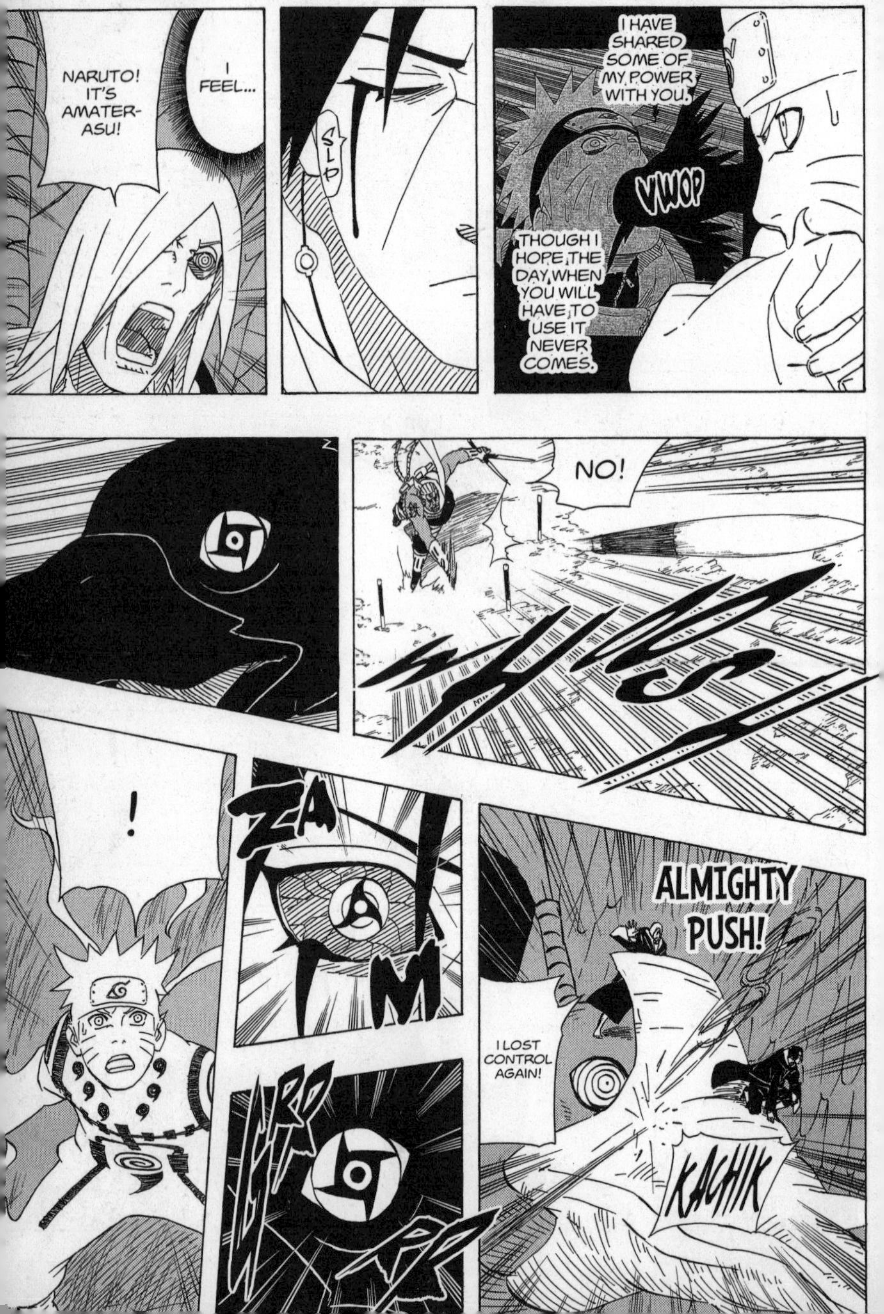
I HAVE SHARED SOME OF MY POWER WITH YOU.
VWOP
THOUGH I HOPE THE DAY WHEN YOU WILL HAVE TO USE IT NEVER COMES.
SLP
I FEEL...
NARUTO! IT'S AMATER-ASU!
NO!
WHUSH
ALMIGHTY PUSH!
I LOST CONTROL AGAIN!
KACHIK
ZAM
!

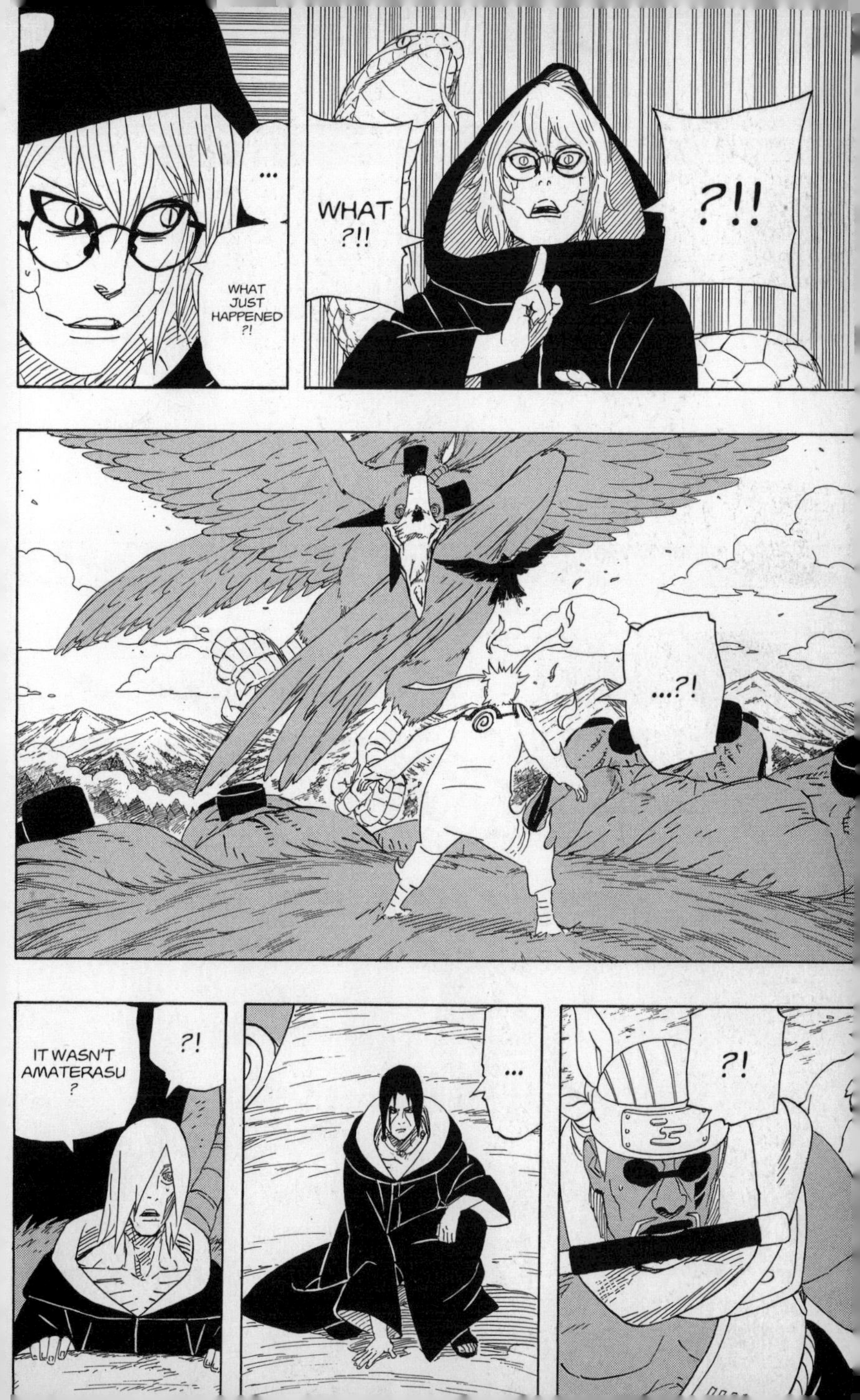
?!!
WHAT ?!!
...
WHAT JUST HAPPENED ?!
...?!
?!
...
?!
IT WASN'T AMATERASU ?

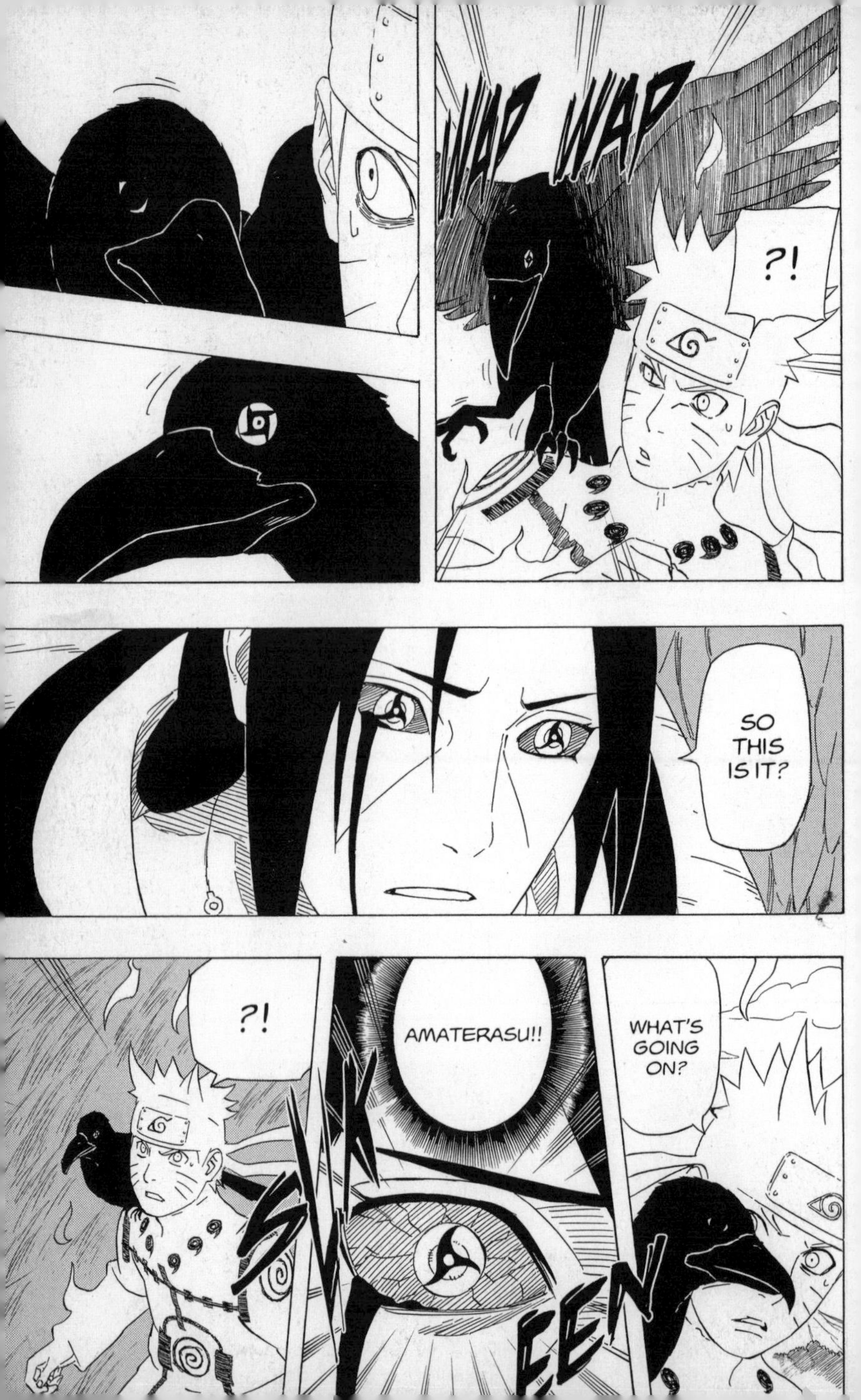
WAP WAP
?!
SO THIS IS IT?
WHAT'S GOING ON?
AMATERASU!!
?!

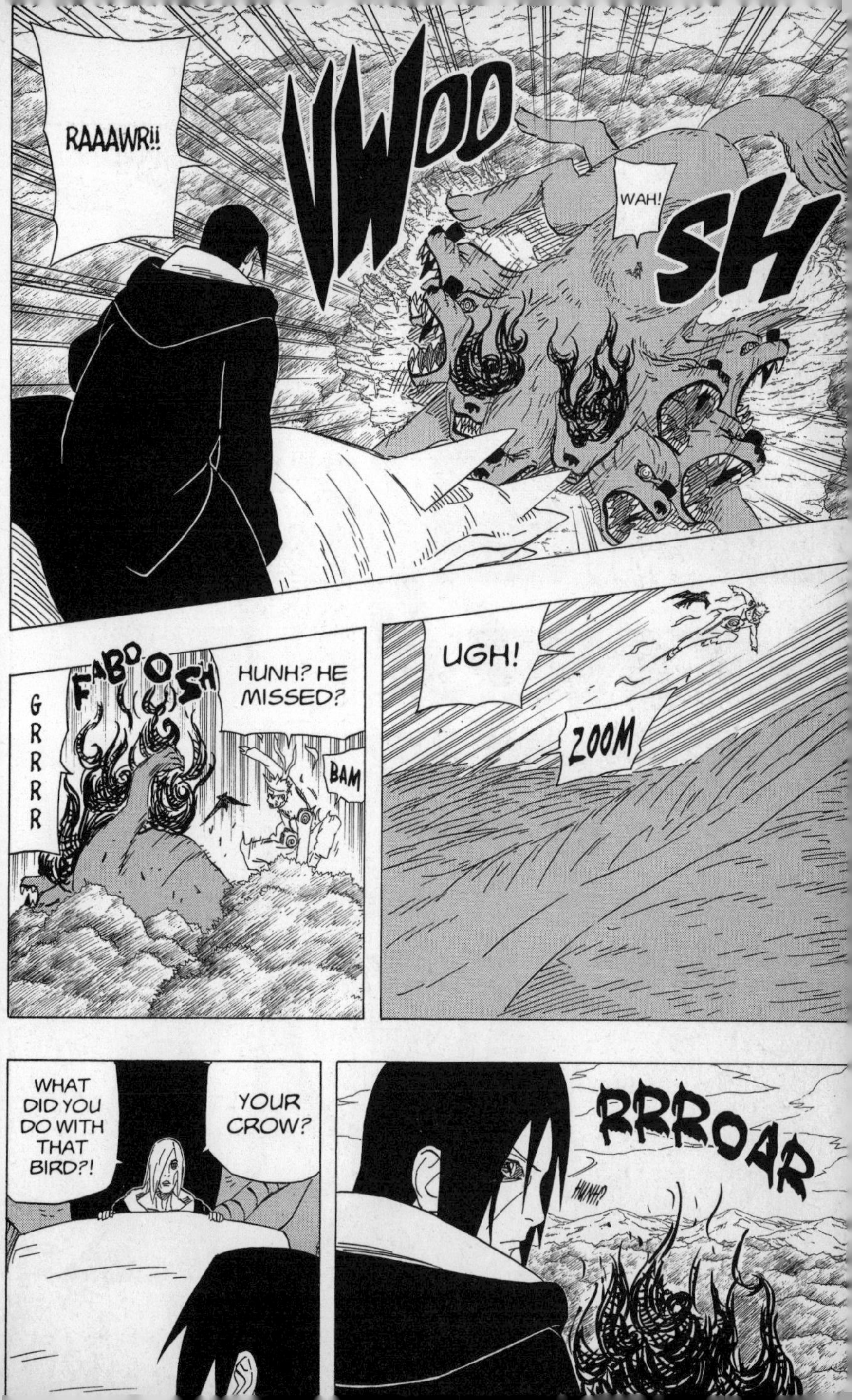
VWOOSH
WAH!
RAAAWR!!
UGH!
ZOOM
HUNH? HE MISSED?
BAM
FABOOSH
GRRRR
RRROAR
HUNH?
YOUR CROW?
WHAT DID YOU DO WITH THAT BIRD?!

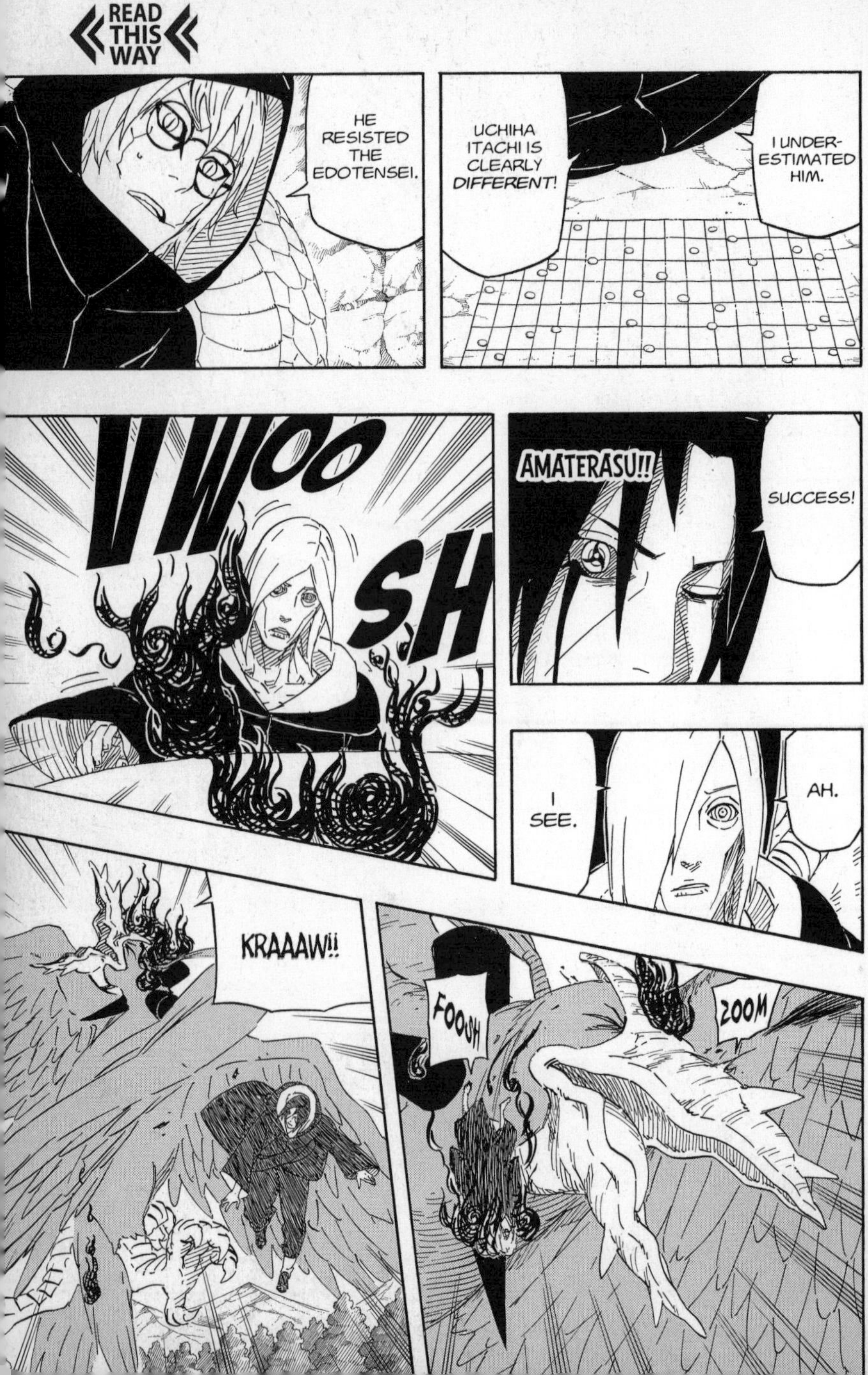
READ THIS WAY
I UNDER-ESTIMATED HIM.
UCHIHA ITACHI IS CLEARLY DIFFERENT!
HE RESISTED THE EDOTENSEI.
SUCCESS!
AMATERASU!!
AH.
I SEE.
VWOOSH
ZOOM
FOOSH
KRAAAW!!

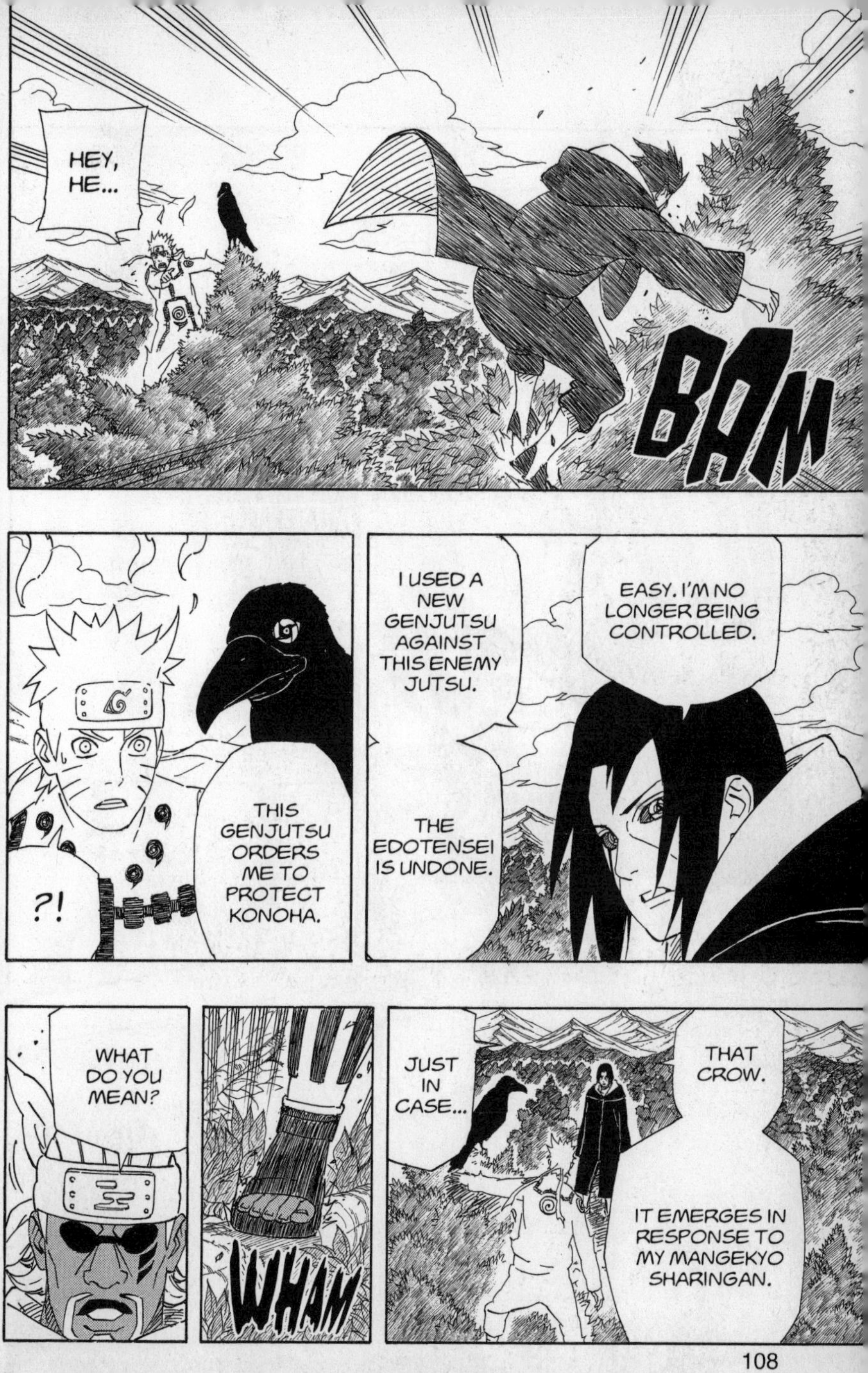
HEY, HE...
BAM
EASY. I'M NO LONGER BEING CONTROLLED.
I USED A NEW GENJUTSU AGAINST THIS ENEMY JUTSU.
THE EDOTENSEI IS UNDONE.
THIS GENJUTSU ORDERS ME TO PROTECT KONOHA.
?!
THAT CROW.
JUST IN CASE...
IT EMERGES IN RESPONSE TO MY MANGEKYO SHARINGAN.
WHAM
WHAT DO YOU MEAN?

READ THIS WAY

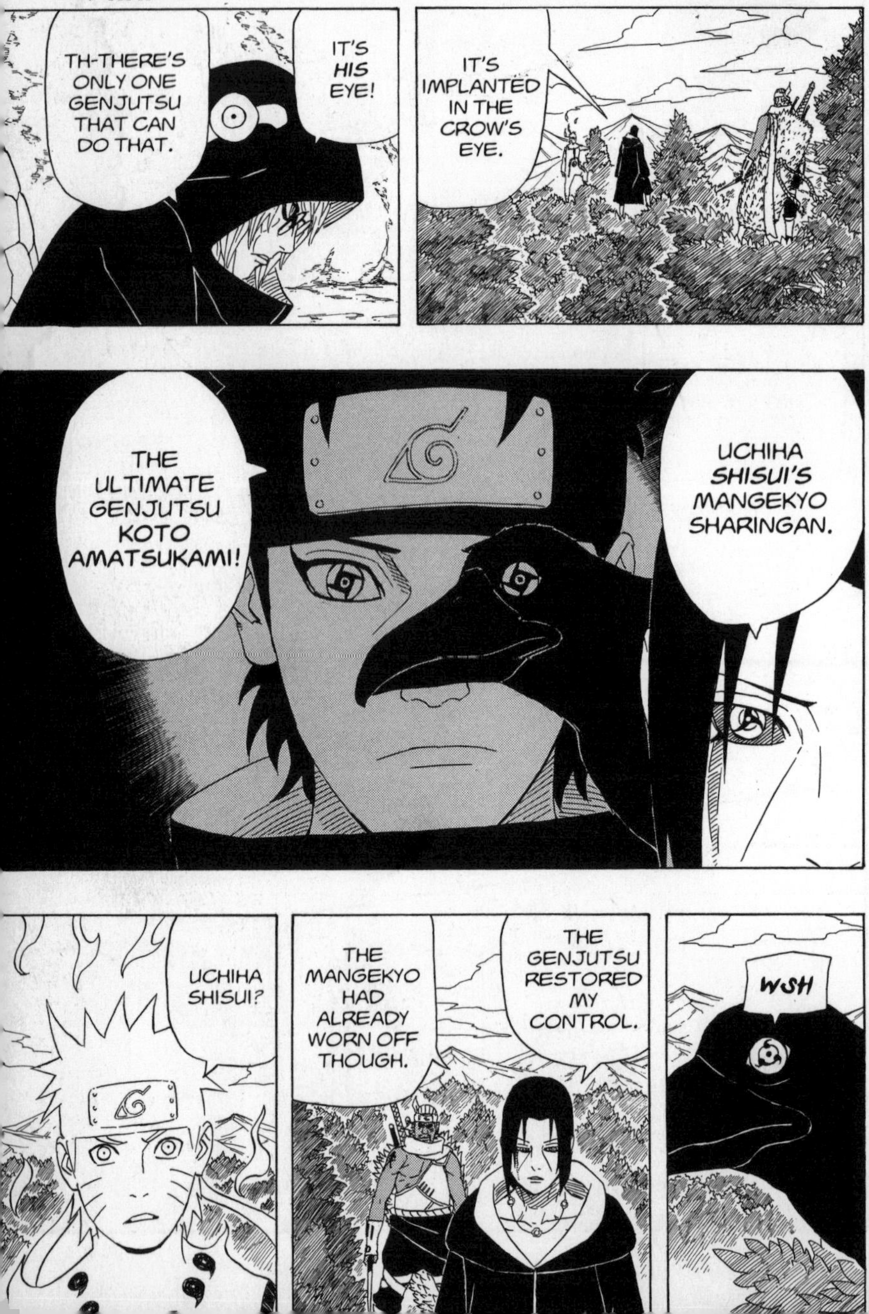
IT'S IMPLANTED IN THE CROW'S EYE.
IT'S HIS EYE!
TH-THERE'S ONLY ONE GENJUTSU THAT CAN DO THAT.
UCHIHA SHISUI'S MANGEKYO SHARINGAN.
THE ULTIMATE GENJUTSU KOTO AMATSUKAMI!
WSH
THE GENJUTSU RESTORED MY CONTROL.
THE MANGEKYO HAD ALREADY WORN OFF THOUGH.
UCHIHA SHISUI?

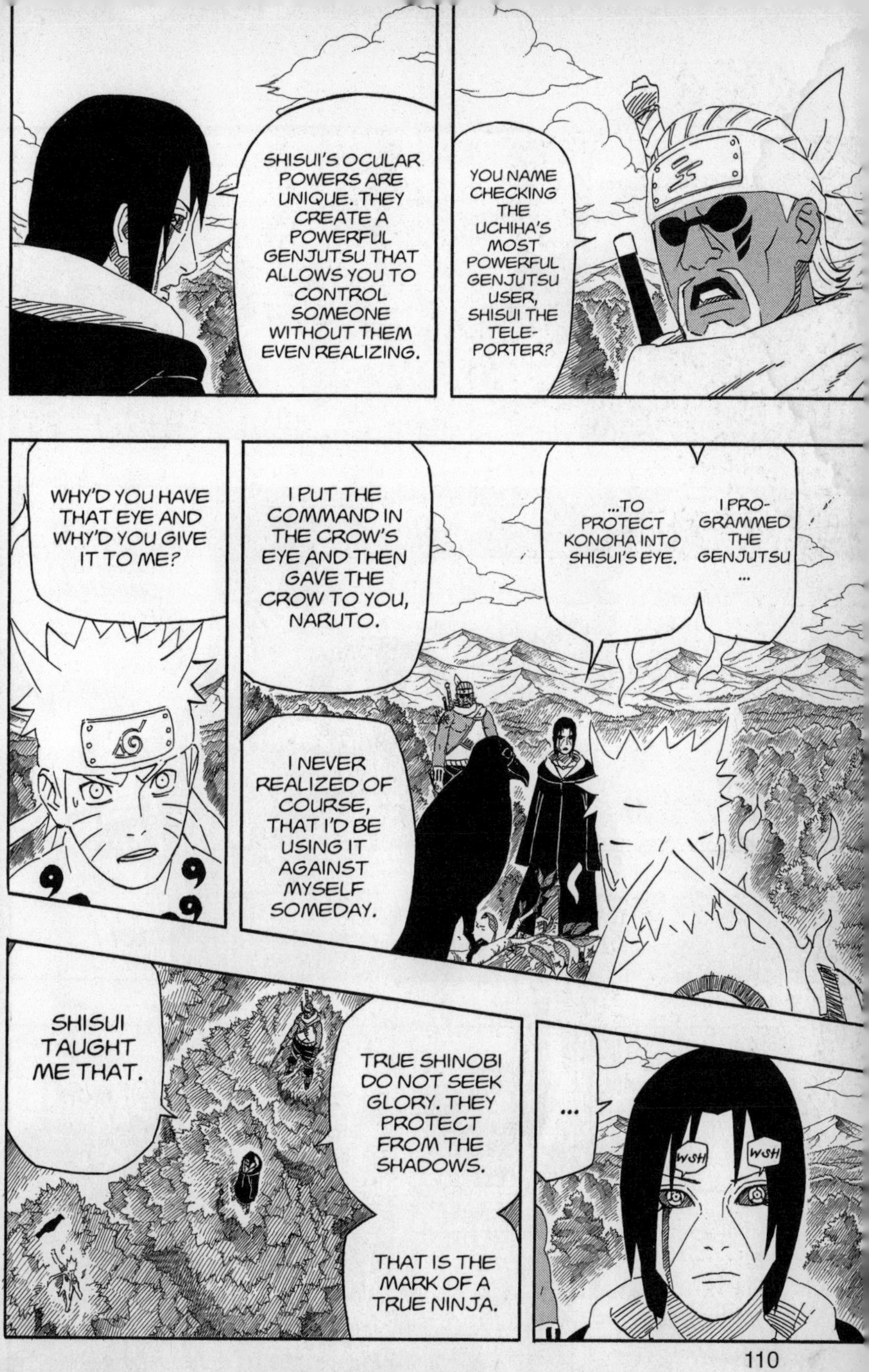
YOU NAME CHECKING THE UCHIHA'S MOST POWERFUL GENJUTSU USER, SHISUI THE TELE-PORTER?
SHISUI'S OCULAR POWERS ARE UNIQUE. THEY CREATE A POWERFUL GENJUTSU THAT ALLOWS YOU TO CONTROL SOMEONE WITHOUT THEM EVEN REALIZING.
I PRO-GRAMMED THE GENJUTSU ...
...TO PROTECT KONOHA INTO SHISUI'S EYE.
I PUT THE COMMAND IN THE CROW'S EYE AND THEN GAVE THE CROW TO YOU, NARUTO.
I NEVER REALIZED OF COURSE, THAT I'D BE USING IT AGAINST MYSELF SOMEDAY.
WHY'D YOU HAVE THAT EYE AND WHY'D YOU GIVE IT TO ME?
...
WSH
WSH
TRUE SHINOBI DO NOT SEEK GLORY. THEY PROTECT FROM THE SHADOWS.
THAT IS THE MARK OF A TRUE NINJA.
SHISUI TAUGHT ME THAT.

READ THIS WAY

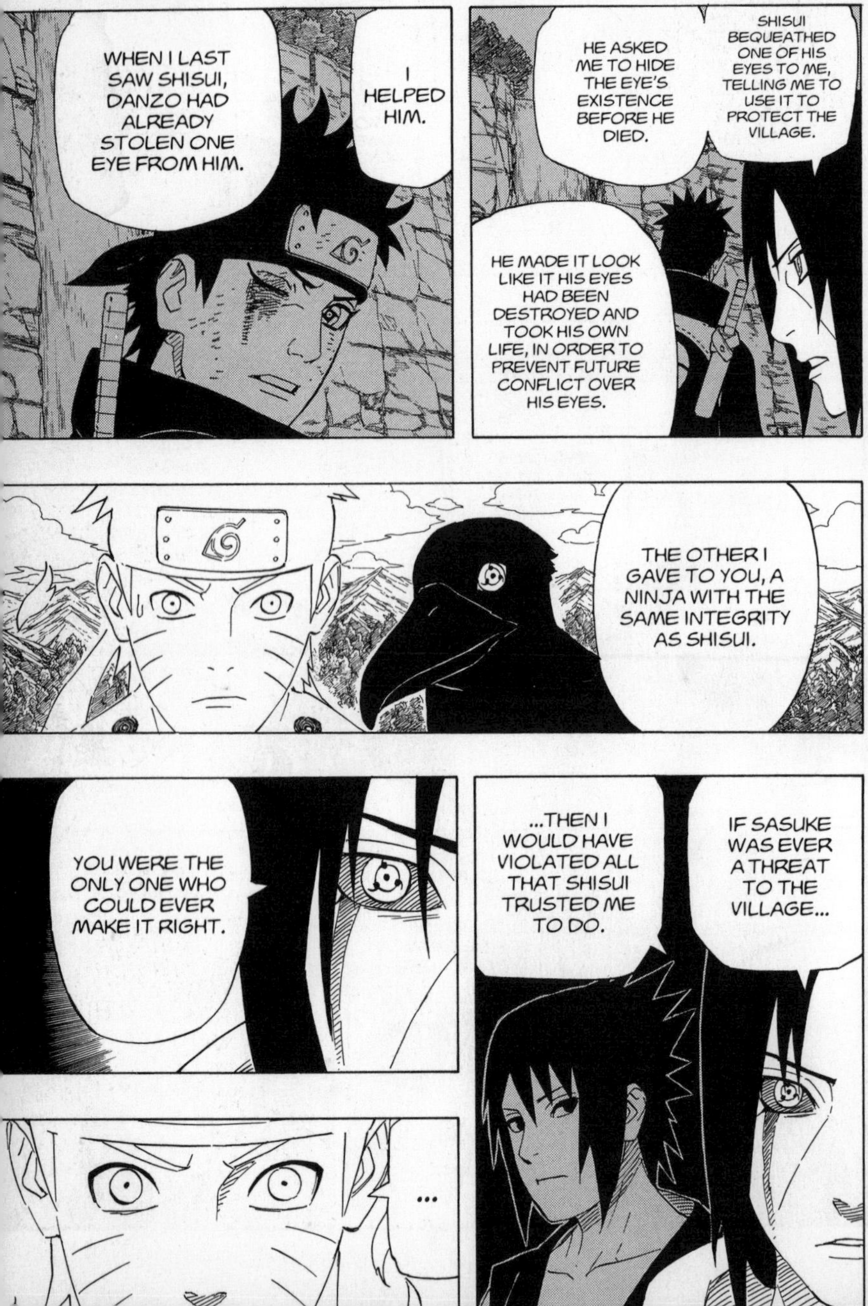
SHISUI BEQUEATHED ONE OF HIS EYES TO ME, TELLING ME TO USE IT TO PROTECT THE VILLAGE.
HE ASKED ME TO HIDE THE EYE'S EXISTENCE BEFORE HE DIED.
HE MADE IT LOOK LIKE IT HIS EYES HAD BEEN DESTROYED AND TOOK HIS OWN LIFE, IN ORDER TO PREVENT FUTURE CONFLICT OVER HIS EYES.
I HELPED HIM.
WHEN I LAST SAW SHISUI, DANZO HAD ALREADY STOLEN ONE EYE FROM HIM.
THE OTHER I GAVE TO YOU, A NINJA WITH THE SAME INTEGRITY AS SHISUI.
IF SASUKE WAS EVER A THREAT TO THE VILLAGE...
...THEN I WOULD HAVE VIOLATED ALL THAT SHISUI TRUSTED ME TO DO.
YOU WERE THE ONLY ONE WHO COULD EVER MAKE IT RIGHT.
...

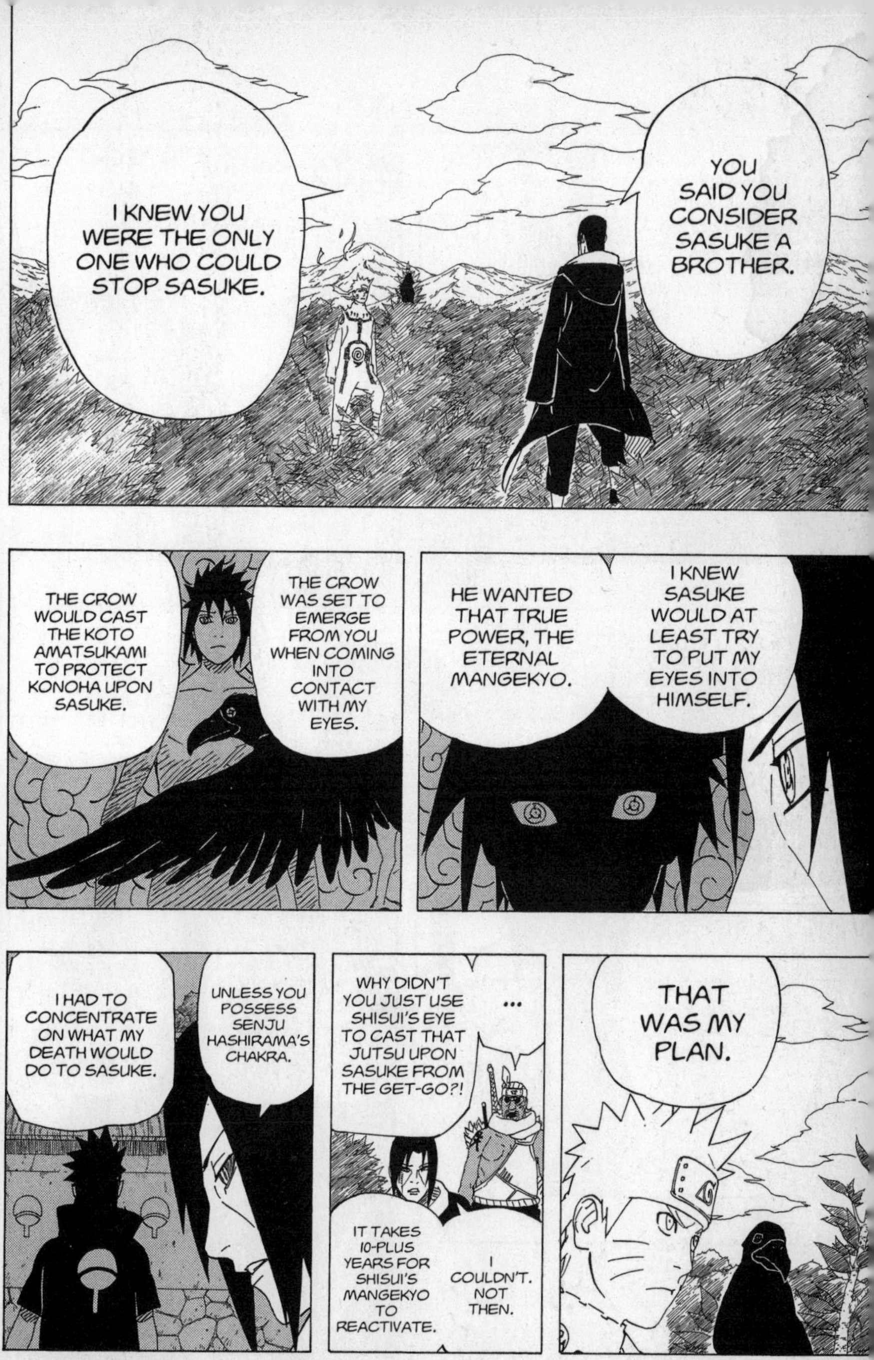
YOU SAID YOU CONSIDER SASUKE A BROTHER.
I KNEW YOU WERE THE ONLY ONE WHO COULD STOP SASUKE.
I KNEW SASUKE WOULD AT LEAST TRY TO PUT MY EYES INTO HIMSELF.
HE WANTED THAT TRUE POWER, THE ETERNAL MANGEKYO.
THE CROW WAS SET TO EMERGE FROM YOU WHEN COMING INTO CONTACT WITH MY EYES.
THE CROW WOULD CAST THE KOTO AMATSUKAMI TO PROTECT KONOHA UPON SASUKE.
THAT WAS MY PLAN.
...
WHY DIDN'T YOU JUST USE SHISUI'S EYE TO CAST THAT JUTSU UPON SASUKE FROM THE GET-GO?!
I COULDN'T. NOT THEN.
IT TAKES 10-PLUS YEARS FOR SHISUI'S MANGEKYO TO REACTIVATE.
UNLESS YOU POSSESS SENJU HASHIRAMA'S CHAKRA.
I HAD TO CONCENTRATE ON WHAT MY DEATH WOULD DO TO SASUKE.

READ THIS WAY

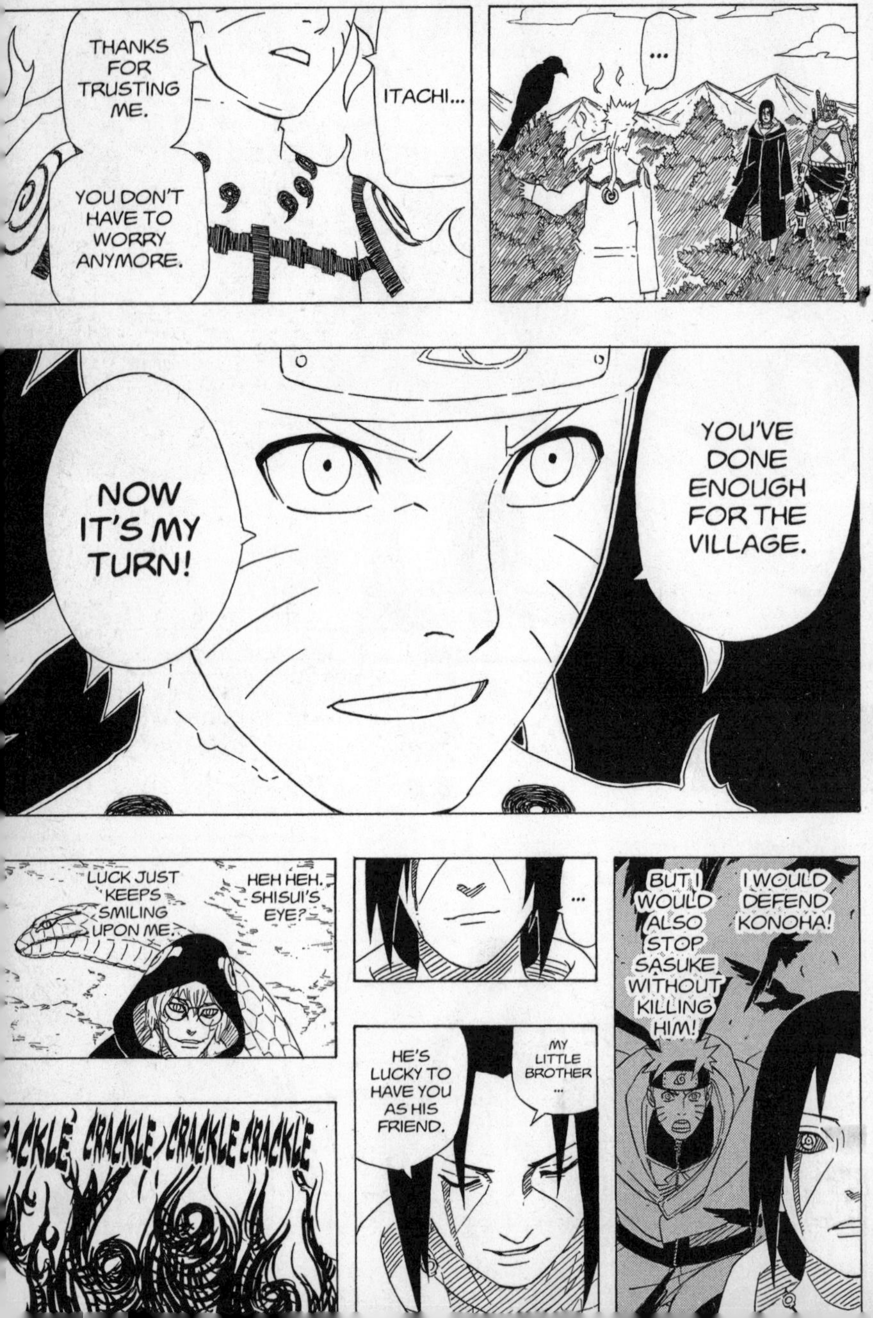
...
ITACHI...
THANKS FOR TRUSTING ME.
YOU DON'T HAVE TO WORRY ANYMORE.
YOU'VE DONE ENOUGH FOR THE VILLAGE.
NOW IT'S MY TURN!
I WOULD DEFEND KONOHA!
BUT I WOULD ALSO STOP SASUKE WITHOUT KILLING HIM!
...
MY LITTLE BROTHER...
HE'S LUCKY TO HAVE YOU AS HIS FRIEND.
HEH HEH. SHISUI'S EYE?
LUCK JUST KEEPS SMILING UPON ME.
CRACKLE CRACKLE CRACKLE CRACKLE

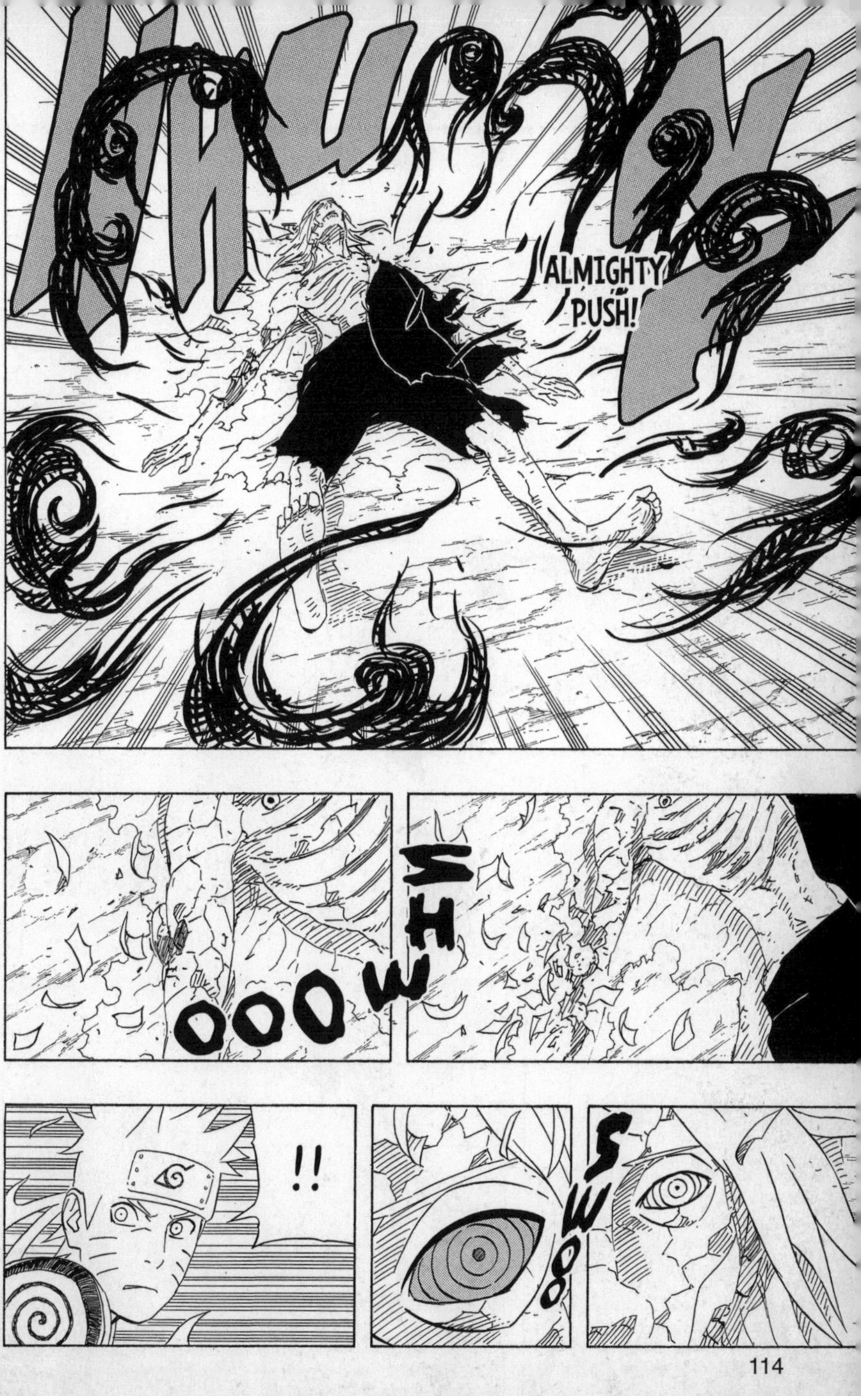
ALMIGHTY PUSH!
SHWOOO
SWOO
!!

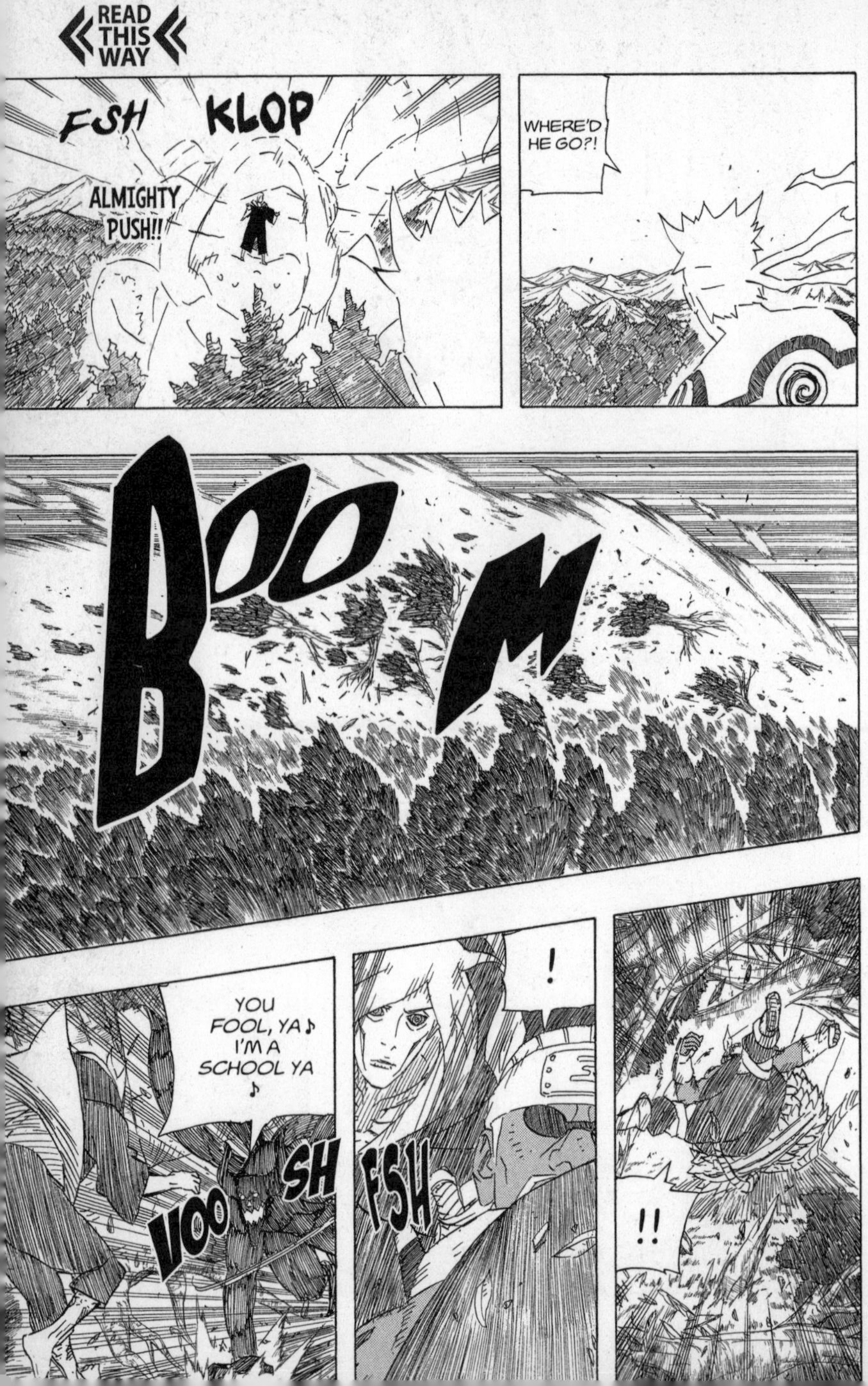
READ THIS WAY
WHERE'D HE GO?!
KLOP
FSH
ALMIGHTY PUSH!!
BOOM
!!
!
FSH
YOU FOOL, YA♪ I'M A SCHOOL YA♪
VOOSH

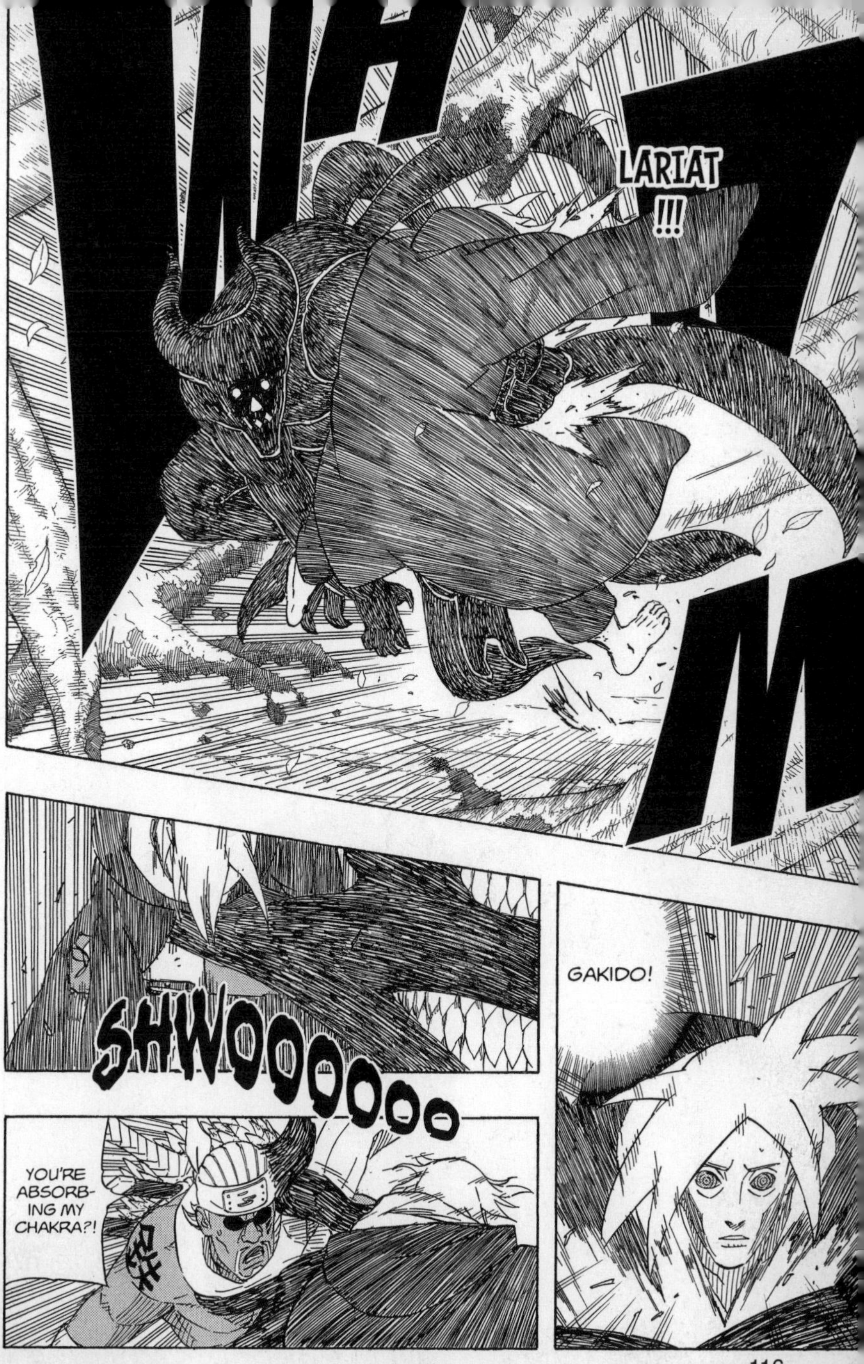
LARIAT !!!
GAKIDO!
SHWOOOOOOOO
YOU'RE ABSORBING MY CHAKRA?!

READ THIS WAY

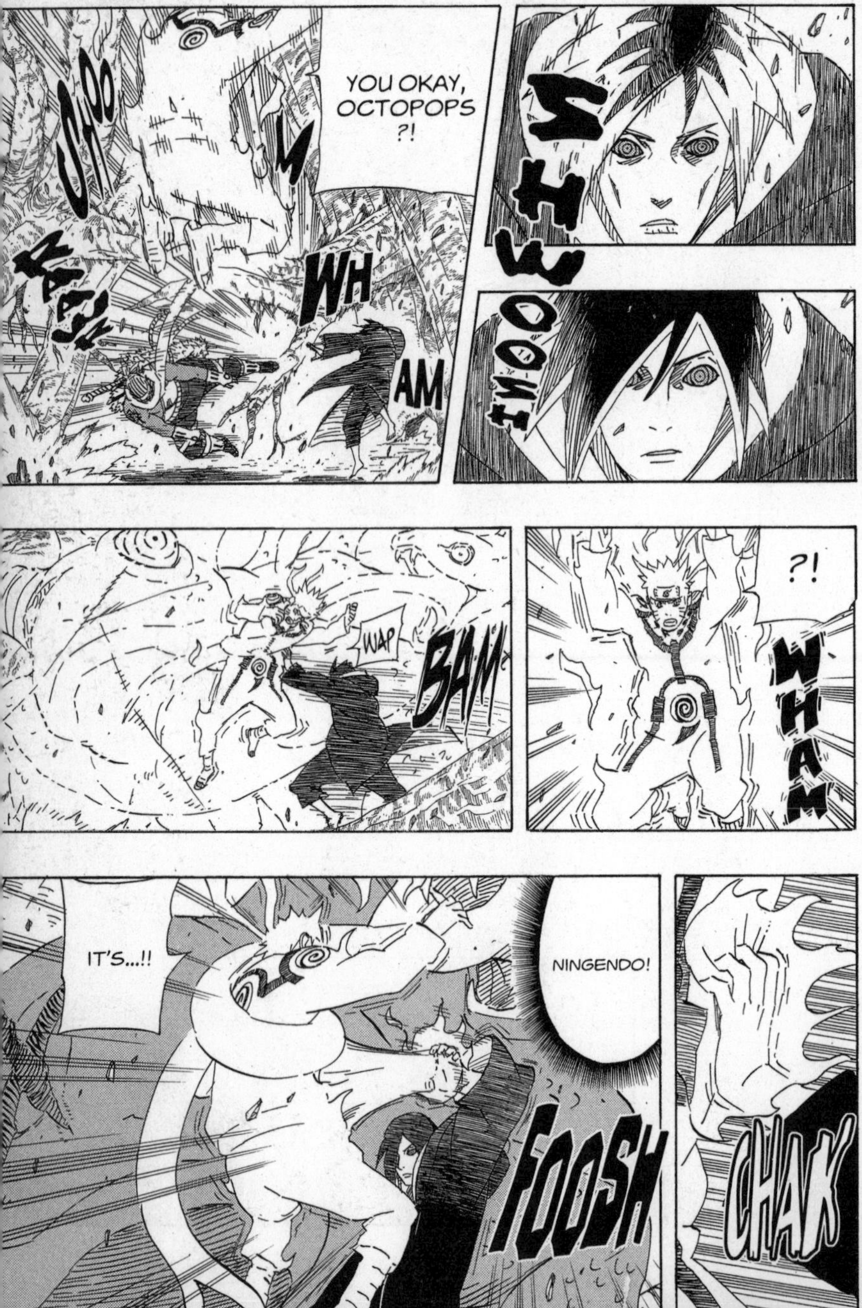
SHWOOSH
YOU OKAY, OCTOPOPS ?!
WHAM
?!
WHAM
WAP
BAM
CHAK
NINGENDO!
IT'S...!!
FOOSH

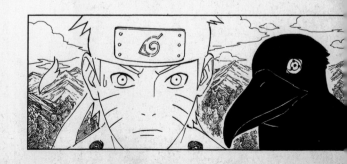

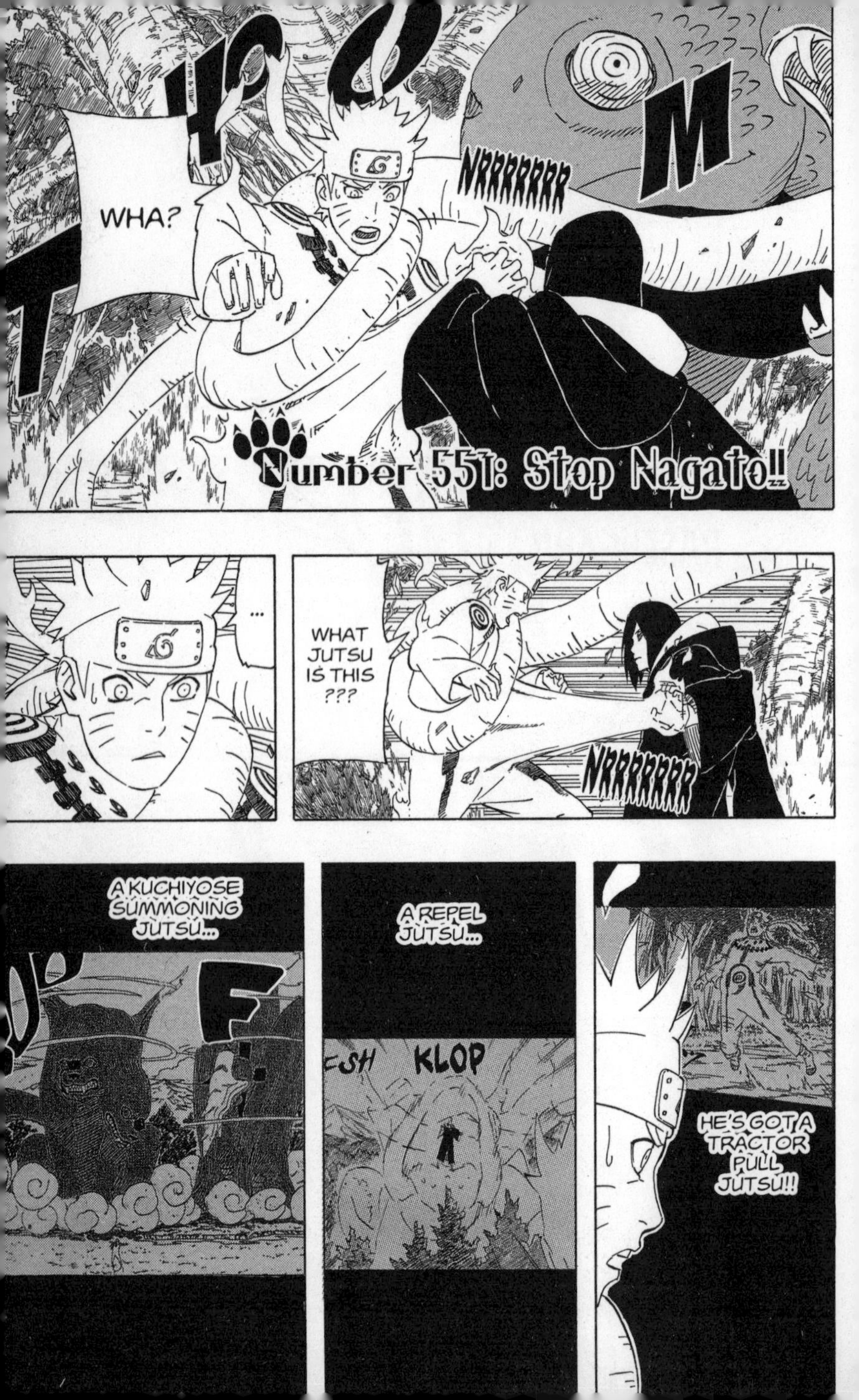

NRRRRRRR
WHA?
Number 551: Stop Nagato!!
WHAT JUTSU IS THIS ???
NRRRRRRR
...
HE'S GOT A TRACTOR PULL JUTSU!!
A REPEL JUTSU...
KLOP
A KUCHIYOSE SUMMONING JUTSU...

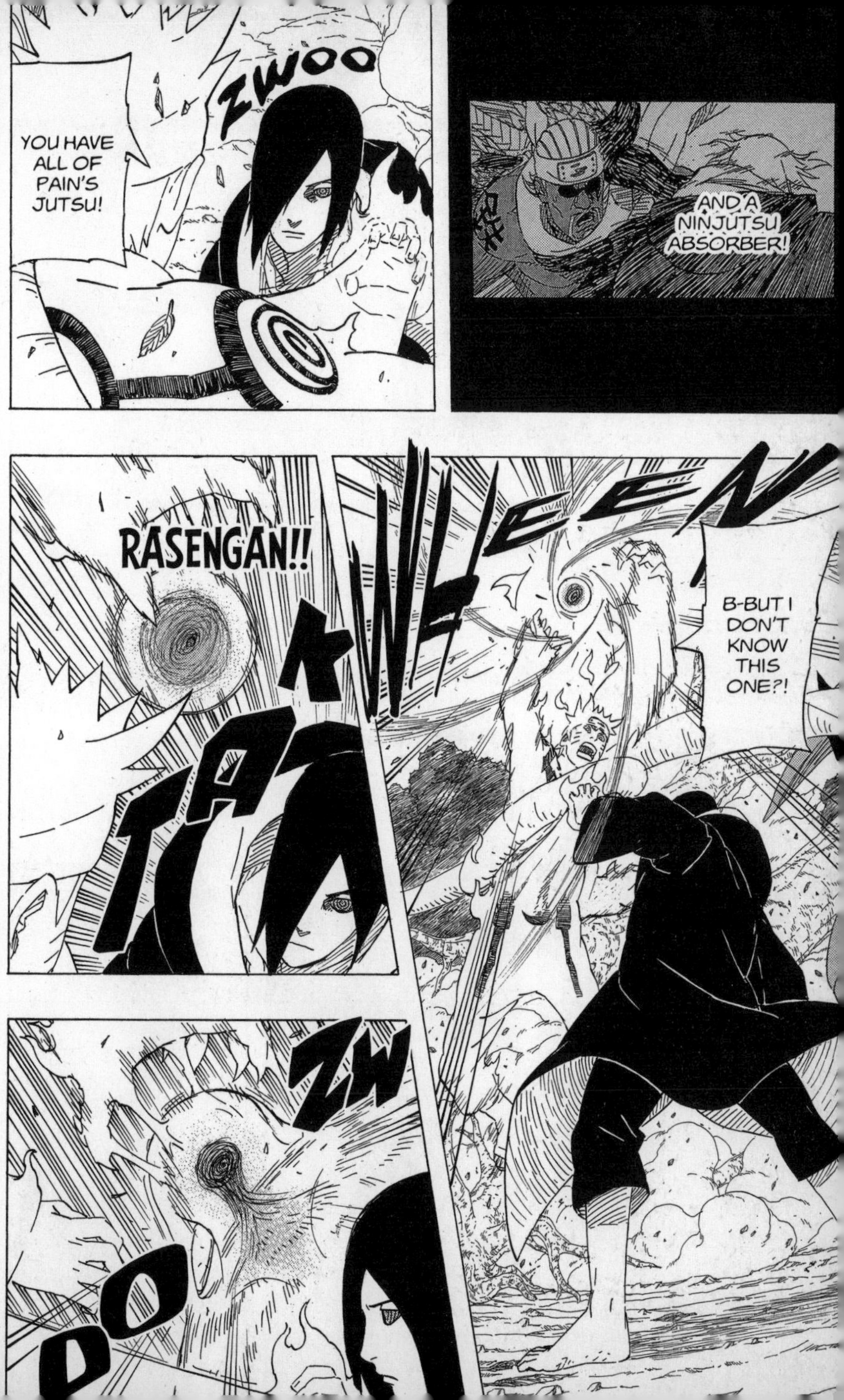
AND A NINJUTSU ABSORBER!
ZWOO
YOU HAVE ALL OF PAIN'S JUTSU!
WHEEEN
B-BUT I DON'T KNOW THIS ONE?!
RASENGAN!!
TA
ZW
DO

READ THIS WAY

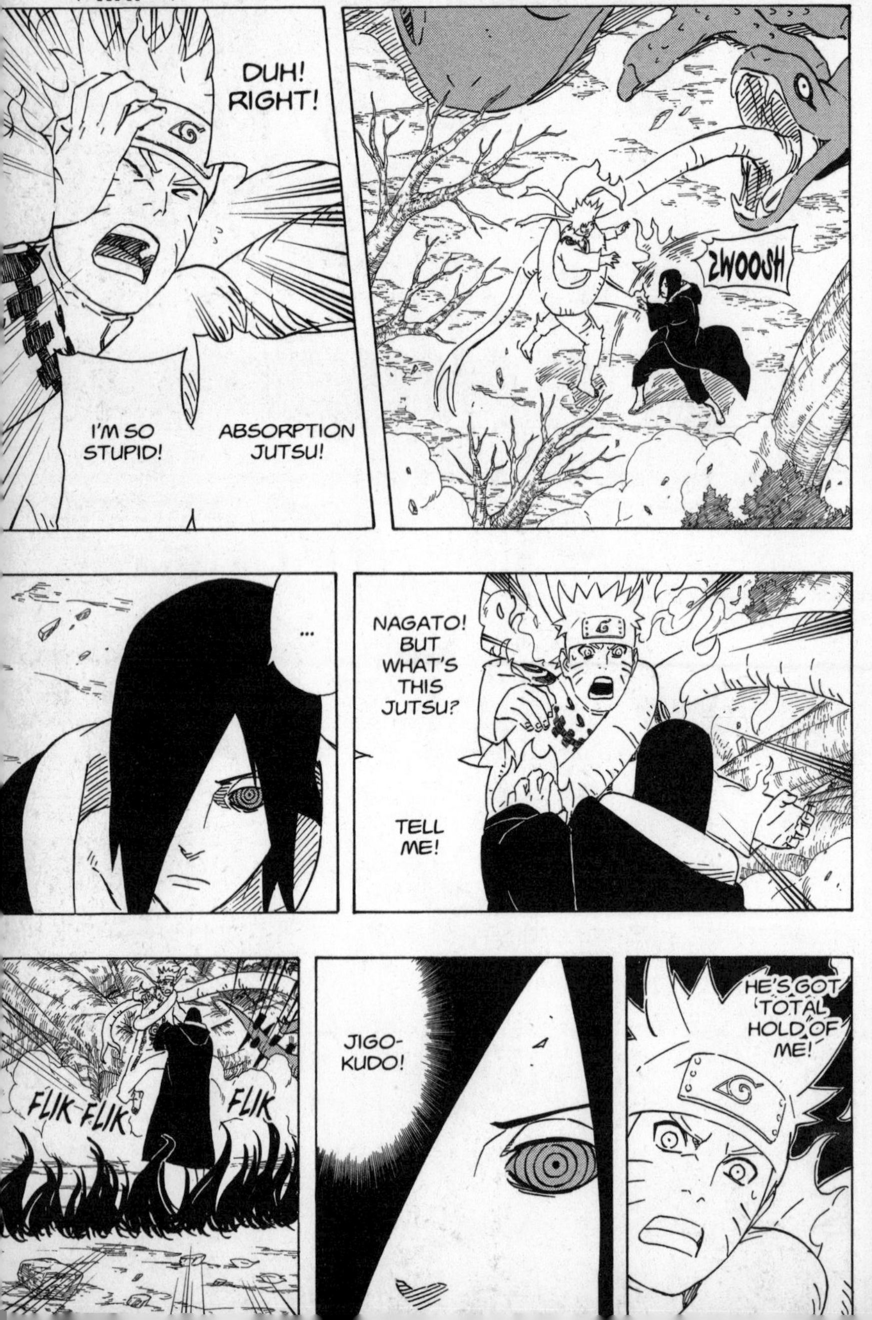
ZWOOSH
DUH! RIGHT!
ABSORPTION JUTSU!
I'M SO STUPID!
NAGATO! BUT WHAT'S THIS JUTSU?
TELL ME!
...
HE'S GOT TOTAL HOLD OF ME!
JIGO-KUDO!
FLIK
FLIK FLIK

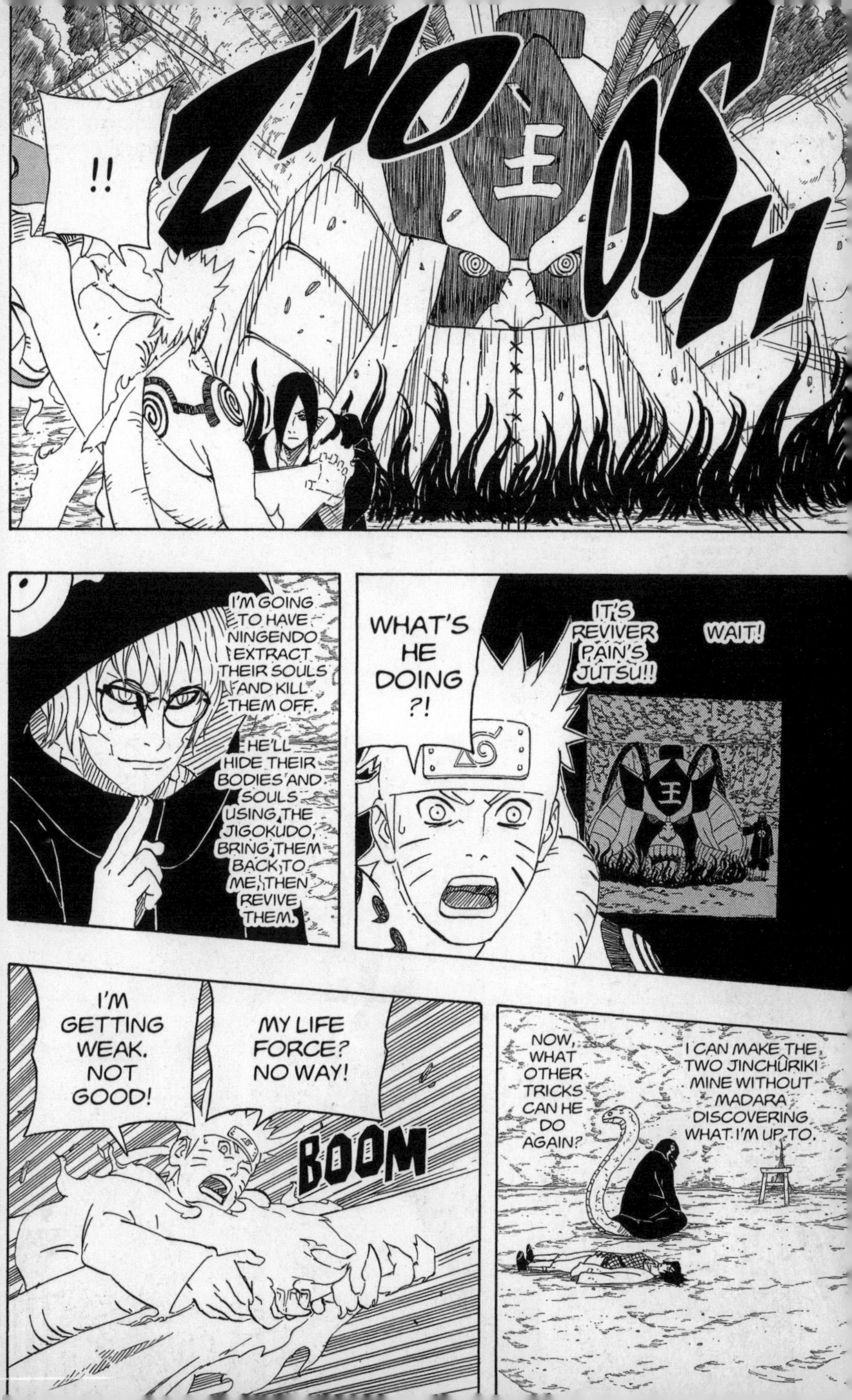
ZWOOSH
!!
WAIT!
IT'S REVIVER PAIN'S JUTSU!!
WHAT'S HE DOING ?!
I'M GOING TO HAVE NINGENDO EXTRACT THEIR SOULS AND KILL THEM OFF.
HE'LL HIDE THEIR BODIES AND SOULS USING THE JIGOKUDO, BRING THEM BACK TO ME, THEN REVIVE THEM.
I CAN MAKE THE TWO JINCHÛRIKI MINE WITHOUT MADARA DISCOVERING WHAT I'M UP TO.
NOW, WHAT OTHER TRICKS CAN HE DO AGAIN?
MY LIFE FORCE? NO WAY!
I'M GETTING WEAK. NOT GOOD!
BOOM

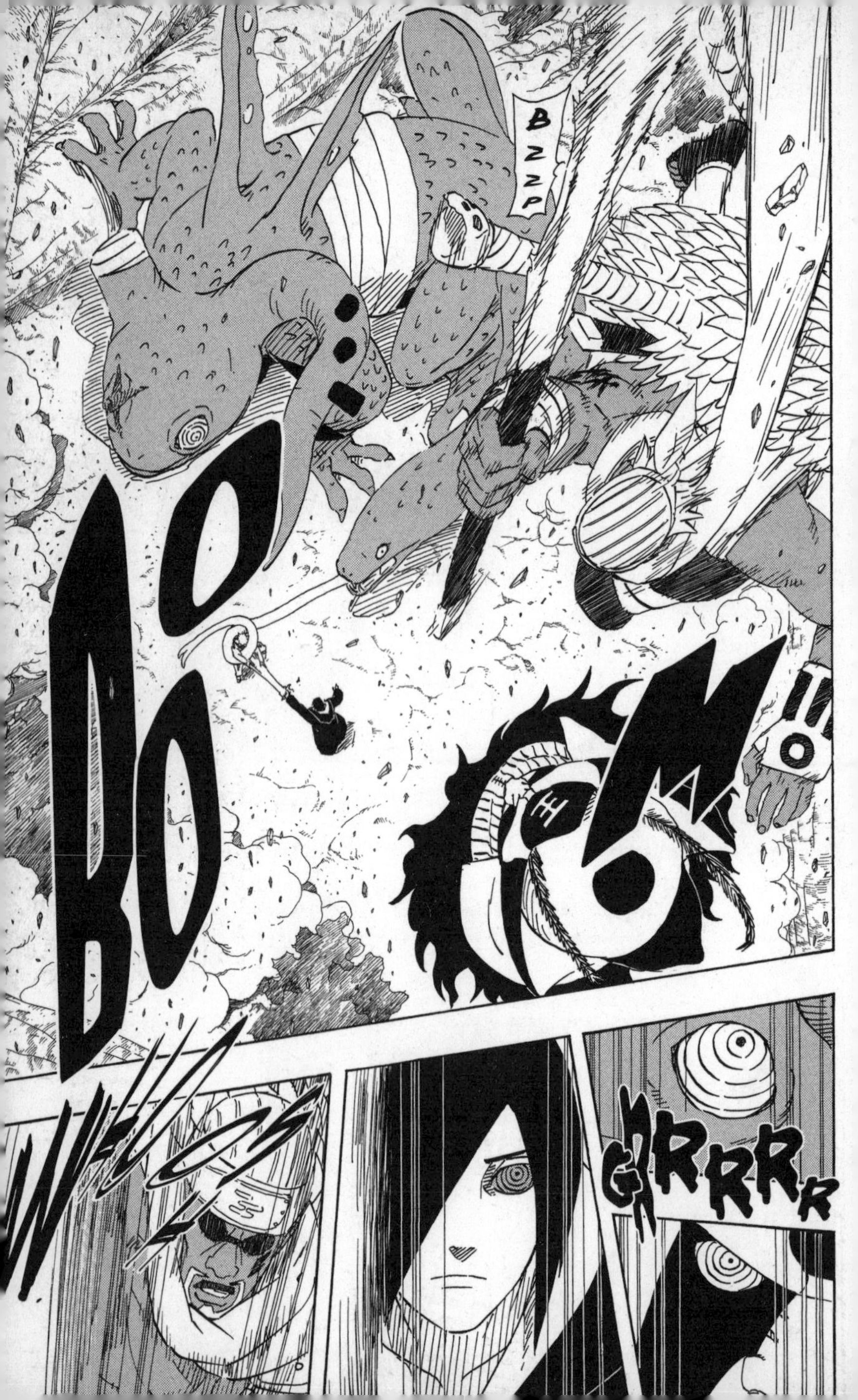
BZZP
BOOM!!
GRRRR

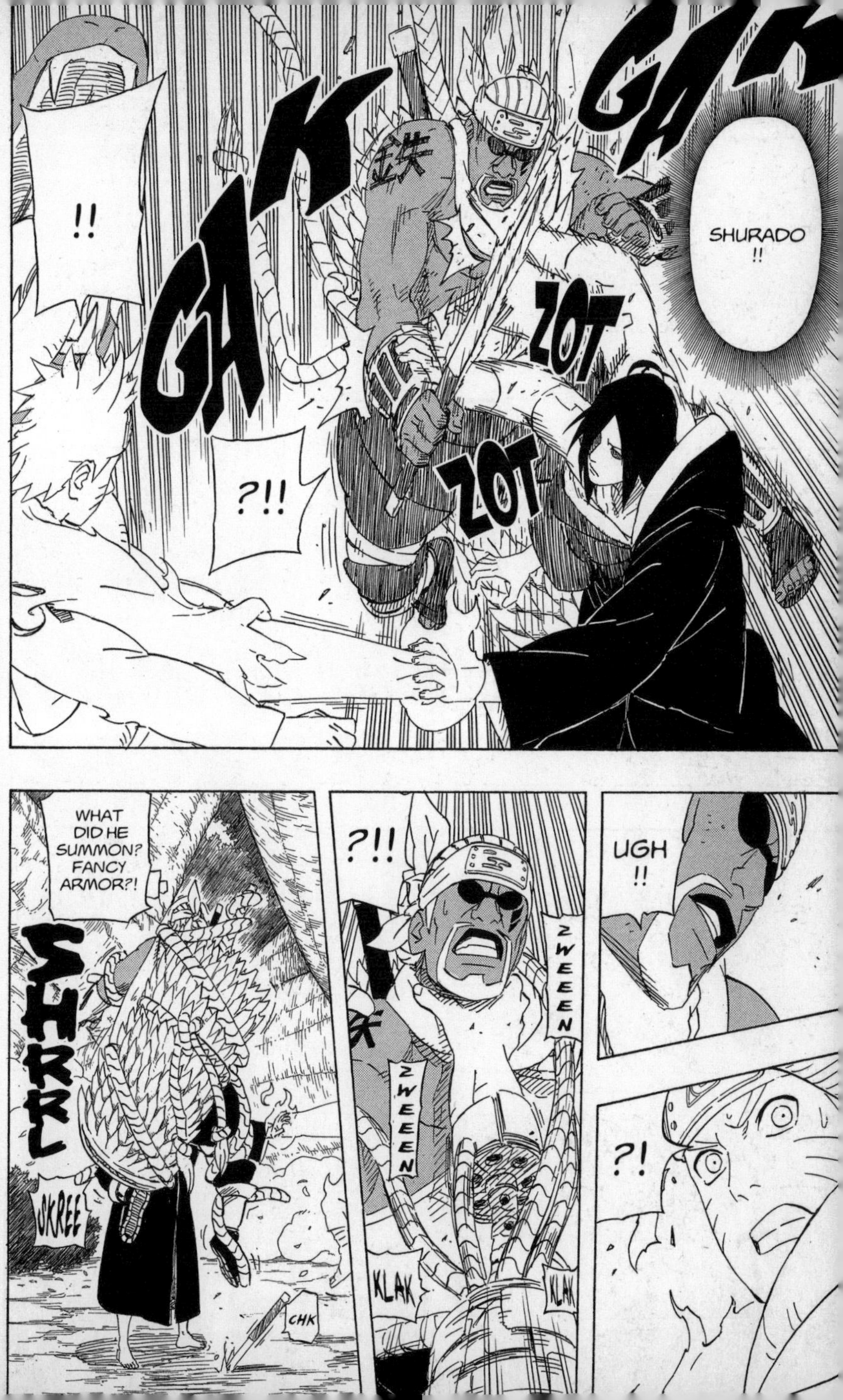
GAK
SHURADO !!
GAK
!!
ZOT
ZOT
?!!
UGH !!
?!
?!!
ZWEEEN
ZWEEEN
KLAK
KLAK
WHAT DID HE SUMMON? FANCY ARMOR?!
SHRRL
SKREE
CHK

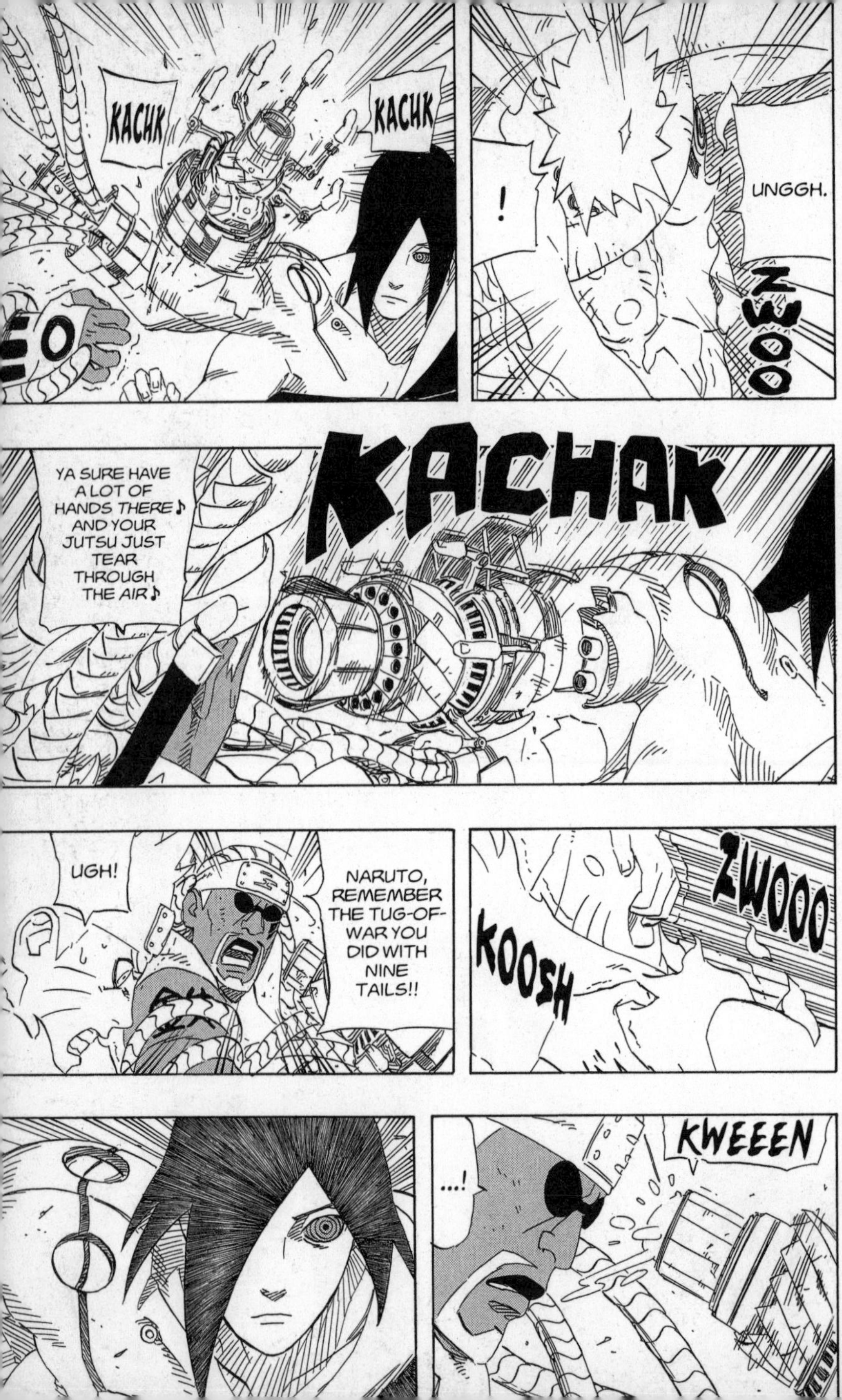
UNGGH.
!
ZWOO
KACHK
KACHK
KACHAK
YA SURE HAVE A LOT OF HANDS THERE♪ AND YOUR JUTSU JUST TEAR THROUGH THE AIR♪
ZWOOO
KOOSH
NARUTO, REMEMBER THE TUG-OF-WAR YOU DID WITH NINE TAILS!!
UGH!
KWEEEN
...!

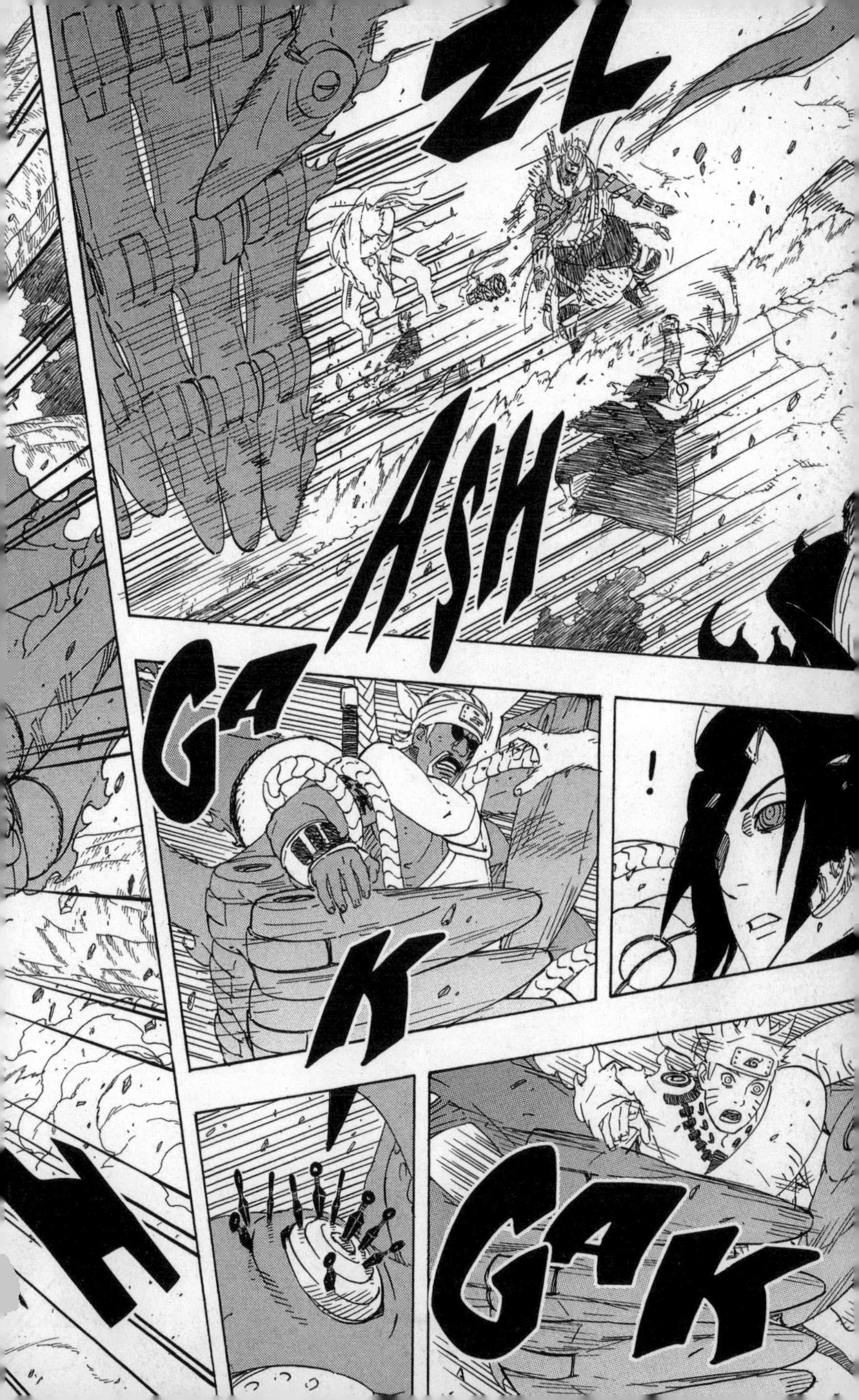

ZZ
ASH
!
GA
K
GAK
H

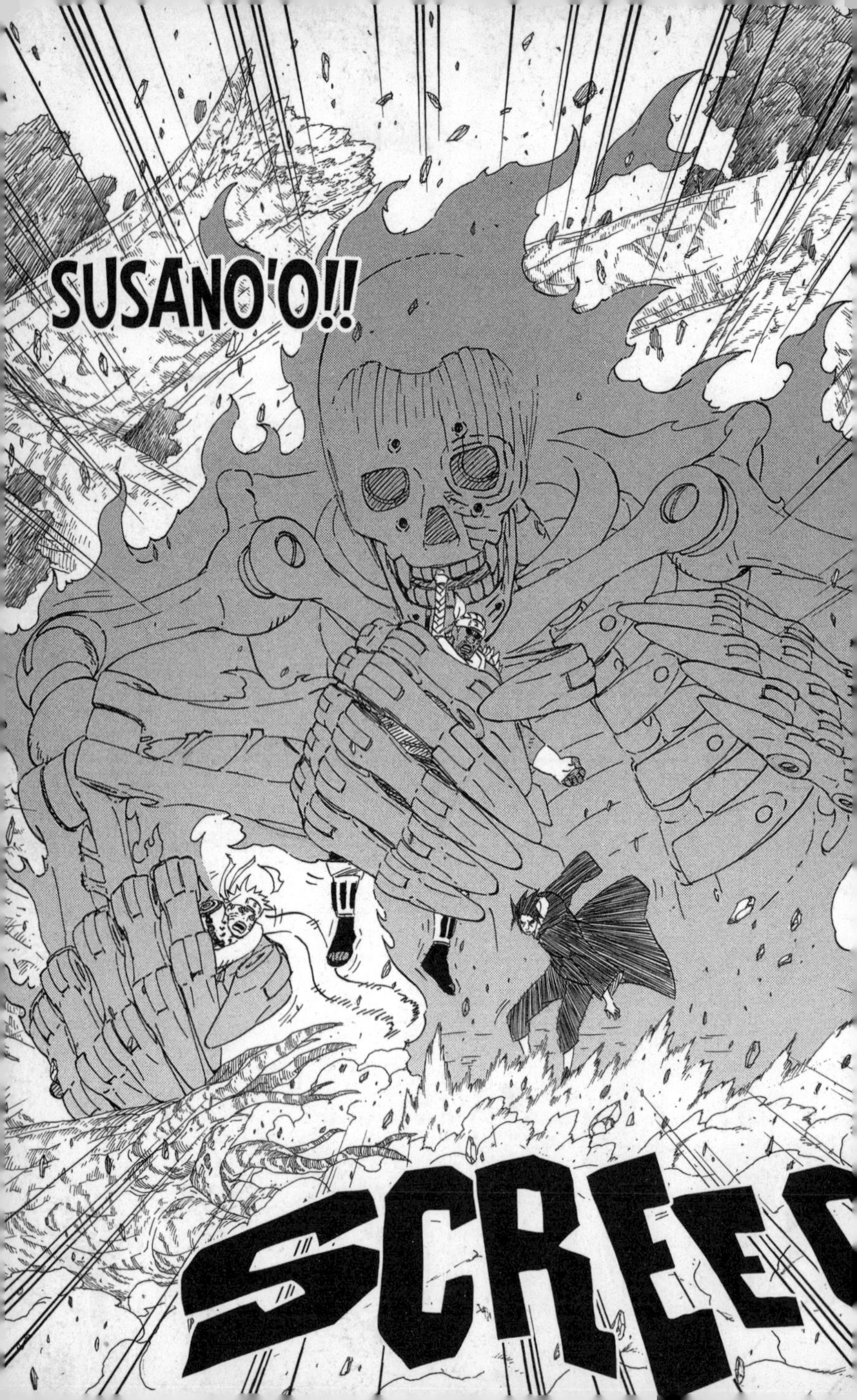
SUSANO'O!!
SCREEC

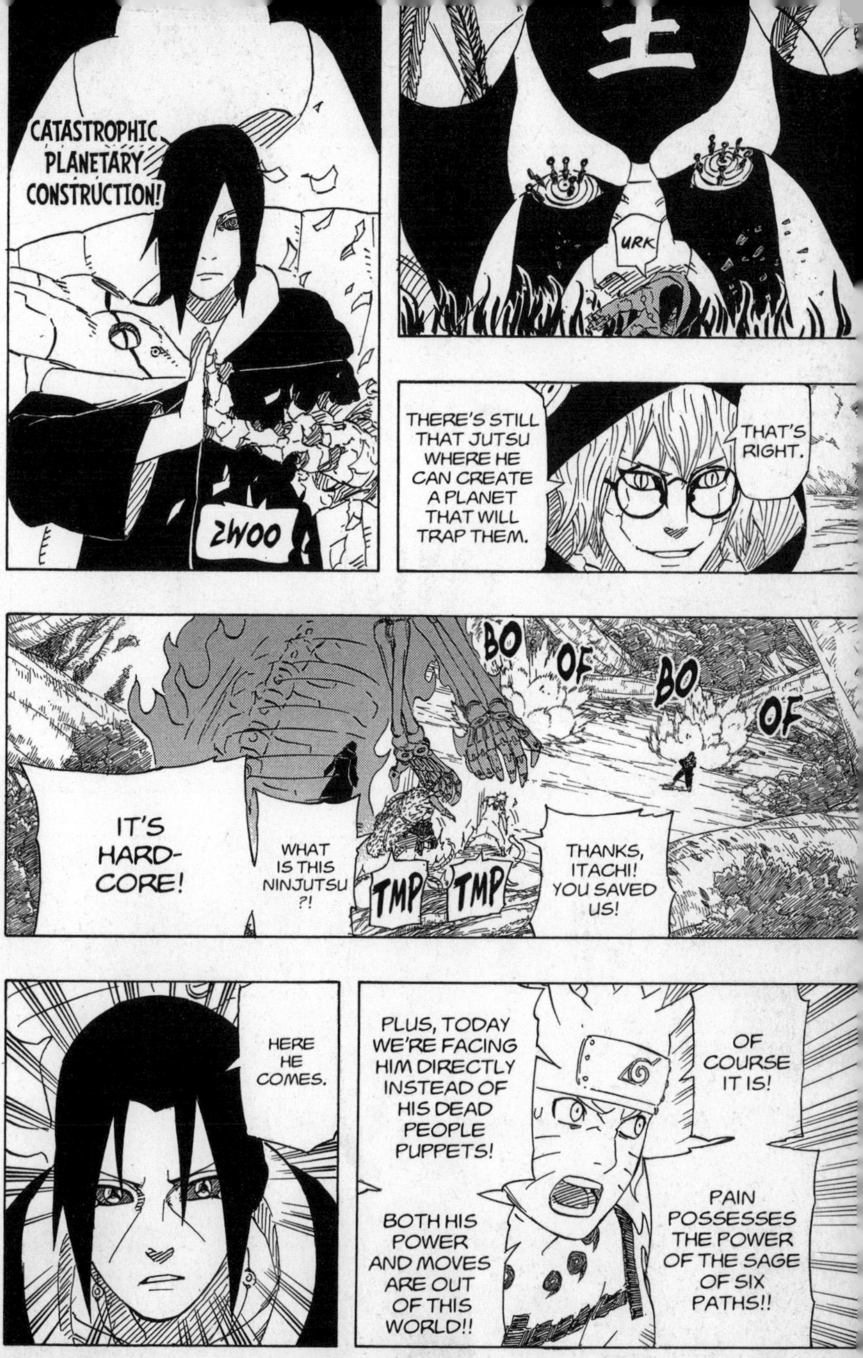
URK
THAT'S RIGHT.
THERE'S STILL THAT JUTSU WHERE HE CAN CREATE A PLANET THAT WILL TRAP THEM.
CATASTROPHIC PLANETARY CONSTRUCTION!
ZWOO
BO OF BO OF
THANKS, ITACHI! YOU SAVED US!
TMP TMP
WHAT IS THIS NINJUTSU?!
IT'S HARD-CORE!
OF COURSE IT IS!
PLUS, TODAY WE'RE FACING HIM DIRECTLY INSTEAD OF HIS DEAD PEOPLE PUPPETS!
PAIN POSSESSES THE POWER OF THE SAGE OF SIX PATHS!!
BOTH HIS POWER AND MOVES ARE OUT OF THIS WORLD!!
HERE HE COMES.

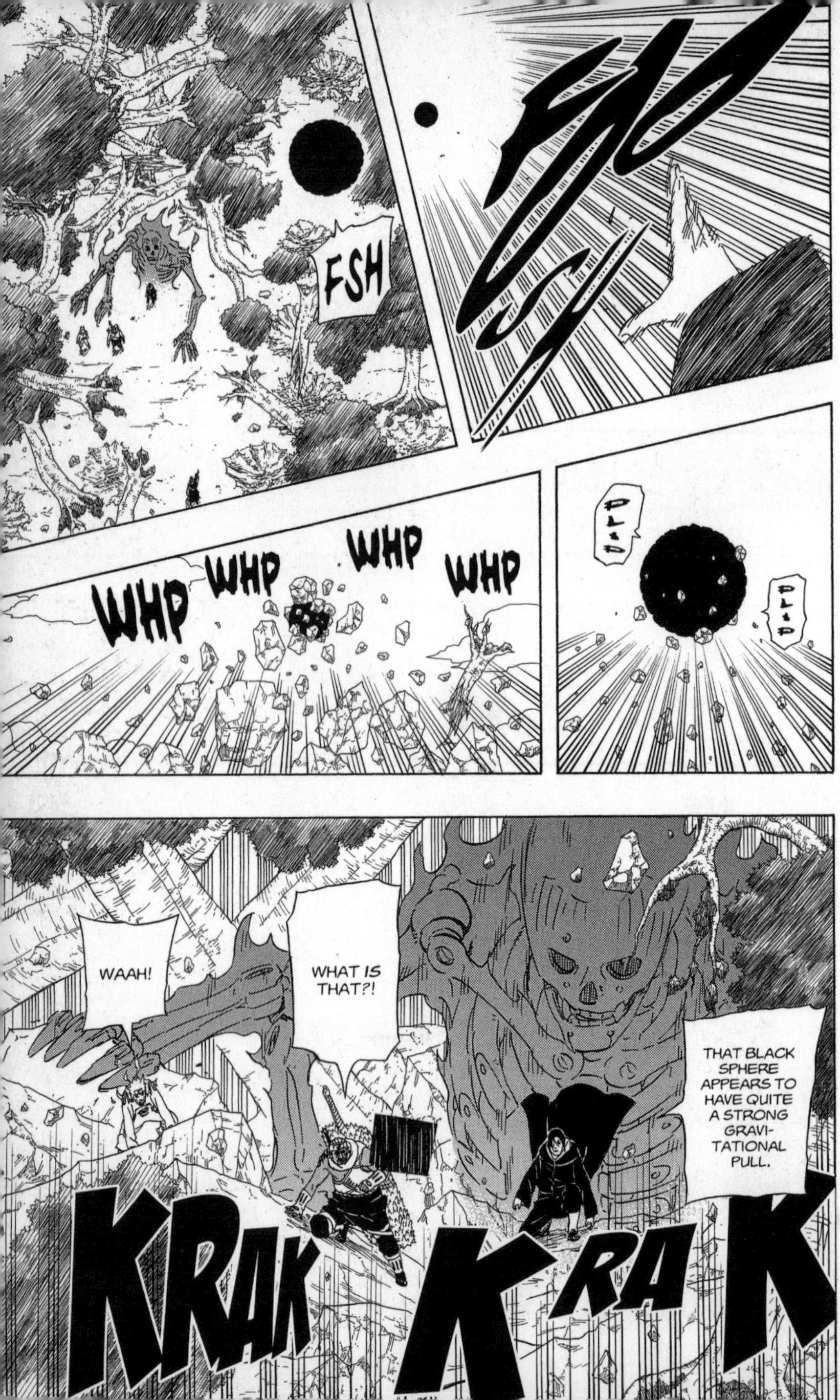
FSH
WHP
WHP
WHP
WHP
THAT BLACK SPHERE APPEARS TO HAVE QUITE A STRONG GRAVITATIONAL PULL.
WHAT IS THAT?!
WAAH!
KRAK
KRAK

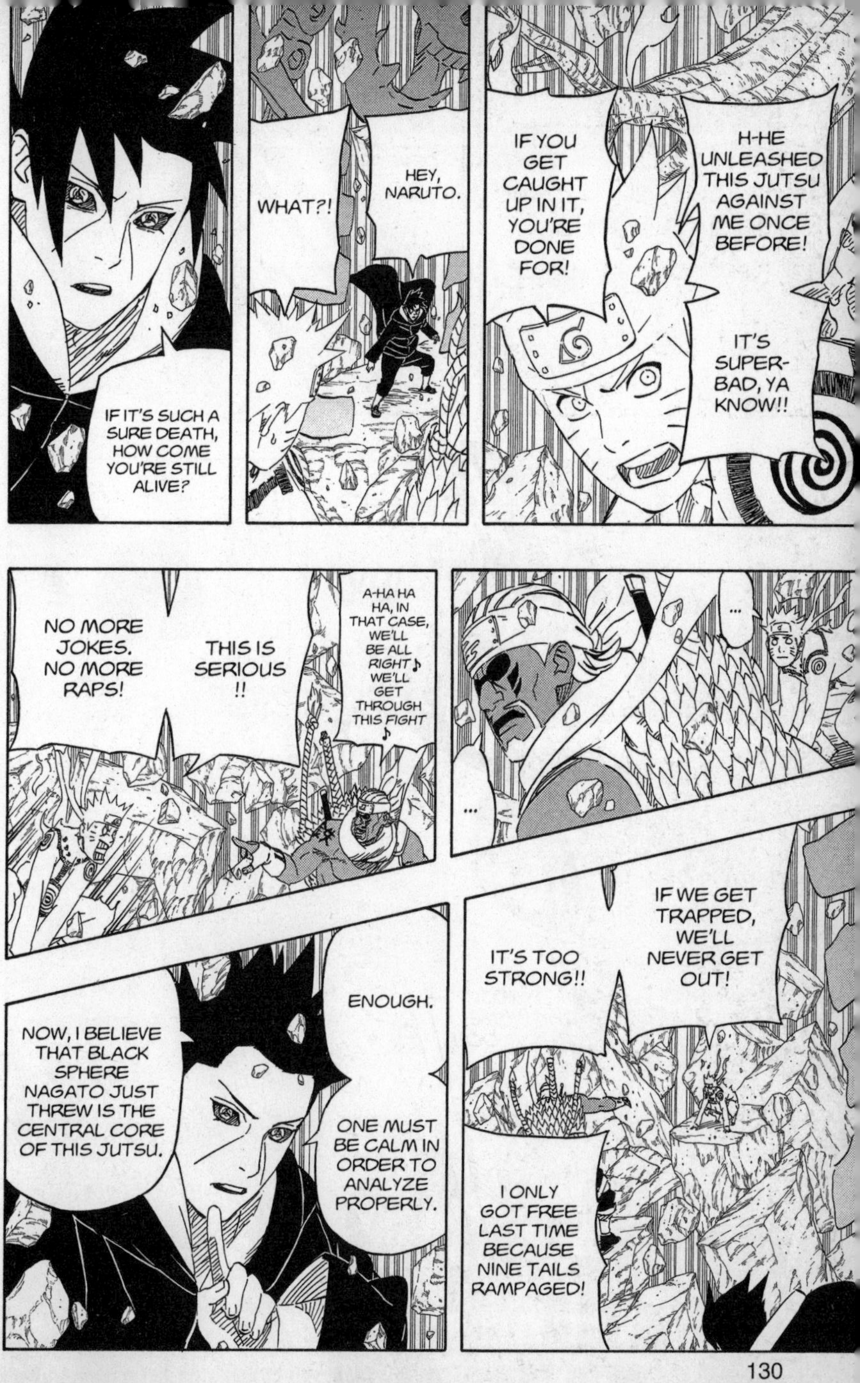
H-HE UNLEASHED THIS JUTSU AGAINST ME ONCE BEFORE!
IF YOU GET CAUGHT UP IN IT, YOU'RE DONE FOR!
IT'S SUPER-BAD, YA KNOW!!
HEY, NARUTO.
WHAT?!
IF IT'S SUCH A SURE DEATH, HOW COME YOU'RE STILL ALIVE?
...
...
A-HA HA HA, IN THAT CASE, WE'LL BE ALL RIGHT♪ WE'LL GET THROUGH THIS FIGHT ♪
THIS IS SERIOUS !!
NO MORE JOKES. NO MORE RAPS!
IF WE GET TRAPPED, WE'LL NEVER GET OUT!
IT'S TOO STRONG!!
I ONLY GOT FREE LAST TIME BECAUSE NINE TAILS RAMPAGED!
ENOUGH.
ONE MUST BE CALM IN ORDER TO ANALYZE PROPERLY.
NOW, I BELIEVE THAT BLACK SPHERE NAGATO JUST THREW IS THE CENTRAL CORE OF THIS JUTSU.

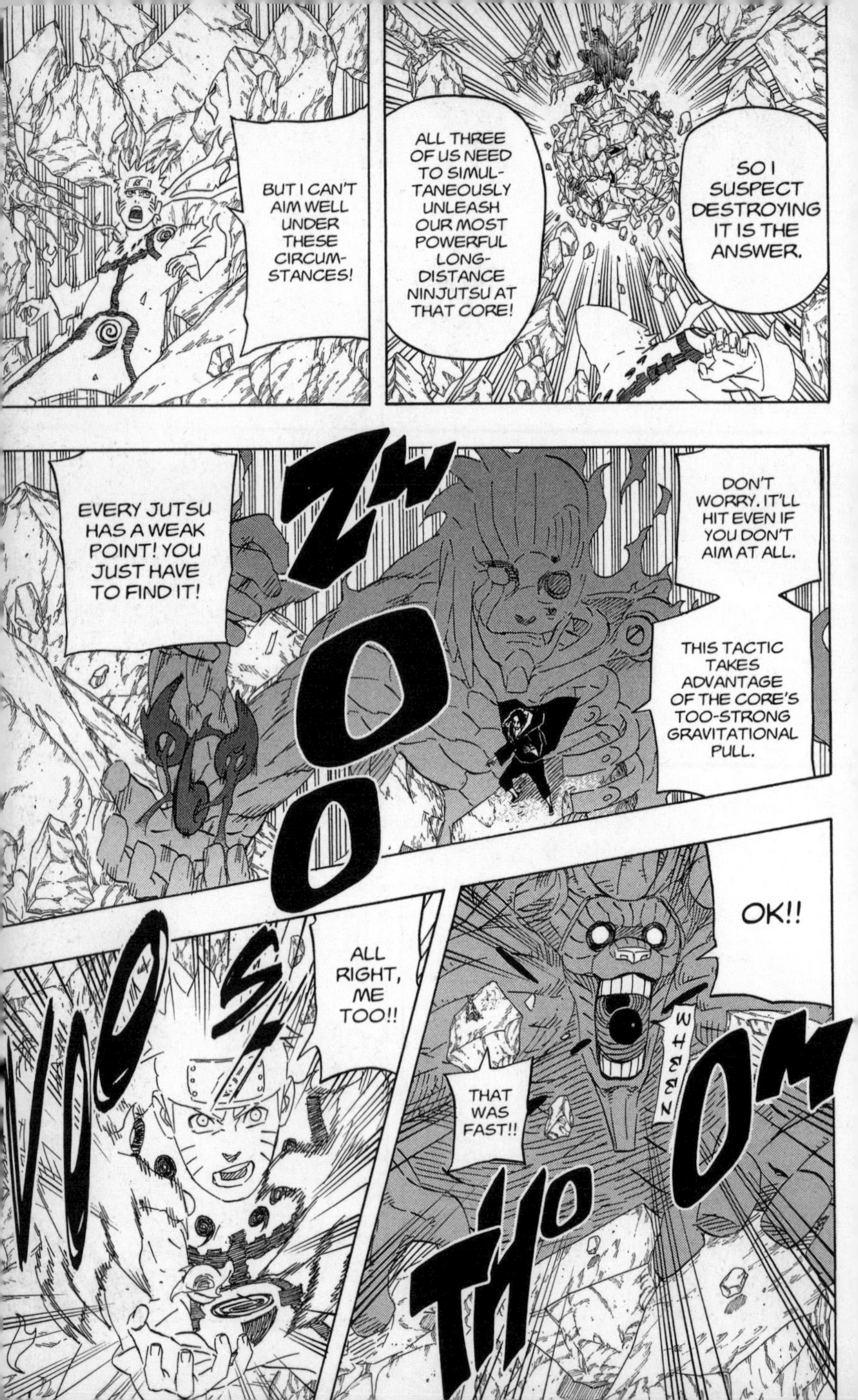
SO I SUSPECT DESTROYING IT IS THE ANSWER.
ALL THREE OF US NEED TO SIMULTANEOUSLY UNLEASH OUR MOST POWERFUL LONG-DISTANCE NINJUTSU AT THAT CORE!
BUT I CAN'T AIM WELL UNDER THESE CIRCUMSTANCES!
DON'T WORRY. IT'LL HIT EVEN IF YOU DON'T AIM AT ALL.
THIS TACTIC TAKES ADVANTAGE OF THE CORE'S TOO-STRONG GRAVITATIONAL PULL.
ZWOOO
EVERY JUTSU HAS A WEAK POINT! YOU JUST HAVE TO FIND IT!
OK!!
WHEEN
THAT WAS FAST!!
THOOOM
ALL RIGHT, ME TOO!!
VOOOSH

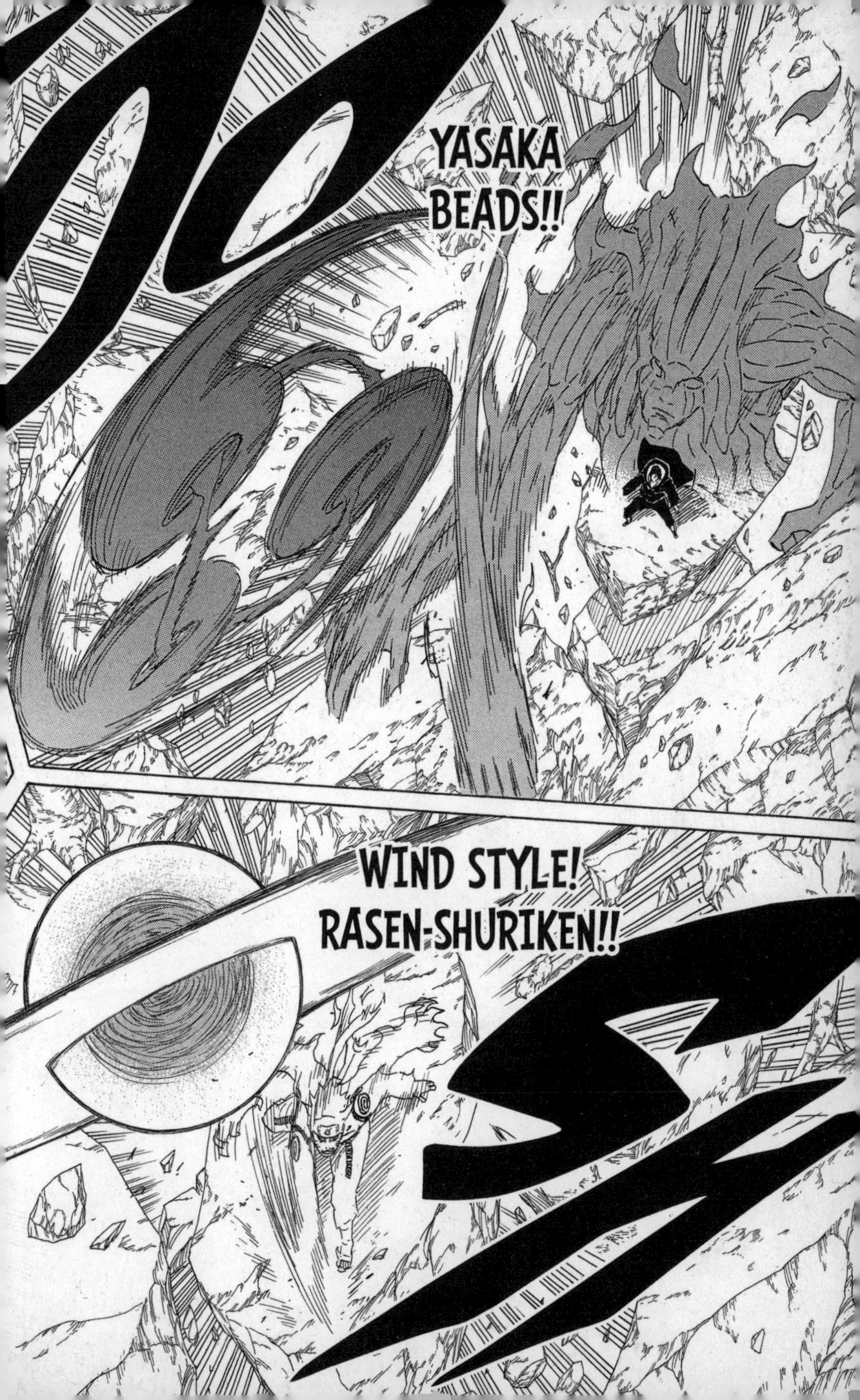
YASAKA BEADS!!
WIND STYLE! RASEN-SHURIKEN!!

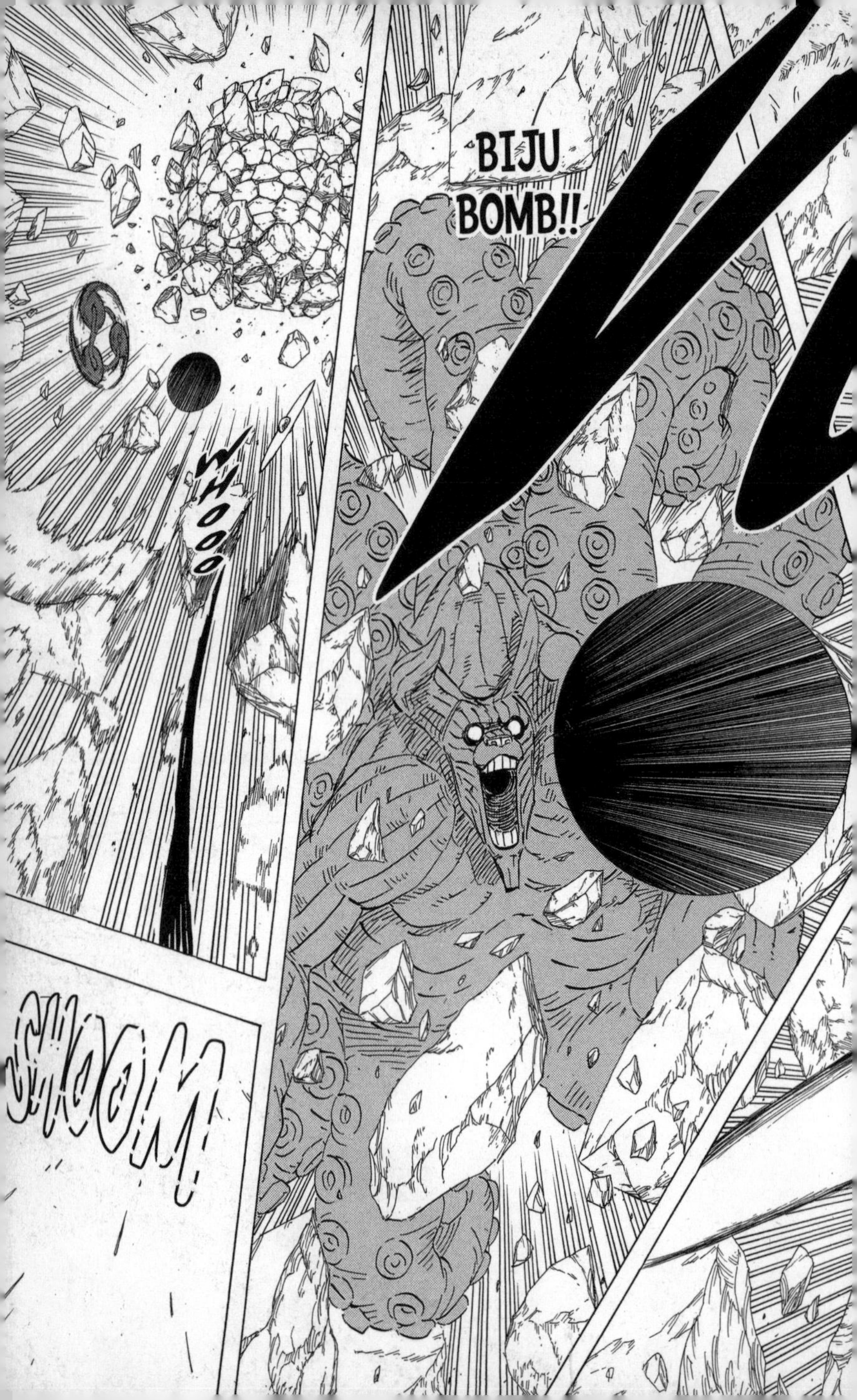
BIJU BOMB!!
WHOOOO
SHOOM

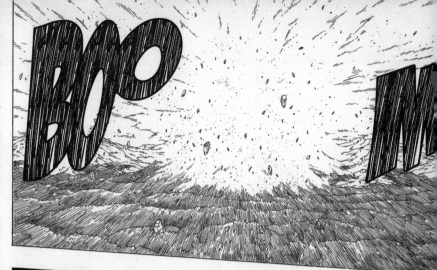

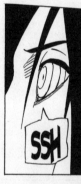

SSH

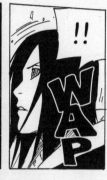

!!

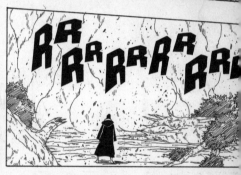

RRRRRRRR RRR

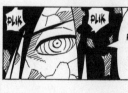

PLIK PLIK

FORGIVE ME, ITACHI.

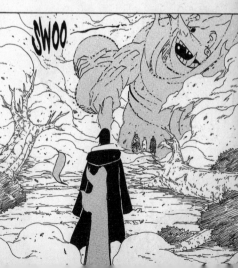

SWOO

IT'S THE TOTSUKA BLADE. YOU'LL BE SEALED AWAY SOON. ANY LAST WORDS?

YOU'RE BACK.

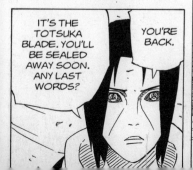

READ THIS WAY

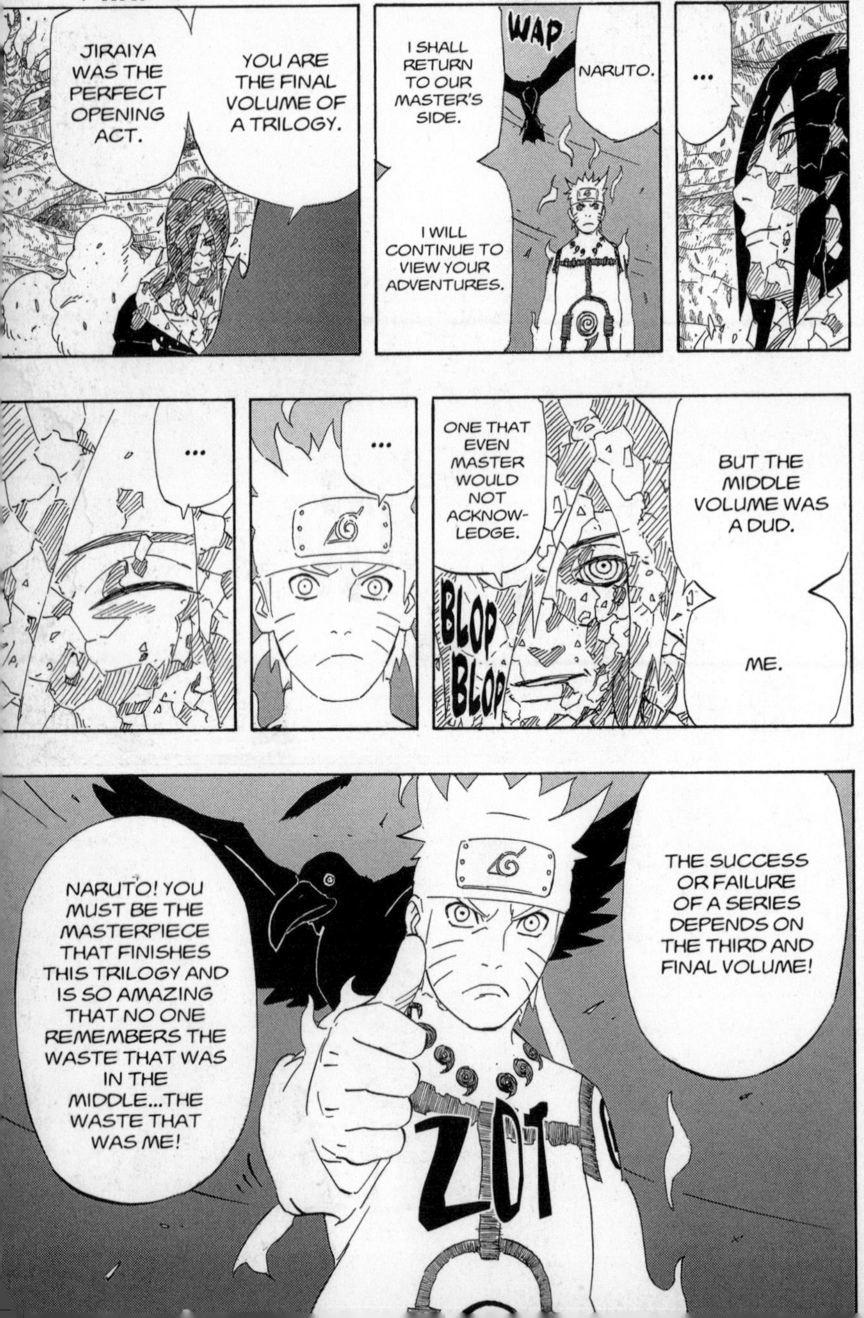

...
WAP
NARUTO.
I SHALL RETURN TO OUR MASTER'S SIDE.
I WILL CONTINUE TO VIEW YOUR ADVENTURES.
YOU ARE THE FINAL VOLUME OF A TRILOGY.
JIRAIYA WAS THE PERFECT OPENING ACT.
BUT THE MIDDLE VOLUME WAS A DUD.
ME.
ONE THAT EVEN MASTER WOULD NOT ACKNOW-LEDGE.
BLOP BLOP
...
...
THE SUCCESS OR FAILURE OF A SERIES DEPENDS ON THE THIRD AND FINAL VOLUME!
NARUTO! YOU MUST BE THE MASTERPIECE THAT FINISHES THIS TRILOGY AND IS SO AMAZING THAT NO ONE REMEMBERS THE WASTE THAT WAS IN THE MIDDLE...THE WASTE THAT WAS ME!
ZOT

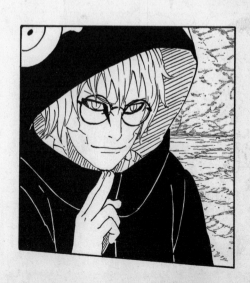

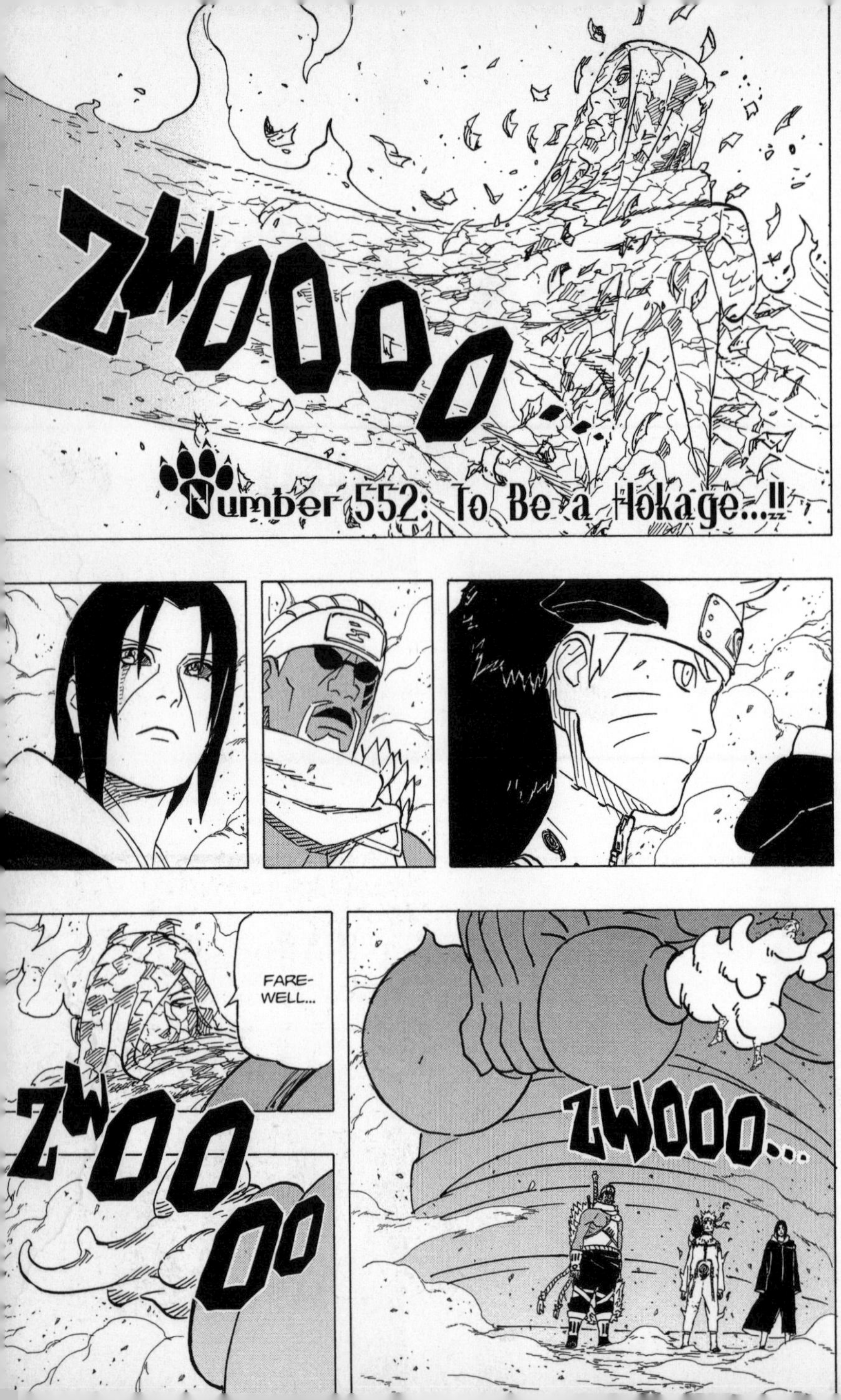
ZWOOOO...
Number 552: To Be a Hokage...!!
ZWOOO...
FARE-
WELL...
ZWOOOO

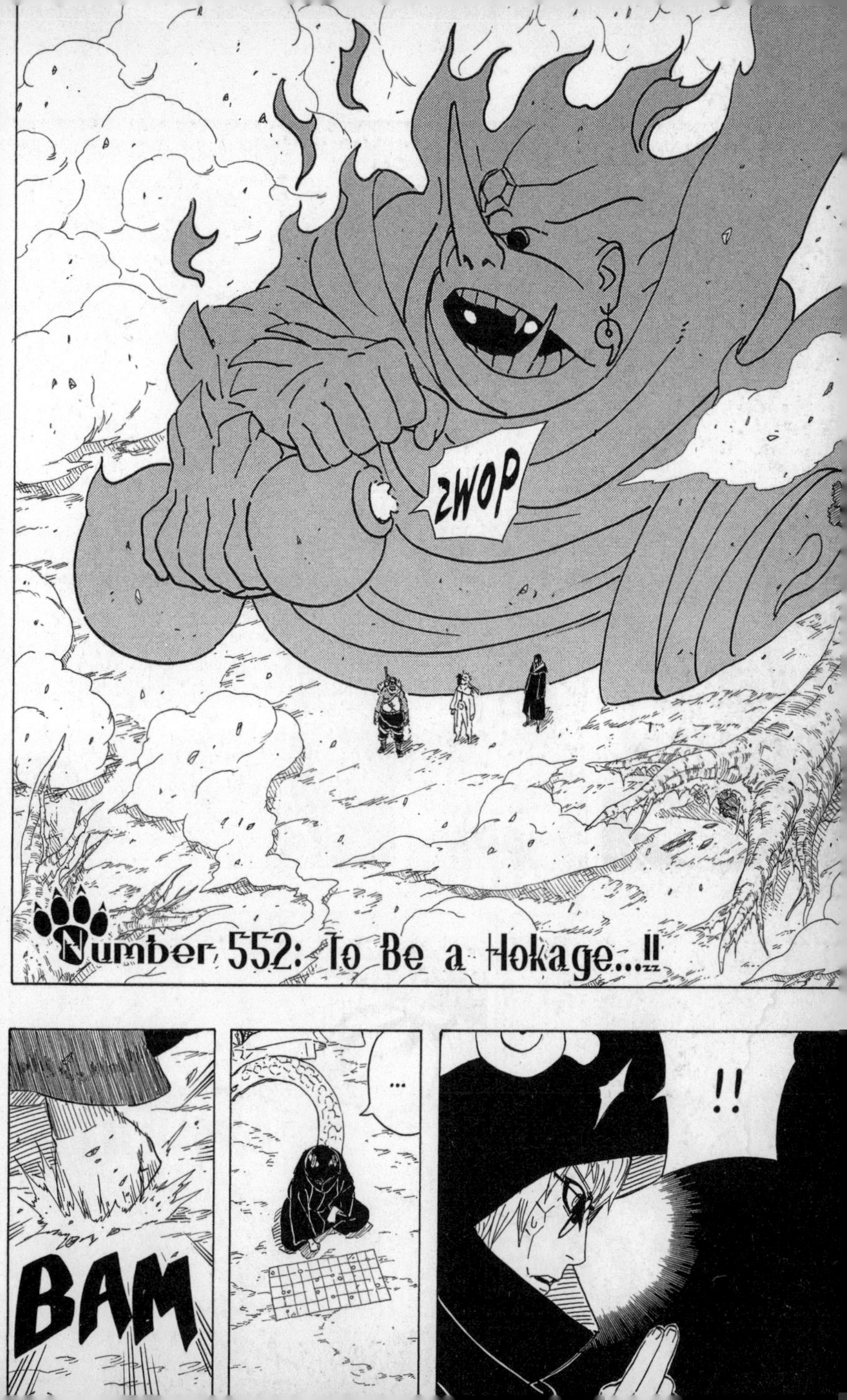
ZWOP
Number 552: To Be a Hokage...!!
!!
...
BAM

READ THIS WAY

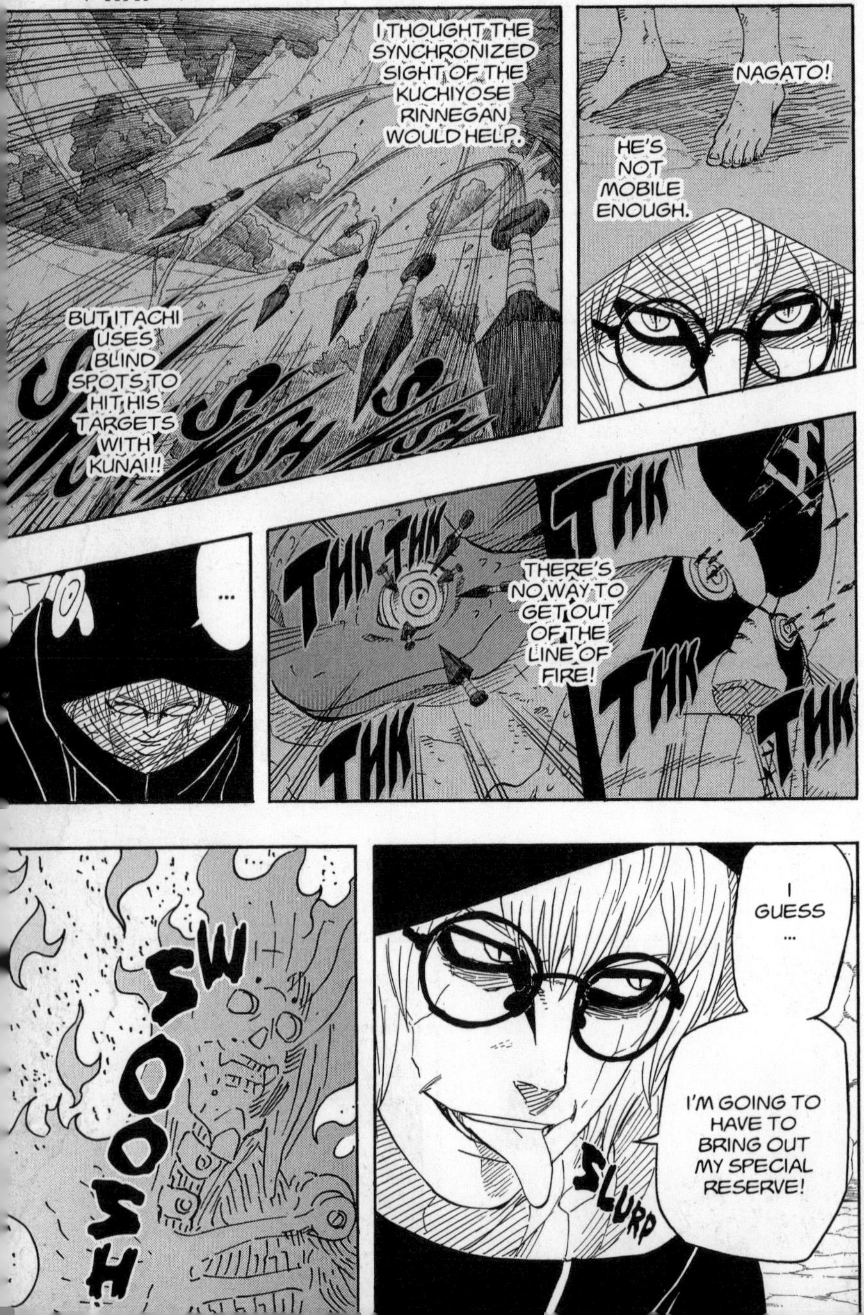
NAGATO!
HE'S NOT MOBILE ENOUGH.
I THOUGHT THE SYNCHRONIZED SIGHT OF THE KUCHIYOSE RINNEGAN WOULD HELP.
BUT ITACHI USES BLIND SPOTS TO HIT HIS TARGETS WITH KUNAI!!
THK
THK
THK
THK
THK
THK
THERE'S NO WAY TO GET OUT OF THE LINE OF FIRE!
...
I GUESS ...
I'M GOING TO HAVE TO BRING OUT MY SPECIAL RESERVE!
SLURP
SWOOSH

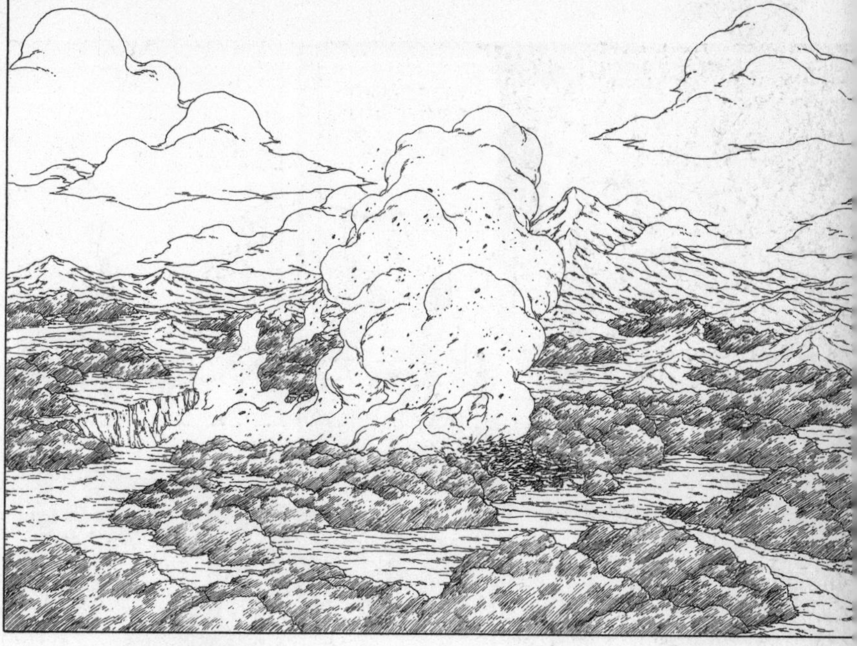

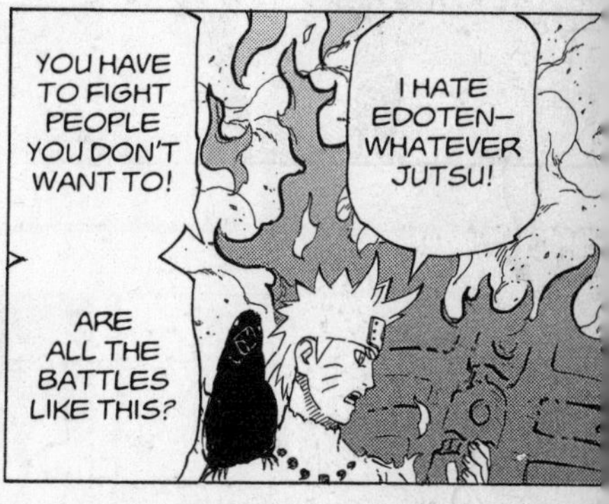
I HATE EDOTEN-WHATEVER JUTSU!
YOU HAVE TO FIGHT PEOPLE YOU DON'T WANT TO!
ARE ALL THE BATTLES LIKE THIS?

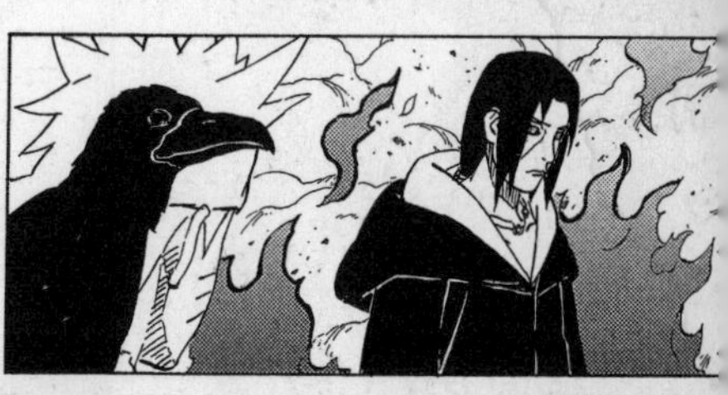

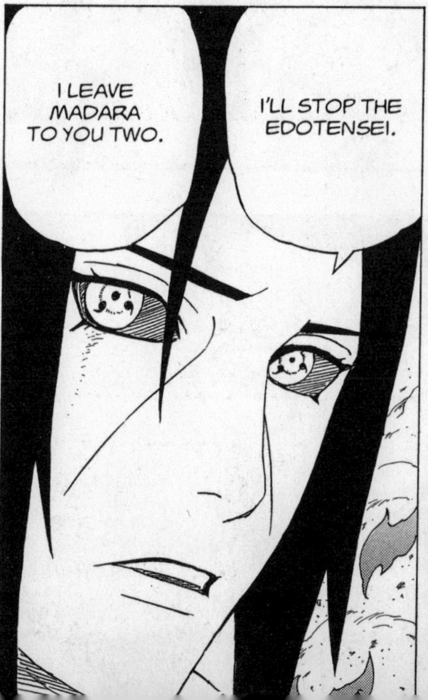
I'LL STOP THE EDOTENSEI.
I LEAVE MADARA TO YOU TWO.

READ THIS WAY

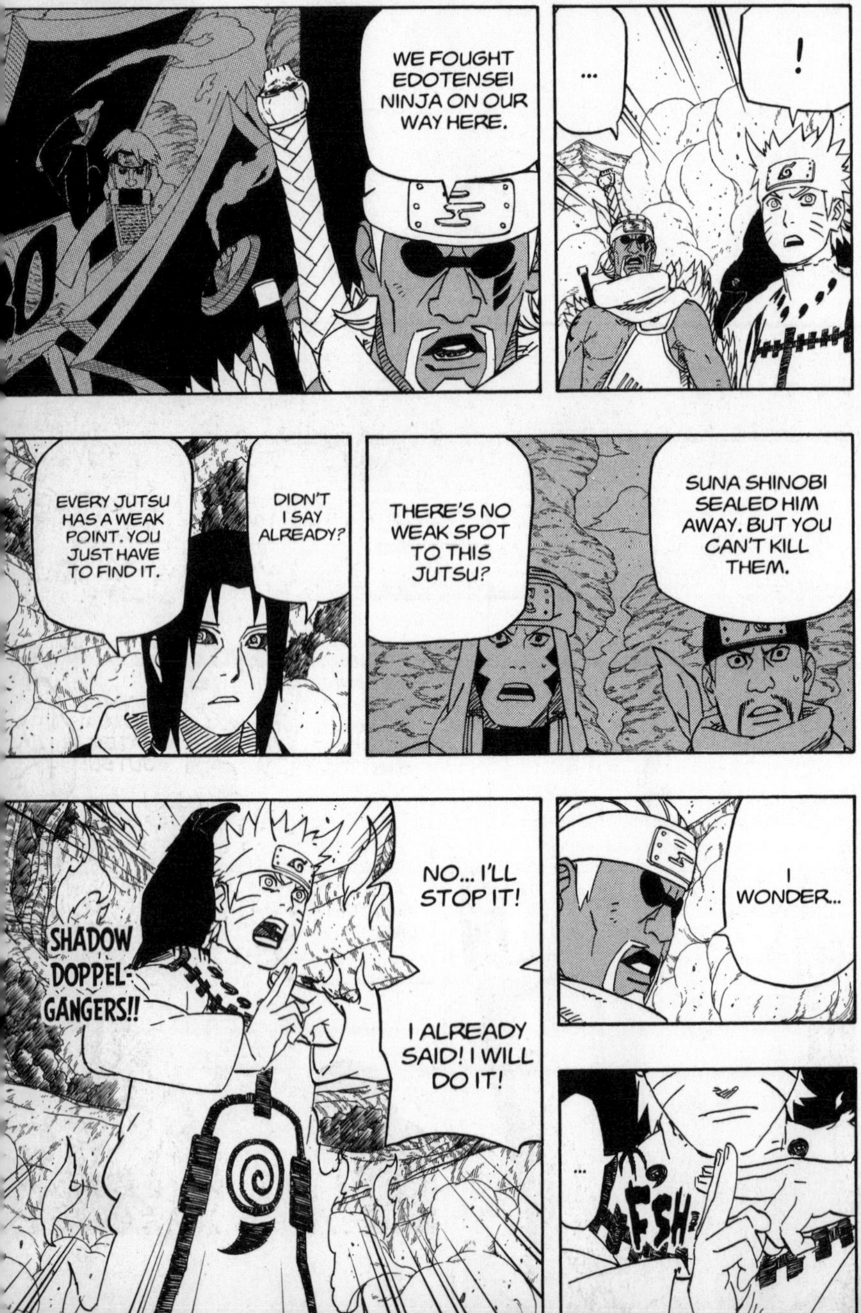
!
...
WE FOUGHT EDOTENSEI NINJA ON OUR WAY HERE.
SUNA SHINOBI SEALED HIM AWAY. BUT YOU CAN'T KILL THEM.
THERE'S NO WEAK SPOT TO THIS JUTSU?
DIDN'T I SAY ALREADY?
EVERY JUTSU HAS A WEAK POINT. YOU JUST HAVE TO FIND IT.
I WONDER...
...
FSH
NO... I'LL STOP IT!
I ALREADY SAID! I WILL DO IT!
SHADOW DOPPEL-GANGERS!!

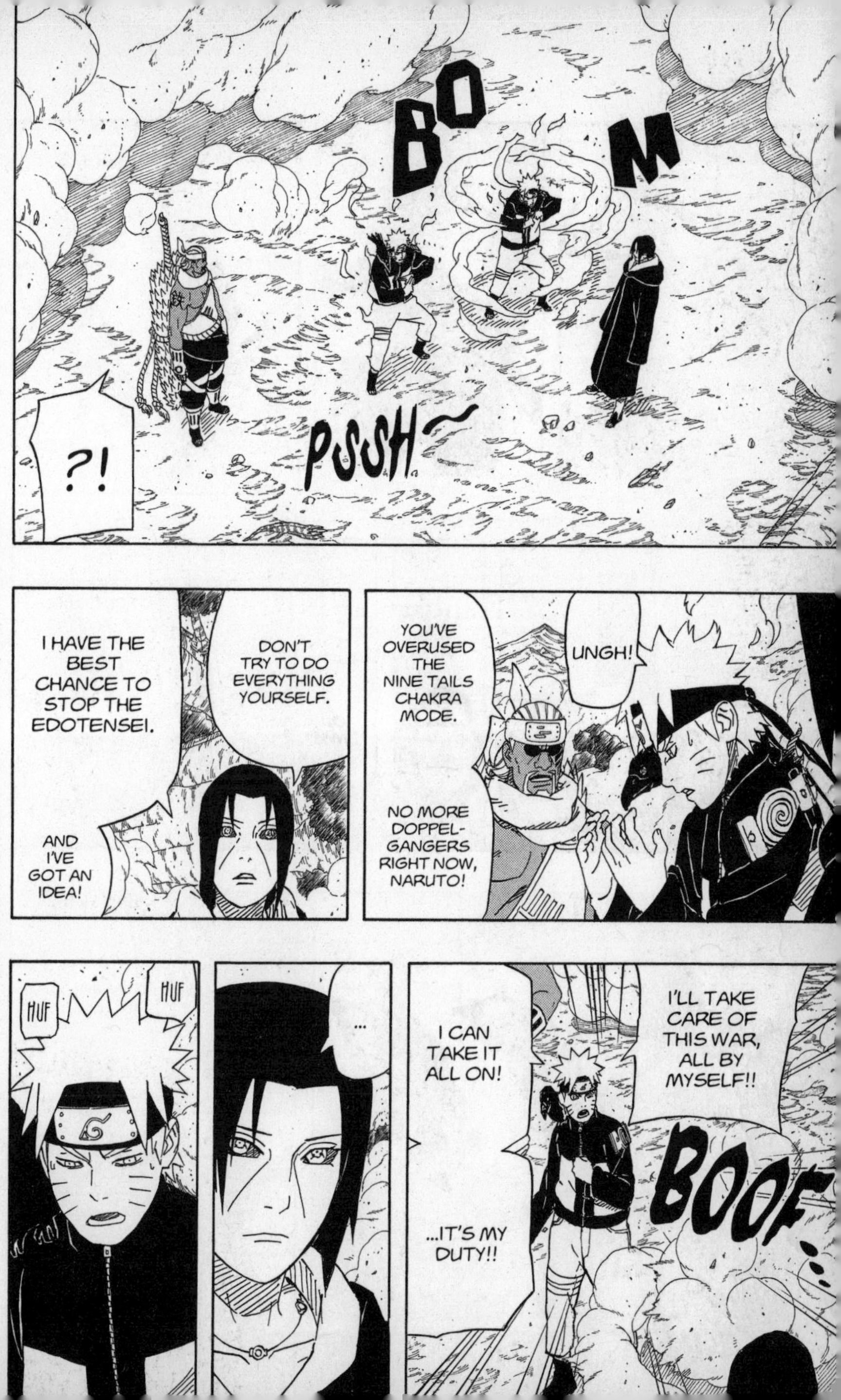
BOOM
PSSH~
?!
UNGH!
YOU'VE OVERUSED THE NINE TAILS CHAKRA MODE.
NO MORE DOPPEL-GANGERS RIGHT NOW, NARUTO!
DON'T TRY TO DO EVERYTHING YOURSELF.
I HAVE THE BEST CHANCE TO STOP THE EDOTENSEI.
AND I'VE GOT AN IDEA!
I'LL TAKE CARE OF THIS WAR, ALL BY MYSELF!!
I CAN TAKE IT ALL ON!
...IT'S MY DUTY!!
BOOF...
...
HUF
HUF

READ THIS WAY

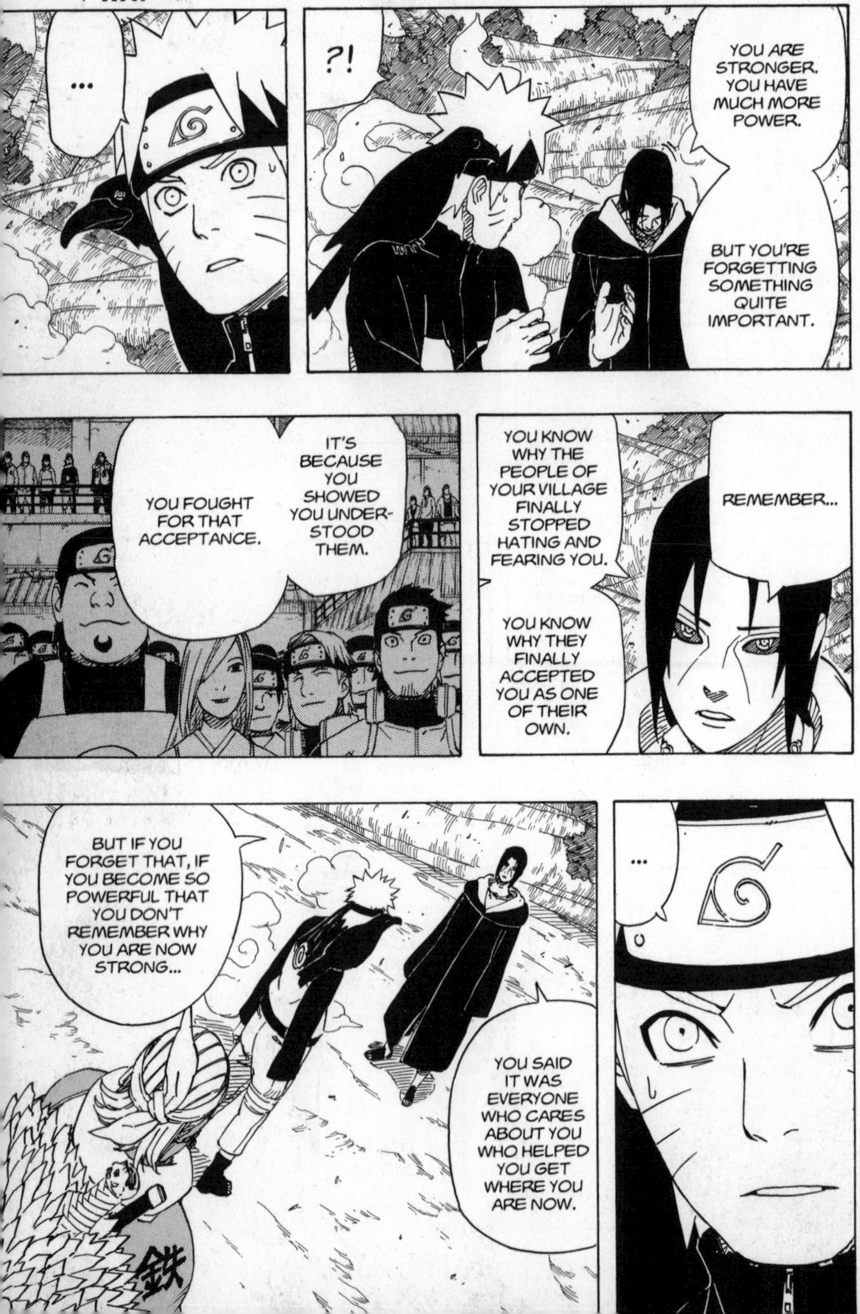
YOU ARE STRONGER. YOU HAVE MUCH MORE POWER.
?!
BUT YOU'RE FORGETTING SOMETHING QUITE IMPORTANT.
...
REMEMBER...
YOU KNOW WHY THE PEOPLE OF YOUR VILLAGE FINALLY STOPPED HATING AND FEARING YOU.
YOU KNOW WHY THEY FINALLY ACCEPTED YOU AS ONE OF THEIR OWN.
IT'S BECAUSE YOU SHOWED YOU UNDER-STOOD THEM.
YOU FOUGHT FOR THAT ACCEPTANCE.
...
BUT IF YOU FORGET THAT, IF YOU BECOME SO POWERFUL THAT YOU DON'T REMEMBER WHY YOU ARE NOW STRONG...
YOU SAID IT WAS EVERYONE WHO CARES ABOUT YOU WHO HELPED YOU GET WHERE YOU ARE NOW.
鉄

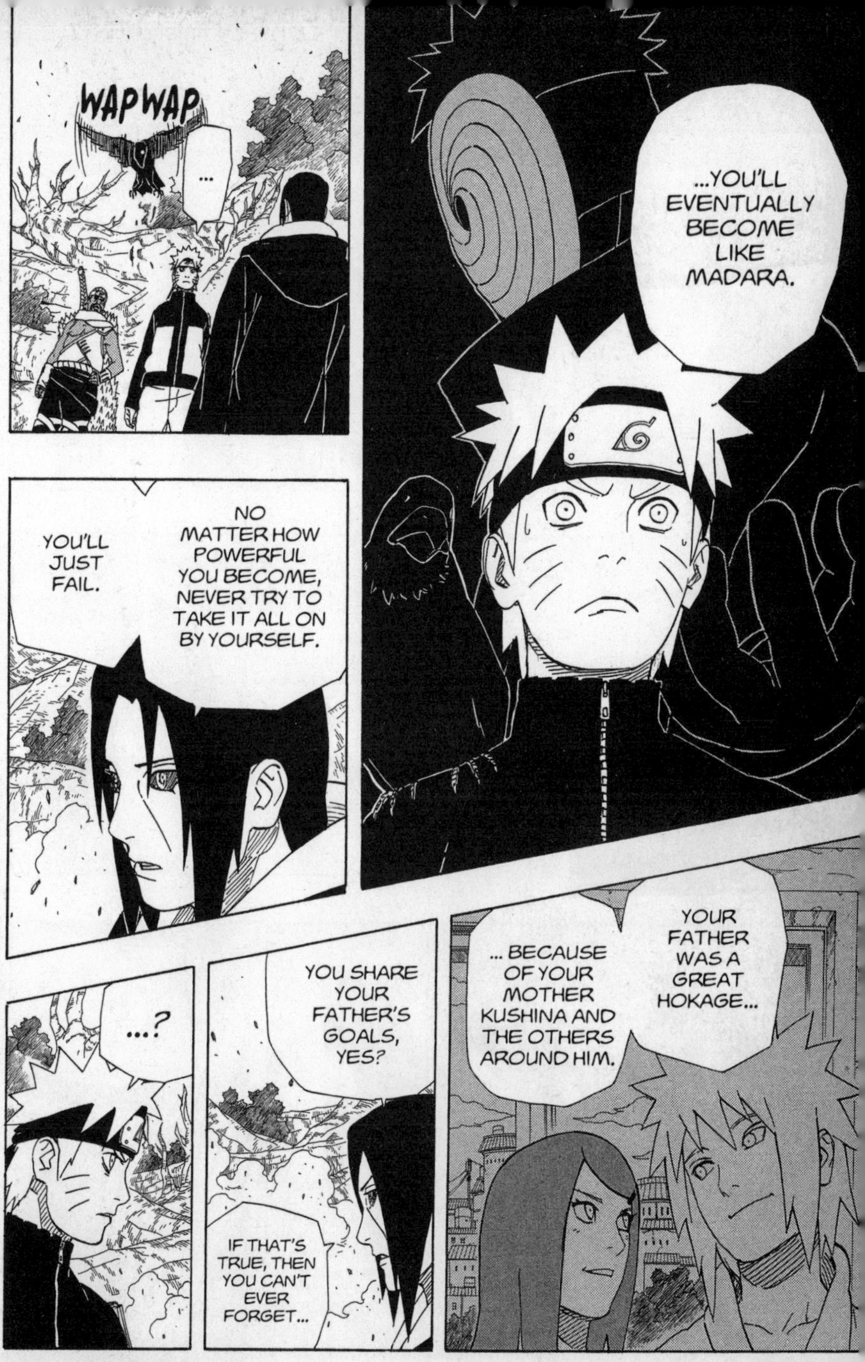
...YOU'LL EVENTUALLY BECOME LIKE MADARA.
WAP WAP
...
NO MATTER HOW POWERFUL YOU BECOME, NEVER TRY TO TAKE IT ALL ON BY YOURSELF.
YOU'LL JUST FAIL.
YOUR FATHER WAS A GREAT HOKAGE...
... BECAUSE OF YOUR MOTHER KUSHINA AND THE OTHERS AROUND HIM.
YOU SHARE YOUR FATHER'S GOALS, YES?
IF THAT'S TRUE, THEN YOU CAN'T EVER FORGET...
...?

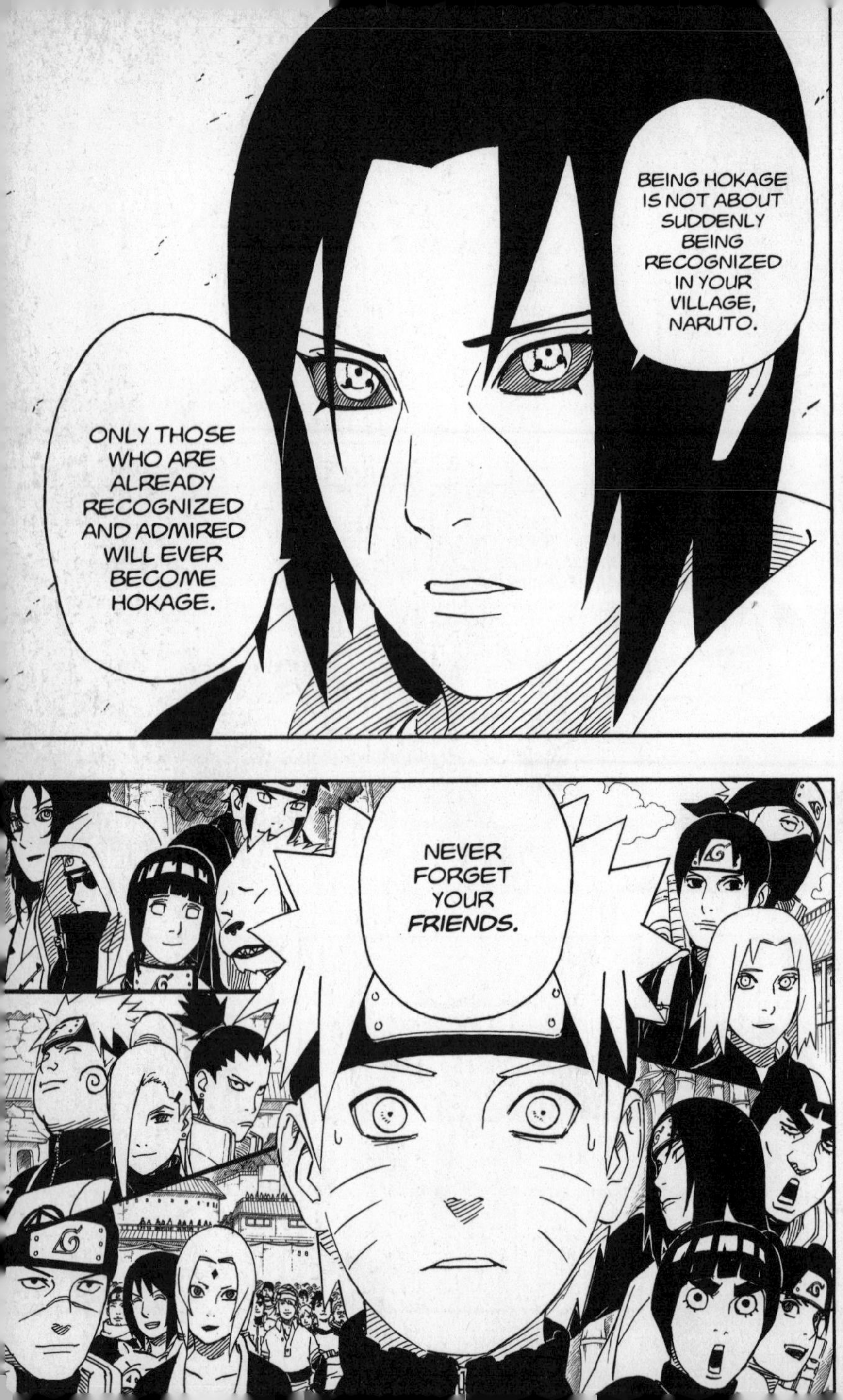
BEING HOKAGE IS NOT ABOUT SUDDENLY BEING RECOGNIZED IN YOUR VILLAGE, NARUTO.
ONLY THOSE WHO ARE ALREADY RECOGNIZED AND ADMIRED WILL EVER BECOME HOKAGE.
NEVER FORGET YOUR FRIENDS.

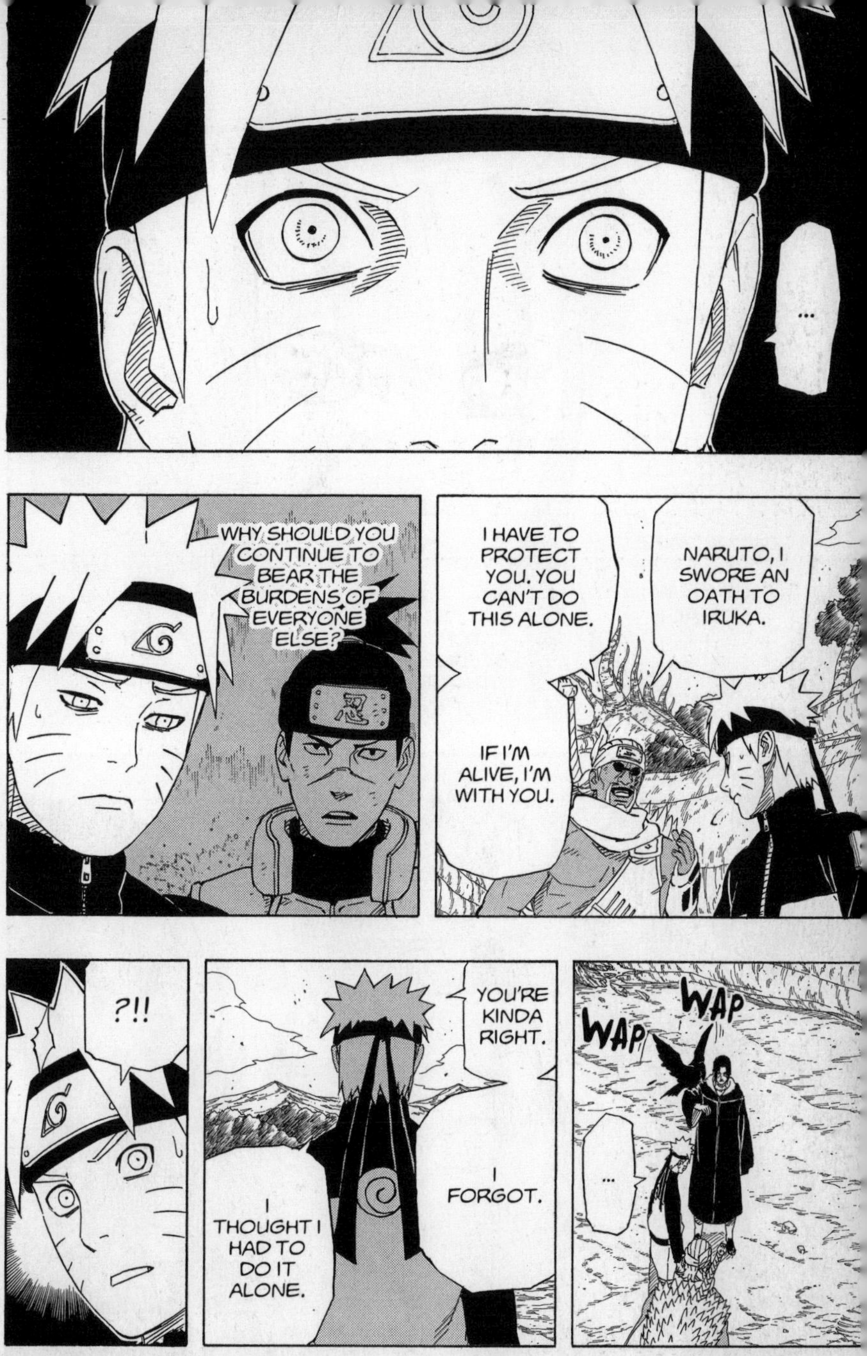
...
NARUTO, I SWORE AN OATH TO IRUKA.
I HAVE TO PROTECT YOU. YOU CAN'T DO THIS ALONE.
IF I'M ALIVE, I'M WITH YOU.
WHY SHOULD YOU CONTINUE TO BEAR THE BURDENS OF EVERYONE ELSE?
WAP
WAP
...
YOU'RE KINDA RIGHT.
I FORGOT.
I THOUGHT I HAD TO DO IT ALONE.
?!!

READ THIS WAY

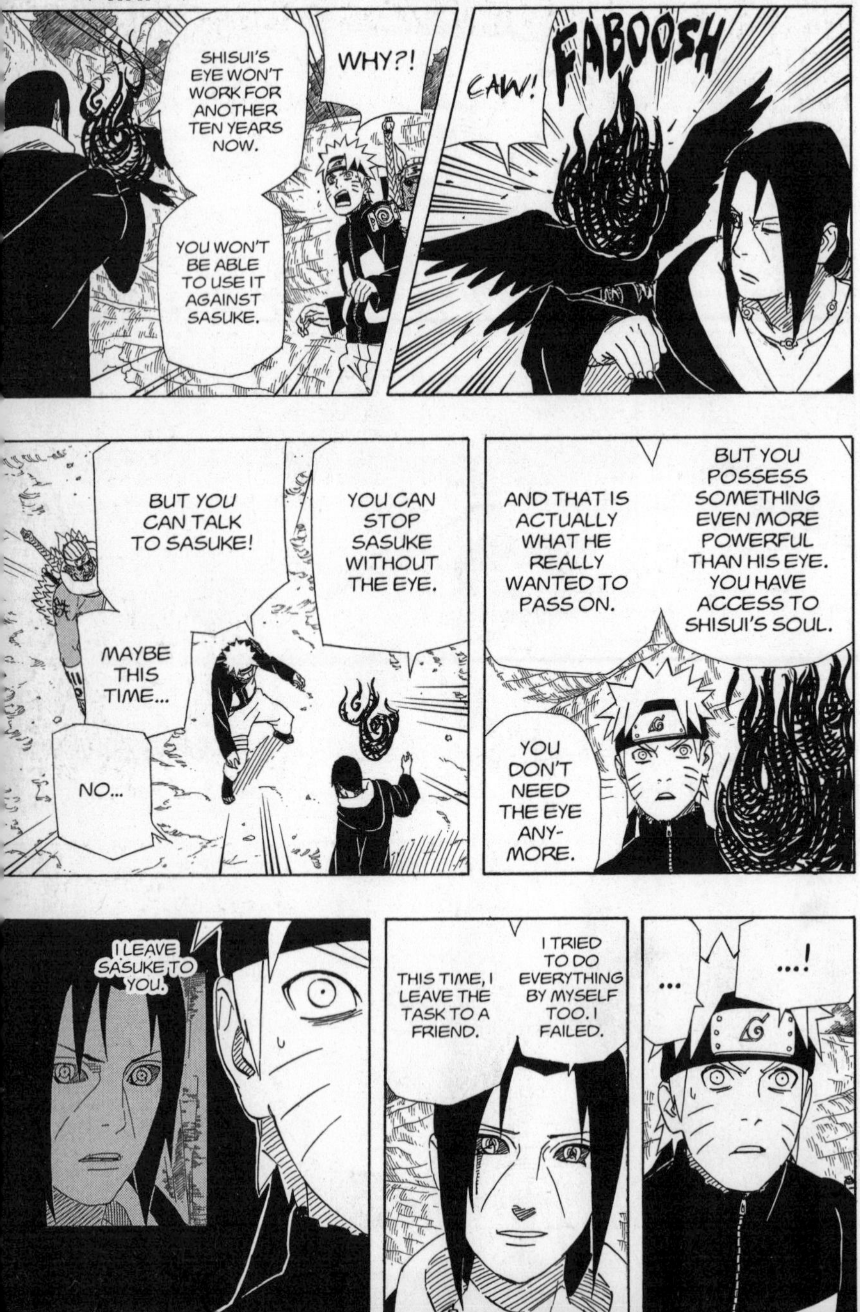
FABOOSH
CAW!
WHY?!
SHISUI'S EYE WON'T WORK FOR ANOTHER TEN YEARS NOW.
YOU WON'T BE ABLE TO USE IT AGAINST SASUKE.
BUT YOU POSSESS SOMETHING EVEN MORE POWERFUL THAN HIS EYE. YOU HAVE ACCESS TO SHISUI'S SOUL.
AND THAT IS ACTUALLY WHAT HE REALLY WANTED TO PASS ON.
YOU DON'T NEED THE EYE ANY-MORE.
YOU CAN STOP SASUKE WITHOUT THE EYE.
BUT YOU CAN TALK TO SASUKE!
MAYBE THIS TIME...
NO...
...!
...
I TRIED TO DO EVERYTHING BY MYSELF TOO. I FAILED.
THIS TIME, I LEAVE THE TASK TO A FRIEND.
I LEAVE SASUKE TO YOU.

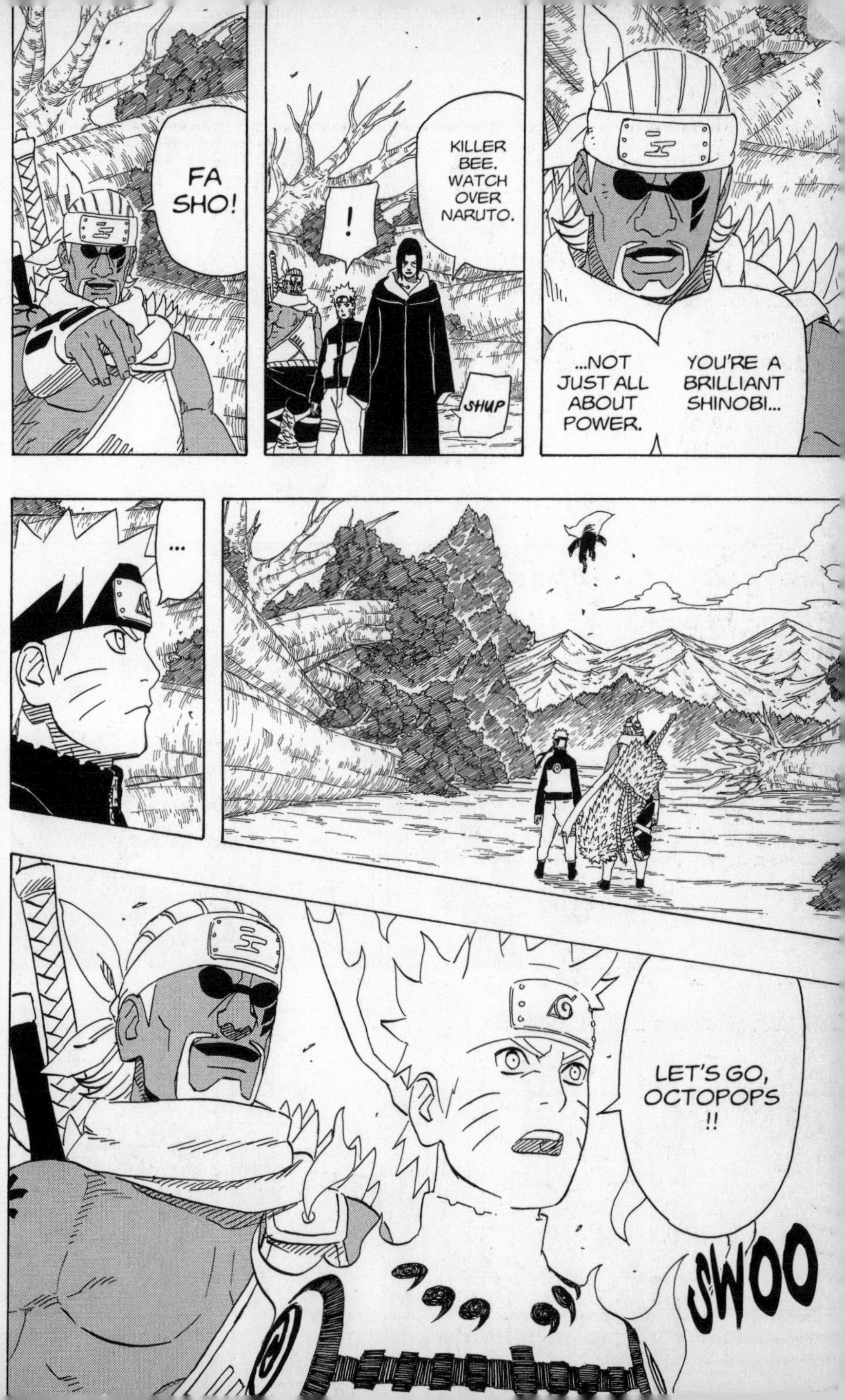
YOU'RE A BRILLIANT SHINOBI...
...NOT JUST ALL ABOUT POWER.
KILLER BEE. WATCH OVER NARUTO.
!
SHUP
FA SHO!
...
LET'S GO, OCTOPOPS !!
SWOO

READ THIS WAY

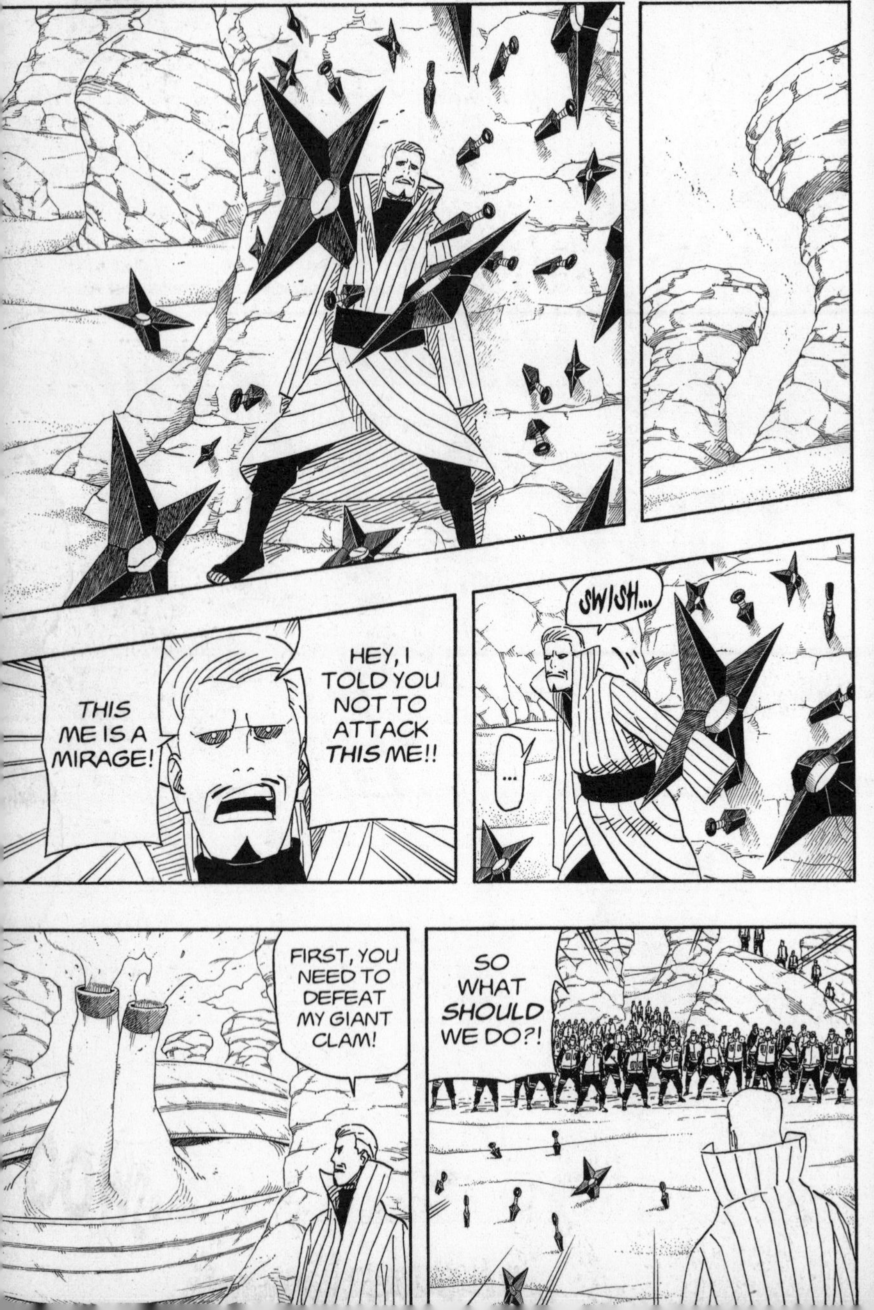
SWISH...
...
HEY, I TOLD YOU NOT TO ATTACK *THIS* ME!!
THIS ME IS A MIRAGE!
SO WHAT *SHOULD* WE DO?!
FIRST, YOU NEED TO DEFEAT MY GIANT CLAM!

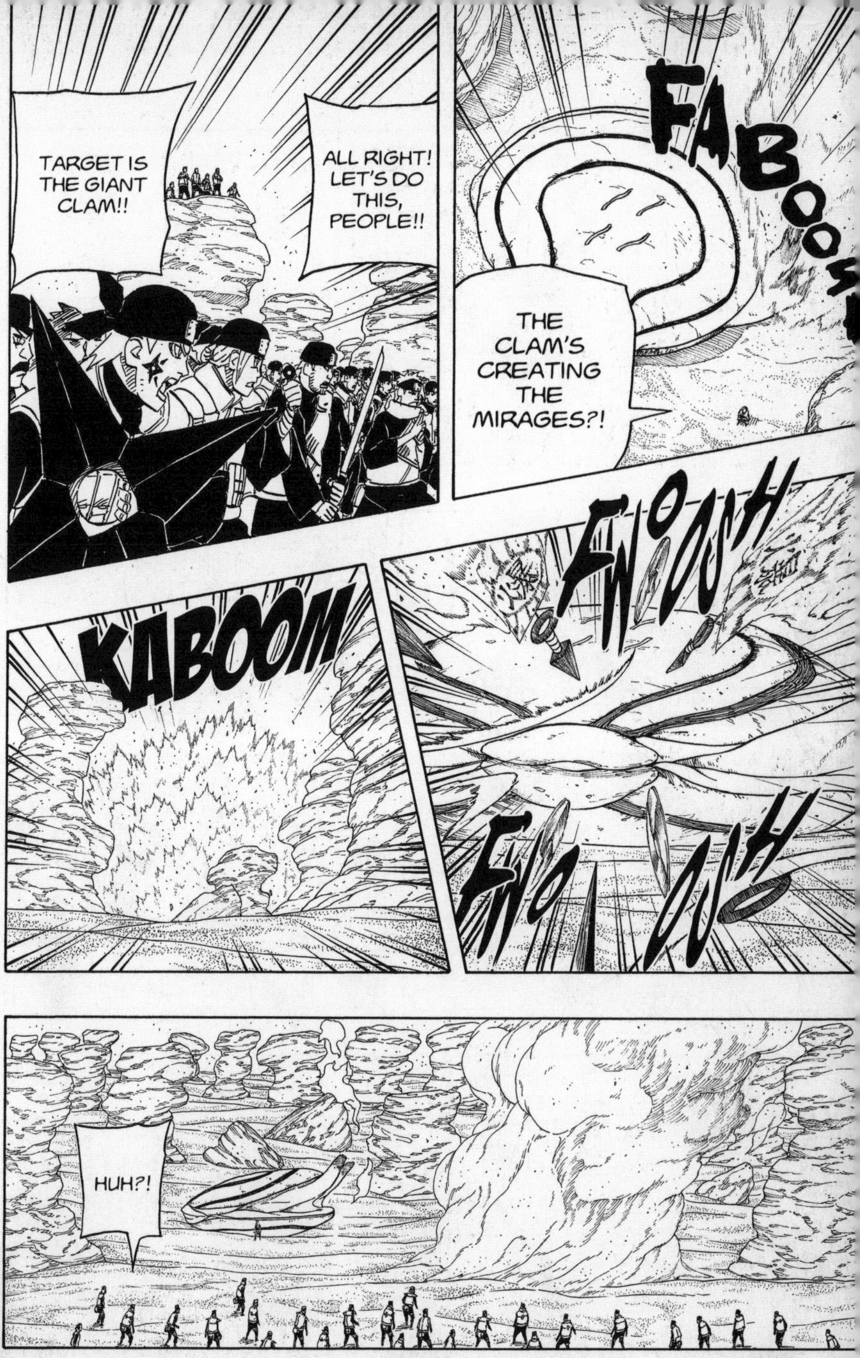
FABOOM
THE CLAM'S CREATING THE MIRAGES?!
ALL RIGHT! LET'S DO THIS, PEOPLE!!
TARGET IS THE GIANT CLAM!!
FWOOSH
FWOOSH
KABOOM
HUH?!

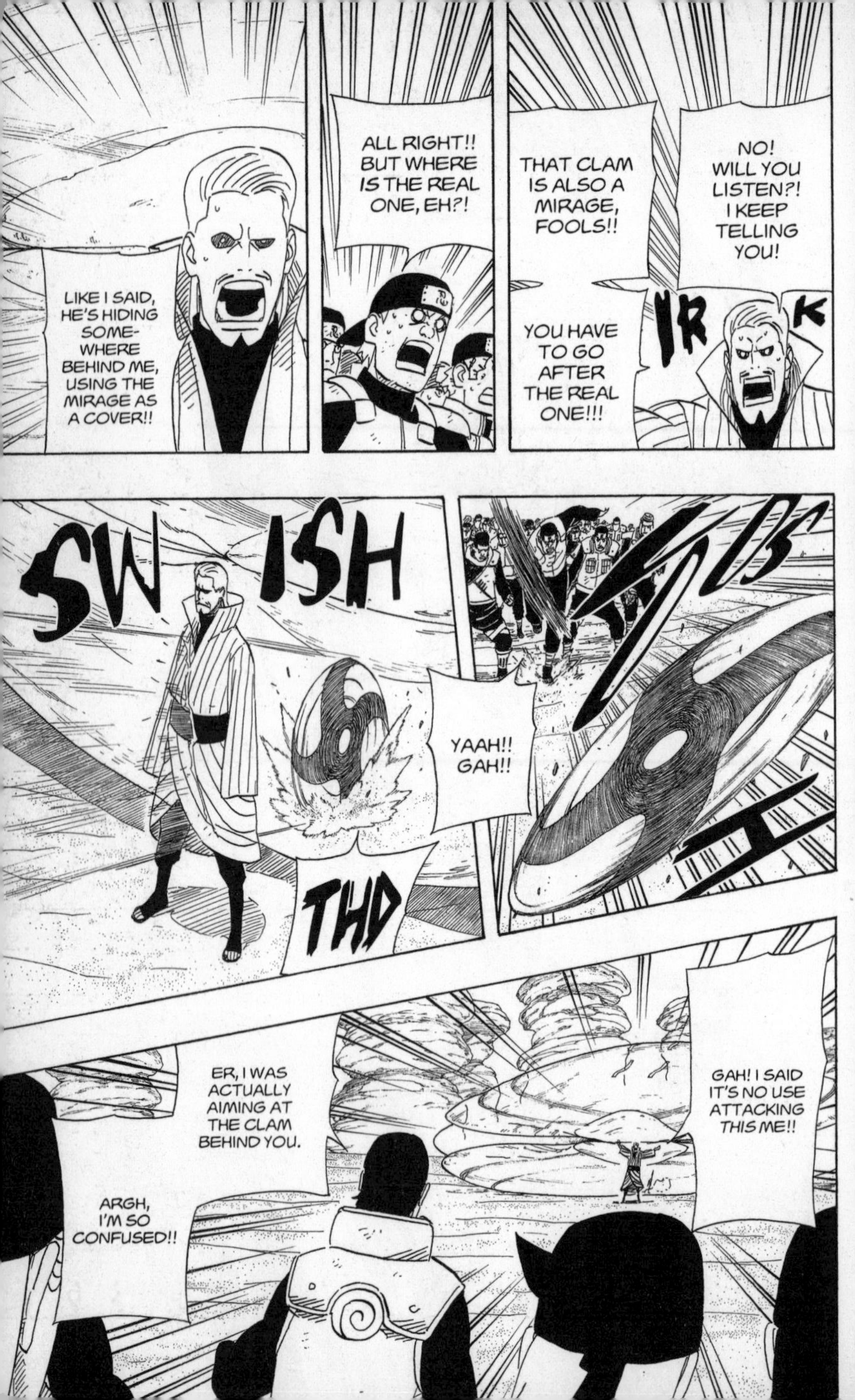
NO! WILL YOU LISTEN?! I KEEP TELLING YOU!
IRK
THAT CLAM IS ALSO A MIRAGE, FOOLS!!
YOU HAVE TO GO AFTER THE REAL ONE!!!
ALL RIGHT!! BUT WHERE IS THE REAL ONE, EH?!
LIKE I SAID, HE'S HIDING SOME-WHERE BEHIND ME, USING THE MIRAGE AS A COVER!!
YAAH!! GAH!!
SWISH
THD
GAH! I SAID IT'S NO USE ATTACKING *THIS* ME!!
ER, I WAS ACTUALLY AIMING AT THE CLAM BEHIND YOU.
ARGH, I'M SO CONFUSED!!

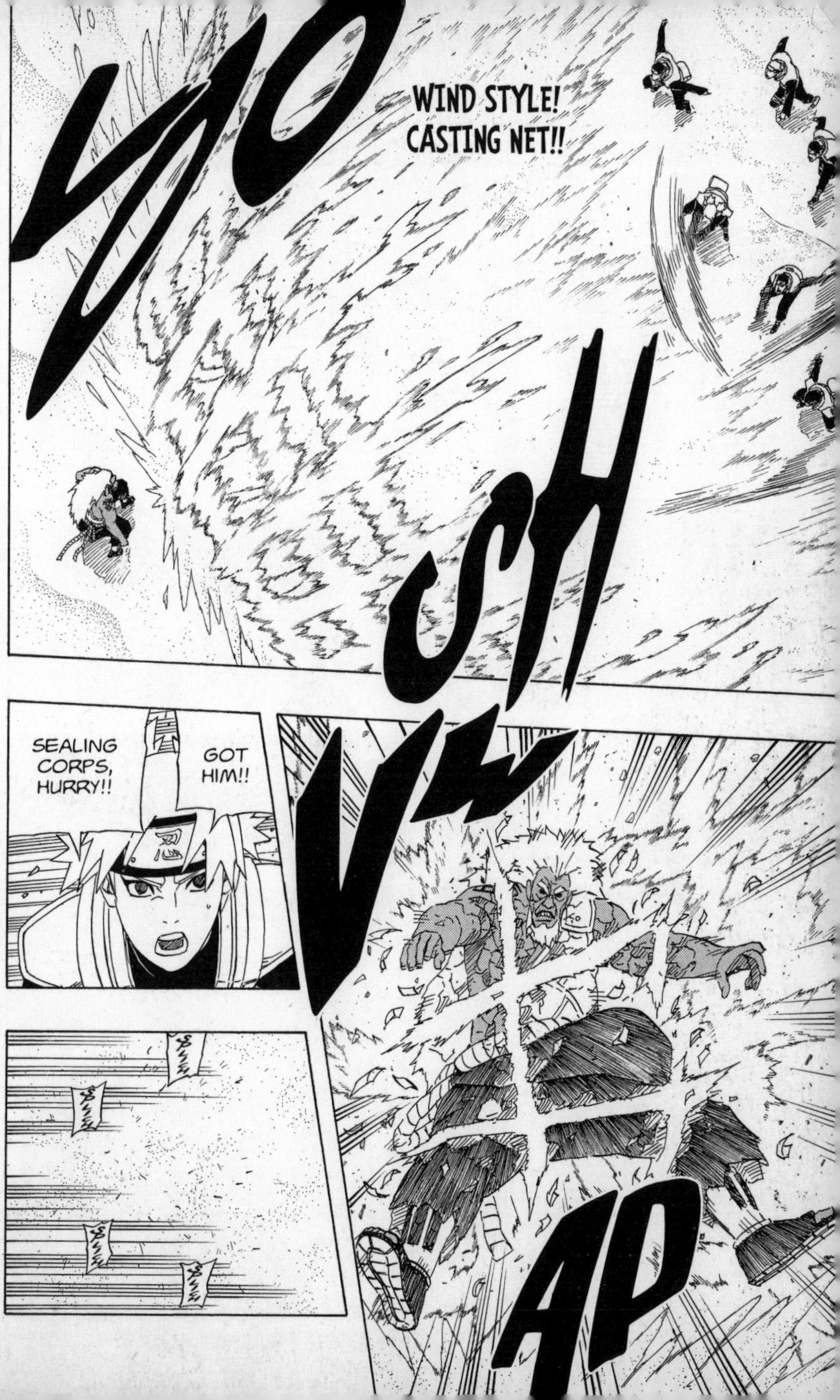
WIND STYLE! CASTING NET!!
GOT HIM!!
SEALING CORPS, HURRY!!

READ THIS WAY

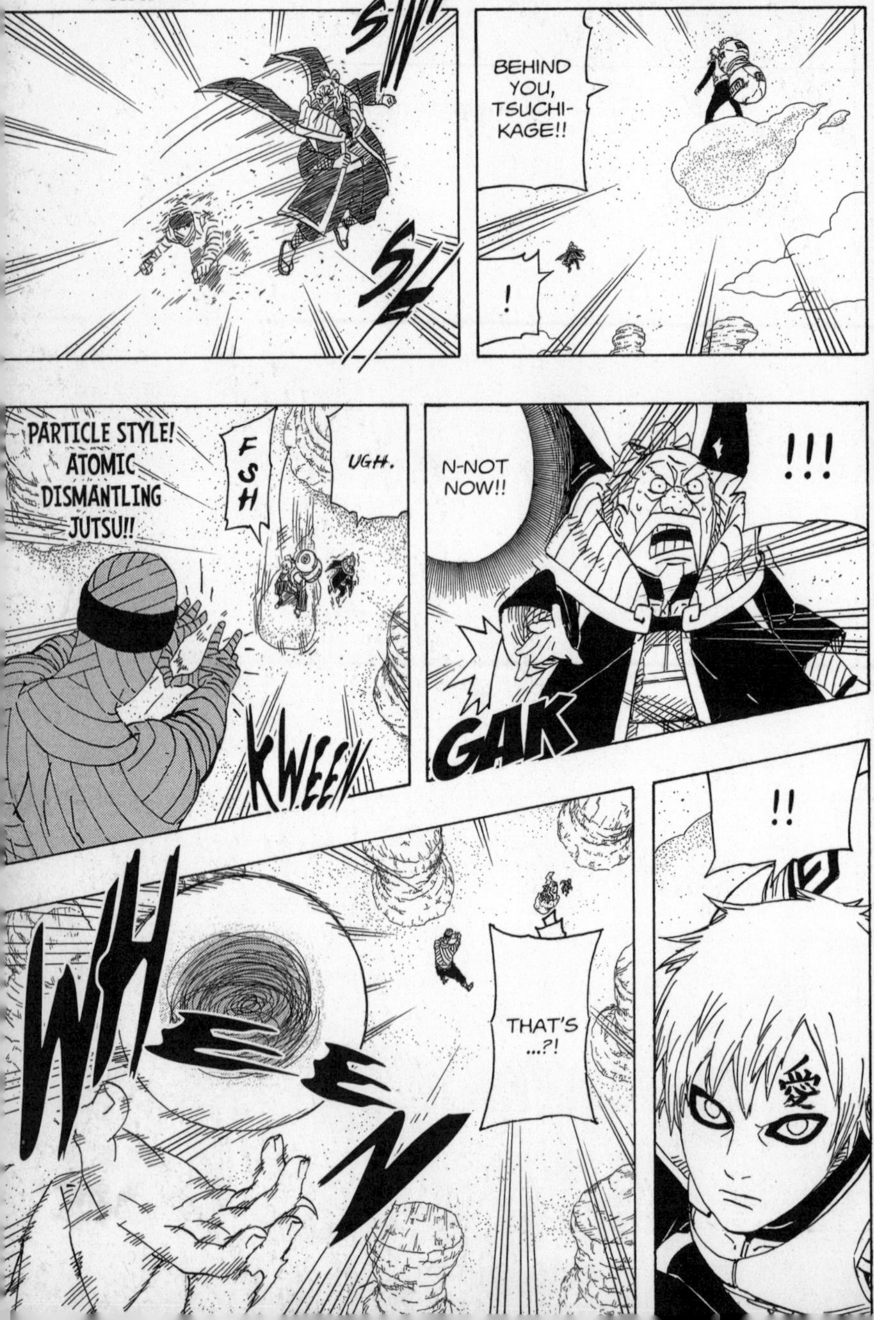
BEHIND YOU, TSUCHI-KAGE!!
!
!!!
N-NOT NOW!!
GAK
UGH.
FSH
PARTICLE STYLE! ATOMIC DISMANTLING JUTSU!!
KWEEN
!!
THAT'S ...?!
WHEEN

NARUTO

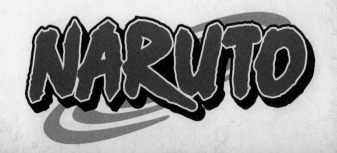

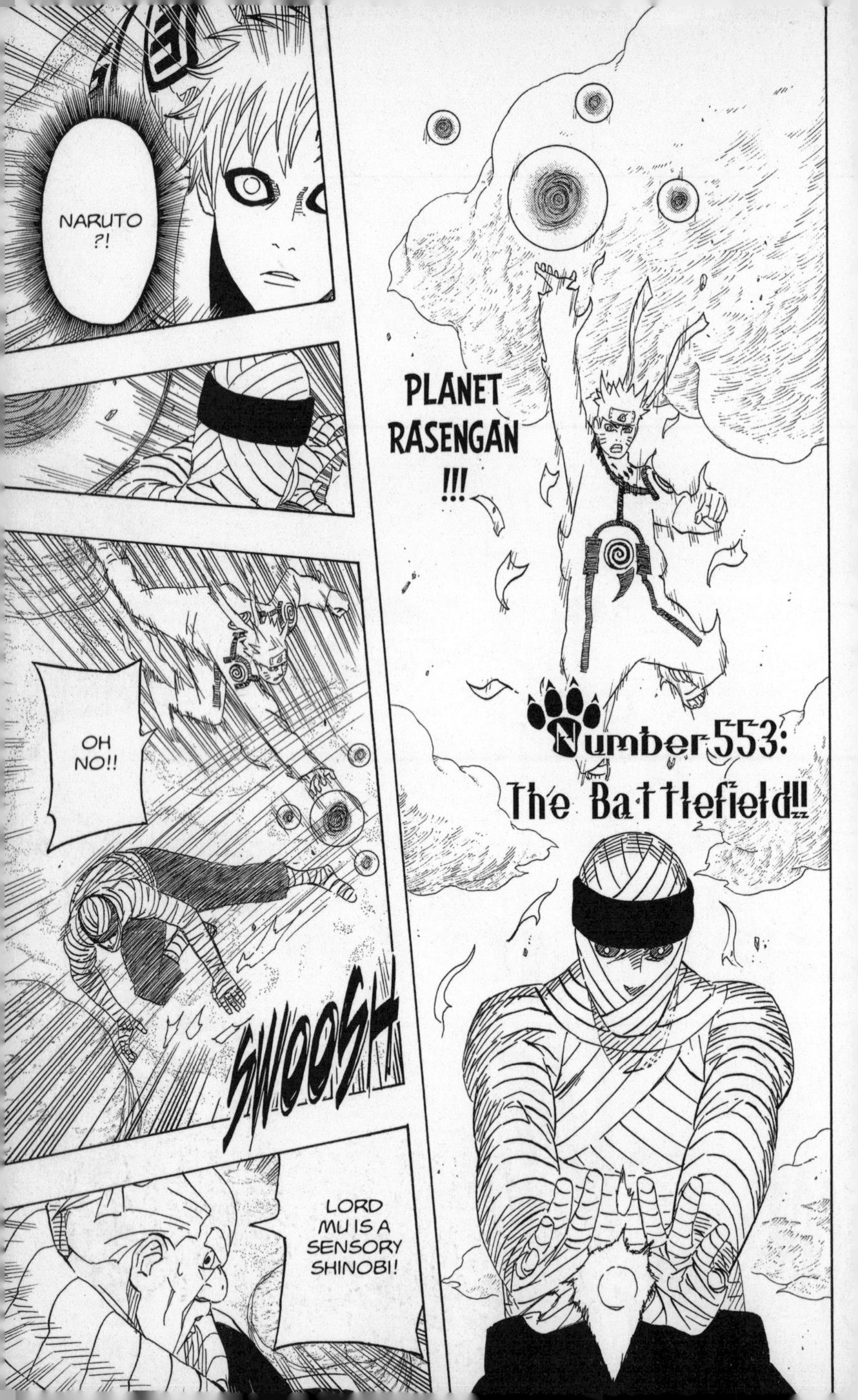
PLANET RASENGAN !!!
Number 553: The Battlefield!!
NARUTO ?!
OH NO!!
SWOOSH
LORD MU IS A SENSORY SHINOBI!

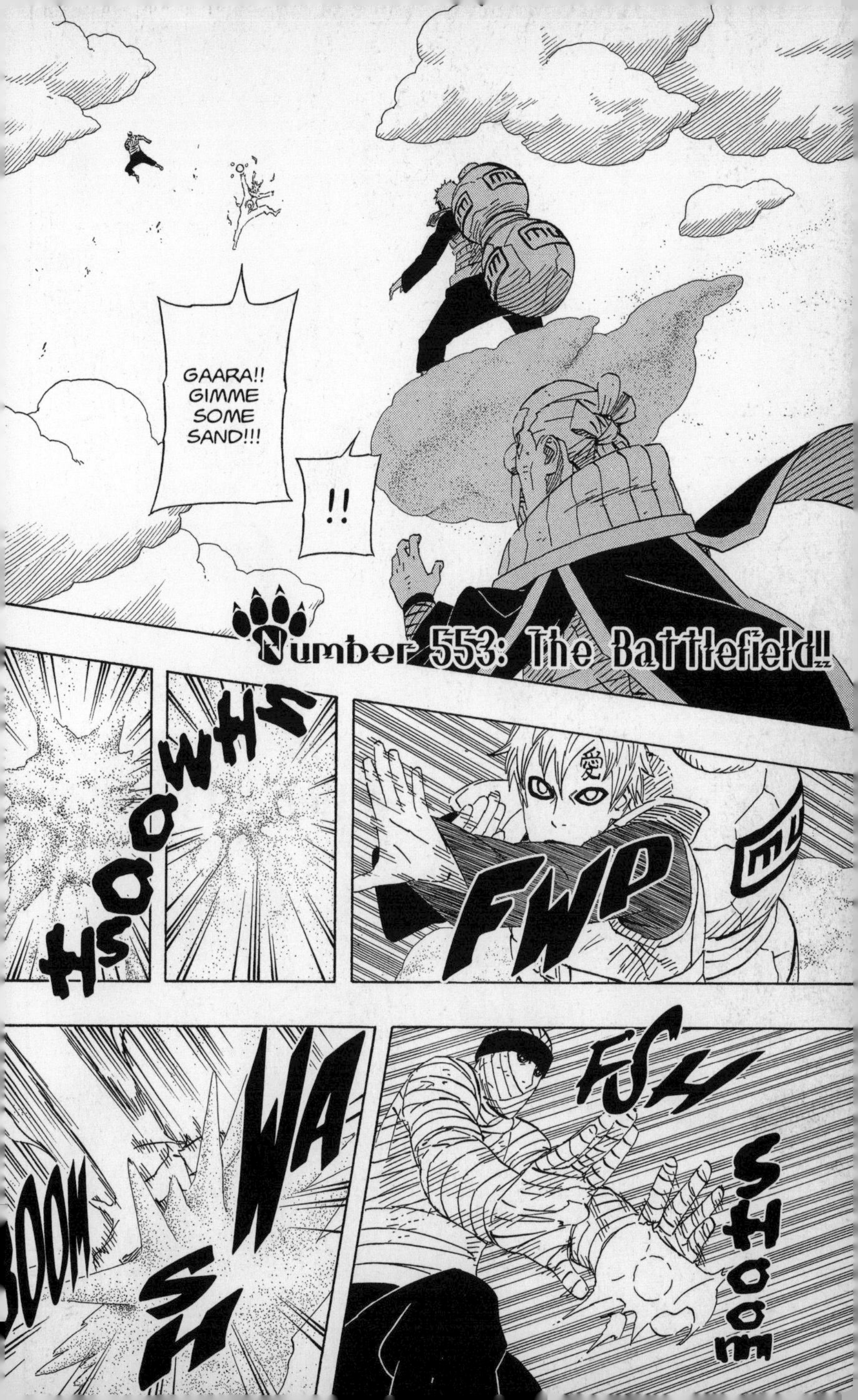
GAARA!! GIMME SOME SAND!!!
!!
Number 553: The Battlefield!!
FWP
SHOOSH
FSH
SHOOM
WASH
BOOM

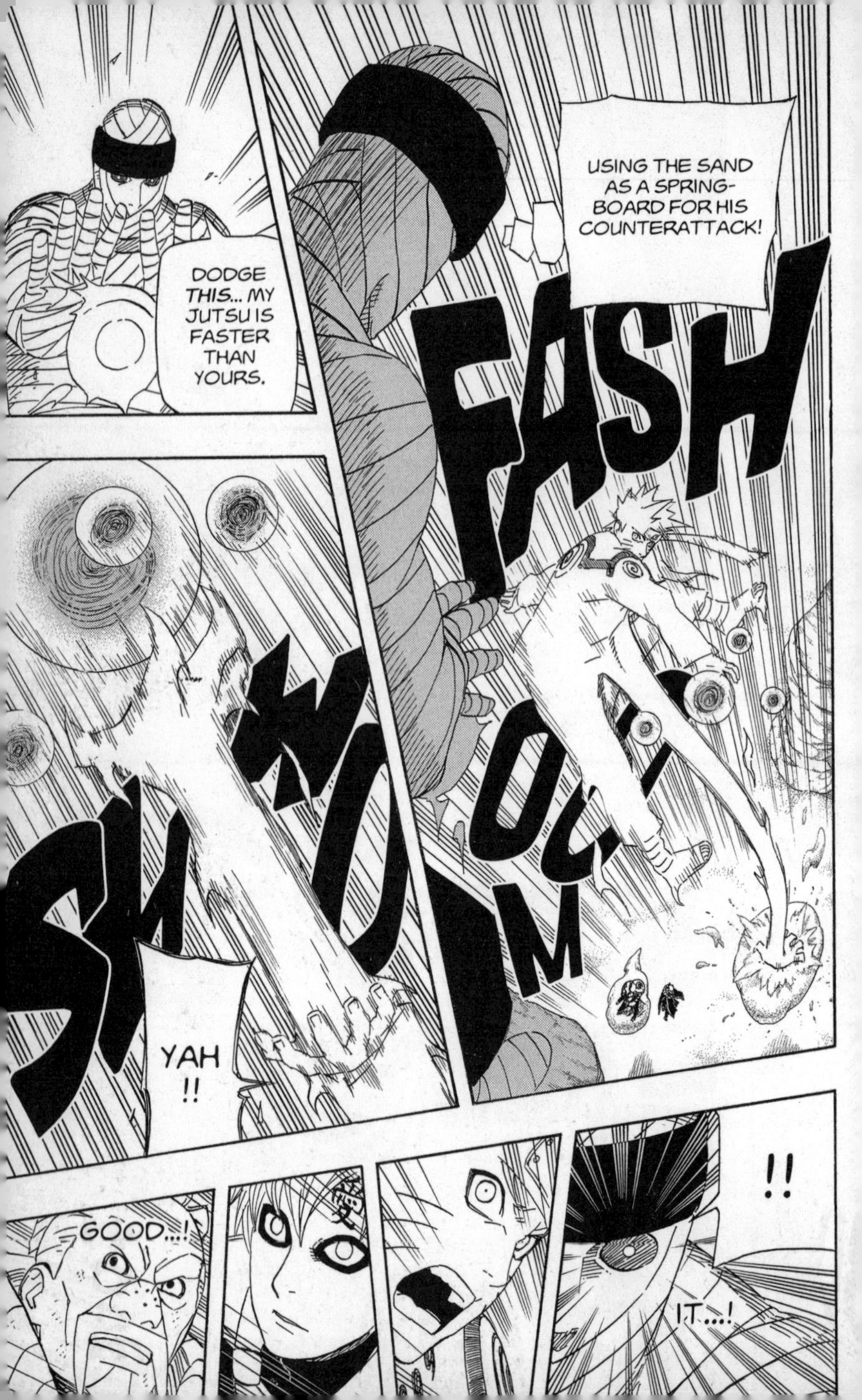
USING THE SAND AS A SPRING-BOARD FOR HIS COUNTERATTACK!
FASH
DODGE THIS... MY JUTSU IS FASTER THAN YOURS.
YAH !!
!!
IT...!
GOOD...!

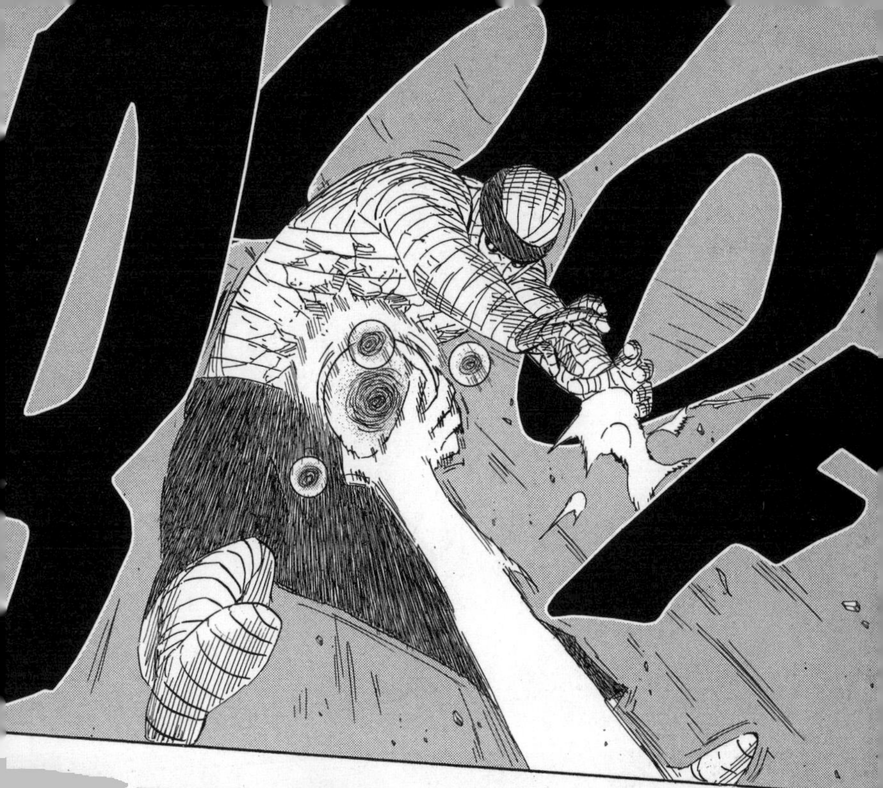

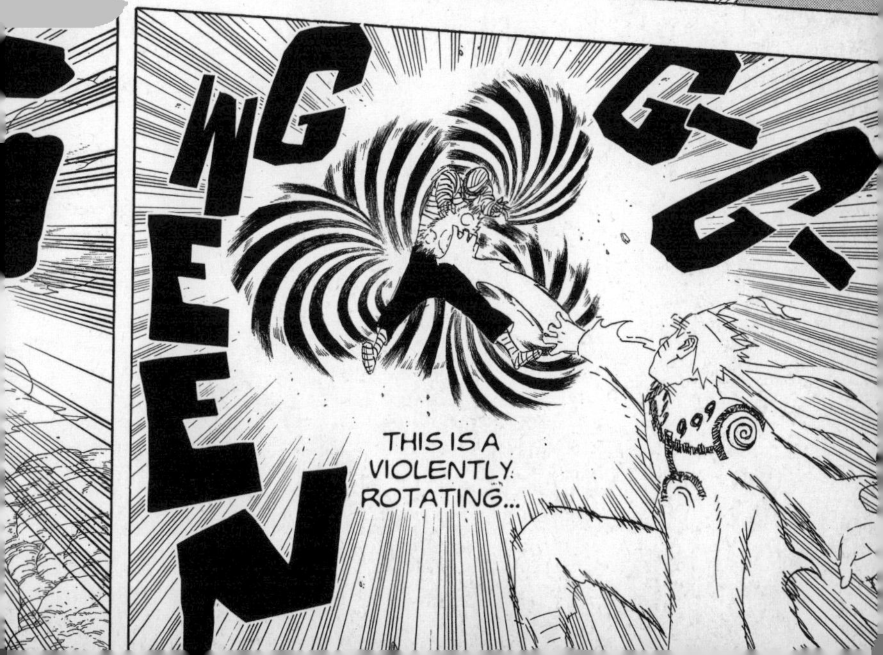
THIS IS A VIOLENTLY ROTATING...

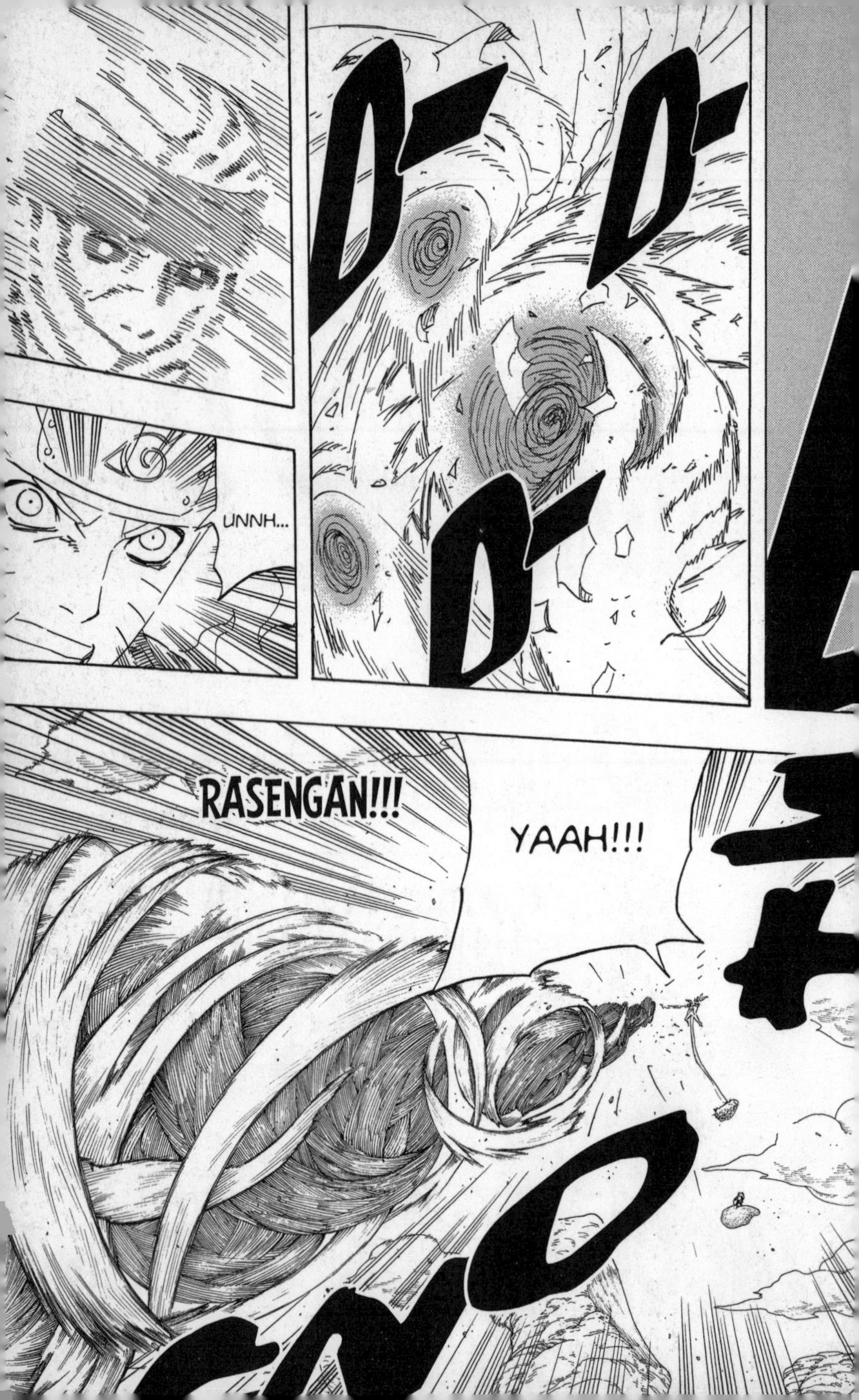
D-D-D-
UNNH...
YAAH!!!
RASENGAN!!!

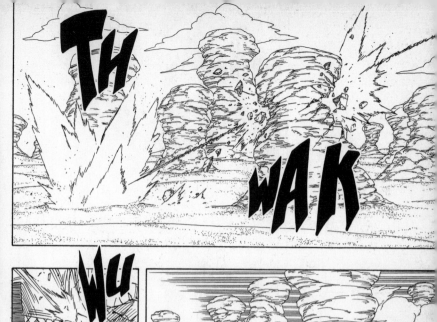

TH

WAK

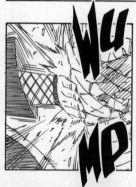

WUMP

T-D T-D T-D T-D T-D T-D T-D T-D

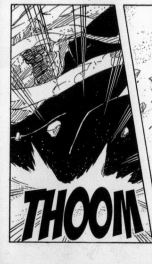

THOOM

EARTH STYLE! BOULDER JUTSU!!

WUMP

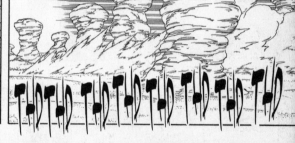

WUMP WUMP

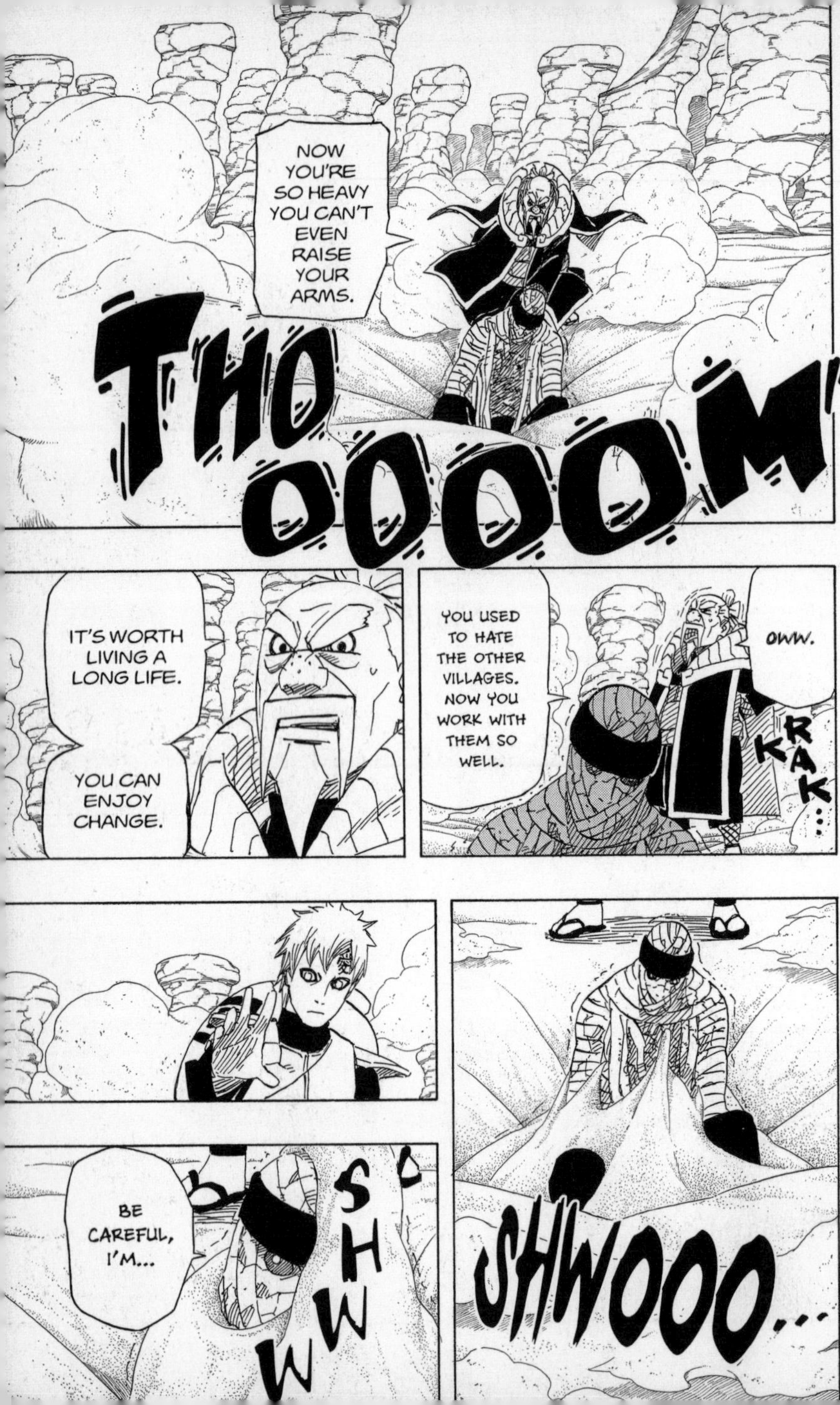
NOW YOU'RE SO HEAVY YOU CAN'T EVEN RAISE YOUR ARMS.
THOOOOOM
OWW.
YOU USED TO HATE THE OTHER VILLAGES. NOW YOU WORK WITH THEM SO WELL.
KRAK...
IT'S WORTH LIVING A LONG LIFE.
YOU CAN ENJOY CHANGE.
SHWOOO...
BE CAREFUL, I'M...
SHWW

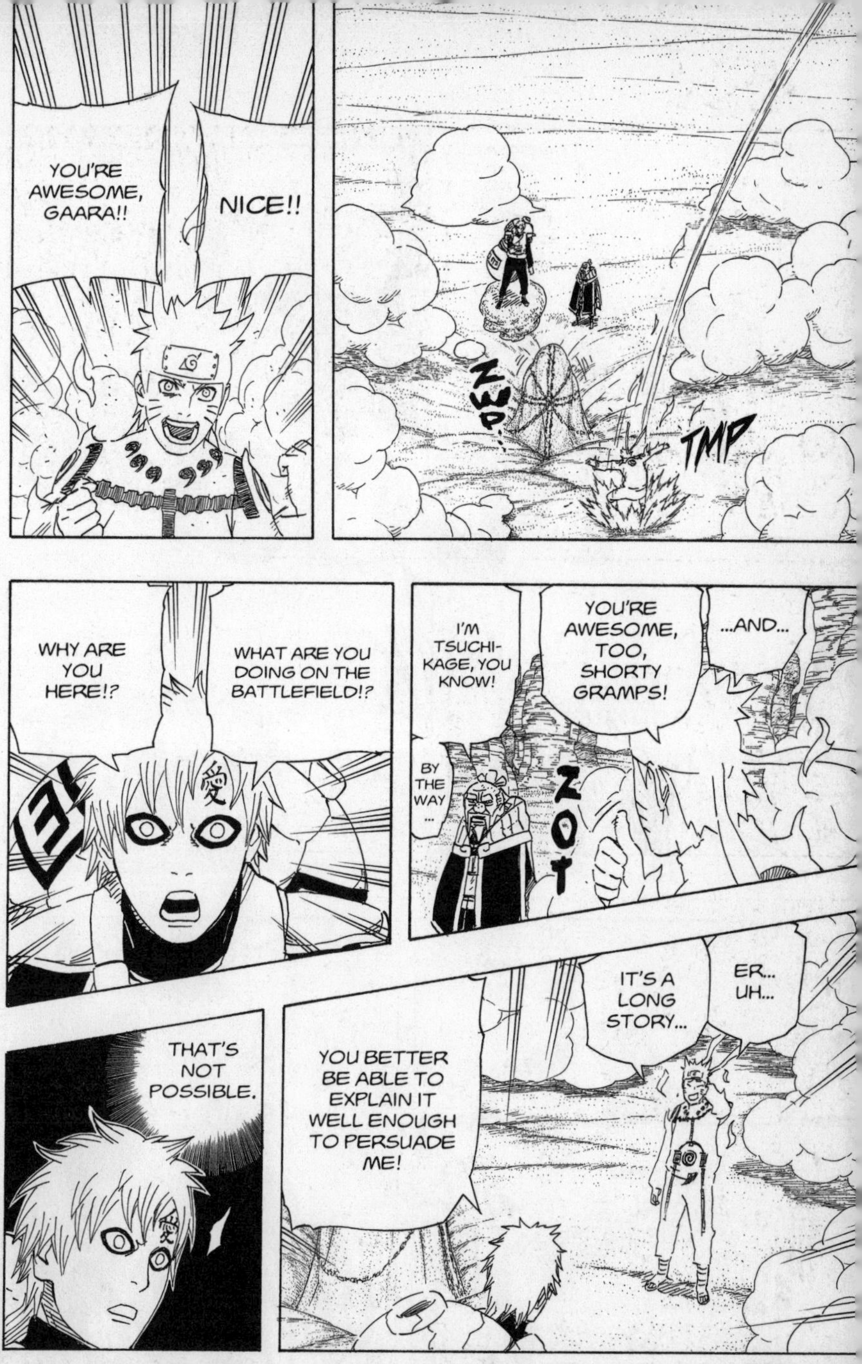
ZWP
TMP
NICE!!
YOU'RE AWESOME, GAARA!!
...AND...
YOU'RE AWESOME, TOO, SHORTY GRAMPS!
I'M TSUCHIKAGE, YOU KNOW!
ZOT
BY THE WAY...
WHAT ARE YOU DOING ON THE BATTLEFIELD!?
WHY ARE YOU HERE!?
ER... UH...
IT'S A LONG STORY...
YOU BETTER BE ABLE TO EXPLAIN IT WELL ENOUGH TO PERSUADE ME!
THAT'S NOT POSSIBLE.

READ THIS WAY

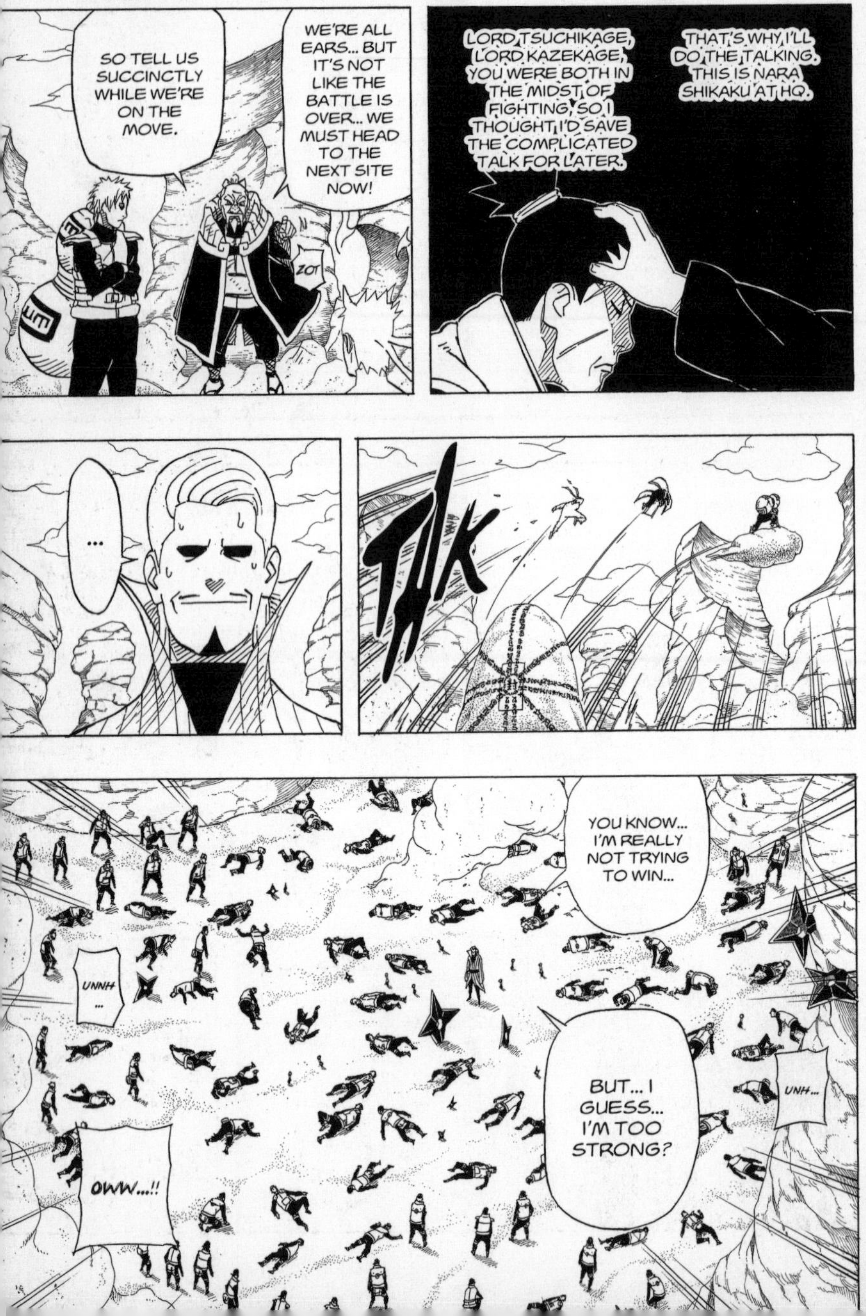
THAT'S WHY I'LL DO THE TALKING. THIS IS NARA SHIKAKU AT HQ.
LORD TSUCHIKAGE, LORD KAZEKAGE, YOU WERE BOTH IN THE MIDST OF FIGHTING, SO I THOUGHT I'D SAVE THE COMPLICATED TALK FOR LATER.
WE'RE ALL EARS... BUT IT'S NOT LIKE THE BATTLE IS OVER... WE MUST HEAD TO THE NEXT SITE NOW!
SO TELL US SUCCINCTLY WHILE WE'RE ON THE MOVE.
ZOT
TAK
...
YOU KNOW... I'M REALLY NOT TRYING TO WIN...
BUT... I GUESS... I'M TOO STRONG?
UNNH...
UNNH...
OWW...!!

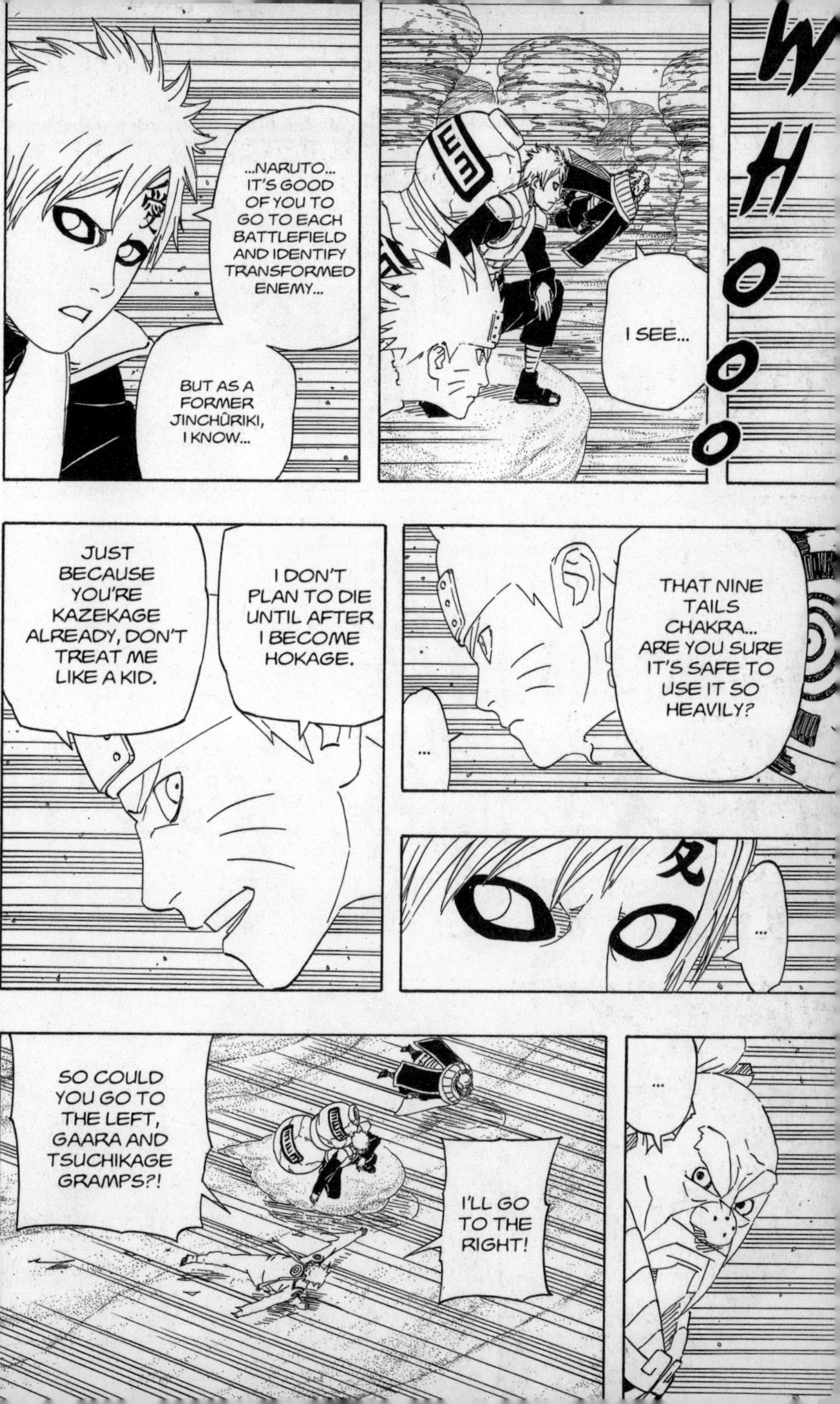
WHOOOOO
I SEE...
...NARUTO... IT'S GOOD OF YOU TO GO TO EACH BATTLEFIELD AND IDENTIFY TRANSFORMED ENEMY...
BUT AS A FORMER JINCHŪRIKI, I KNOW...
THAT NINE TAILS CHAKRA... ARE YOU SURE IT'S SAFE TO USE IT SO HEAVILY?
...
...
I DON'T PLAN TO DIE UNTIL AFTER I BECOME HOKAGE.
JUST BECAUSE YOU'RE KAZEKAGE ALREADY, DON'T TREAT ME LIKE A KID.
...
SO COULD YOU GO TO THE LEFT, GAARA AND TSUCHIKAGE GRAMPS?!
I'LL GO TO THE RIGHT!

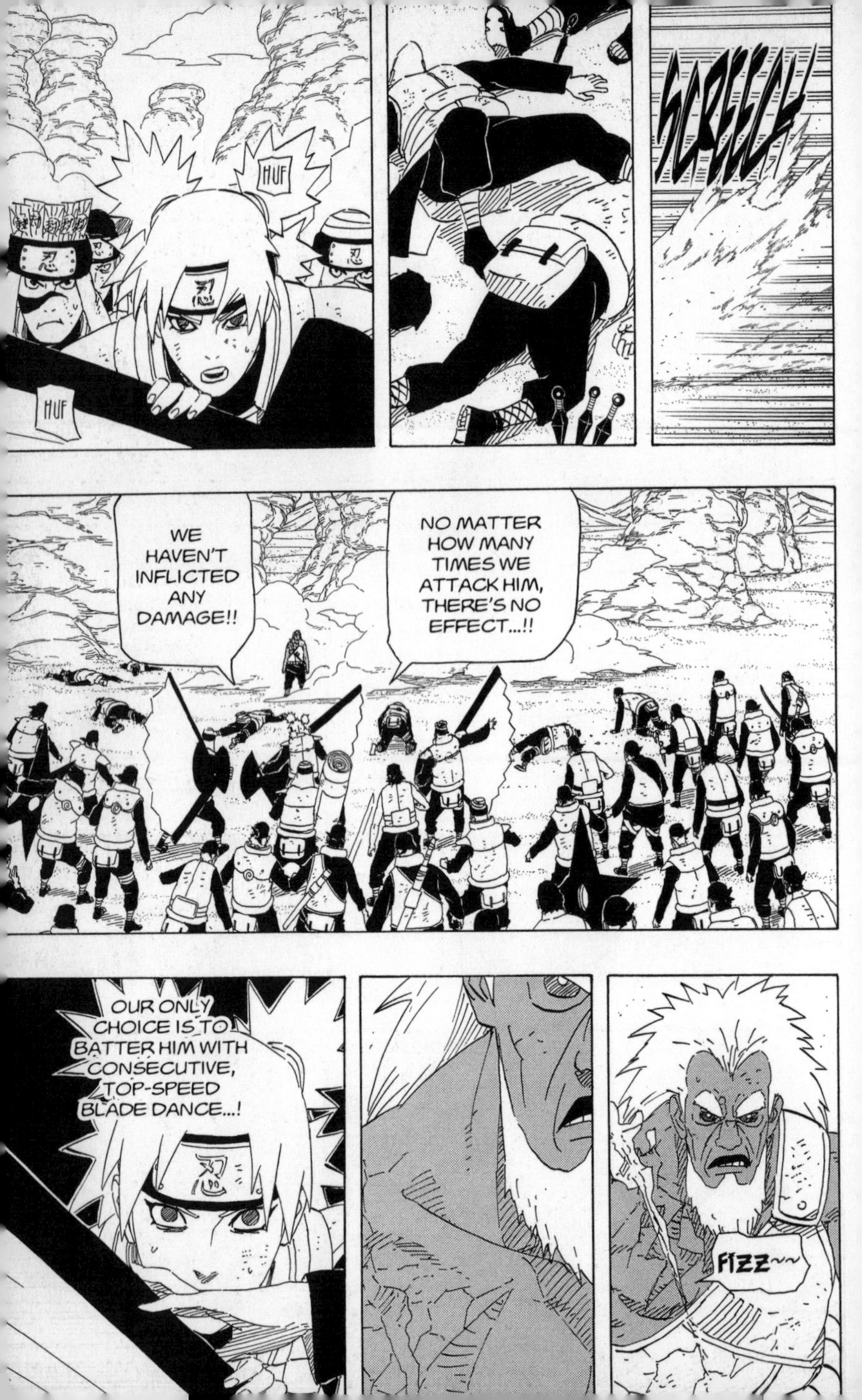
SCREECH
HUF
HUF
NO MATTER HOW MANY TIMES WE ATTACK HIM, THERE'S NO EFFECT...!!
WE HAVEN'T INFLICTED ANY DAMAGE!!
FIZZ~~
OUR ONLY CHOICE IS TO BATTER HIM WITH CONSECUTIVE, TOP-SPEED BLADE DANCE...!

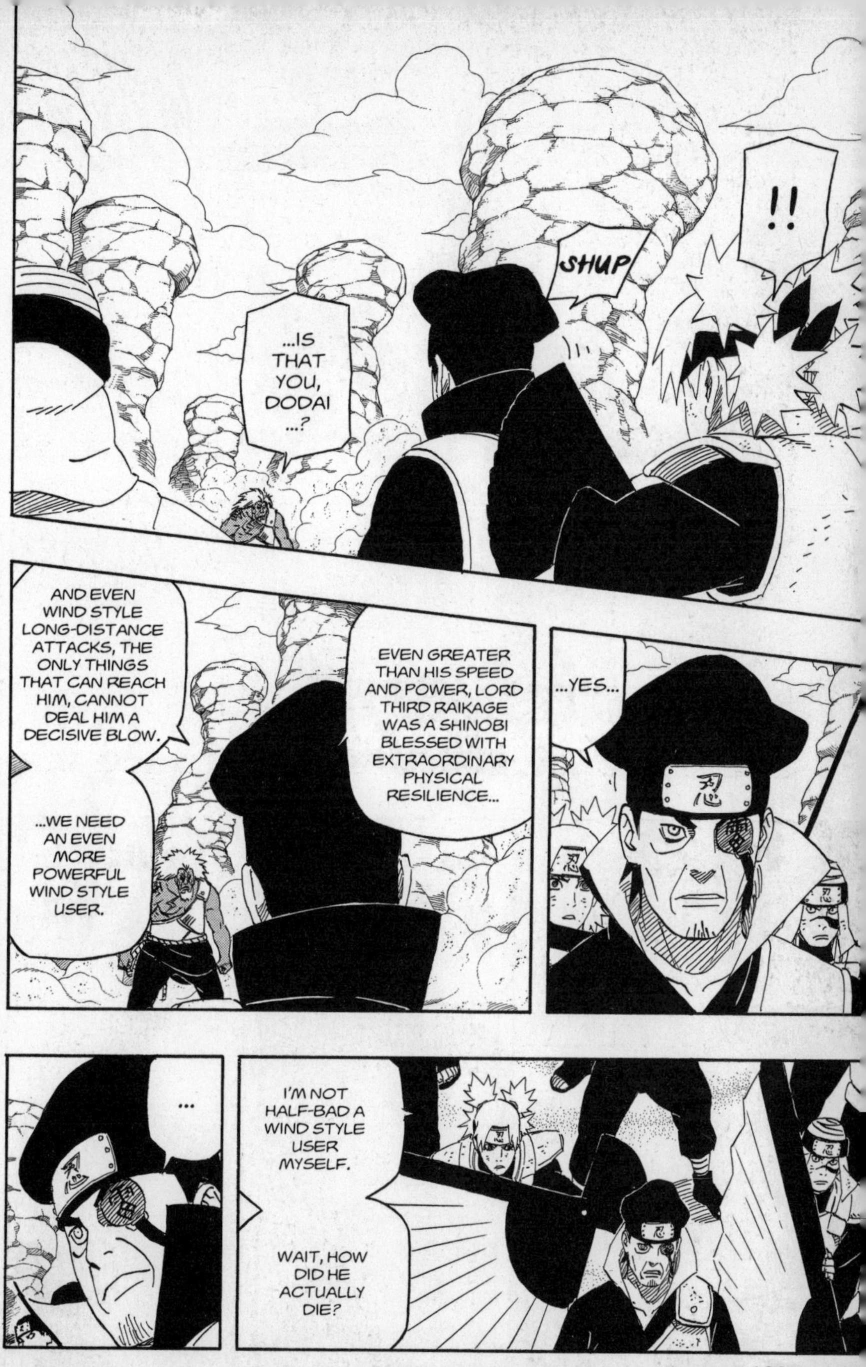
!!
SHUP
...IS THAT YOU, DODAI ...?
...YES...
EVEN GREATER THAN HIS SPEED AND POWER, LORD THIRD RAIKAGE WAS A SHINOBI BLESSED WITH EXTRAORDINARY PHYSICAL RESILIENCE...
AND EVEN WIND STYLE LONG-DISTANCE ATTACKS, THE ONLY THINGS THAT CAN REACH HIM, CANNOT DEAL HIM A DECISIVE BLOW.
...WE NEED AN EVEN MORE POWERFUL WIND STYLE USER.
I'M NOT HALF-BAD A WIND STYLE USER MYSELF.
WAIT, HOW DID HE ACTUALLY DIE?
...

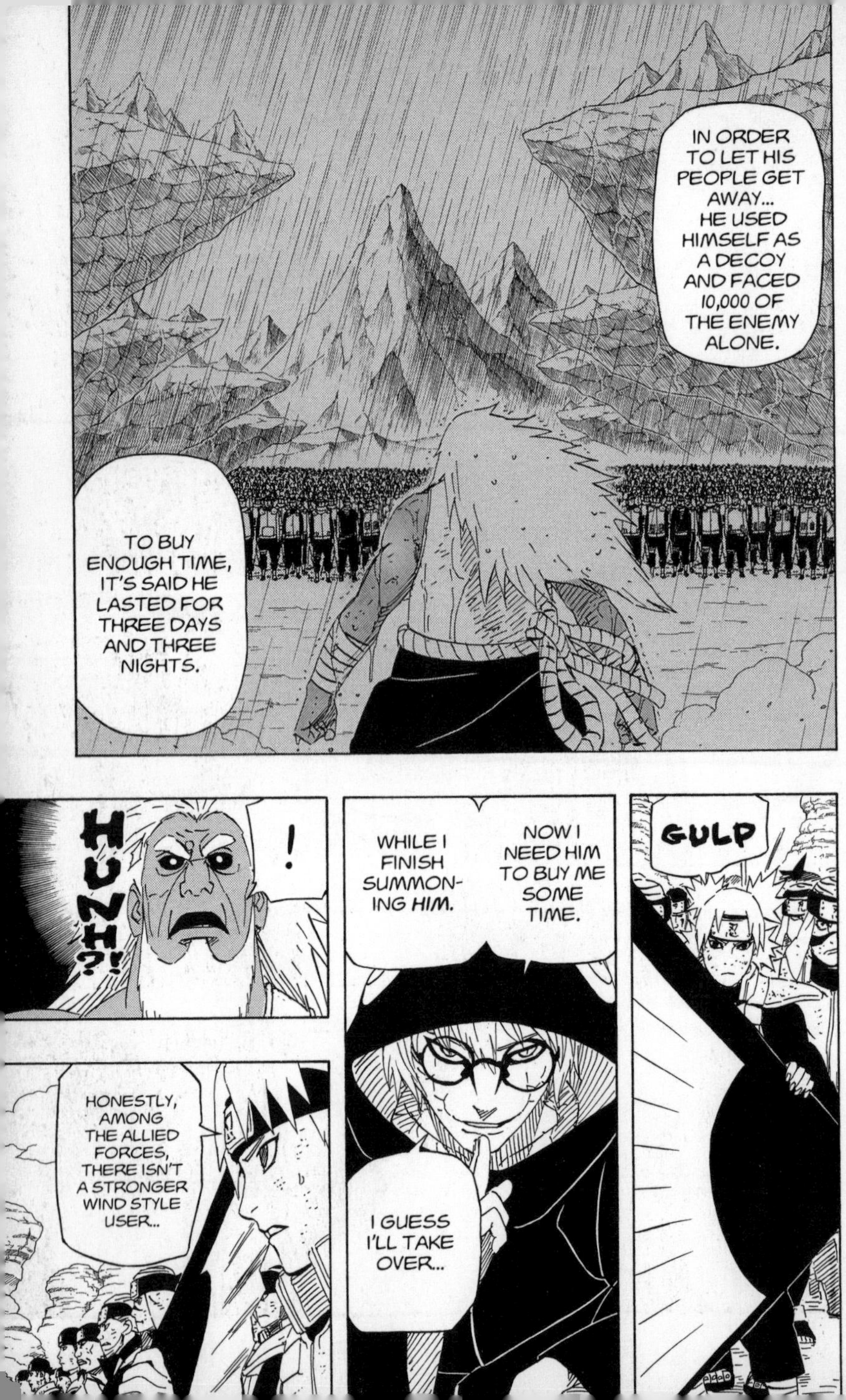
IN ORDER TO LET HIS PEOPLE GET AWAY... HE USED HIMSELF AS A DECOY AND FACED 10,000 OF THE ENEMY ALONE.
TO BUY ENOUGH TIME, IT'S SAID HE LASTED FOR THREE DAYS AND THREE NIGHTS.
GULP
NOW I NEED HIM TO BUY ME SOME TIME.
WHILE I FINISH SUMMON-ING HIM.
I GUESS I'LL TAKE OVER...
!
HUNH?!
HONESTLY, AMONG THE ALLIED FORCES, THERE ISN'T A STRONGER WIND STYLE USER...

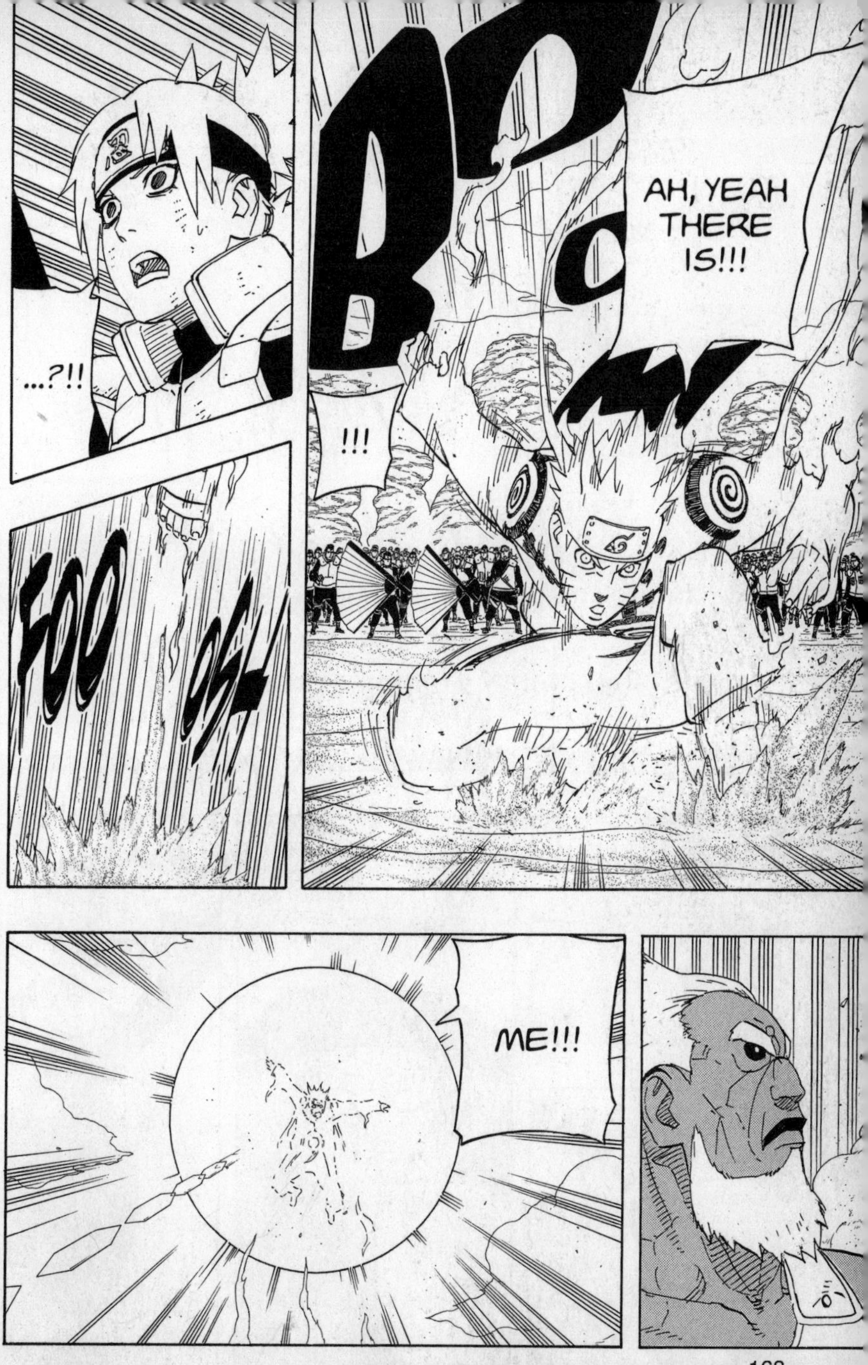
BOOM
AH, YEAH THERE IS!!!
!!!
...?!!
FOOOSH
ME!!!

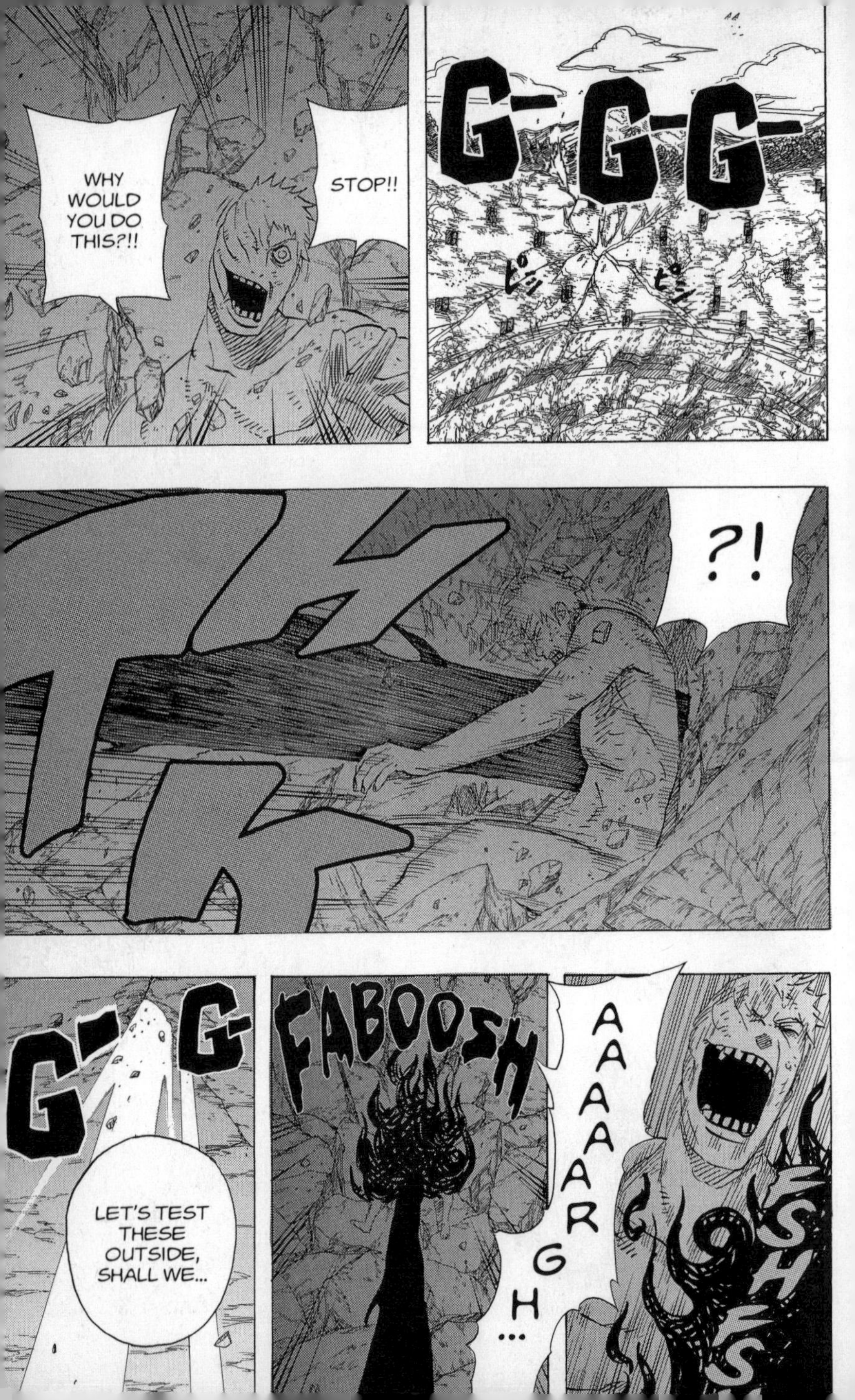
G-G-G-
STOP!!
WHY WOULD YOU DO THIS?!!
?!
AAAAARGH...
FABOOSH
G-G-
LET'S TEST THESE OUTSIDE, SHALL WE...

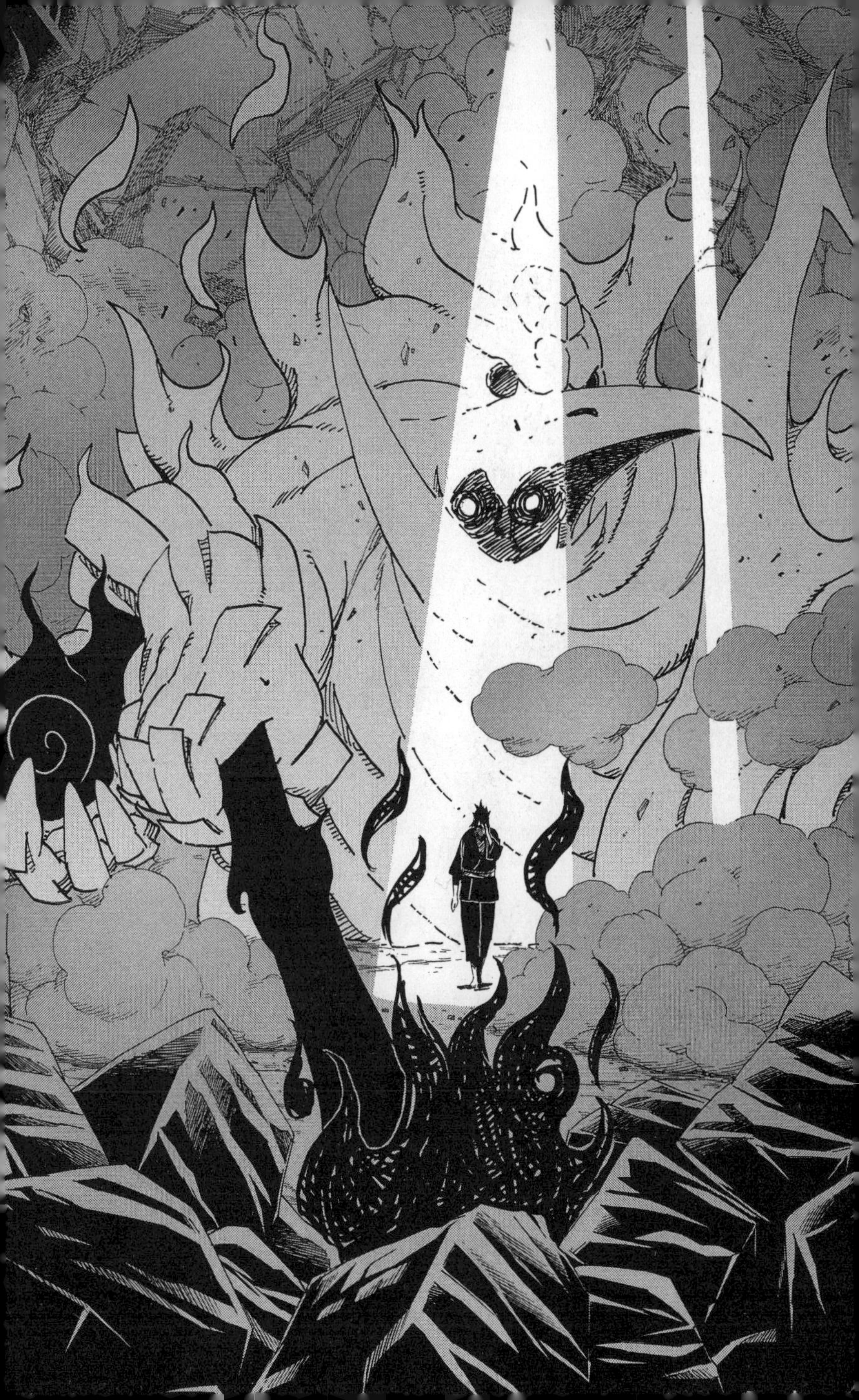

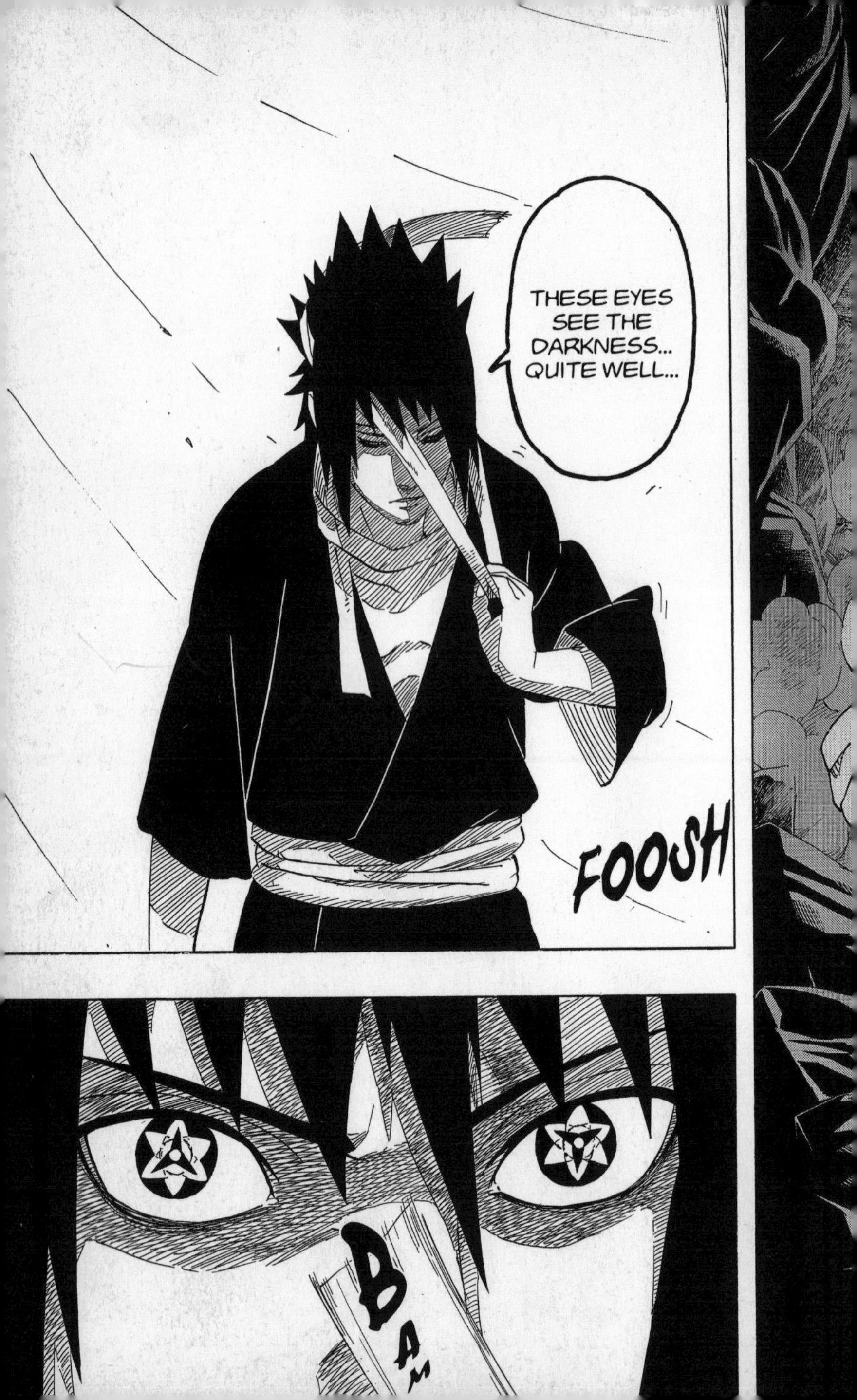
THESE EYES SEE THE DARKNESS... QUITE WELL...
FOOSH
BAM

NARUTO

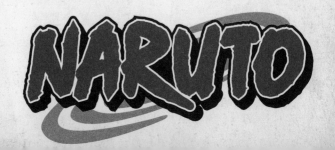

Number 554: The Rasen-Shuriken Limit!!

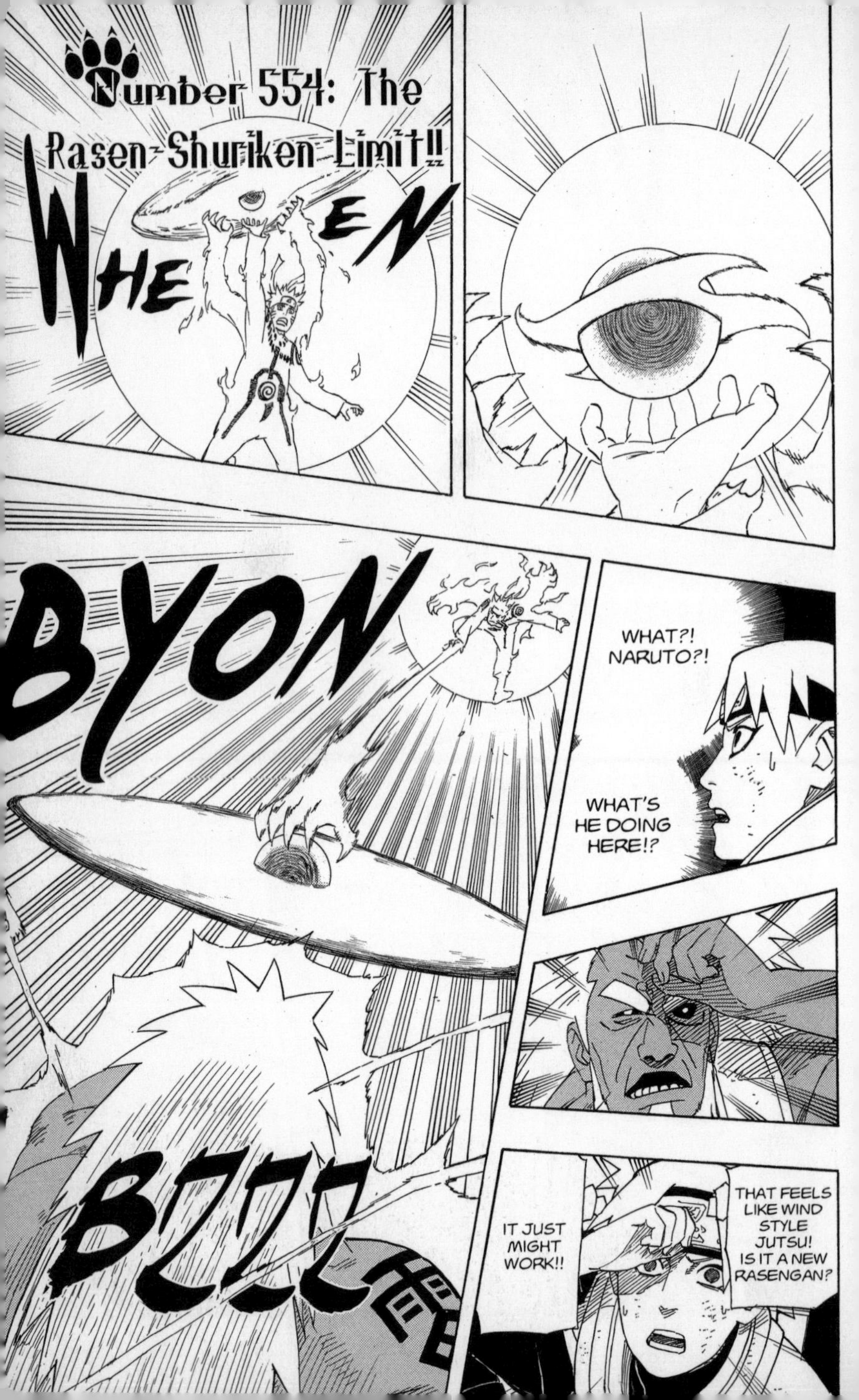
WHEEN
WHAT?! NARUTO?!
WHAT'S HE DOING HERE!?
THAT FEELS LIKE WIND STYLE JUTSU! IS IT A NEW RASENGAN?
IT JUST MIGHT WORK!!
BYON
BZZZ

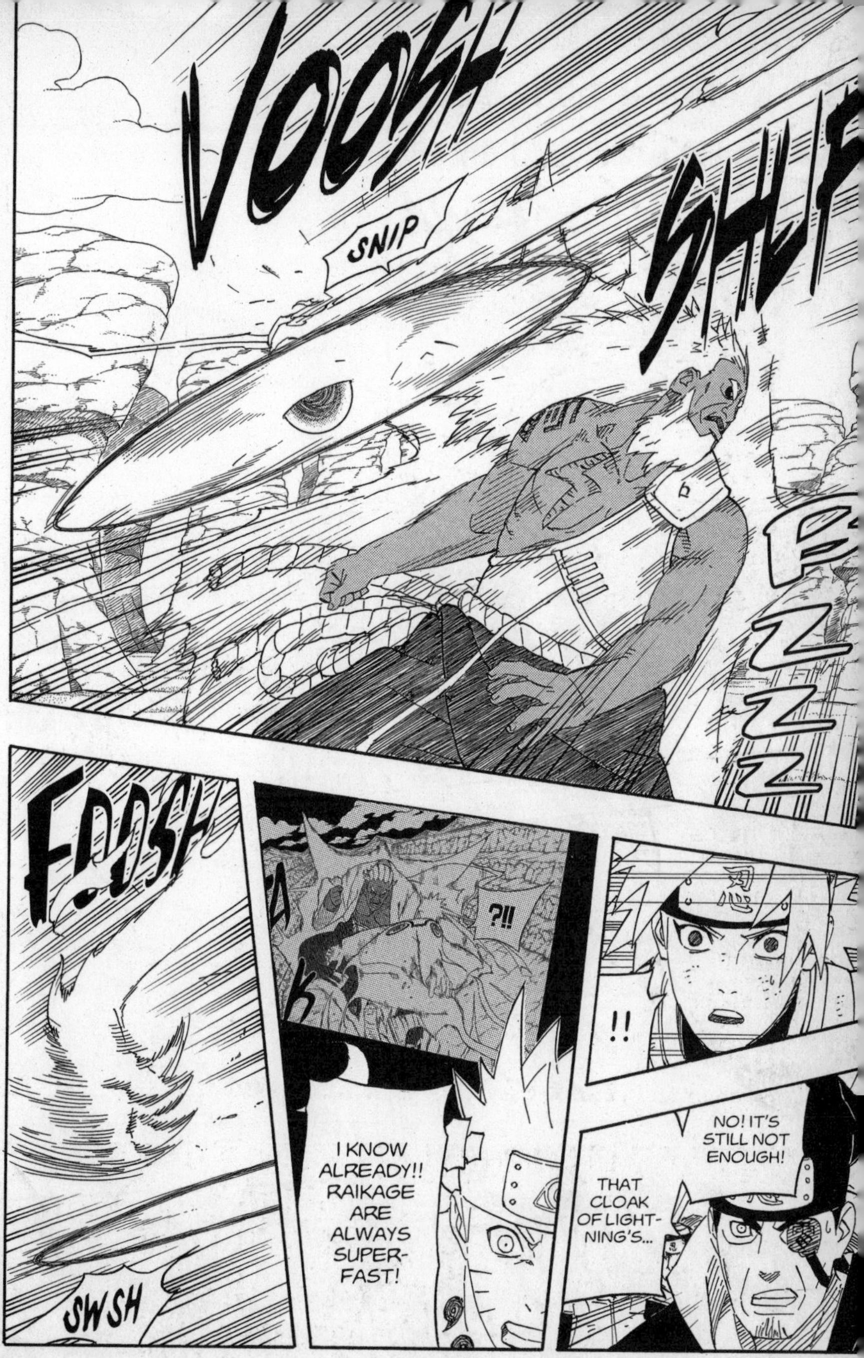
VOOSH
SNIP
BZZZZ
!!
NO! IT'S STILL NOT ENOUGH!
THAT CLOAK OF LIGHT-NING'S...
?!!
I KNOW ALREADY!! RAIKAGE ARE ALWAYS SUPER-FAST!
FOOSH
SWSH

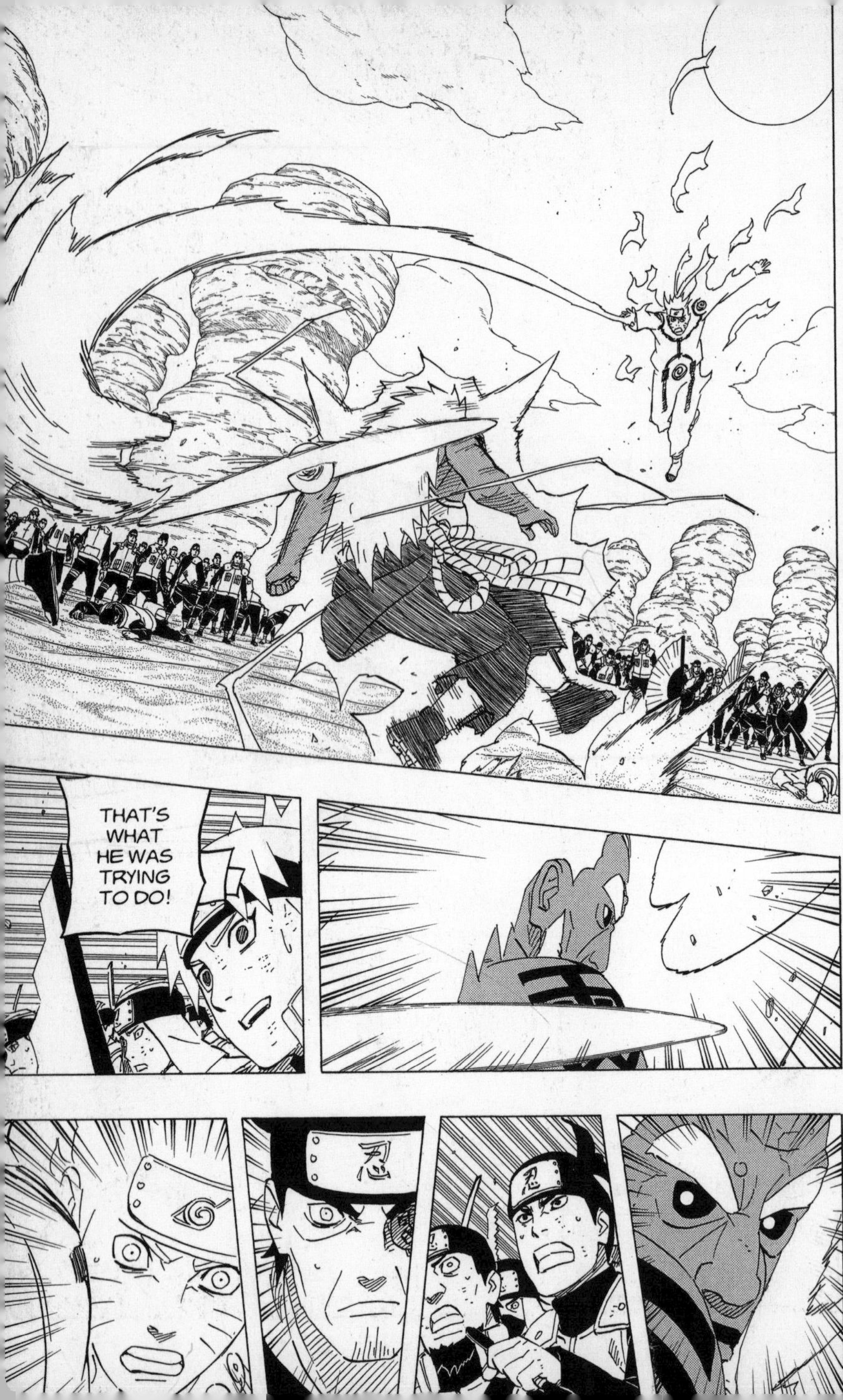
THAT'S WHAT HE WAS TRYING TO DO!

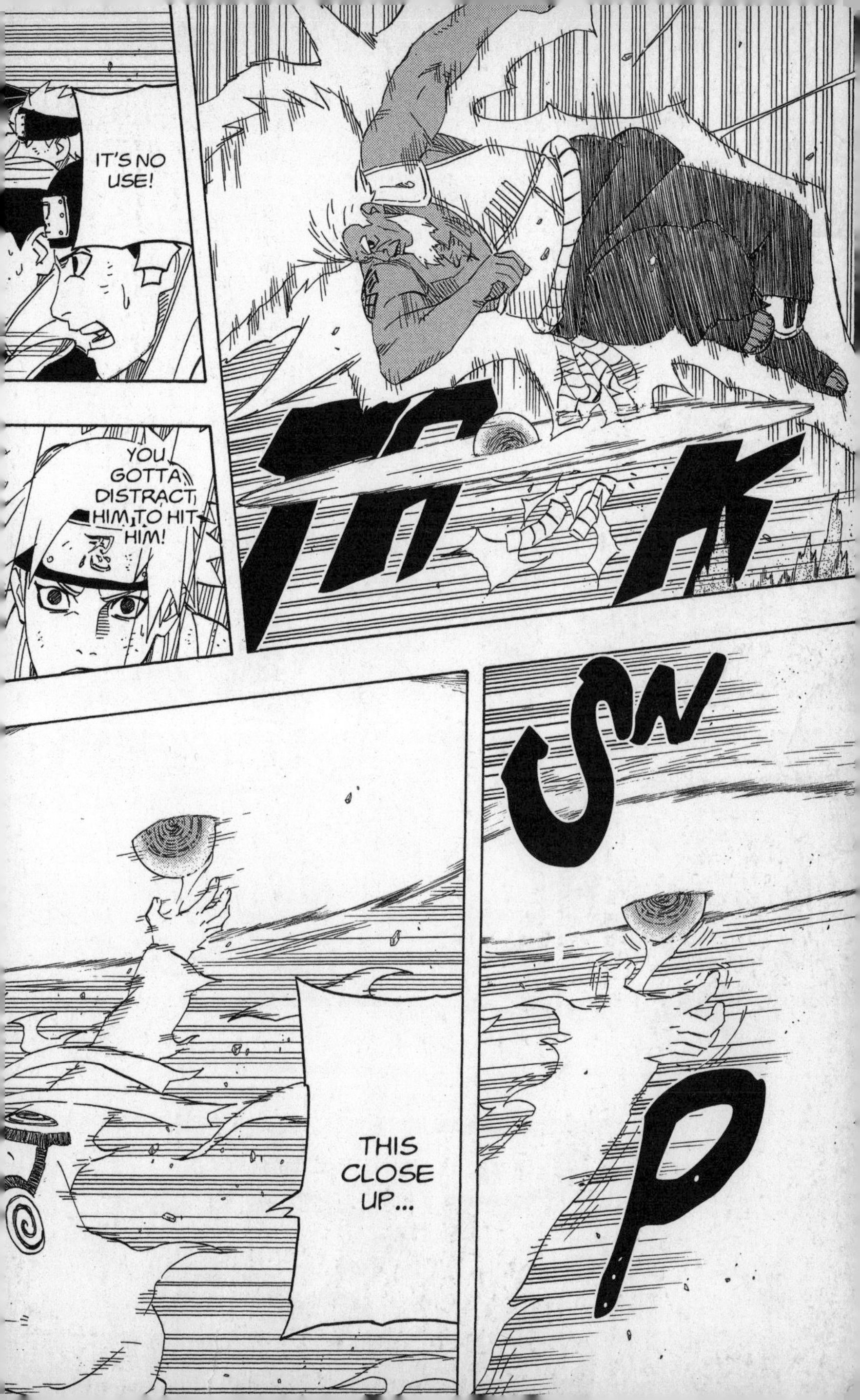
IT'S NO USE!
YOU GOTTA DISTRACT HIM TO HIT HIM!
THIS CLOSE UP...

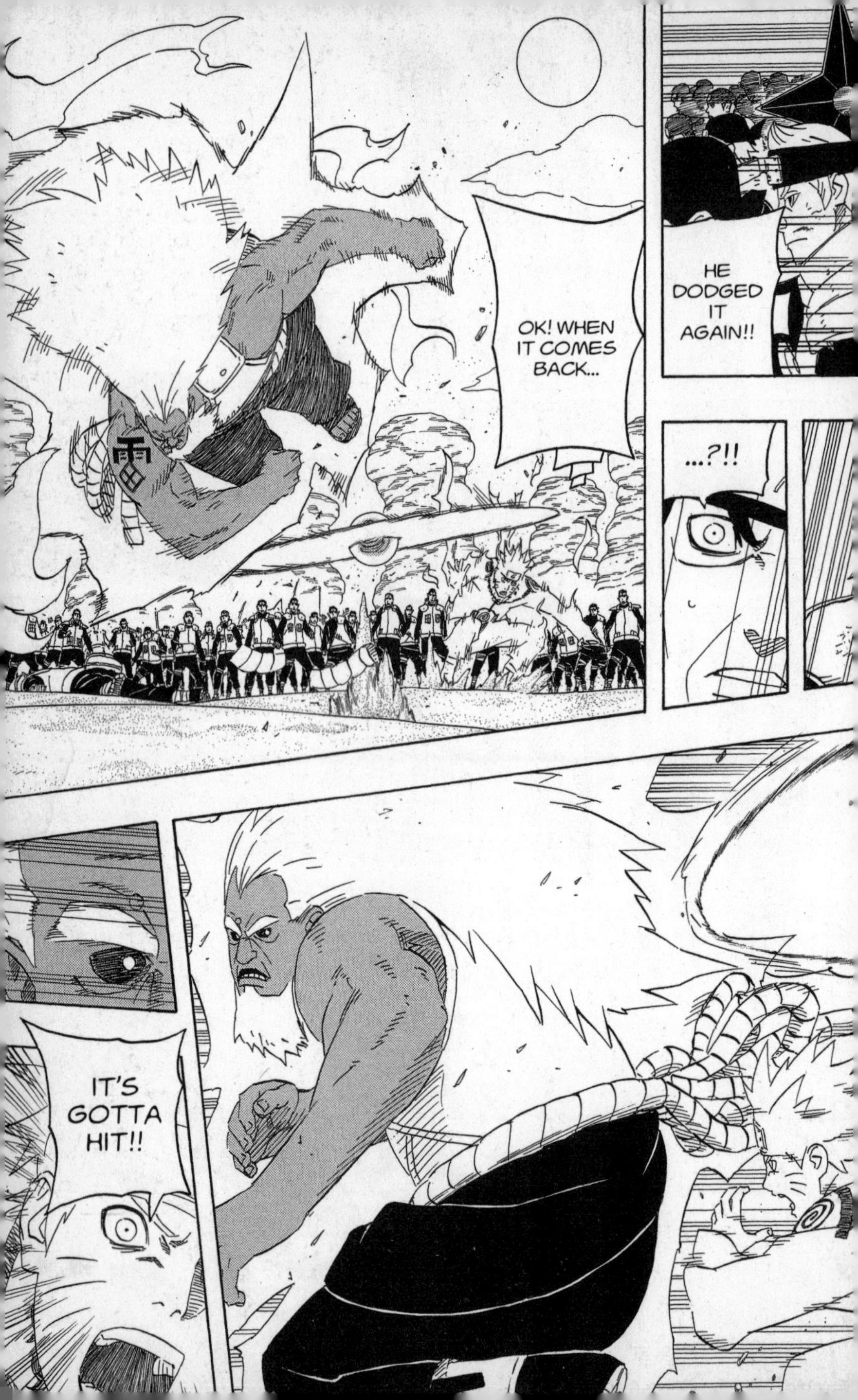
HE DODGED IT AGAIN!!
...?!!
OK! WHEN IT COMES BACK...
IT'S GOTTA HIT!!

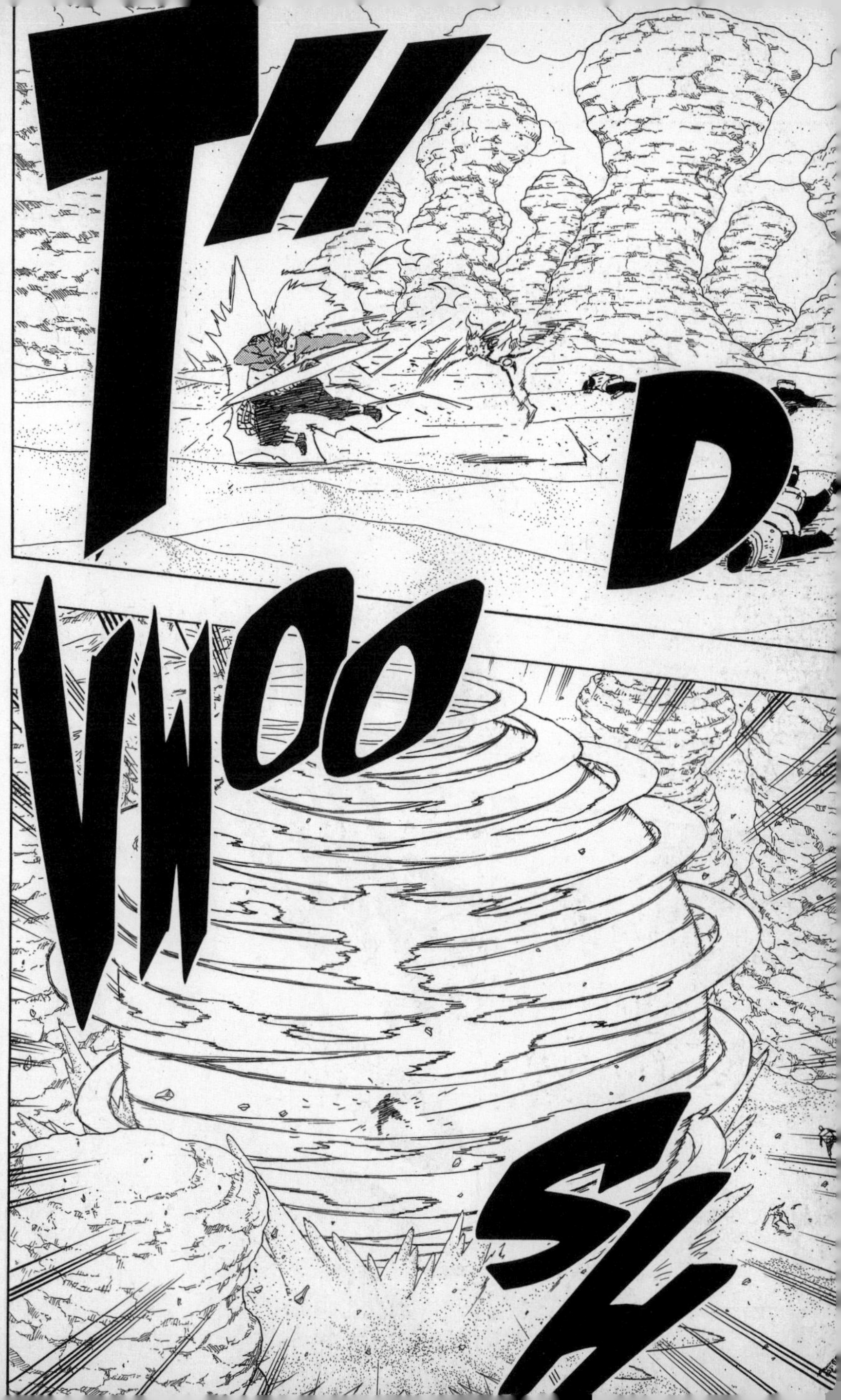
THD
VWOOSH

READ THIS WAY

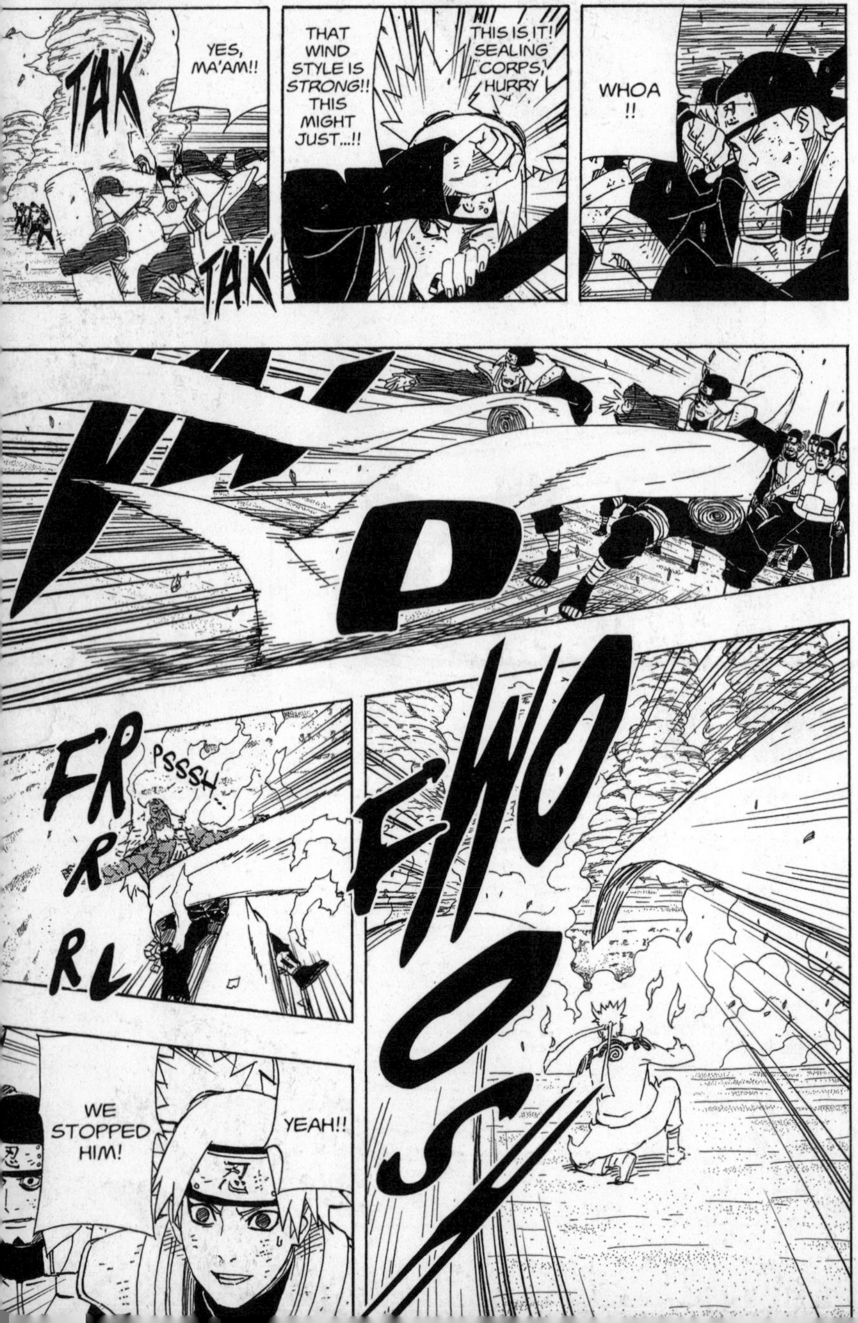
WHOA !!
THIS IS IT! SEALING CORPS, HURRY
THAT WIND STYLE IS STRONG!! THIS MIGHT JUST...!!
TAK
YES, MA'AM!!
TAK
FWOOSH
PSSSH
FRRRL
YEAH!!
WE STOPPED HIM!

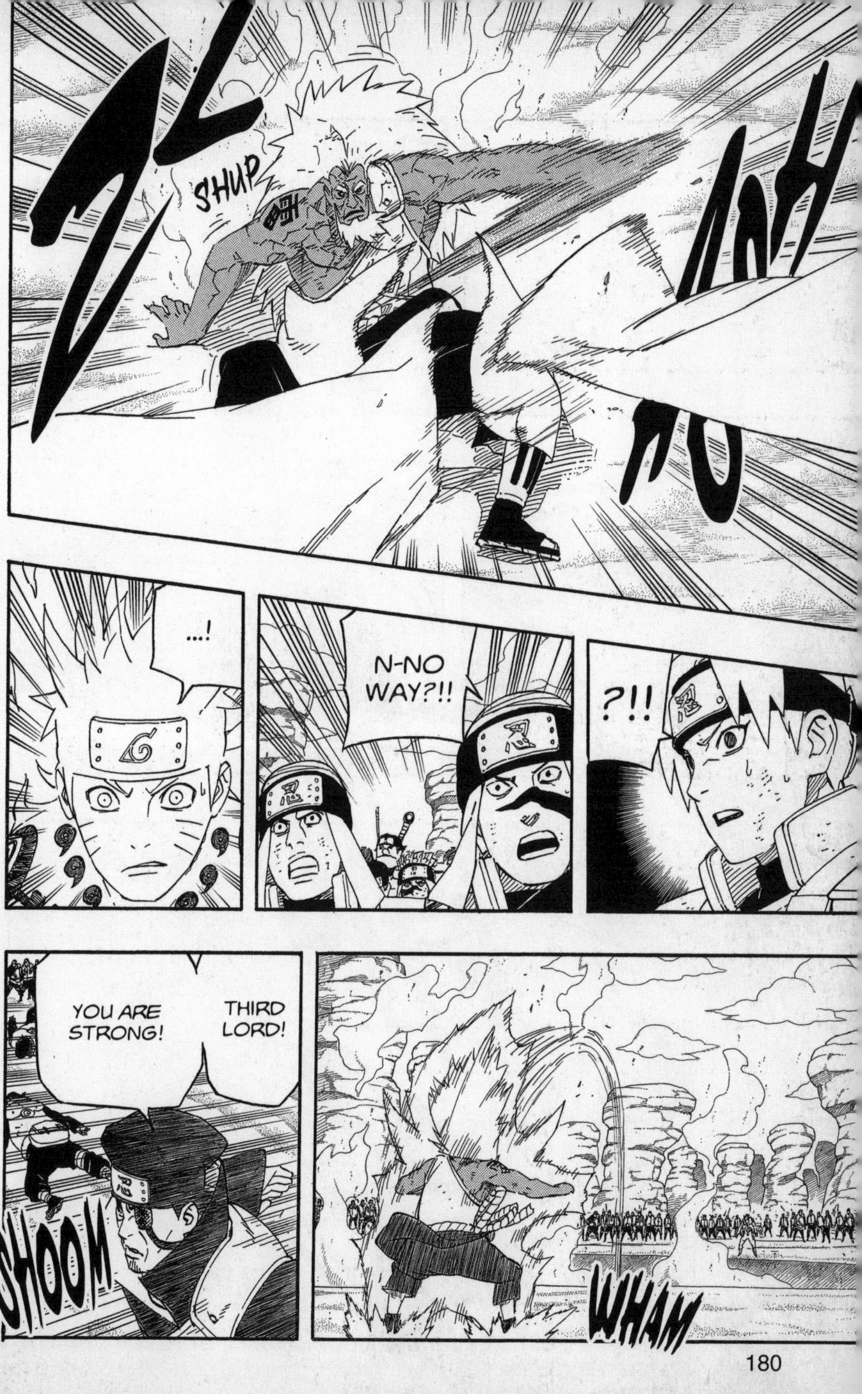
SHUP
?!!
N-NO WAY?!!
...!
WHAM
THIRD LORD!
YOU ARE STRONG!
SHOOM

READ THIS WAY

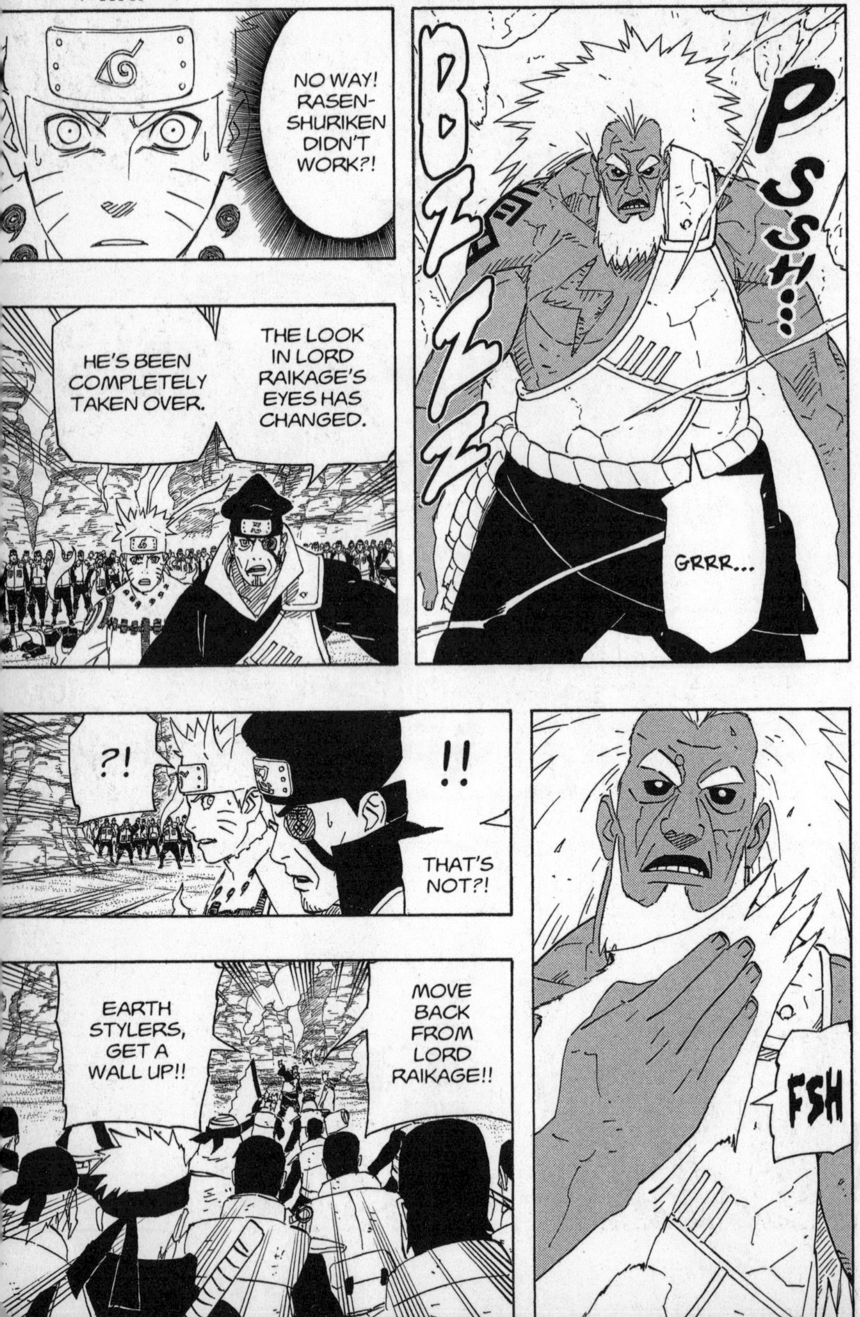
PSSH...
GRRR...
NO WAY! RASEN-SHURIKEN DIDN'T WORK?!
THE LOOK IN LORD RAIKAGE'S EYES HAS CHANGED.
HE'S BEEN COMPLETELY TAKEN OVER.
FSH
!!
THAT'S NOT?!
?!
MOVE BACK FROM LORD RAIKAGE!!
EARTH STYLERS, GET A WALL UP!!

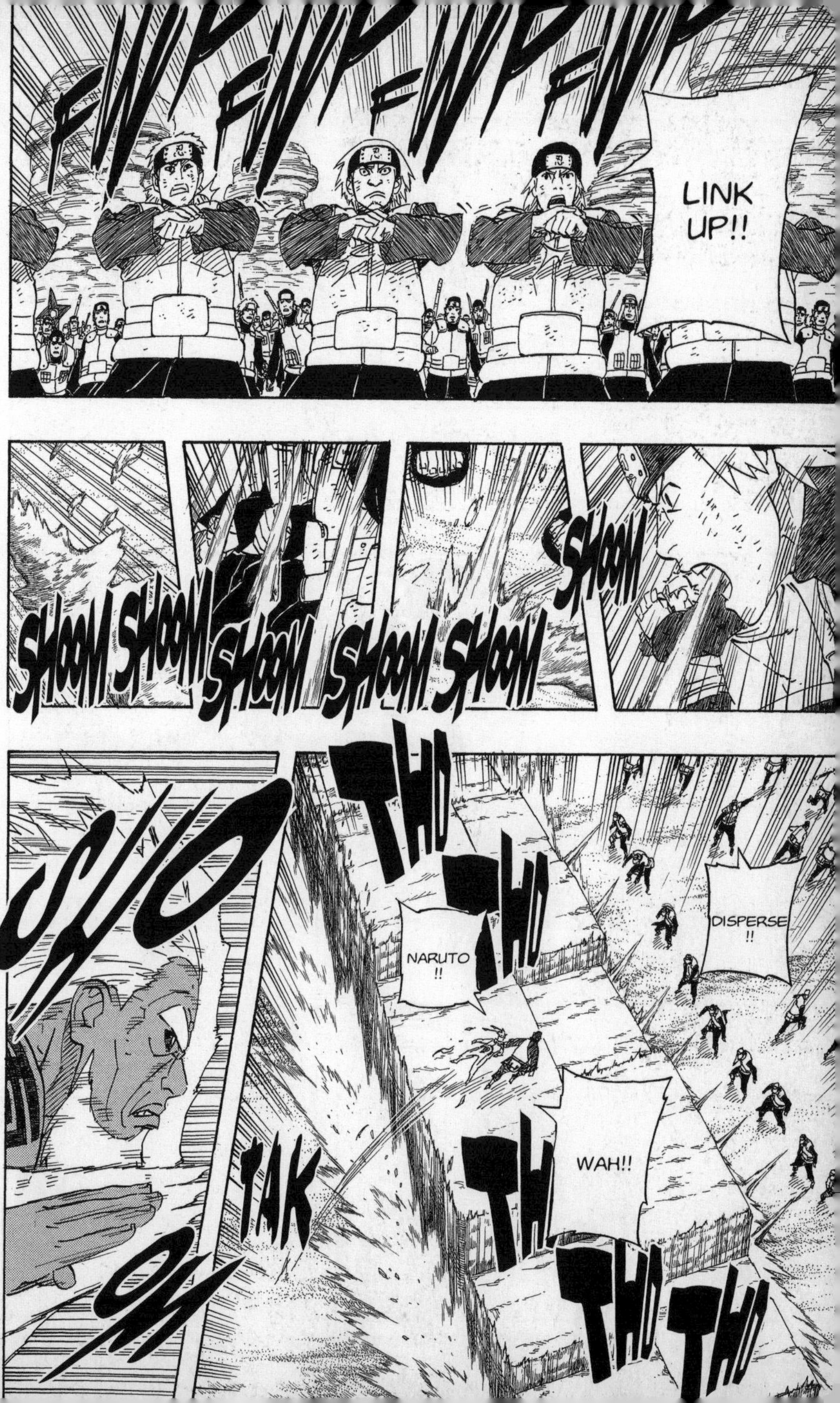
LINK UP!!
FWP
FWP
FWP
FWP
SHOOM
SHOOM SHOOM
SHOOM
SHOOM SHOOM
SHOOM
DISPERSE!!
NARUTO!!
THD
THD
THD
WAH!!
TH
THD
THD
TAK
SHOOM

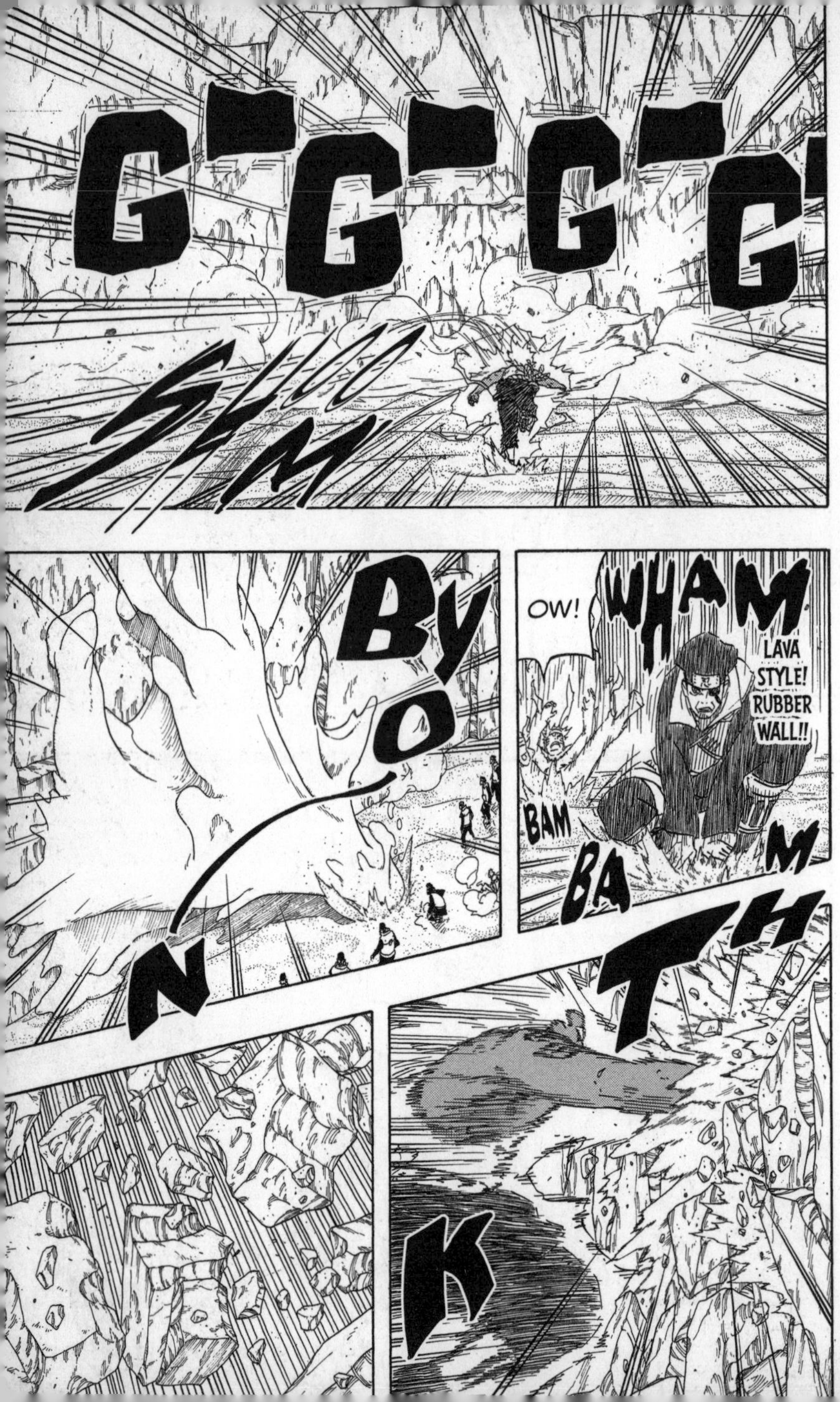
G'G'G'G
SHUOOM
OW!
WHAM
LAVA STYLE! RUBBER WALL!!
BAM
BAM
BYOON
TH
K

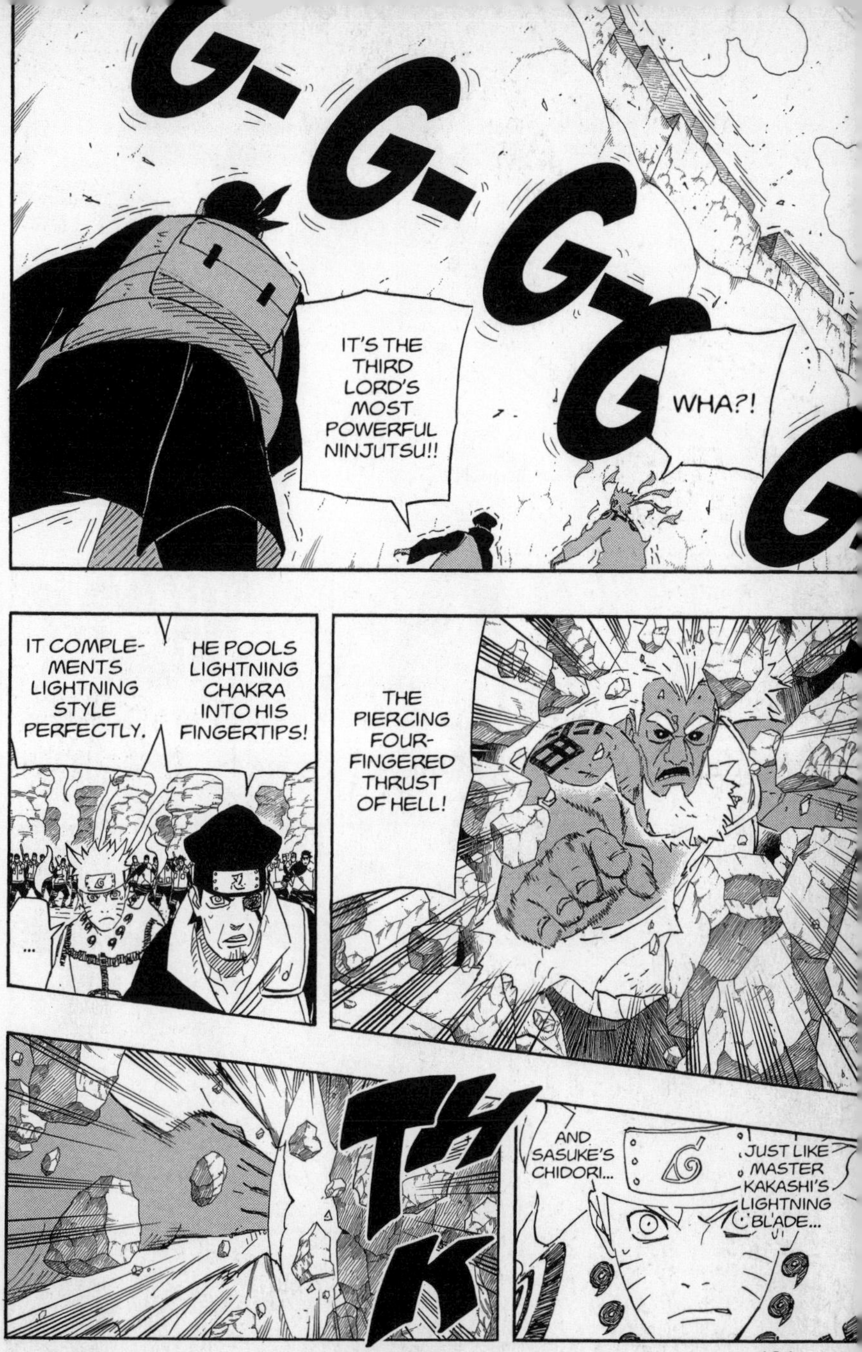
WHA?!
IT'S THE THIRD LORD'S MOST POWERFUL NINJUTSU!!
G-G-G-G-G
THE PIERCING FOUR-FINGERED THRUST OF HELL!
HE POOLS LIGHTNING CHAKRA INTO HIS FINGERTIPS!
IT COMPLE-MENTS LIGHTNING STYLE PERFECTLY.
...
JUST LIKE MASTER KAKASHI'S LIGHTNING BLADE...
AND SASUKE'S CHIDORI...
THK

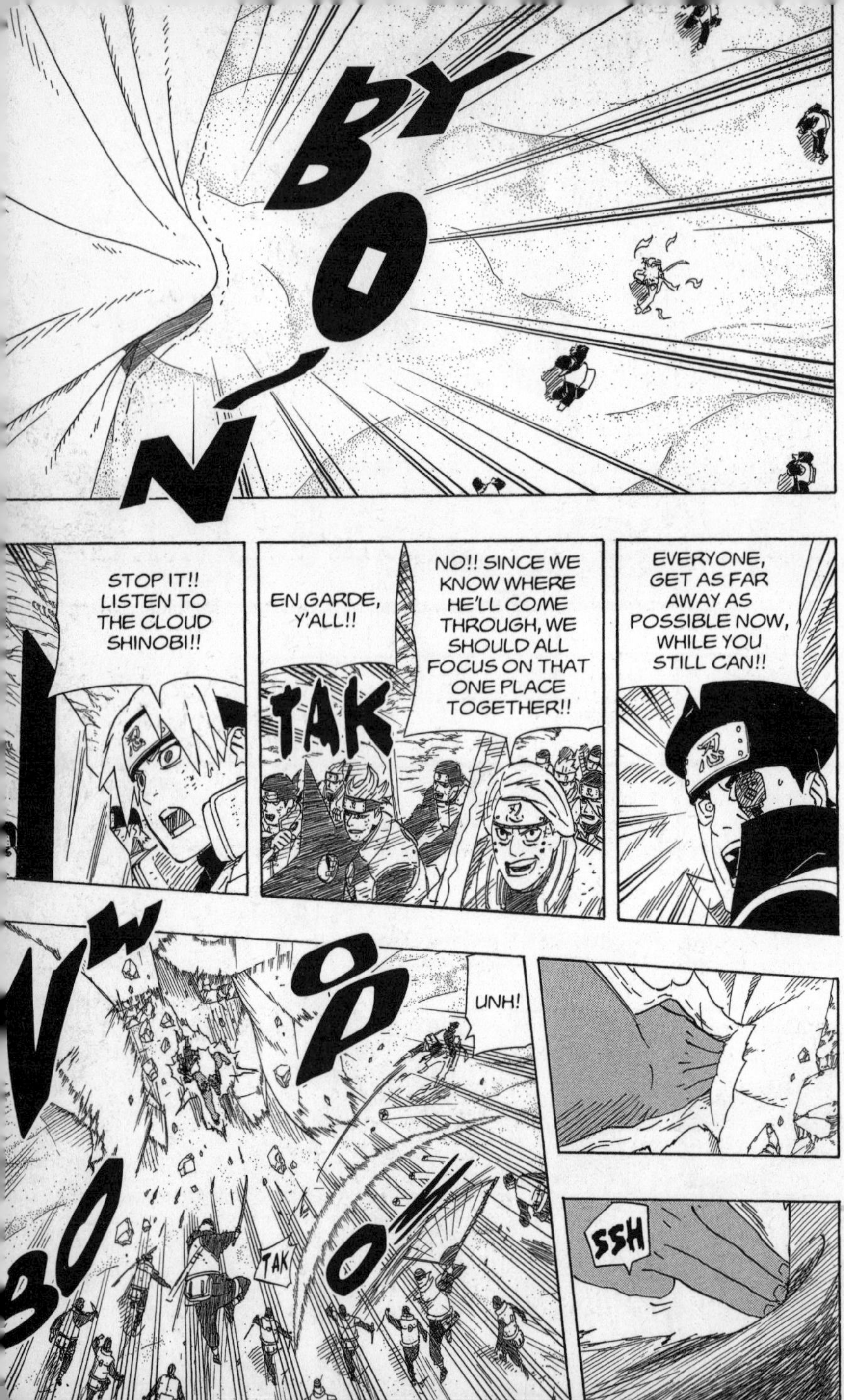
EVERYONE, GET AS FAR AWAY AS POSSIBLE NOW, WHILE YOU STILL CAN!!
NO!! SINCE WE KNOW WHERE HE'LL COME THROUGH, WE SHOULD ALL FOCUS ON THAT ONE PLACE TOGETHER!!
EN GARDE, Y'ALL!!
TAK
STOP IT!! LISTEN TO THE CLOUD SHINOBI!!
SSH
UNH!
TAK

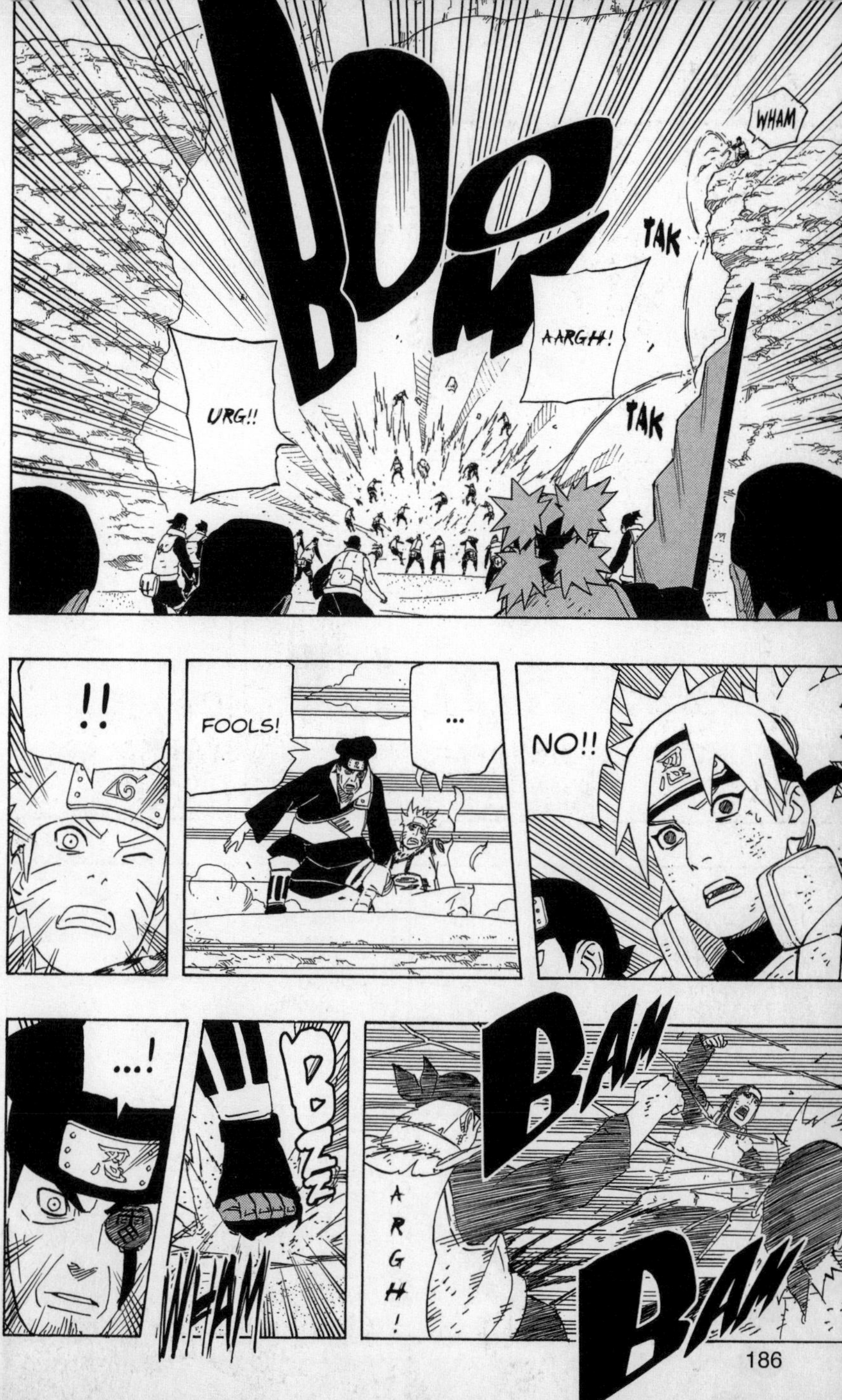
WHAM
TAK
BOOM
AARGH!
TAK
URG!!
NO!!
...
FOOLS!
!!
BAM
ARGH!
BAM
BONK
WHAM
....!

READ THIS WAY

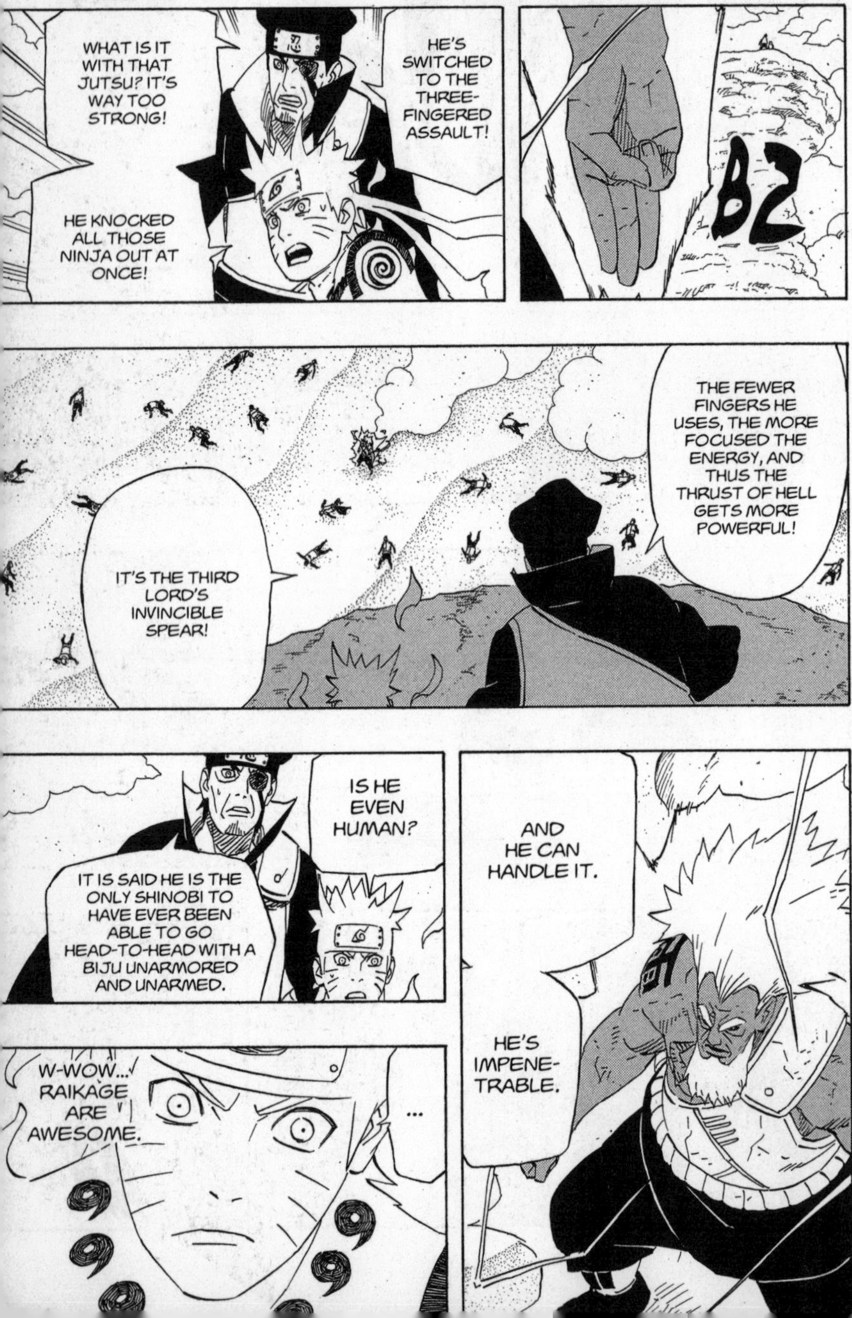
B2
HE'S SWITCHED TO THE THREE-FINGERED ASSAULT!
WHAT IS IT WITH THAT JUTSU? IT'S WAY TOO STRONG!
HE KNOCKED ALL THOSE NINJA OUT AT ONCE!
THE FEWER FINGERS HE USES, THE MORE FOCUSED THE ENERGY, AND THUS THE THRUST OF HELL GETS MORE POWERFUL!
IT'S THE THIRD LORD'S INVINCIBLE SPEAR!
AND HE CAN HANDLE IT.
HE'S IMPENE-TRABLE.
IS HE EVEN HUMAN?
IT IS SAID HE IS THE ONLY SHINOBI TO HAVE EVER BEEN ABLE TO GO HEAD-TO-HEAD WITH A BIJU UNARMORED AND UNARMED.
...
W-WOW... RAIKAGE ARE AWESOME.

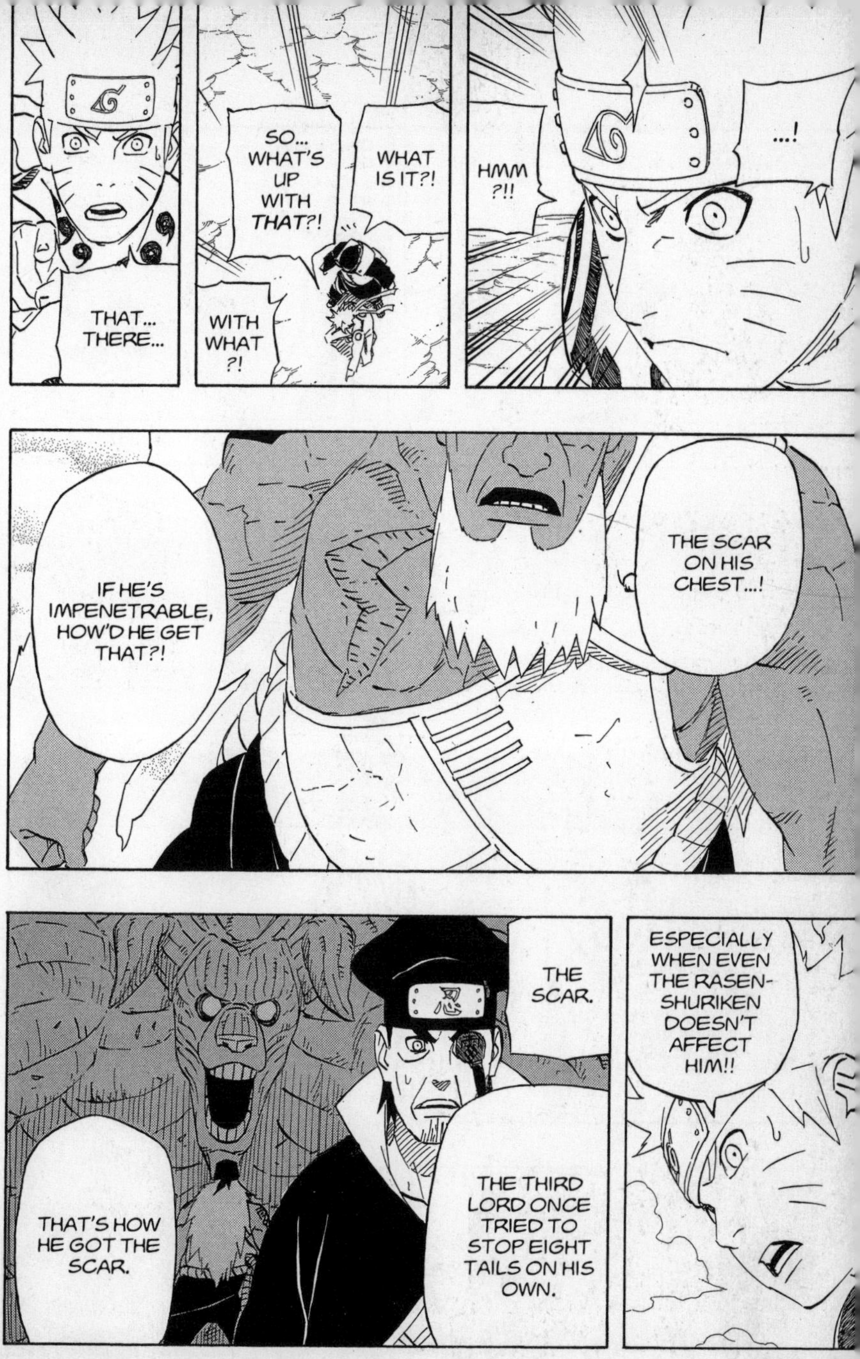
...!
HMM ?!!
WHAT IS IT?!
SO... WHAT'S UP WITH *THAT*?!
WITH WHAT ?!
THAT... THERE...
THE SCAR ON HIS CHEST...!
IF HE'S IMPENETRABLE, HOW'D HE GET THAT?!
ESPECIALLY WHEN EVEN THE RASEN-SHURIKEN DOESN'T AFFECT HIM!!
THE SCAR.
THE THIRD LORD ONCE TRIED TO STOP EIGHT TAILS ON HIS OWN.
THAT'S HOW HE GOT THE SCAR.

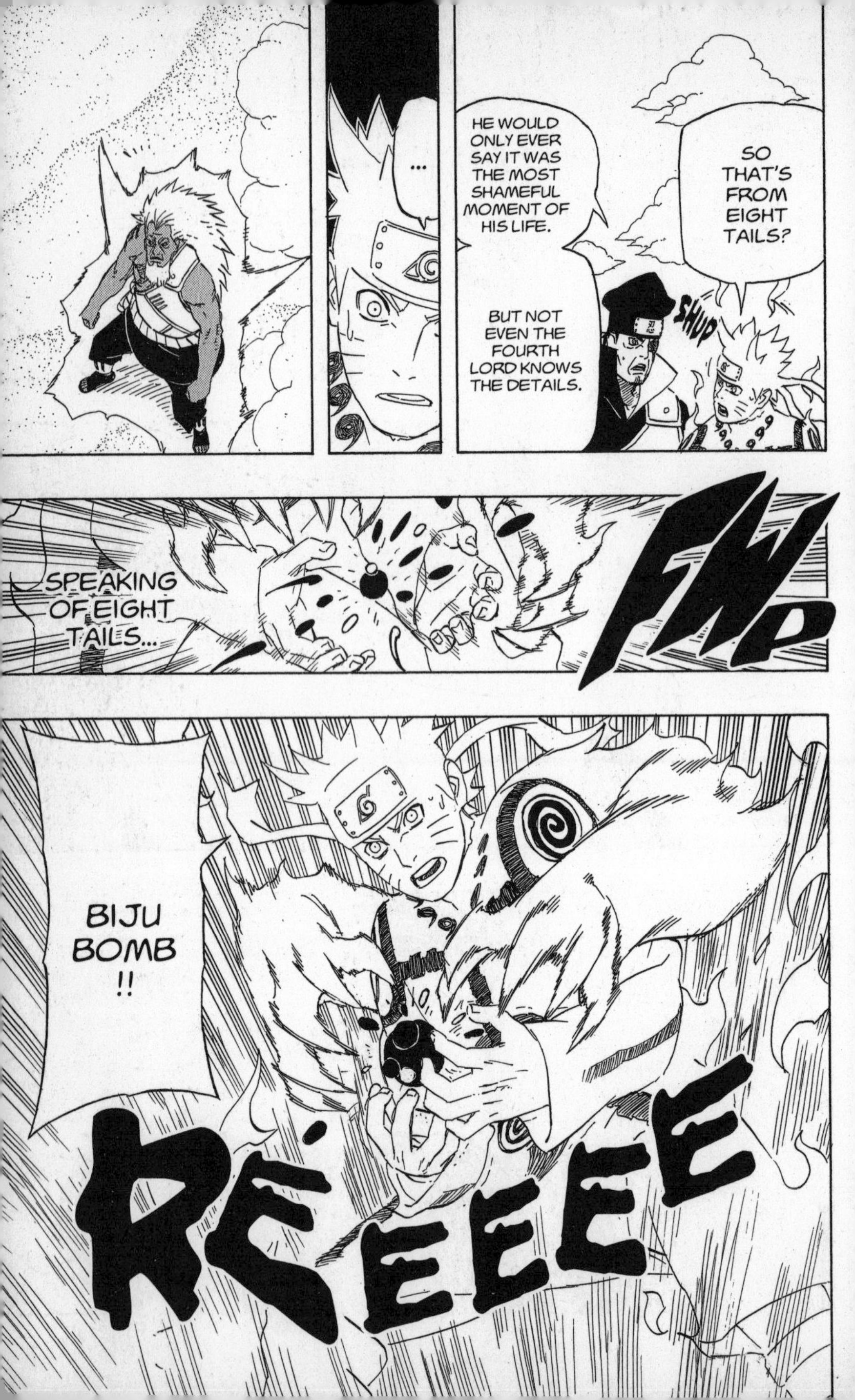
SO THAT'S FROM EIGHT TAILS?
SHUP
HE WOULD ONLY EVER SAY IT WAS THE MOST SHAMEFUL MOMENT OF HIS LIFE.
BUT NOT EVEN THE FOURTH LORD KNOWS THE DETAILS.
...
FWP
SPEAKING OF EIGHT TAILS...
BIJU BOMB !!
REEEEE

NARUTO

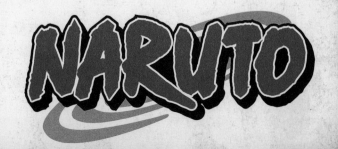

Number 555: Paradox

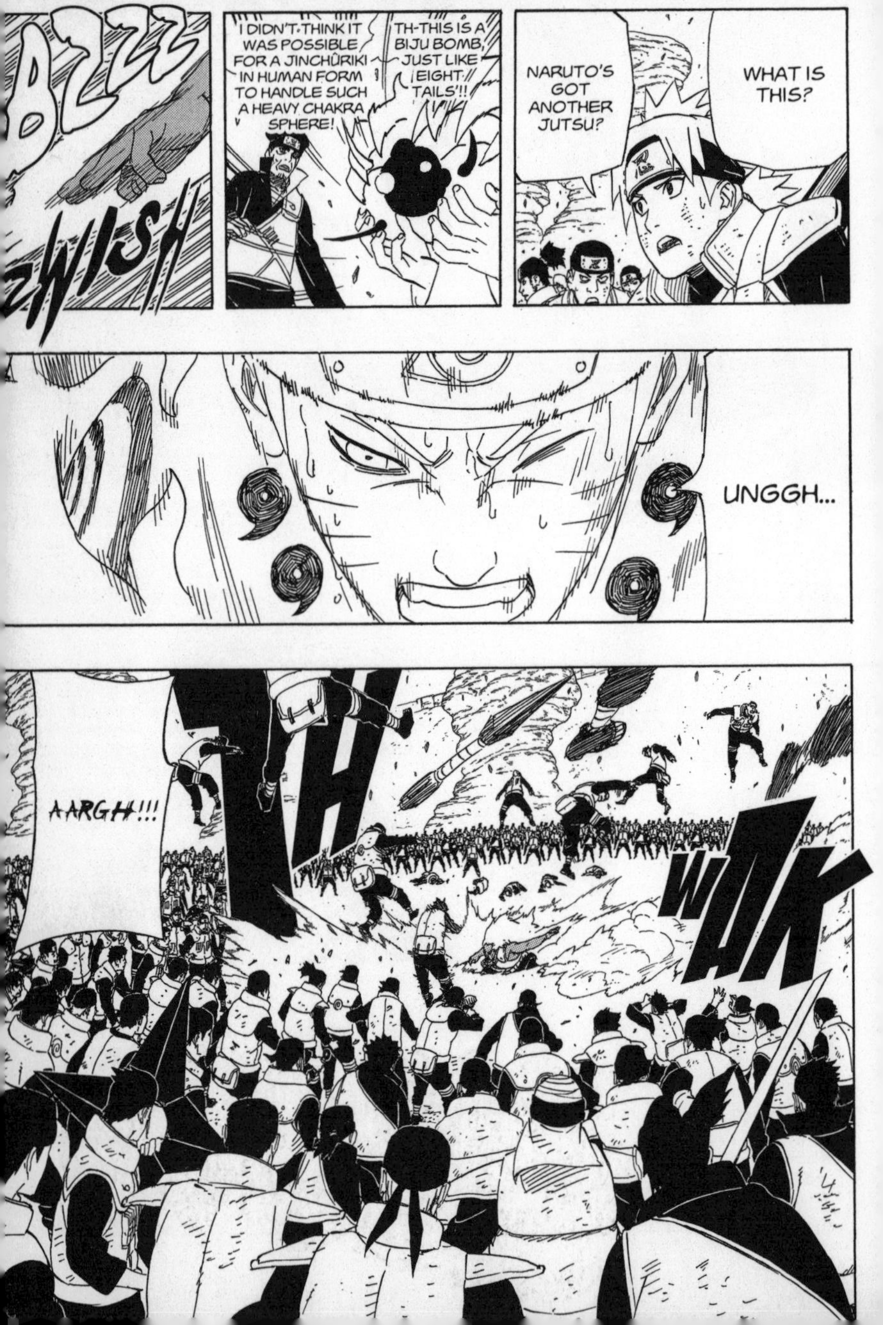
WHAT IS THIS?
NARUTO'S GOT ANOTHER JUTSU?
TH-THIS IS A BIJU BOMB, JUST LIKE EIGHT TAILS'!!
I DIDN'T THINK IT WAS POSSIBLE FOR A JINCHÛRIKI IN HUMAN FORM TO HANDLE SUCH A HEAVY CHAKRA SPHERE!
BZZZZ
ZWISH
UNGGH...
WHAK
TH
AARGH!!!

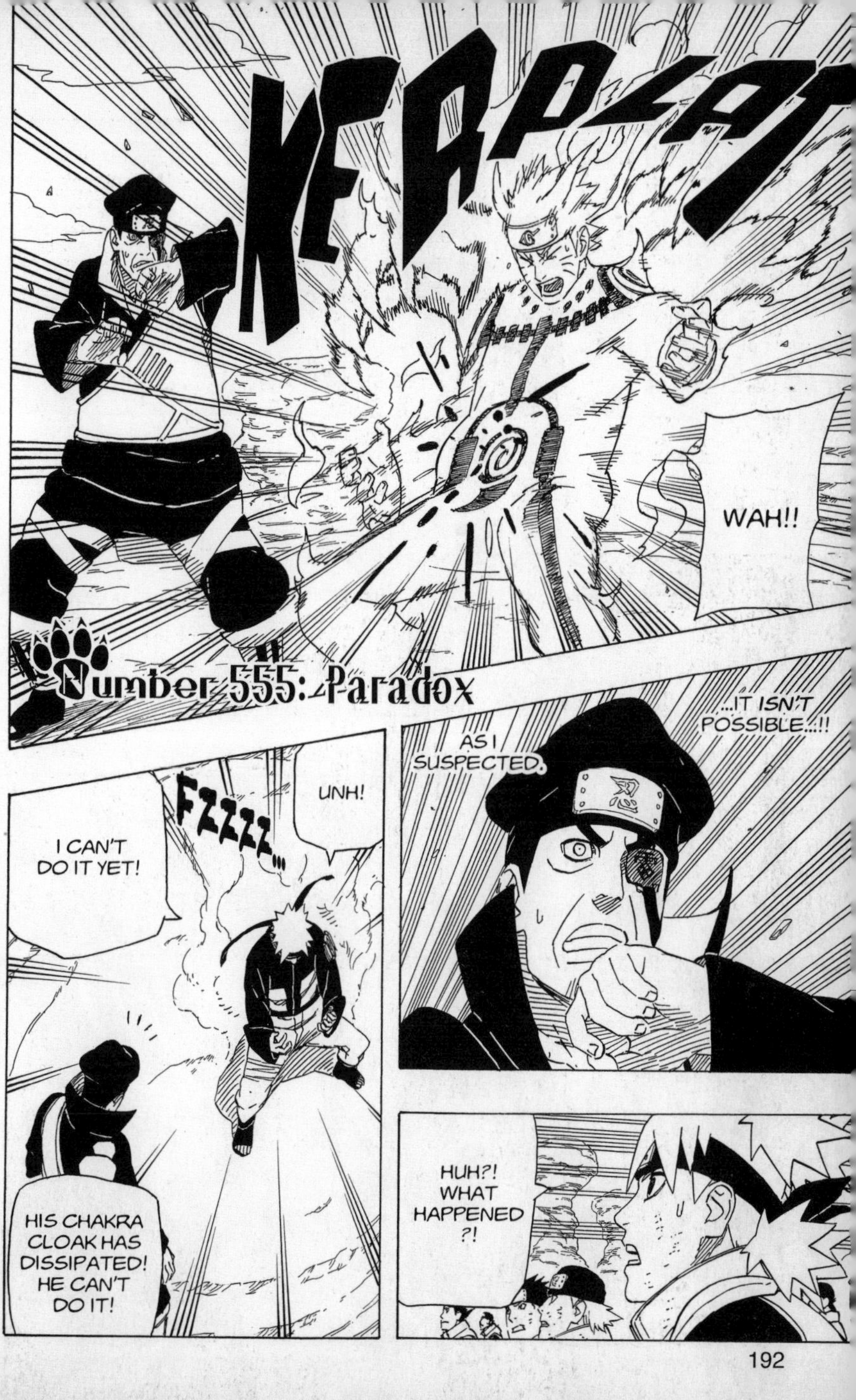
KERPZAT
WAH!!
Number 555: Paradox
...IT ISN'T POSSIBLE...!!
AS I SUSPECTED.
HUH?! WHAT HAPPENED ?!
UNH!
FZZZZ...
I CAN'T DO IT YET!
HIS CHAKRA CLOAK HAS DISSIPATED! HE CAN'T DO IT!

READ THIS WAY

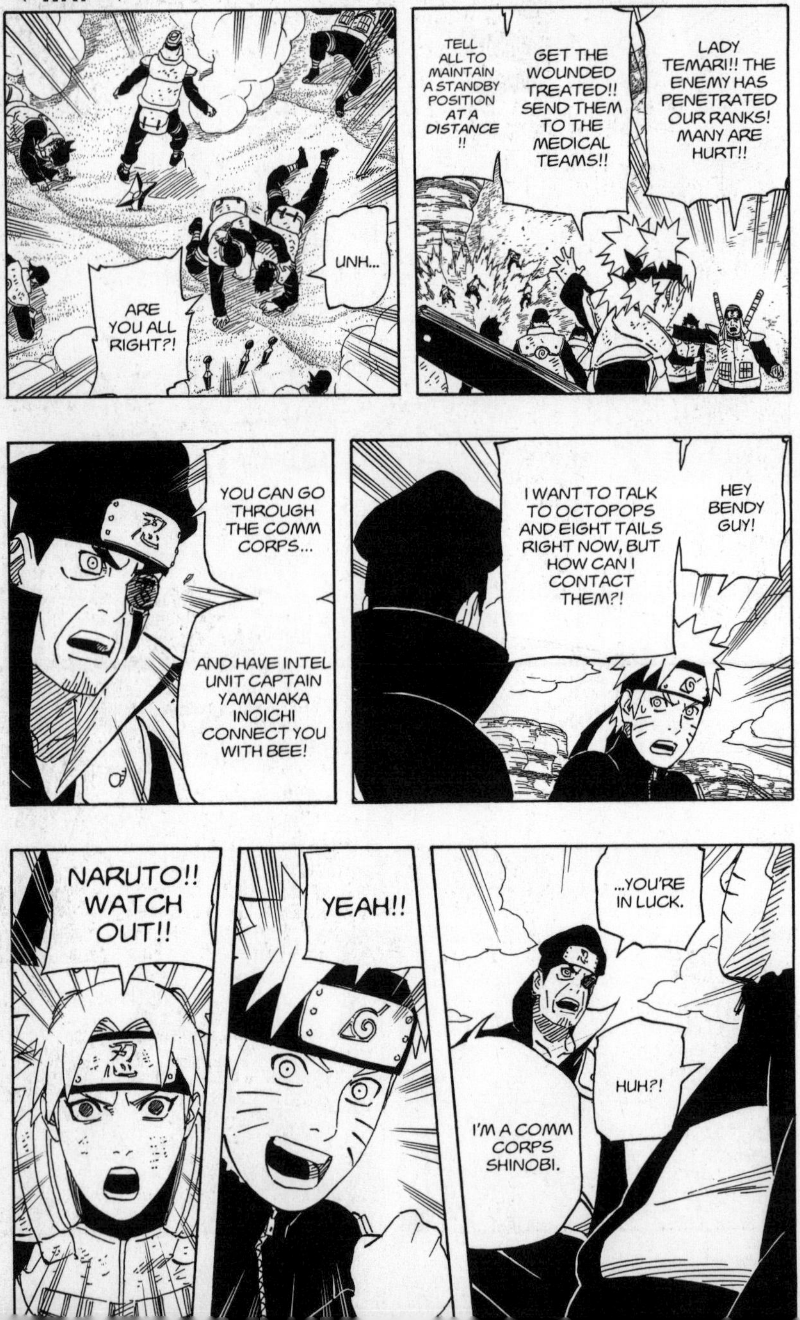

LADY TEMARI!! THE ENEMY HAS PENETRATED OUR RANKS! MANY ARE HURT!!
GET THE WOUNDED TREATED!! SEND THEM TO THE MEDICAL TEAMS!!
TELL ALL TO MAINTAIN A STANDBY POSITION AT A DISTANCE !!
UNH...
ARE YOU ALL RIGHT?!
HEY BENDY GUY!
I WANT TO TALK TO OCTOPOPS AND EIGHT TAILS RIGHT NOW, BUT HOW CAN I CONTACT THEM?!
YOU CAN GO THROUGH THE COMM CORPS...
AND HAVE INTEL UNIT CAPTAIN YAMANAKA INOICHI CONNECT YOU WITH BEE!
...YOU'RE IN LUCK.
HUH?!
I'M A COMM CORPS SHINOBI.
YEAH!!
NARUTO!! WATCH OUT!!

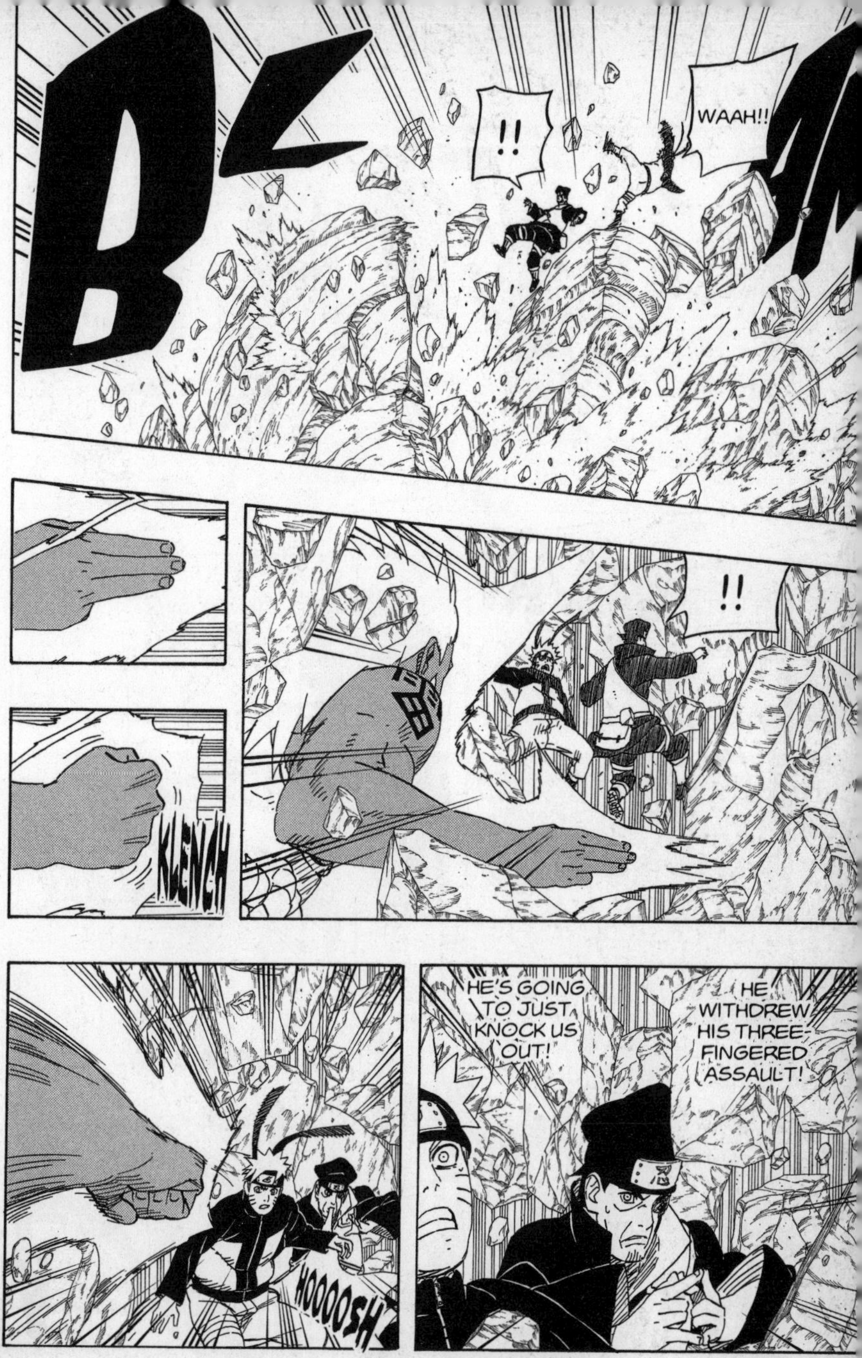
WAAH!!
!!
!!
KLENCH
HE WITHDREW HIS THREE-FINGERED ASSAULT!
HE'S GOING TO JUST KNOCK US OUT!
HOOOOSH

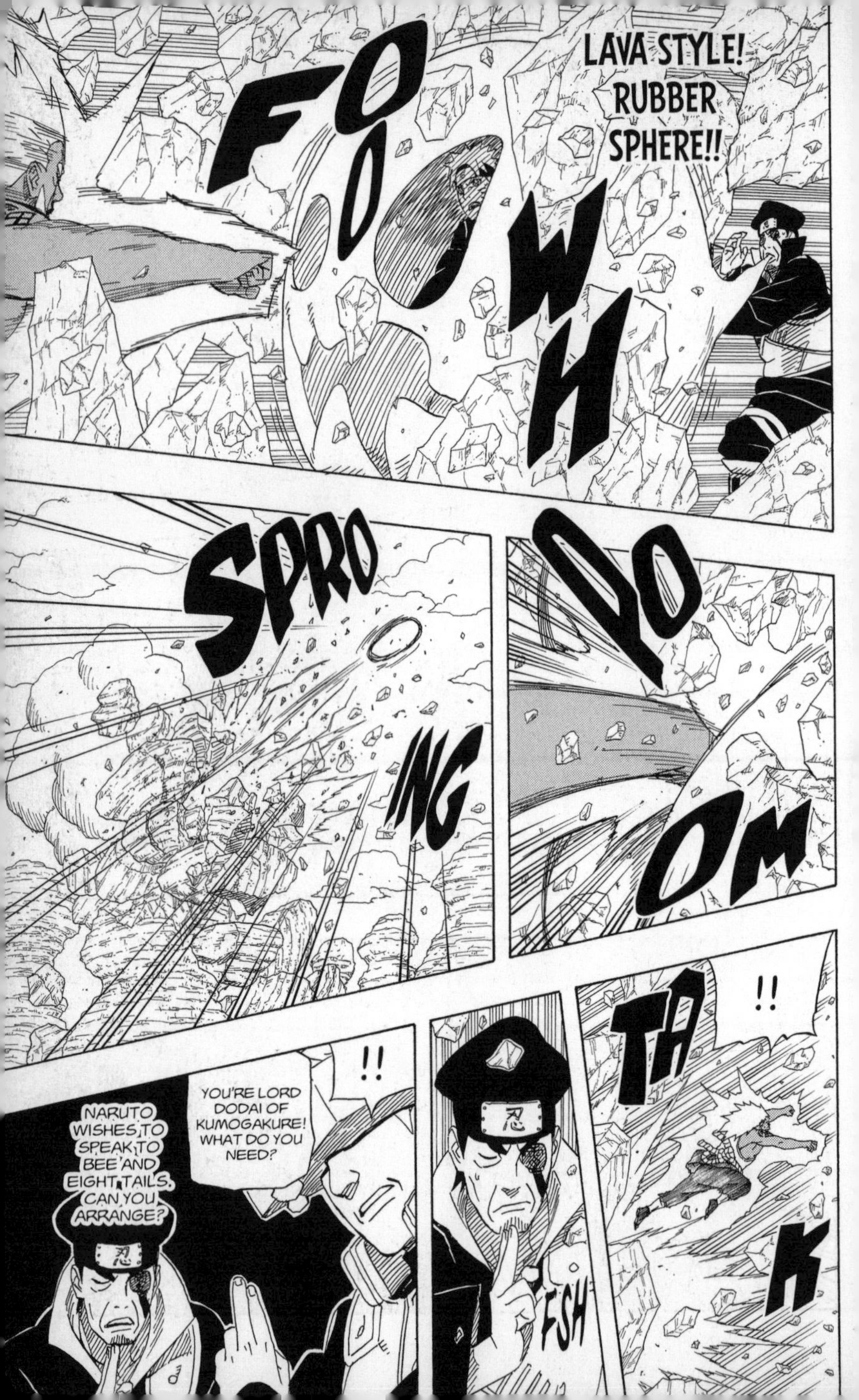
LAVA STYLE! RUBBER SPHERE!!
FOOWH
DOOM
SPROING
!!
TAK
FSH
!!
YOU'RE LORD DODAI OF KUMOGAKURE! WHAT DO YOU NEED?
NARUTO WISHES TO SPEAK TO BEE AND EIGHT TAILS. CAN YOU ARRANGE?

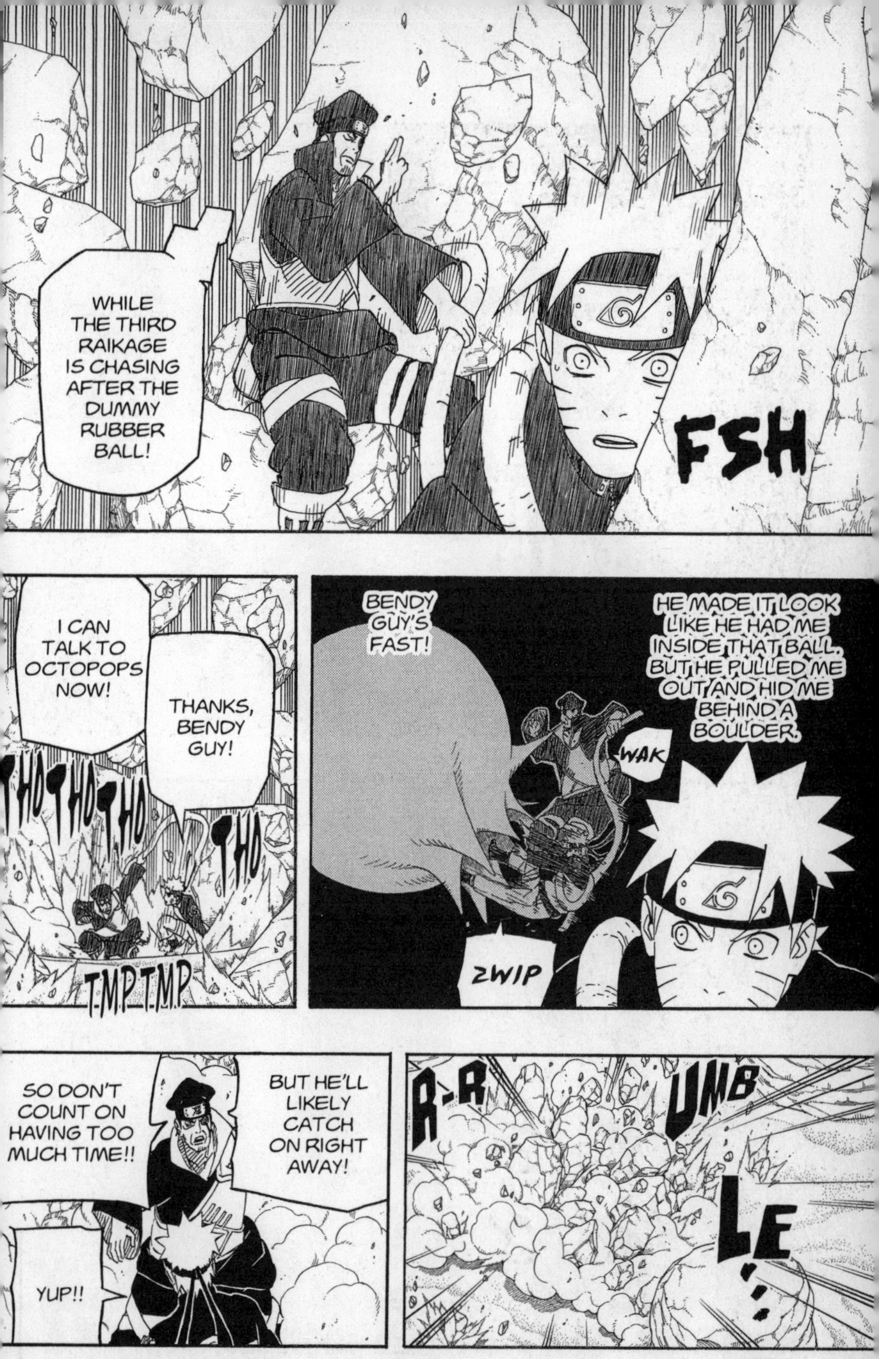
WHILE THE THIRD RAIKAGE IS CHASING AFTER THE DUMMY RUBBER BALL!
FSH
HE MADE IT LOOK LIKE HE HAD ME INSIDE THAT BALL, BUT HE PULLED ME OUT AND HID ME BEHIND A BOULDER.
BENDY GUY'S FAST!
WAK
ZWIP
I CAN TALK TO OCTOPOPS NOW!
THANKS, BENDY GUY!
THO THO THO THO
TMP TMP
R-RUMBLE
BUT HE'LL LIKELY CATCH ON RIGHT AWAY!
SO DON'T COUNT ON HAVING TOO MUCH TIME!!
YUP!!

READ THIS WAY

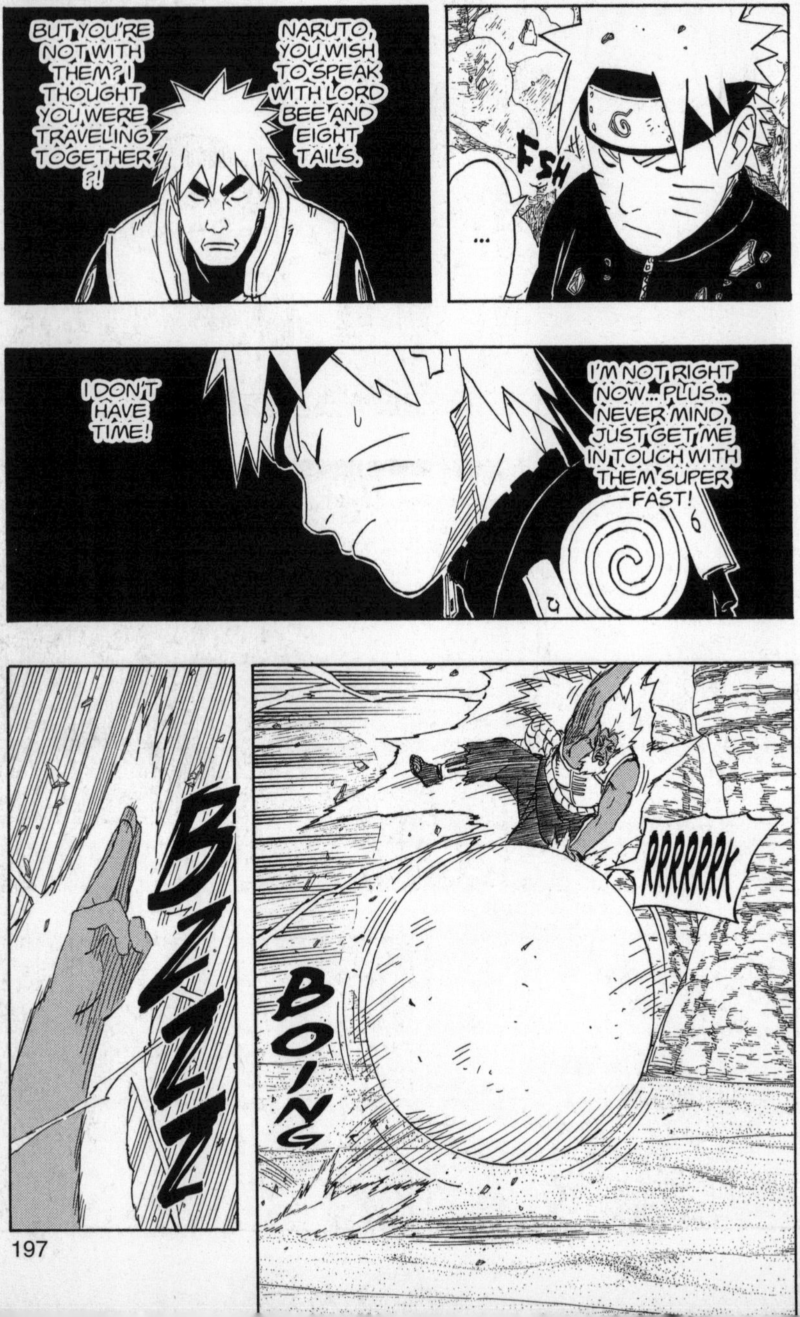

FSH
...
NARUTO, YOU WISH TO SPEAK WITH LORD BEE AND EIGHT TAILS.
BUT YOU'RE NOT WITH THEM?! I THOUGHT YOU WERE TRAVELING TOGETHER?!
I'M NOT RIGHT NOW... PLUS... NEVER MIND, JUST GET ME IN TOUCH WITH THEM SUPER FAST!
I DON'T HAVE TIME!
RRRRRRK
BOING
BZZZZ

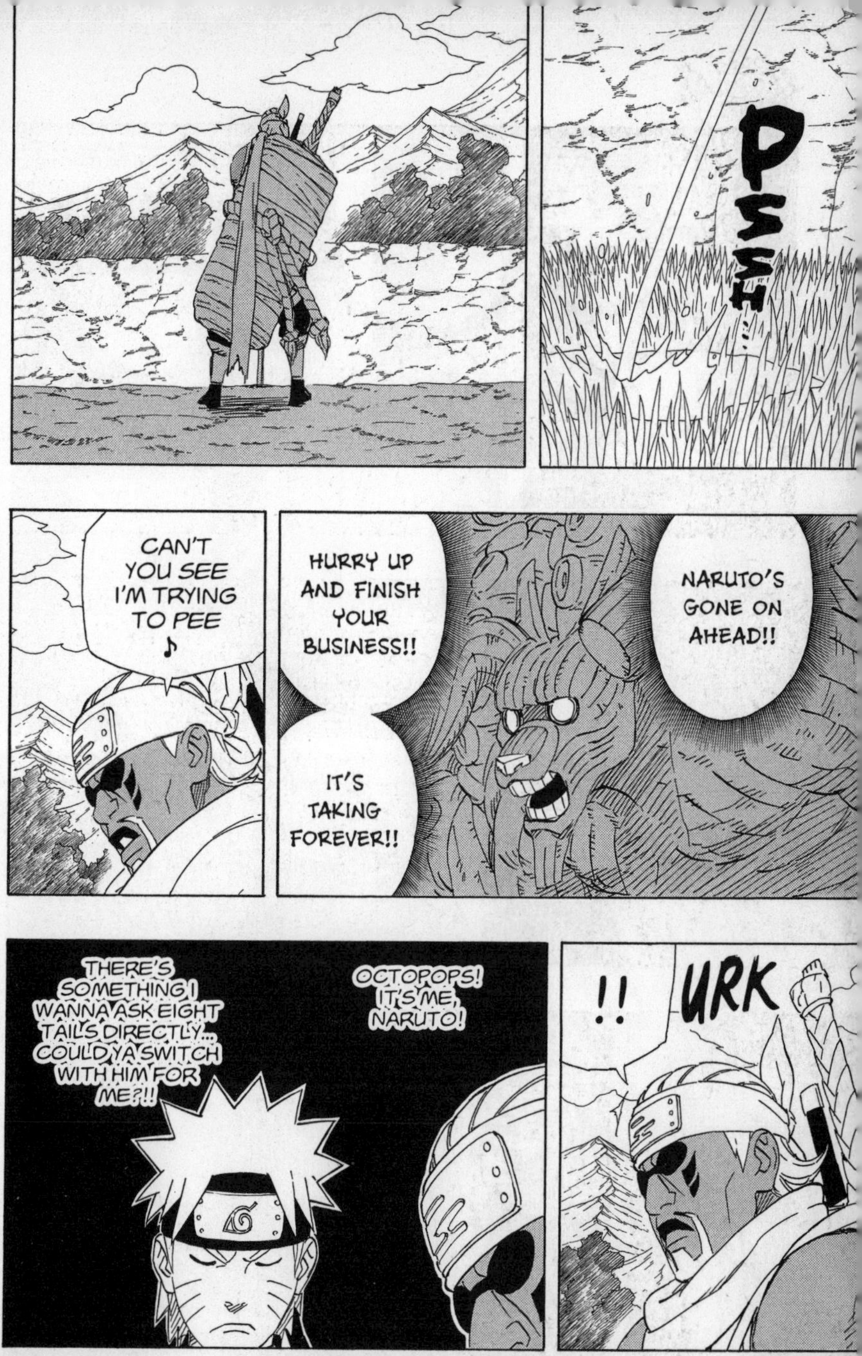
PSSH...
NARUTO'S GONE ON AHEAD!!
HURRY UP AND FINISH YOUR BUSINESS!!
IT'S TAKING FOREVER!!
CAN'T YOU SEE I'M TRYING TO PEE ♪
URK
!!
OCTOPOPS! IT'S ME, NARUTO!
THERE'S SOMETHING I WANNA ASK EIGHT TAILS DIRECTLY... COULD YA SWITCH WITH HIM FOR ME?!!

READ THIS WAY

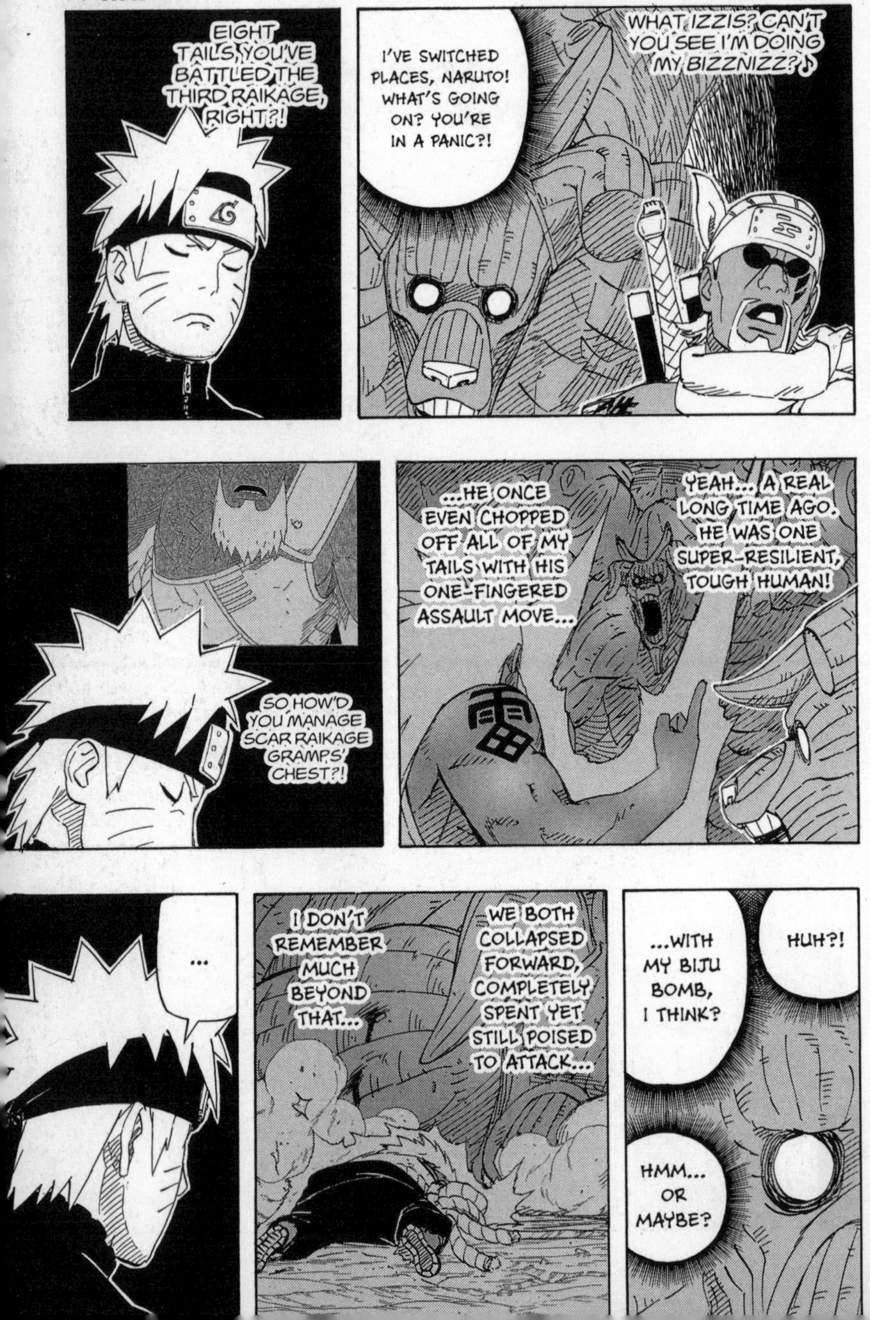
WHAT IZZIS? CAN'T YOU SEE I'M DOING MY BIZZNIZZ? ♪
I'VE SWITCHED PLACES, NARUTO! WHAT'S GOING ON? YOU'RE IN A PANIC?!
EIGHT TAILS, YOU'VE BATTLED THE THIRD RAIKAGE, RIGHT?!
YEAH... A REAL LONG TIME AGO. HE WAS ONE SUPER-RESILIENT, TOUGH HUMAN!
...HE ONCE EVEN CHOPPED OFF ALL OF MY TAILS WITH HIS ONE-FINGERED ASSAULT MOVE...
SO HOW'D YOU MANAGE SCAR RAIKAGE GRAMPS' CHEST?!
HUH?!
...WITH MY BIJU BOMB, I THINK?
HMM... OR MAYBE?
WE BOTH COLLAPSED FORWARD, COMPLETELY SPENT YET STILL POISED TO ATTACK...
I DON'T REMEMBER MUCH BEYOND THAT...
...

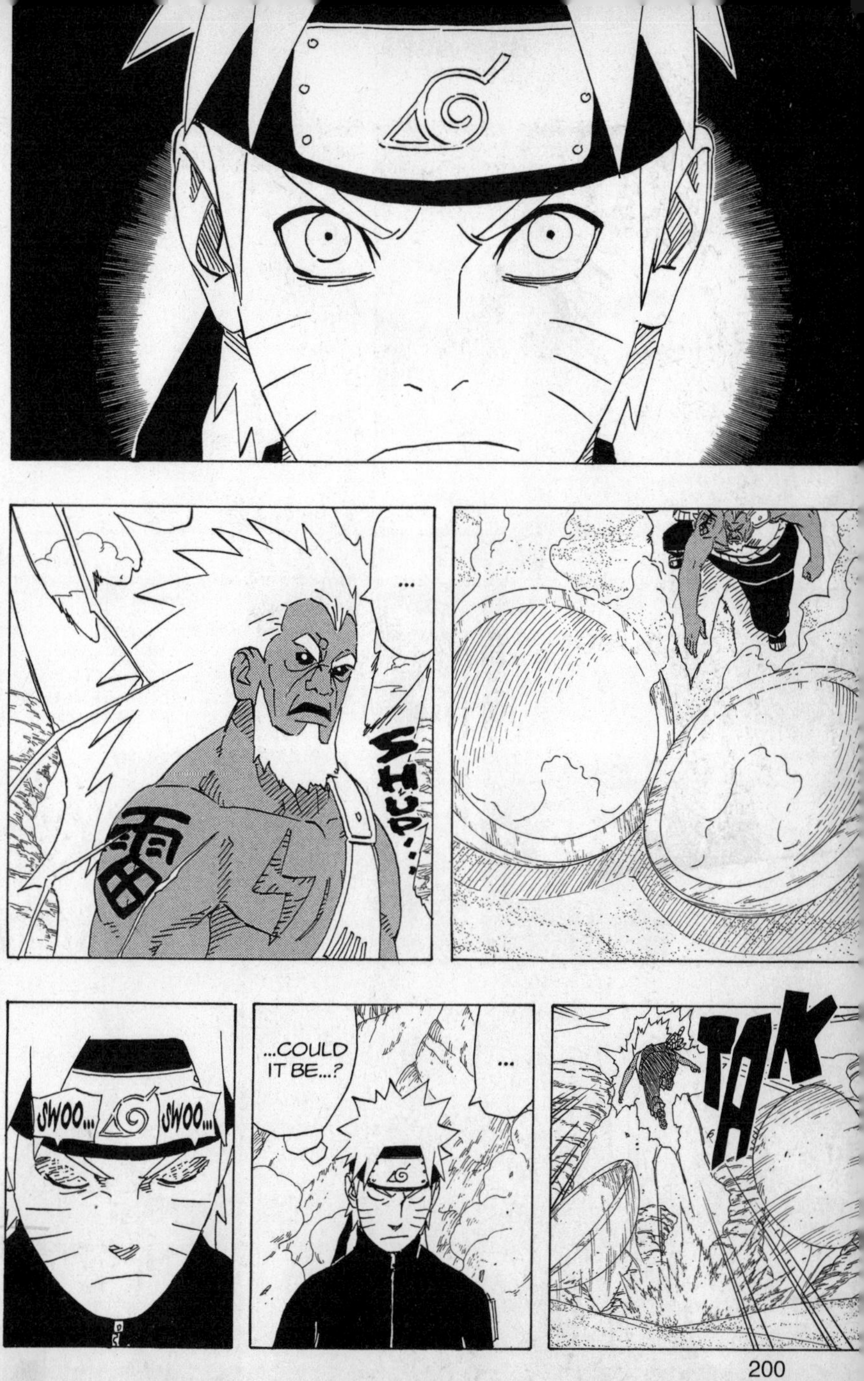
...
SHUP...
TAK
...
...COULD IT BE...?
SWOO...
SWOO...

READ THIS WAY

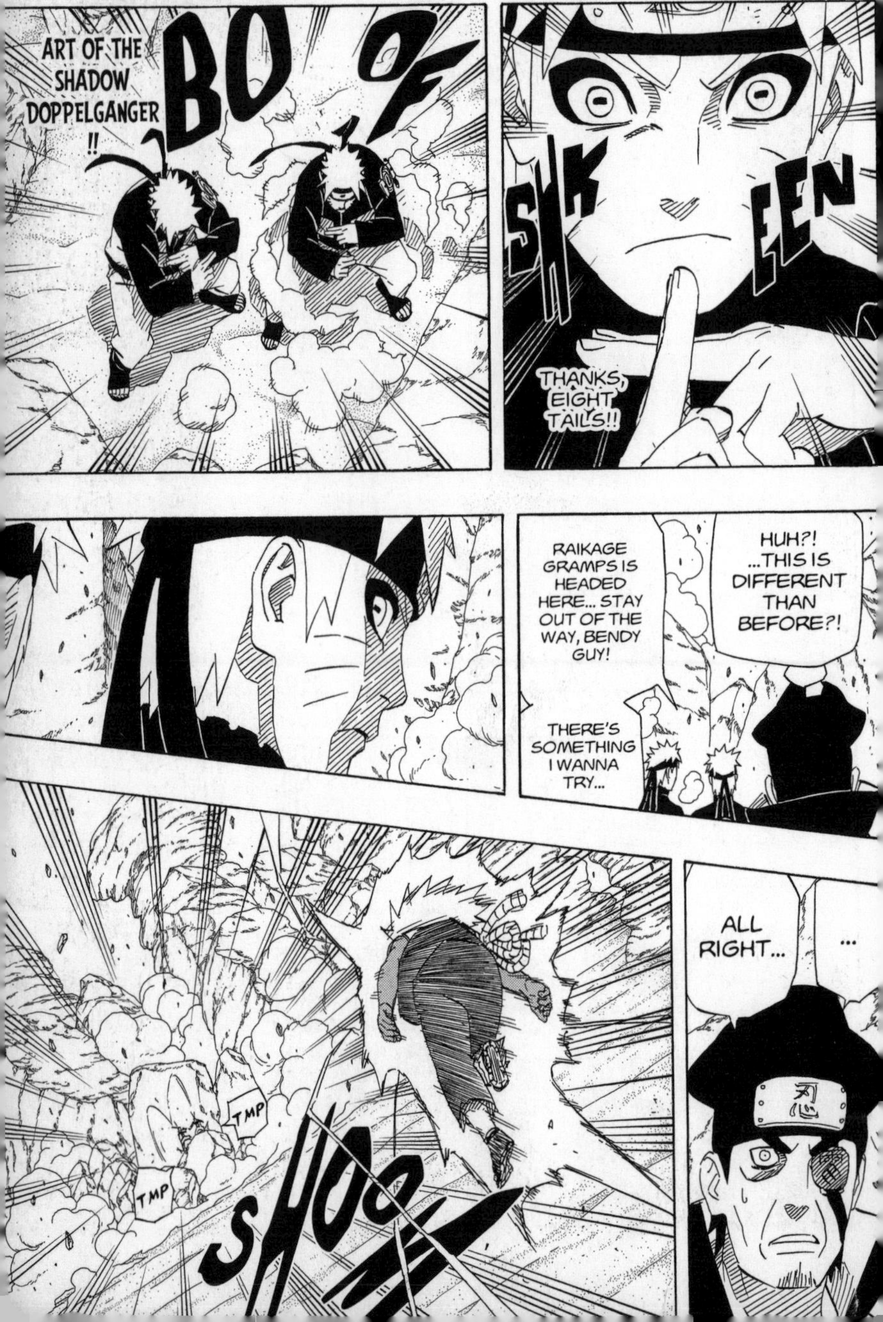
SHKEEN
THANKS, EIGHT TAILS!!
ART OF THE SHADOW DOPPELGANGER !!
BOOF
HUH?! ...THIS IS DIFFERENT THAN BEFORE?!
RAIKAGE GRAMPS IS HEADED HERE... STAY OUT OF THE WAY, BENDY GUY!
THERE'S SOMETHING I WANNA TRY...
...
ALL RIGHT...
SHOOM
TMP
TMP

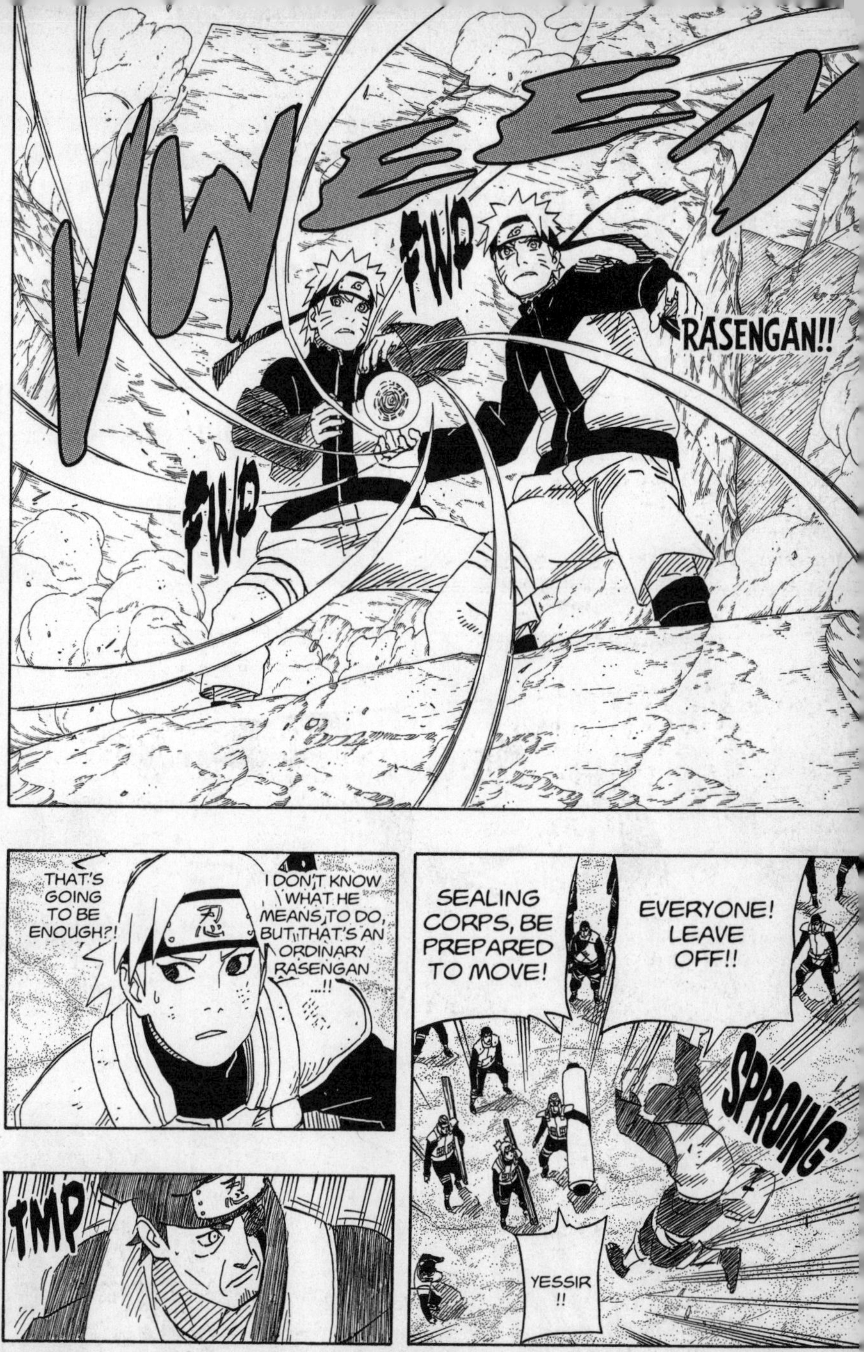
VWEEEN
FWP
RASENGAN!!
FWP
EVERYONE! LEAVE OFF!!
SEALING CORPS, BE PREPARED TO MOVE!
SPROING
YESSIR!!
THAT'S GOING TO BE ENOUGH?!
I DON'T KNOW WHAT HE MEANS TO DO, BUT THAT'S AN ORDINARY RASENGAN ...!!
TMP

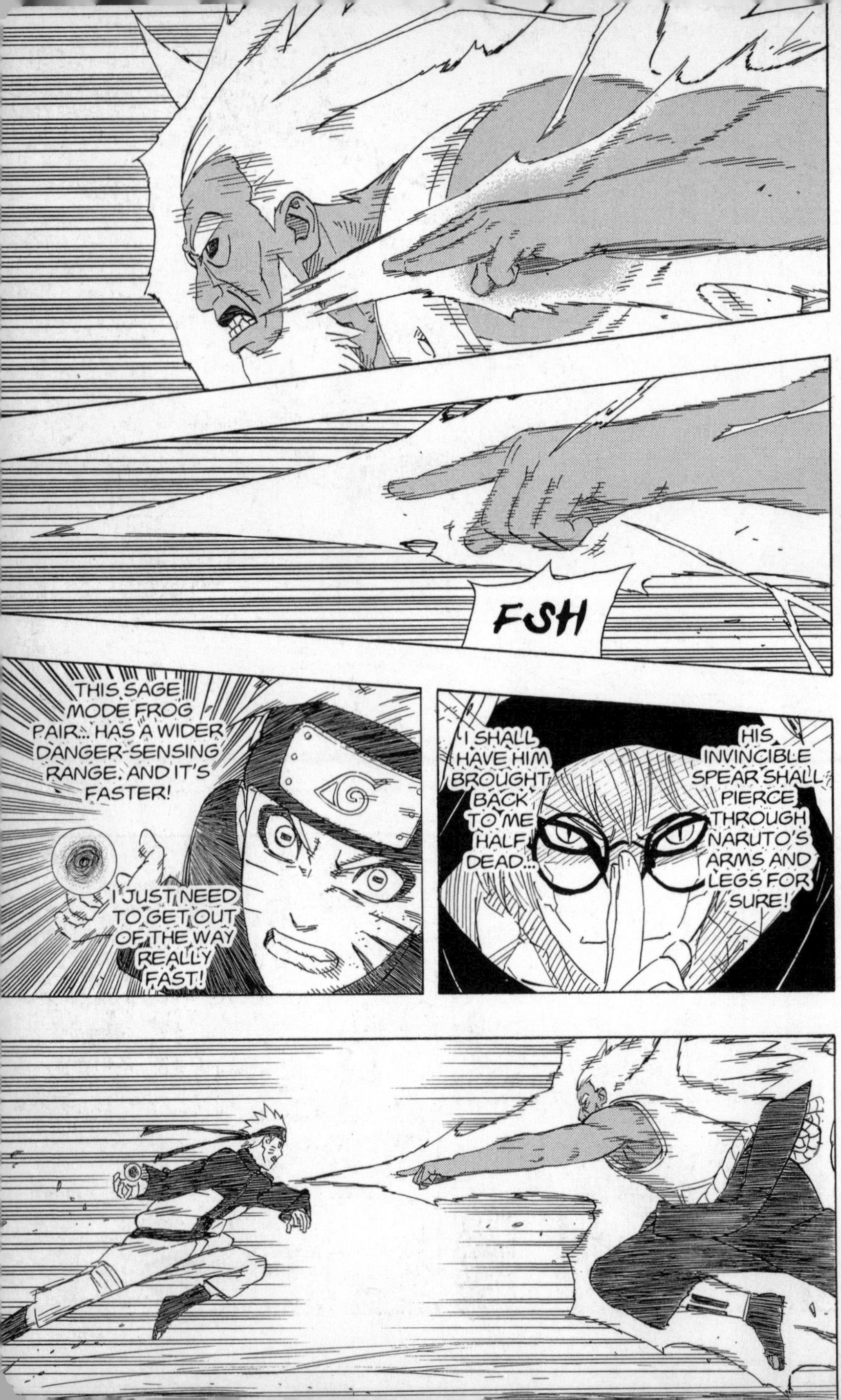
FSH
HIS INVINCIBLE SPEAR SHALL PIERCE THROUGH NARUTO'S ARMS AND LEGS FOR SURE!
I SHALL HAVE HIM BROUGHT BACK TO ME HALF DEAD...
THIS SAGE MODE FROG PAIR... HAS A WIDER DANGER-SENSING RANGE. AND IT'S FASTER!
I JUST NEED TO GET OUT OF THE WAY REALLY FAST!

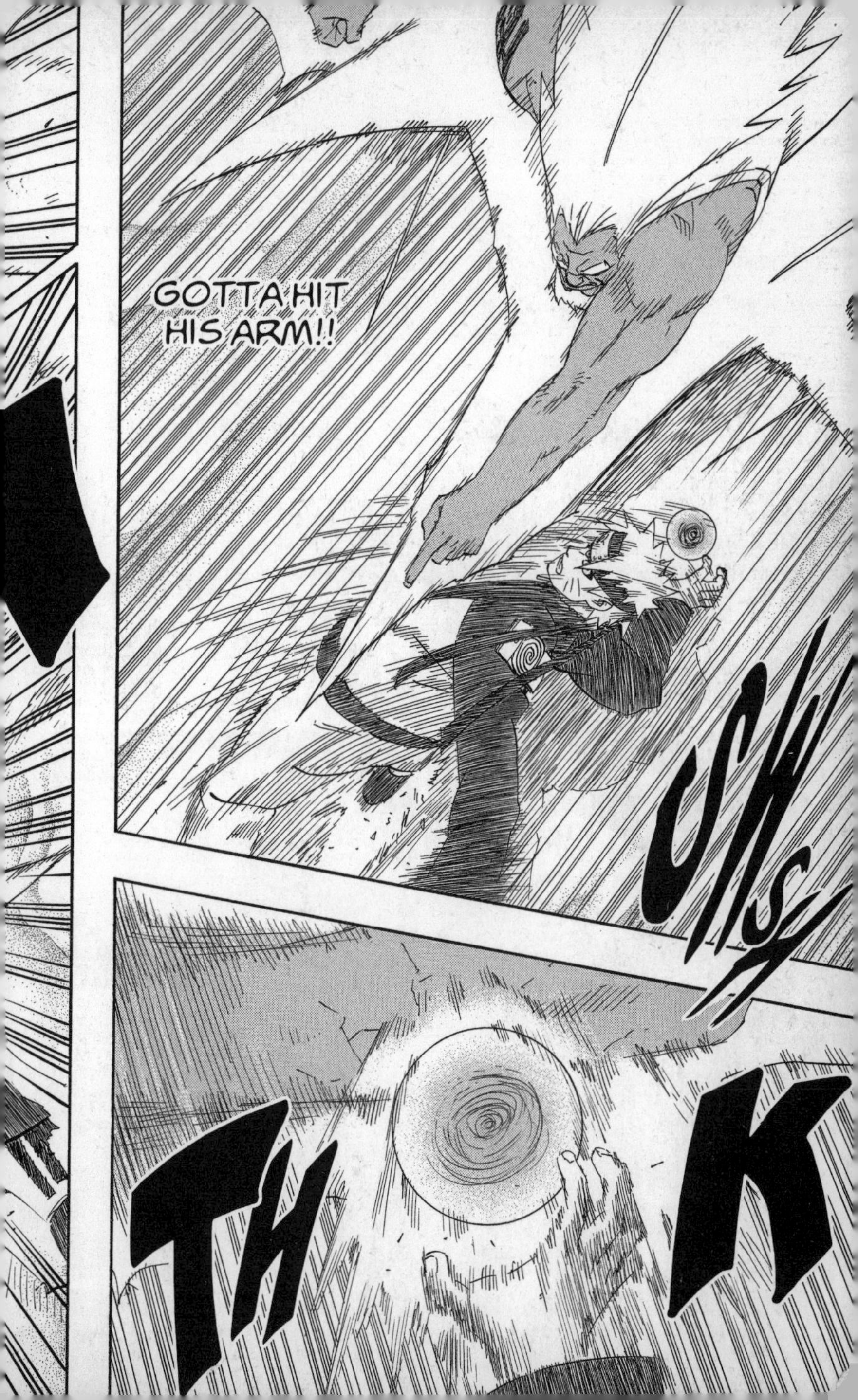
GOTTA HIT HIS ARM!!
SWISH
TH
K

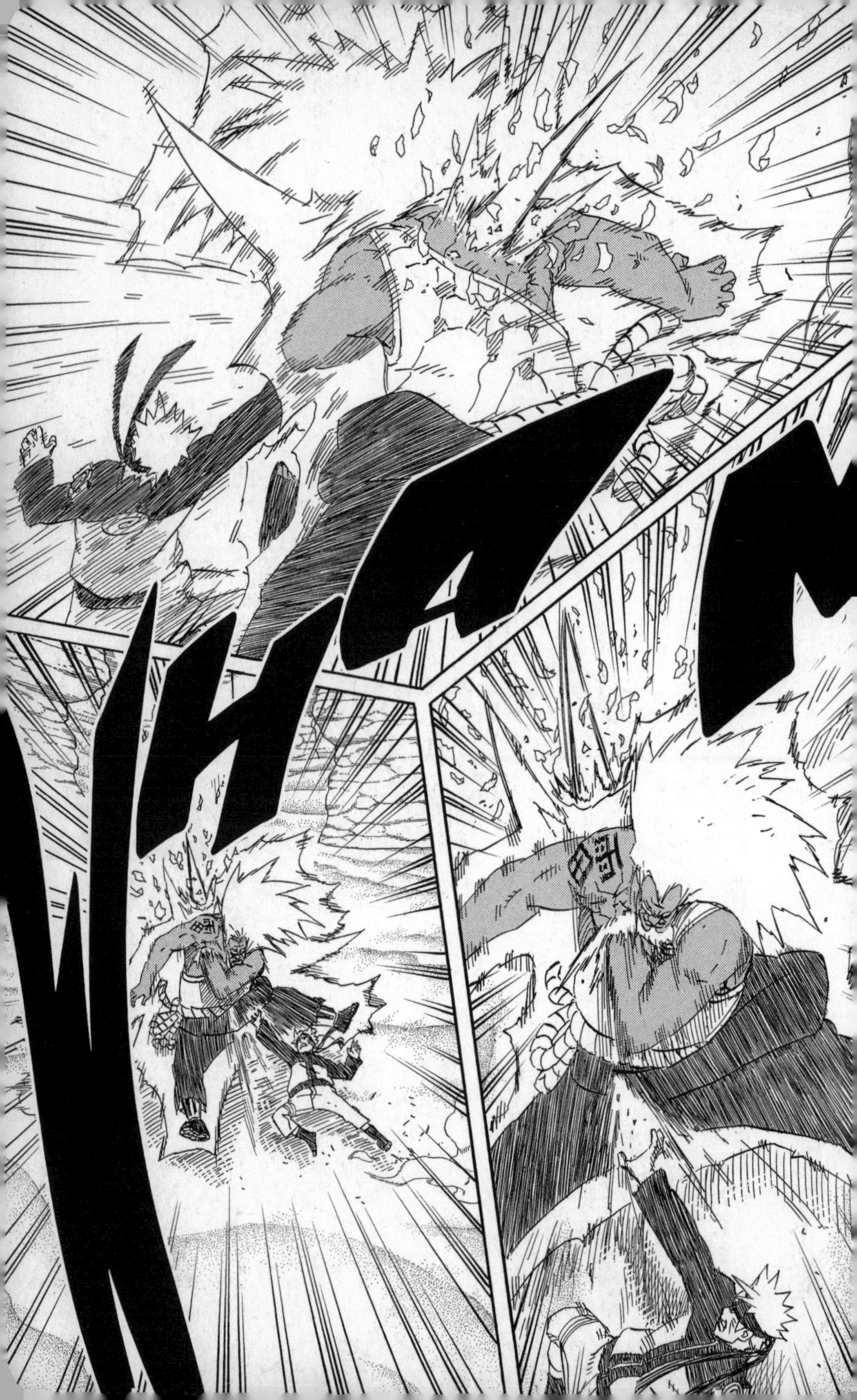
WHAM

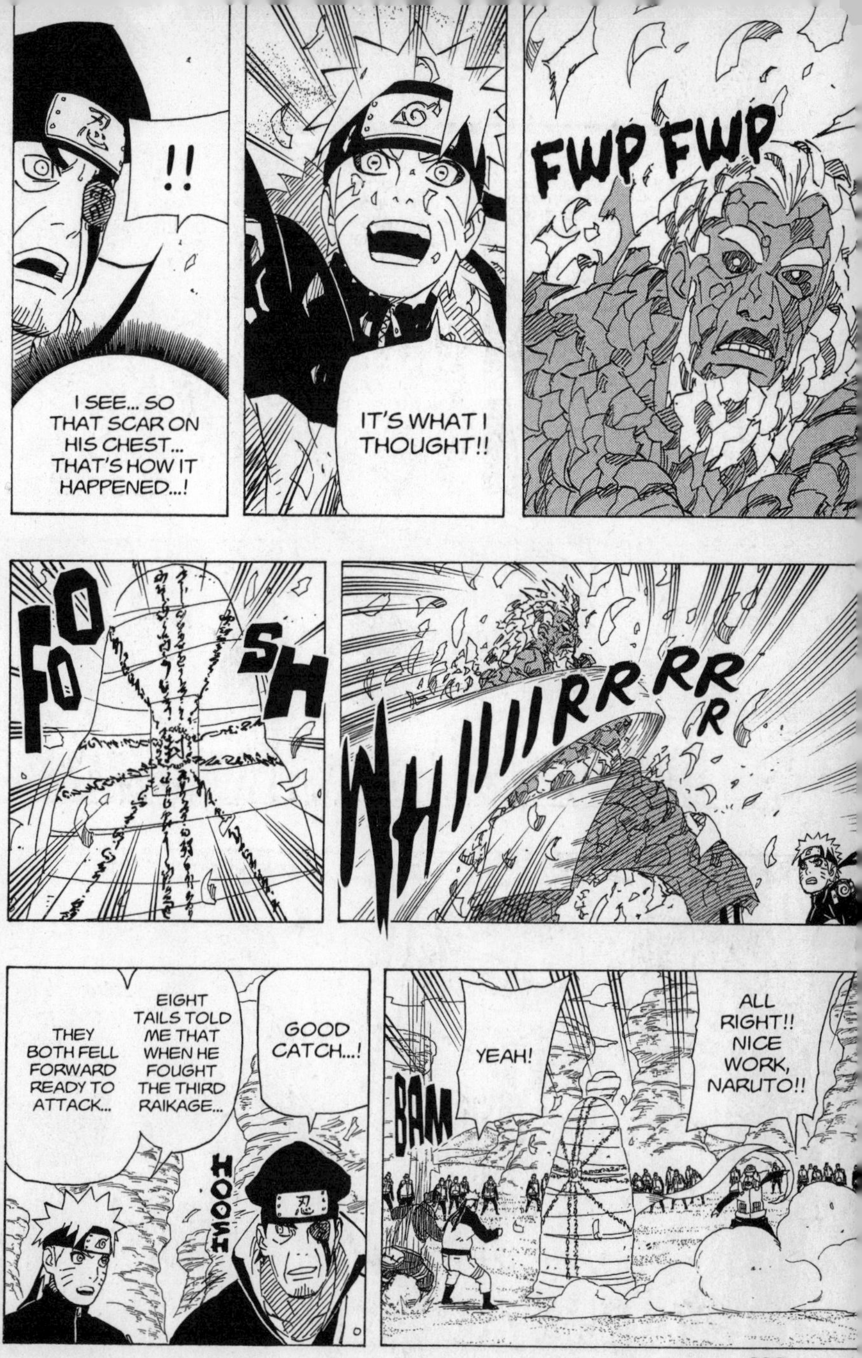
FWP FWP
IT'S WHAT I THOUGHT!!
!!
I SEE... SO THAT SCAR ON HIS CHEST... THAT'S HOW IT HAPPENED...!
WHIIIIRRRRR
FOOSH
ALL RIGHT!! NICE WORK, NARUTO!!
YEAH!
BAM
GOOD CATCH...!
EIGHT TAILS TOLD ME THAT WHEN HE FOUGHT THE THIRD RAIKAGE...
THEY BOTH FELL FORWARD READY TO ATTACK...
HOOSH

READ THIS WAY

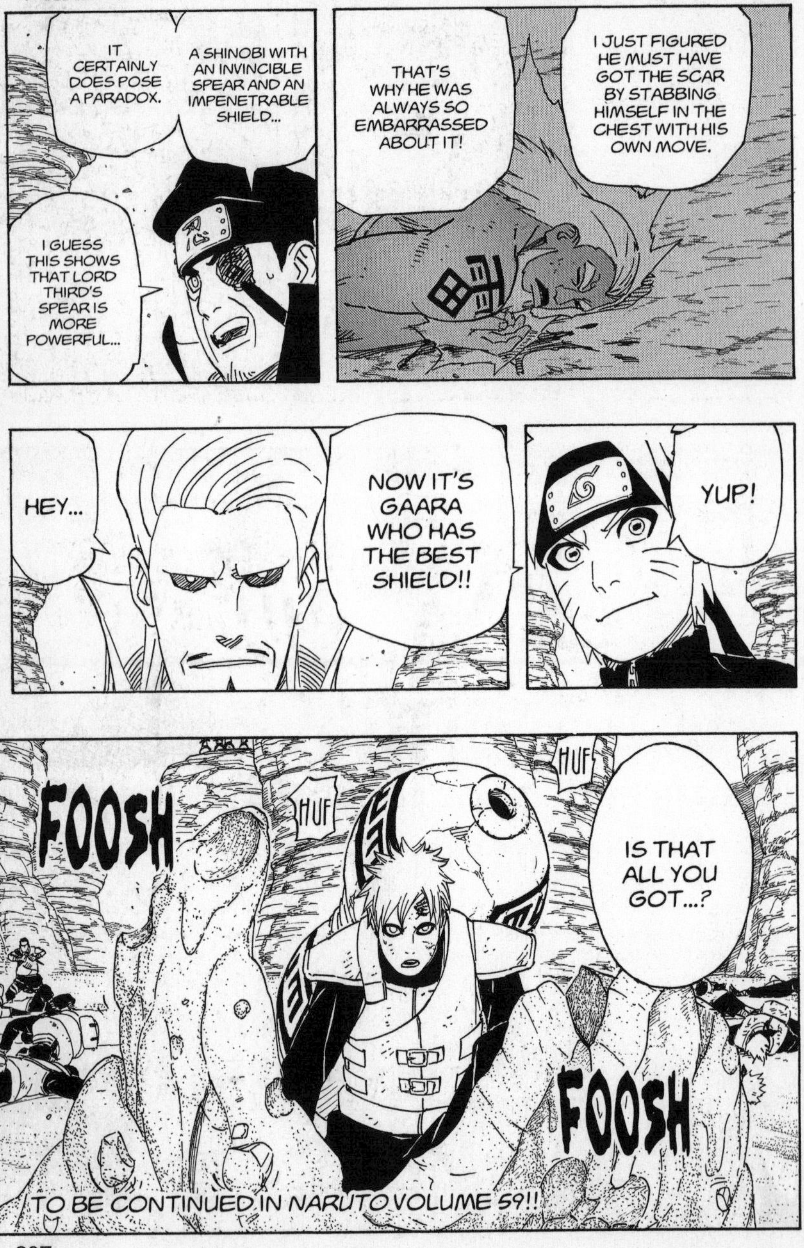

I JUST FIGURED HE MUST HAVE GOT THE SCAR BY STABBING HIMSELF IN THE CHEST WITH HIS OWN MOVE.
THAT'S WHY HE WAS ALWAYS SO EMBARRASSED ABOUT IT!
A SHINOBI WITH AN INVINCIBLE SPEAR AND AN IMPENETRABLE SHIELD...
IT CERTAINLY DOES POSE A PARADOX.
I GUESS THIS SHOWS THAT LORD THIRD'S SPEAR IS MORE POWERFUL...
YUP!
NOW IT'S GAARA WHO HAS THE BEST SHIELD!!
HEY...
HUF
IS THAT ALL YOU GOT...?
HUF
FOOSH
FOOSH
TO BE CONTINUED IN NARUTO VOLUME 59!!

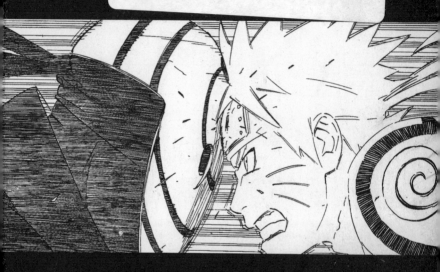

IN THE NEXT VOLUME...

REINFORCEMENTS

As powerful as they are, Naruto and his friends, including all five village Kage, can't seem to gain ground over Kabuto's army of undead ninja. And now, the biggest surprise resurrection of all makes them have to ask a question they all thought had already been answered: just who is Madara and what does he really want?!

AVAILABLE NOVEMBER 2012!

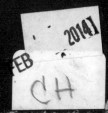